Viriathus

Viriathus

and the Lusitanian Resistance
to Rome 155-139 BC

Luis Silva

Pen & Sword
MILITARY

First published in Great Britain in 2013 by
Pen & Sword Military
an imprint of
Pen & Sword Books Ltd
47 Church Street
Barnsley
South Yorkshire
S70 2AS

Copyright © Luis Silva 2013

ISBN 978 1 78159 128 4

Printed and bound by CPI Group (UK) Ltd, Croydon, CR0 4YY

Pen & Sword Books Ltd incorporates the Imprints of Pen & Sword
Aviation, Pen & Sword Maritime, Pen & Sword Military, Wharncliffe Local
History, Pen and Sword Select, Pen and Sword Military Classics and Leo
Cooper.

For a complete list of Pen & Sword titles please contact:
PEN & SWORD BOOKS LIMITED
47 Church Street, Barnsley, South Yorkshire, S70 2AS, England
E-mail: enquiries@pen-and-sword.co.uk
Website: www.pen-and-sword.co.uk

Contents

List of Maps

Introduction
The Lusitanian War
(155–139 BC)

Viriathus the Iberian against Rome

The Roman conquest of the Iberian Peninsula lasted for 200 years (218 BC–19 BC). It began when the two Scipio brothers, Gnaeus and Publius Cornelius Scipio, landed at Ampurias, on the Catalonian coast in southeastern Spain, at the start of the Second Punic War, and ended with the final Roman military campaign against the Cantabrians in northern Spain.

During this long period of conquest, classical historians recorded the names, places and actions associated with the indigenous resistance to Roman control. Among the autochthonous groups led by Iberian commanders against Rome, the most prominent mentioned were the Celtiberians and the Lusitanians. The story begins with an early Lusitanian leader, Punicus, who incited another native group, the Vettones, to join him in his fight against Rome in 155 BC. Together they drove the conflict deep into Baetica, where they attacked the Blastofenicios, Roman subjects occupying the Spanish Mediterranean coast. Upon Punicus' death in battle, he was succeeded by another Lusitanian, Cesarus, who incited the Celtiberians to continue the war against the Romans. The next major Lusitanian warrior mentioned was Cauceno. The troops of this elected tribal leader travelled the whole region south of the Tagus River, attacking the Conii, who were allies of Rome, and the Conii city of Conistorgis.

Other Iberian warrior chiefs were mentioned in Roman historiography, such as Curius, Apuleius, Connoba, Retogenes, Megaravico, Tautalus and Corocota, but during the entire period of Rome's conquest of Hispania no other warrior chief or military commander was more celebrated or more dangerous to the Romans than a Lusitanian named Viriathus. Viriathus' guerrilla tactics gave him an enormous mobility that bewildered the Romans. His actions and military victories embraced a very wide area of the peninsula's territory and his successes incited other tribes to either join his cause or start their own rebellions against Rome. Viriathus became a great leader and tactician because he knew his people and the Romans very well. With this knowledge he was able to transform a disordered group of individual warriors into a disciplined army. Although guerilla warfare in the ancient world is occasionally mentioned in texts about Alexander the Great's campaigns and the Jugurthine War (112-150 BC), the Lusitanian War, driven by Viriathus, is said to have made such an impact that it was passed down throughout the centuries as a model of guerrilla campaigning.

Justinus, summarizing the account of the Lusitanian War by Gnaeus Trogus Pompeius, a Gallic historian writing during Augustus' reign, declared that the Lusitanians did not have a better general than Viriathus. All of the Greco-Roman authors that wrote about the Lusitanian War agreed that Viriathus was of humble origins, a shepherd and a bandit, and that in time he became a great leader of men. He was also unanimously praised for his virtue and austerity.

The late Iberian historian Adolf Schulten, as well as other twentieth-century historians and scholars, rank Viriathus among the great barbarian leaders —similar to Armínius, Vercingetorix, Boudica, Tacfarinas and Decebalus. But Viriathus was the first barbarian on record to unite and integrate warriors from different tribes to fight against Rome for their liberty.

Viriathus' death, due to betrayal, marked the end of the organized resistance movement against Rome's power in Hispania, with the result that Rome imposed its imperialistic policies all across the Iberian Peninsula.

Maurico Pastor Muñoz, a professor of history at Spain's University of Granada, has written two important books on Viriathus that document both the historical facts as they are known and stories that may be fictitious or mythical. As happens with many great persons of the past, various aspects of Viriathus' life were transformed into legend. Writing about the life and exploits of a person whose life was half history and half legend is not an easy task, for it requires a meticulous analysis of the classical sources and the modern interpretations in order to fully understand who the subject was and what he represents in the historical record. In this work I will attempt to separate the historical facts from legend and fiction, but at times this may not be possible.

Portugal and Spain did not exist in Viriathus' time; the land that encompasses much of them was known as Lusitania. Therefore he was neither Portuguese nor Spanish, but Lusitanian. The classical authors present him as an intelligent, strong leader who rose up to defend a particular political and military unification (an entity we might call a state today) against Rome and perhaps even create the idea of a 'monarchy' in Lusitania.

Roman historiography presents Viriathus as a strong personality, similar to other military commanders of the time, including Hannibal, Sertorius and Julius Ceasar. Thanks to this personality, during the ten years his war lasted he led the Lusitanians not just as a military commander but as a 'king'.

Viriathus was part of a society that was fundamentally made up of warriors, of which we know very little apart from a small amount of information from ancient Roman texts and archaeological data. Although we know something about the Lusitanian family system, the ownership of land, the position of women, and the tribe's class structure, it is hard to distinguish whether the classes intertwined with one another or not. We also know that these people had iron weapons, gold and jewellery that were works of art. The data that exists about the Lusitanians, though small, gives us a glimpse into their social, political and economic life.

The Lusitanians were an aristocratic society, and one which dedicated itself mainly to war. Like many other ancient Celtic societies, war was the road for social promotion, but it was a hard and risky road in which only few succeeded. This was the case for Viriathus.

Because of his personality and fighting prowess, Viriathus became leader of not just his Lusitanian clan but of all Lustianians living between the Douro and Tagus Rivers. The consolidation of his power was recognized by the Roman Senate who named him *amicus poplui romani* in 140 BC, putting Viriathus at the same level as other detached allied kings. With this recognition, Lusitanian society transformed, evolving and integrating itself, becoming Roman. It also began to form a political entity that transformed from a motley group of clans into the beginnings of a monarchy, headed by Viriathus, something unheard of in Iberian-Celtic societies. Though others before and after him were nominated leaders of the Lusitanians, no other gained such fame for his actions.

In conclusion, for everything that Viriathus did within the realm of the Iberian Peninsula's history, it is important to remember that his life and times played and still play an important role in Portugal's and even Spain's early history and society. But if nothing is learned from this book, at the very least one should remember Viriathus, the Lusitanian, who lead the first tentative organized resistance to Rome's imperialistic policies during its early endeavours to grow beyond the borders of Italy.

Map 1: The Pre-Roman Populi of Iberia

CARPETANI = Large/Generic Populus
Deitanni = Local Gens/Civitas

Chapter 1
Hispania at the End of the Second Punic War

The End of the Punic War in Hispania

With the Carthaginian defeat at the Battle of Ilipa and the naval defeat of Hannibal's youngest brother, Mago Barca, off the coast of southern Spain near Gades (modern-day Cadiz) in 206 BC, the Romans had successfully driven out the Carthaginians from Hispania.[1] With Hispania now under their control, the Romans planned to consolidate this newly acquired territory and stabilize it from any further violence. Rome thus inherited its wealth as well as its problems, most notably the rebellious Iberian tribes. The year 206 BC marked the end of the first period of Roman involvement in the peninsula. They were now ready to begin their second phase: consolidation and pacification of the natives. Prior to the start of the Second Punic War in 218 BC, Rome had no interest in Hispania except to maintain a watch over the growth of Barcas family power and its influence in the Mediterranean.[2] But after the war, the status quo had changed.

As all powerful nations and empires have discovered, breaking off from an involvement of such magnitude is not so simple, even if one wants to. The Romans had realized that their presence in the Iberian Peninsula for the last twelve years had altered the status quo in the Mediterranean. Rome, which had formed alliances with the Iberians, was now obligated to support its allies on the peninsula, and disregarding those obligations might have weakened Rome's ability to control what had become an important area strategically and economically. Their so-called Iberian 'allies' were disobedient, unruly and unpredictable, so they could not be trusted to keep out the Carthaginians. It was important for the Romans to maintain some sort of governance and military presence in Hispania because its distance from Italy would prevent Rome from quickly responding to any crisis.[3] Thus direct control from within Hispania by Senate elected officials was the only practical solution. Furthermore, Roman presence had resulted in the creation of commercial avenues of interests, such as trading and mining, which brought considerable additional wealth into Rome.

Rome decided to stay on, fearing that if it withdrew from Hispania the Carthaginians would quickly return. To maintain a long-term presence, it became clear to Rome that it needed to replace the military consular *imperium* (power) given to military commanders with some form of an organized government.[4] But for this to happen, Hispania had first to be labelled a *provincia* by the Senate. Its unofficial designation as a Roman province (though this would not be officially ratified until 197 BC when Hispania became an official state of the empire) enabled Rome to quickly gain some control over this new addition to its growing empire by stationing soldiers within its borders to combat any future Carthaginian or indigenous threat.

With the war over, military commanders also became administrators and began contacting local tribal leaders, developing a structure that would determine the life of the province. Besides caring for and training their army, they began to collect taxes and tributes, set up and maintain friendly relations with local tribes, institute laws and practices, and establish new settlements. As Roman influence grew in Hispania's coastal areas, the appearance of more Roman settlers led to the exploitation of the peninsula's mineral and agricultural resources and peoples. This would cause the indigenous population to rebel against the new occupier within a year of the war's end.

Rome and the Indigenous People of Hispania

The decision to get involved in Hispania in 218 BC came primarily from the Senate after the fall of Saguntum, an Iberian city that had become an ally of Rome, at the start of the Second Punic War.[5] While the Senate provided a command structure, supply and manpower, and sent its elected commanders onto the shores of Hispania, all decisions were then made by the commanders in the field, particularly the Scipio family, which was in charge of the entire military operation.[6] A military commander was delegated senatorial power once assigned to Hispania due to the Senate's concurrent war against Hannibal in Italy and the fact that the Spanish campaign was in a remote area, distant from senatorial supervision or control.[7] Because of distance and the need to make rapid and immediate decisions, an ad hoc mechanism of a military government was set up in 217 BC.[8] Despite the Senate's interest in the war, its advice and decisions appear to have had no effect on the conduct of military operations. In the end, it was the commander's decision that counted, for he was the one who was there fighting the Carthaginians.

After the war, according to Professor J.S. Richardson, the governmental/military command structure in Spain remained the same, but how governors were elected changed. Richardson's study of the Roman campaign and occupation of Hispania shows that from the year 206 BC military governors were elected by a popular assembly, either the *comitia centuriata* or the *comitia tributa*.[9] With the war over, the Senate wanted decision making to be shared by senators and military governors, but this proved impractical for the same reasons as before. It was decided that the military governors would continue to be the deciding governing body on Roman policies in Hispania, but would have to inform the Senate of what they had instituted.

While at the time of the invasion, manpower, supplies and money for the army came from Rome, by 215 BC there were signs that the Romans had begun to take root in Hispania, making them a self-sufficient force.[10] By the end of the war, not only was P. Scipio Africanus, the son of Publius Scipio, obtaining sufficient supplies, troops and money from Rome, he was also able to levy fresh troops from his allies and requisition land and money from defeated tribes allied to the Carthaginians.[11] It was from these exactions of money and provisions from the Iberian tribes that Scipio Africanus was able to pay a *stipendium* to his army.[12]

Maintaining good relations with the indigenous people proved to be the hardest job of the Roman commanders in Hispania. Although it is difficult to assess the type of relations that existed because reports and histories were susceptible to being reworked by Romans to either favour or disfavour a people, several accounts state that when the Romans arrived in Hispania they were determined to win local backing.[13] It was in the Romans' best interests to persuade the Iberians to support them, and during the war they won over as many allies as they could.[14] One of the main reasons Scipio was successful in gaining tribal support was the harsh rule the Carthaginians imposed on the Iberians.[15] In addition, the Romans commissioned Iberian soldiers, who were mostly Carthaginian defectors, to fight as mercenaries rather than conscripting them as the Carthaginians had.[16] In some cases, these mercenaries were better paid than they were by the Carthaginians.[17]

In the aftermath of the Roman victory at Ilipa (modern-day Alcalá del Río, near Seville), Scipio decided to make an example of tribes or towns that had sided with Carthage. The two Iberian towns selected to be the first to feel Rome's power were Castulo and Ilurco.[18] The reason these two cities were chosen was because their citizens had participated, respectively, in Scipio's father's death at the Battle of the Upper Baetis (211 BC) and his uncle's at Ilorco (210 BC).[19]

M. Junius Silanus, Scipio's deputy, along with a legion from Tarraco (modern-day Tarragona), was sent to Castulo to make sure its inhabitants accepted Roman rule.[20] They refused to swear allegiance to Rome, and soon became enraged and hostile. When this was communicated to Scipio, he immediately set out from Carthago Nova (modern-day Cartagena) to assist Silanus' attack on Castulo. On his way, he decided to change direction and attacked the town of Ilurco, which was 19 miles (30 km) from Castulo.[21] In Livy's account, Scipio marched from Carthago Nova to the outskirts of Ilurco in five days, covering about 124 miles (200 km) through mountainous terrain. His change of plan was because during his father's time in Hispania, Ilurco had been friendly to the Romans, but after his father was killed in battle, the city had welcomed a Roman legion only to hand it over to the Carthaginians.[22] Perhaps he also changed his battle plan because he thought Castulo may have warned Ilurco of his coming and that when Castulo was taken by Silanus, Ilurco might rally its forces against the Romans. Both Livy and Appian say that Ilurco was taken in four hours, and that although he was wounded in the neck, Scipio did not desist until the city was in his hands. In their desire to take the city as quickly as possible his legionnaires killed everyone, including women and children. Even though they had not received orders to, they razed the entire town on their own initiative in search of plunder.[23] But according to Appian, Scipio seemed to have been in such a rush that his soldiers did not get the chance to collect any booty, as he quickly reorganized and redirected his troops toward Castulo.[24] We can only assume that he did this to reach Castulo before any survivors of Ilurco could.

Arriving at Castulo to support Silanus' siege, Scipio divided his army into three and set up camp around the city. At first he did not press the siege, but watched the town to see if it would surrender to him, for he had received intelligence that the Castacians had intended to give in to his demands. After hearing what had happened at Ilurco from several of its survivors, the Castacians quickly and quietly gave up. Scipio then stationed a garrison there and placed the town under a pro-Roman government made up of Castacian citizens under the leadership of a man named Cerdubelus.[25] Scipio returned to Carthago Nova and sent Silanus and L. Marcius Septimius into Hispania's unconquered northern central regions to devastate, plunder and take control of as much territory as they could.[26]

Moving west into the Baetis Valley (now Guadalquivir River Valley) the two commanders took several Iberian cities and continued to move in a southwesterly direction to deal with Gades (today Cadiz), the last pro-Carthaginian stronghold. The best recorded siege of this campaign concerns the town of Astapa, another pro-Carthaginian town (today it is an ancient ruin on the Guadalquivir River, north of Astigi, modern Écija). Appian writes:

> Marcius Septimius on arriving at Astapa quickly laid siege to the city, and the inhabitants foreseeing that when the city was taken by the

Romans, they would be reduced to slavery. To deny the Romans that victory, they brought all their valuables into the marketplace, piled wood around it, the men then placed the elderly, their wives and their children on the heap while calling out to their gods for what they had done. Fifty of their best men took an oath that whenever they should see that the city was about to fall, they would kill everyone, set fire to the pile, and slay themselves.[27]

From Livy's account of the battle, which is more detailed than Appian's, he writes:

committed to their word, the Astapians warriors flung open the town gates and burst out in a tumultuous charge, which Marcius Septimius did not anticipate anything of the kind. On seeing the human wave coming, he quickly deployed the entire cavalry and light infantry against them. Fierce fighting ensued in which the legionnaires, who had been first to come into contact with the enemy were soon routed; this created a panic amongst the light infantry. The Iberian attack would have been pushed to the foot of the Roman camp's defence perimeter if it had not been for Marcius' leadership in getting his men back on line.[28]

He goes on to write:

at first there was some wavering amongst the Roman front ranks, for the enemy, blinded by rage, fury and desperation rushed with mad recklessness upon wounds and death, allotting the Romans a few minutes to get into a line formation. On seeing the human wave, many of the inexperienced Roman soldiers at the front rank began to waver. Unshaken by the frantic onset, the veterans came up in support and cut down the enemy's front ranks. When the Roman line began to waver due to the Astapians' ferocity, Marcius extended his lines and outflanked the enemy. With sheer numbers, the Iberians fighting in a compact body and the Roman's tactical manoeuvering, the Romans wiped them all out.[29]

When all had fallen, the fifty who remained behind killed the women and children, kindled the fire, and flung the bodies of the dead as well as themselves on it. Livy says that by the time the Romans arrived on the scene, all had perished:

At first the Romans stood horror-stricken at such a fearful sight, then, seeing the melted gold and silver flowing amongst the other articles which made up the heap, the greediness common to human nature impelled them to try and snatch what they could out of the fire. Some were caught by the flames, others were scorched by the heated air, and those in front could not retreat owing to the crowd pressing on behind to get a look.[30]

Appian writes that although Astapa was taken and practically destroyed, the legionnaires left without any plunder and Marcius received a barren victory. In admiration of the Astapians' bravery, Marcius spared the town's structures.[31]

After taking Astapa and accepting the surrender of the remaining pro-Carthaginian cities in the area, Marcius led his victorious army back to Carthago Nova. At the same time some Carthaginian deserters came from Gades promising to deliver the city with its Carthaginian garrison and its commandant, who had anchored his ships in the city's harbour.[32] The commandant of Gades was Mago Barca, Hannibal's brother. After the Battle of Ilipa, Mago decided he would continue to take up arms against the Romans and took up quarters in the fortified city of Gades. With the help of the ships he had assembled, along with an army made up of Carthaginian soldiers and Iberian allies, he had a considerable force to face the Romans. After guarantees of good faith had been given between the Carthaginians and Romans, Scipio sent Marcius Septimius with a cohort of light infantry and Laelius with seven triremes and one quinquereme to conduct joint operations against Gades.[33] But this was delayed when Scipio became sick and either Silanus or Marcius took command, depending on which ancient text one reads.[34]

For this discussion I will use Appian's work. During Marcius' very short generalship two incidents took place. Soon after he took charge of the army many legionnaires had spent all their money and had not been paid; a large number of men stationed at Surco mutinied, saying that Scipio had taken from them what they had worked for and the glory that came with it.[35] Some went to join Mago Barca at Gades and soon returned to their garrisons with money urging the rest of the army to desert and join Mago's army.[36] Mago, as we shall soon see, was planning on making a move against the Romans. Many of the Roman soldiers took the money, but instead of joining Mago, took it upon themselves to swear an oath of allegiance to one another and elect their own officers.[37]

In Livy's version of the same story, Scipio was overtaken by a serious illness that was rumoured to have killed him. The whole of Spain, especially the Roman-controlled parts, were joyous at the news. At Surco, these rumours had a dangerous affect on the Romans' legionnaires. This camp, according to Livy, held a force of 8,000 men who were stationed there to protect the peaceful tribes on the south side of the Ebro River.[38]Although there were rumours about their commander's death, it was not the primary cause of the mutiny. Accustomed to living on captured enemy plunder, bored due to long periods of inactivity and chafed by the restraints of peace and horrors of war, many of the legionnaires were becoming demoralized. At first their discontent was confined to simply murmurs.[39] But as time passed, they began to demand to be paid with an insolence quite inconsistent with military discipline and at some point soldiers went out on their own to steal from the peaceful surrounding inhabitants. Although they committed crimes and fought to get paid, Livy writes that they still continued to do their duties such as guard duty.[40] Livy goes on to say that the mutiny occurred when they found that the tribunes in Rome had censured and reprobated their pay in an endeavour to repress them, at which the legionnaires openly declared that they would have nothing to do with the Senate's insensate folly and broke out into open mutiny. They drove out the tribunes from the camp, and amid universal acclamation appointed as camp commanders the mutiny's ringleaders, two common soldiers, C. Albius of Cales and C. Atrius, an Umbrian.[41] Livy states that the false belief that Scipio had died without paying his army would spread and kindle the flames of mutiny throughout Hispania, and thus the Romans levied contributions on their Iberian allies, while plundering their enemies.[42]

When the sick Scipio heard this, he wrote to the rebellious soldiers that he was alive and getting better and because of his illness he was not able to pay them, but if they came to Carthago Nova he would reward them properly and all would be forgiven. But Scipio had other plans for these men. He ordered several of his officers to head out to Surco and befriend the mutiny's ringleaders so as to gain their confidence. Once that was accomplished, they would be brought to Carthago Nova and arrested before they realized what was going on.[43]A party of seven military tribunes arrived in Surco to read the letters and dictate Scipio's terms.[44] Some were suspicious, but others trusted Scipio's word and decided to proceed to Carthago Nova.

At Carthago Nova, the trap was sprung.[45] With the mutineers assembled, waiting for their fearless and sick leader to compensate them, they were taken. Scipio then appeared, spoke to the men and released them back to their units, while the ringleaders were shackled in chains and later executed. Amnesty was announced to the rest who did not show up at his camp, thus ending the mutiny, restoring order to his army.[46]

With the mutiny ongoing, along with the rumours of Scipio's 'death', former Iberian allies to the Romans decided not to preserve their fidelity. This was the case for Mandonius and Indibilis, chiefs of the Ilergetes tribe. After the expulsion of the Carthaginians from Hispania these two brothers believed that Hispania's sovereignty would be passed on to them. But when they found that the Romans were establishing permanent bases and settlements, and realized that Scipio had delivered empty promises, they became somewhat disgruntled. When Scipio became sick and rumours spread that he had died, they decided this was their chance to shake off Rome's imperial yoke just as they had shaken off Carthage. This means the two men understood Scipio's intention of making their country a Roman province.

Believing that Scipio's 'death' would cause disorganization among the Roman soldiers for they had no leader, they encouraged a general revolt among their own subjects, as well as several neighbouring Iberian tribes such as the Lacetani and Celtiberians. Once aroused, Mandonius and Indibilis' army began to ravage the territories of the Suessitanians and Sedetanians, both of which were Roman allies.[47] When the two brothers heard that Scipio was still alive, they gave up their enterprise and retired within their frontiers.[48] Over the years there have been suggestions as to why they did this. Their actual reasoning is lost forever to history, but it could have been out of fear or respect for Scipio's fighting prowess.

Although Mandonius and Indibilis had returned to their lands, the recovered Scipio was not inclined to leave their disloyalty unpunished. According to Livy and Appian, soon after the mutiny had been quelled, Scipio marched against the two brothers. On hearing that Scipio was coming, they summoned their tribesmen to arms and gathered an army of 20,000 infantry and 2,500 cavalry, with which they crossed their frontiers and marched into Sedetania to meet Scipio.[49]

From his camp at Carthago Nova, Scipio marched for several weeks until he reached the Ebro River where he met the rebel army. Both armies met and a battle was fought, but unfortunately the classical records do not provide many battle details, only the results. It was a costly Roman victory. According to Livy the Romans suffered over 5,000 casualties but took 3,000 prisoners and booty.[50] Livy says the victory would not have been so costly for the Romans had the battle been fought in a wider plain, to allow room for the Iberians to retreat—their better choice if they saw themselves in trouble. But it seems that the Roman battle plan had worked, for the Iberians were surrounded and strategically outmanoeuvred. They fought harder in the enclosed area and suffered to the higher number of casualties. Appian claims that the Romans suffered 1,200 casualties and killed as many as 20,000 Iberians, but this seems exaggerated as the Iberian army, according to Livy, numbered 22,500 and 3,000 were taken prisoner.[51] If one believes these numbers then not a single Iberian warrior survived.

Facing defeat, the brothers decided it would be better to lay aside all ideas of continuing their campaign against Scipio, and that the safest course to take would be to throw themselves on Scipio's clemency. Having trusted that their strength and cause would lead them to victory, they were now hopeless. Indibilis sent Mandonius to discuss making peace with Scipio.

Throwing himself before Scipio, Mandonius declared that he and his brother and the rest of their countrymen were in such a bad state that if Scipio spared them, they would devote the whole of their lives to the man they owed them to.[52] Scipio, after sternly reprimanding Mandonius and the absent Indibilis at considerable length, said that their lives were justly forfeited by their crime, but through his own kindness and that of the Roman people, they would be spared.[53] He did not demand hostages or take away their arms; instead he would take an indemnity. Scipio would let them decide whether they preferred the favour or the wrath of Rome.[54] Dismissed, Mandonius returned to his brother with Scipio's terms and his only condition: an indemnity 'sufficient enough to furnish the pay which was owed to the troops', according to Livy.[55]

It is important to understand why Scipio had to punish his former allies. A hostile enemy force in this position could easily disrupt the communication and supply lines along the coastal strip and Ebro River. In addition, had he not made an example of these two men, there would perhaps be more native insurrections. Lastly, it made clear to the Iberians that the Romans 'were here to stay', showing the Iberian tribes the type of power Rome had. These actions against the Iberian population suggest that Scipio had intentions of controlling them.

Once Scipio had quieted the rebellious Iberians, his thoughts returned to Gades. He sent Marcius on ahead into southern Spain to capture the city from Mago Barca, while he himself, with a light-armed force, stayed behind a few days until the Ilergetes paid their indemnity in full. He then set out to meet Marcius, who was already nearing Gades.[56]

Unaware of what the Romans had in store for him, Mago decided to take advantage of the Iberian insurrection under Indibilis and Mandonius and the mutiny of the Roman troops along the Surco River.[57] Believing that these events might help restore Carthaginian power on the peninsula, he led a raid against Carthago Nova, which was thought to be lightly defended. Having received erroneous intelligence about the city's defence, his forces were repulsed with severe losses.[58] While Mago was at Carthago Nova, Marcius took Gades without a fight. Mago returned to find the gates of Gades barred, and sailed away to the Balearic Islands.[59]

The Romans had finally ousted the Carthaginians from a vital land base filled with mineral resources and agricultural wealth. They now were able to lay down their own foundation for a continuous Roman presence on the Iberian Peninsula with the establishment of military bases at Tarraco (modern-day Tarragona), Carthago Nova, and Gades, along with the newly established settlement at Italica (modern-day Santiponce), which provided an outline for the colonization of the entire peninsula. Moreover, the way the Scipio family had set about the tasks of supplying themselves with provisions and money for the troops and determining their relations with the various Iberian tribes was to shape Roman policy and begin the emergence of Roman institutions in the peninsula.[60]

To the indigenous people of the peninsula, Scipio's actions, such as the founding of Italica, the establishment of a Roman *praefectus* and the placement of Roman troops in former Carthaginian strongholds, brought a feeling that perhaps confirmed that the Romans had intentions of staying.[61] As Scipio had fought hard to establish a permanent presence on the Iberian Peninsula in the name of Rome, holding on to what the Romans had gained during twelve years of war against Carthage naturally became important. These events foreshadowed future developments in the peninsula, but before they could happen Rome would have to conquer and pacify the entire peninsula.

The Roman Conquest of Hispania Begins

Before Scipio Africanius left in 206 BC, to be elected as consular for his success in defeating the Carthaginians, he had shown the Iberians that the end of the fight against Carthage in Hispania did not mean the end of Roman interests in the peninsula. The Roman occupation of Hispania during the war had substantial cultural and technological influences over the tribes under Roman control. The practices and ideas employed by the three Scipios established a foundation that subsequent governors would continue to employ or modify. To solidify Hispania as part of the Roman Empire, he presented to the Senate several reasons why it was important to remain in Hispania and brought with him an embassy from the city of Saguntum to thank the Romans for the benefits of their alliance with Rome and for relieving them from the Carthaginian menace.[62] Scipio's petition was answered, for the Senate decided to send two military commanders, L. Cornelius Lentulus and L. Manlius Acidinus, to Hispania instead of one to govern the place.[63] It was clear that Rome's presence was now permanent.

During this new phase of Roman occupation, Rome saw Hispania as quite primitive and the pacification of its indigenous tribes as requiring time. It became important to Rome that their elected official to Hispania undertake certain obligations and policies to 'Romanize' the Iberian tribes. Rome felt that if these commitments were ignored it may have weakened Rome's ability to control an important area in the known world, as well as leave the Peninsula open for Carthaginian reoccupation, which was still a threat. Furthermore, Rome's twelve-year presence in Hispania had resulted in the emergence of further Roman imperial interests, such as increasing trading connections with the peninsula to introduce Iberian products and new varieties of food to Rome, thus enhancing Roman quality of life. But for this to happen, it would have to find a way to pacify and control the Iberian tribes.

With this in mind, the Romans launched an imperialistic endeavour to take advantage of the enormous wealth that Hispania had to offer. In antiquity, the Iberian Peninsula was famous for its richness in metal ores, such as silver, gold, tin and copper. The resources of the metal-rich western area of Iberia had been in high demand since the Bronze Age.[64] Besides Hispania's abundance in mineral deposits, its soil, in certain areas, was rich and fertile for growing crops to feed Rome's growing population. After the Roman victory over Carthage, the Senate and its Roman patrician oligarchy began to reorganize the land that they had conquered. One example of this was Scipio's establishment of Italica, far away from any significant strategic areas of the eastern route to the Pyrenees. This shows that he was aware of the benefits that might be accrued to the state from the control of the fertile Baetis Valley in southern Spain and the silver mines of the Sierra Morena.[65] The Romans thus developed a great economic diversification and subsistence strategy based on the exploitation of all the resources available: agriculture, livestock breeding, hunting, mining as well as handicrafts.

By the early part of the second century BC, Rome controlled the eastern fertile plains of the Baetis River Valley and the Ebro and began to produce crops in these areas. As for mineral deposits that were in the areas controlled by the Romans, they were exploited to their full capacity while the rest of the peninsula was still far from being under Roman control. To reach deeper into the peninsula, the Romans needed to launch military expeditions to make contact with the other Iberian tribes to begin some type of communication that would later form a social structure that would determine the life of the province in the years to come. While the Romans attempted to pacify Hispania's remote areas, they began to collect taxes and tributes, building political and social relations with the local Iberian communities and their leaders, and establishing new Roman settlements in areas already in their hands.

By the latter part of the second century BC, the actions and decisions made by the Roman governors gave way to abuses, exploitation, spoliation and violations that harmed, harassed and intimidated the Iberian population.[66]

This, together with the obligation of paying heavy annual taxes, awoke the rebellious spirit of the natives. The greed and inexperience of many governors and government officials, the short-term nature of the position and the scarce knowledge of the autochthonous world provoked serious disorder among the population. In Rome, the Senate tried to end these abuses but failed entirely.[67]

Though Roman governmental representatives caused dissension among the Iberian population, it was the Roman soldiers and their allies that had the most significant effect on the local populace's actions, particularly in places where troops were stationed such as Tarraco, Carthago Nova and Emporion. During the lull in fighting, Roman influence spread across the country as the soldiers intensified Roman habits and culture among the population, while merchants brought the Iberians new wares and products and technological advances they had never seen before. With troops stationed in Hispania and traders lurking at every port across the eastern and southern Spanish coastline, many opportunities arose for those Iberians who were skilled craftsmen, artists and entrepreneurs. For entrepreneurial Romans, freedmen and aspiring politicians, Hispania presented itself as a golden opportunity to get ahead and become wealthy. Rome's culture gradually spread across the eastern and southern coastal lands of the Iberian Peninsula and the Iberians began to take on the patterns of Roman life. As for the rest of the country, this wave of Roman influence was still years away.

A year after the Carthaginian expulsion from the peninsula, the Roman provincial government under L. Cornelius Lentulus and L. Manlius Acidinus faced its second major rebellion. According to Livy, Indibilis and Mandonius, continuing to witness Rome's takeover of their land, once again rallied up their tribes, along with the Ausetani and other neighbouring tribes, to take up arms against the Romans. They brought together an army of 34,000 warriors and marched into Sedetani territory north of the Ebro River.[68]

Livy says that Lentulus and Acidinus were determined not to let the rebellion spread. They united their forces and marched through Ausetanian territory, without inflicting any hostility upon the peaceable districts, until they came to where the enemy was encamped. Pitching camp 3 miles away, the Romans sent envoys to persuade the brothers to surrender. Indibilis asked the envoys to give him time to discuss the surrender terms with his captains. A few days later the Romans got their answer, for a group of Iberian cavalry attacked a party of Roman foragers. In support, a Roman cavalry squadron was quickly dispatched and a skirmish took place.[69]

The following day, the Iberian army marched within a mile of the Roman camp. According to Livy their battle formation consisted of the Ausetani in the centre, the Ilergetes on the right flank, with the left flank made up of various indigenous tribes. Meanwhile between the wings and the centre, open spaces were left wide enough to allow cavalry through when the signal was given for such an attack.[70]

The Romans took their usual battle formation, except that they copied the enemy's formation by also leaving spaces between the legions so that their cavalry could pass through.[71] Both sides moved in to attack. Seeing that his infantry was making no progress and his left wing was beginning to give ground to the Ilergetes, Lentulus decided to bring up his reserves. At the same time, he realized that whoever was first to use their cavalry through the wide gaps against the opposing line would probably have a chance in defeating the enemy. As soon as the left wing was restored, Lentulus gave one of his military tribunes, Servius Cornelius, orders to send the cavalry at full speed through the openings. Lentulus then rode up to Acidinus, who was at the front encouraging his men, and informed him of the situation. Livy writes that he had hardly finished his commands when the Roman cavalry slammed into the middle of the enemy formation throwing the enemy infantry into confusion, barring the passage for an Iberian cavalry counter-attack.[72]

Finding themselves unable to act as mounted cavalry, the Romans dismounted and fought on foot. When the Roman commanders saw the enemy's ranks in disorder, they instructed their men to break up the enemy into segments so as not to let them re-form their lines. Confusion and panic began to spread among the Iberians. Not being able to withstand the furious attack much longer, Indibilis and his cavalry also dismounted and placed themselves in front to screen and protect the infantry, so that his brother Mandonius could regroup his battle formation.[73] The fighting lasted for some time, neither side giving way. Indibilis, wounded and fatigued, kept his ground till he was killed by a javelin. After seeing their great leader killed, many of the Iberians lost hope and withdrew. With many of the Iberians individually withdrawing from the battle, the battle turned into a rout on the battlefield. The Iberians quickly dispersed and stealthily returned to their respective communities. By the end of the battle, 13,000 Iberians were killed and about 1,800 taken prisoner. Of the Romans and allies a little more than 200 fell, mainly on the left wing.[74] Mandonius escaped with the remnants of the army.

On his return to his village, Mandonius summoned a tribal meeting. Loud complaints were uttered about the disaster incurred, and all the blame was thrown upon Indibilis for starting the rebellion, and on the other chieftains, most of whom had fallen in the battle. After the meeting, envoys were sent to the Romans to formally surrender and plead for permission to retain their arms.[75] The reply was that their surrender would only be accepted on condition that they give up Mandonius and the other instigators of the rebellion; if not, the Roman army would march into Ilergetes and Ausetani country and wreck havoc upon their kingdoms.[76] When this was reported to the tribal council, Mandonius and several other chiefs were arrested and handed over for punishment. Peace was re-established among the Iberian tribes. Under the peace agreement, the Iberians were required to pay double tribute to the Roman troops that year, plus a six month supply of corn, and cloaks and togas for the army. The Romans also took away their weapons and demanded hostages from the noble families of about thirty tribes, so as to keep the tribes in line.[77] To make matters worse a strong Roman garrison was installed in the territory to watch over them, according to Appian. Roman Spain's second major revolt had been crushed without any further serious disturbance.[78] As for Mandonius, according to Appian, he was brought to trial, found guilty for instigating the rebellion and put to death along with the others.[79]

Nothing more is heard of Lentulus and Acidinus until 201 BC. After six years in Hispania, Lentulus was finally recalled to Rome[80] and replaced by C. Cornelius Cethegus, who only served two years.[81] Cethegus, having been elected *curule aedile* in 199 BC, was replaced by Cn. Cornelius Blasio (Hispania Citerior) who served until 196 BC.[82] As for Acidinus, he remained in Hispania until 199 BC, and was replaced by L Sertinius (Hispania Ulterior) who served until 196 BC.[83] In between all these governors, Livy mentions C. Sergius,who had taken command of the province in the year 200 BC when Cethegus and Acidinus left for Rome. According to Livy he stayed behind to award land to veteran soldiers that had served for many years in Hispania.[84] Not much is known of these other proconsuls'exploits in Hispania except of their ovations in Rome, which indicates that they had conducted some type of military campaign against the Iberians.[85] Although much is not said about these men, we can see changes happening within Hispania's occupied areas, such as the formation of two provinces for administrative purposes instead of one huge and uncontrolled province.[86]

Peace settled into Hispania after the rebellion and the benefits of Roman civilization quickly began to exhibit results upon those so-called 'barbarians'. Tribal villages became towns and cities, and roads began to be built along with aqueducts and bridges. Hispania would provide hardy soldiers and cavalry as well as poets, rhetoricians, geographers, historians and a series of successful emperors such as Trajan, Hadrian and Marcus Aurelius. Due to large food demands, the Romans initiated improvements in irrigation and agriculture, imported new crops, and introduced animal husbandry. Lastly, advanced mining techniques were brought in to extract the peninsula's mineral wealth. The newly formed province of Hispania had much to offer, and Rome would benefit greatly in the years to come.

With the Carthaginian threat diminished after the Battle of Zama, peace settled throughout Hispania, bringing into question the necessity of a Roman military presence there.[87] Prior to Hispania becoming a permanent chess piece in Rome's growing empire, it was important to have two military commanders with a large army within each command structure of their area of operation, which would later turn into a province. Having two commanders was seen as essential by the Senate as Rome was involved in a major conflict and only controlled the coastal areas of eastern and southern Hispania. Rome's Spanish allies were new and unreliable, thus leaving essential strategic points such as certain coastal routes and cities open to enemy attacks and raids.

But with the changes in Hispania after the war, including its designation as a Roman province and thus a permanent fixture of Rome's growing empire, the Senate decided that its vast military presence in Hispania needed to be downsized from two armies to one legion and 15 cohorts of Latin allies. The remaining veterans were to be brought back to Italy with the returning proconsul.[88] This proposed change in policy, given the size of the territory controlled by the Romans in 201 BC, suggests that the Senate questioned the necessity of having such a large army to protect Hispania against disorganized and undisciplined bands of barbarians. This was perhaps derived from the amazing victory of Lentulus and Acidinus, which had enforced the Senate's belief that a small force of professional Roman soldiers could control the area with no problem. The other reason for the suggested force reduction was political. Richardson states that it was linked to cutting back the number of commanders, for there were two men in Hispania with *imperium pro consule* that controlled large armies.[89] A change of *imperium* (power) was perhaps a way for the Senate to control these men who, with such large armies, may have hungered for absolute power so as to establish their own independent state or pose a threat to Rome in a bid to become emperor. It released a decree to decrease the size of its military presence and reduce its commanders to one.[90]

We will never know exactly what the Senate's intentions were, for Livy is silent on the matter, but it seems this reduction in force was never carried out. Unfortunately the absence of details on the matter makes interpretation difficult and shows that this policy change may have not been important enough to be addressed. Perhaps Rome's new and unreliable 'allies' still meant that flexibility in deploying troops throughout strategic points in the realm, which was beginning to expand further inland, was necessary. It would be difficult for a small army to cover or fight against indigenous tribes over such as vast area. It is also possible, but undocumented, that the Senate changed its mind because it realized that with Rome's imperialistic attitude the two commanders would be kept busy enough with an unruly populace and at the same time gain Rome's favour for expanding the empire. In the end, whatever intentions the Senate had about withdrawing troops and a commander, it never occurred.

During the Punic War, Scipio had laid out the foundations of how Hispania would be governed until the end of the Republic era in 27 BC, when Augustus became emperor. The militaristic-governmental structure put in place by Scipio was based on the need to pay, feed and supply the army.[91] The command structure during the war came under a single commander with *consular imperium*, who had to send reports to keep the Senate informed of the war's progress and of their needs.[92] During the war, it was better to have one man in control instead of two or more, so as to conduct successful military operations against an enemy, for if there were two commanding generals there would always be one who would try to either outdo the other or counter the other's orders, causing chaos within the command structure. As mentioned before, the major decisions that shaped the progress of the war in Hispania were taken by the commanders on the spot and not by Rome. The only thing the Senate could do from such a long distance was express its approval, disapproval or grief.

But after the war it seems that the pattern set by Scipio continued, for there is little information about Hispania's early administrative developments with the exception of a few changes, as we shall see. Scipio established policies and a governmental structure in Hispania to administer a huge piece of land and its people. With such a vast area for one man, the Senate would allow two men to act as governors and establish Roman policies and institutions within the province's two regions, making Romanization of the area much easier.

The next change came in the form of paying 'taxes'. During the war, Rome sent money, food and supplies to support and maintain the army in Hispania. But after the war, to be self-sufficient, the Romans began to collect a tax, which was actually more of a *stipendium* used to pay the army.[93] This seems to have been the beginning of more systematic taxation that would later be used in Hispania as well as the rest of the empire, but at this stage it was an ad hoc levy to pay soldiers.[94] To obtain this *stipendium* the Romans collected food, clothes, and at times gold and silver from Iberian tribes that had revolted against them, as the Ilergetes and Ausetani did in 205 BC. The penalties suffered by the Iberians were beneficial to Rome. For example the price of corn was reduced because of the large quantity being sent from Spain. Rome did not have to send as much money as it had done during the Second Punic War, because by 203 BC the army was self-sustaining from the constant collection of clothing, corn, weapons and various supplies.[95]

With governmental administrative policy somewhat installed, the next step was to instill Senate policy within the realm. At first we see one proconsul being elected by the Senate, empowered with *consular imperium*, and upon reaching Hispania's shores governing as he saw fit. After 201 BC this was somewhat modified. We begin to see two men rule with *imperium* after the Punic War, as Rome had captured so much Spanish territory that two men were needed to run the country. But around 201 BC the Senate, thinking about downsizing its forces in Hispania, put forward the idea of just having one man governing the entire province and enforcing actual Senatorial policies made in Rome rather than by men conducting the day-to-day governmental business in Hispania. But that policy also never materialized, for it would have been difficult for the Senate to keep control and manage its policies from so far away, compared to what a praetor did or did not do while stationed in Spain. So the final outcome was left to the governors, who would instill Senatorial policies on their arrival in Hispania.

It is difficult to know when the Senate made its decision about having one instead of two governors, but it probably happened after Cethegus and Acidinus were reassigned back to Rome.[96] If the Senate was going to replace both men, the Senate would have sent two others to replace them, but it did not. Here C. Sergius, who was *praetor urbanus* during 200 BC, comes into play, for Livy states that his term as praetor was extended, providing him with not just the power of *praetor urbanus*, for the purpose of allotting land to the veterans that had served in Hispania, but giving him *imperium* to run the country.[97] This was perhaps the Senate's attempt to install one governor for one province but it seems to have failed, for the following year, 199 BC, we see two new governors in the written record: Cornelius Blasio and L. Stertinius.[98] Perhaps after consultation with Lentulus, Cethegus and Acidinus about what was happening in Hispania, the Senate changed its mind and went back to two praetors instead of one. The sending out of two praetors in 199 BC and the fact that their tenure lasted only two years suggests that a regular pattern for Hispania's administration was beginning to evolve.[99]

Another interesting change occurring around this time can be seen in Livy's *History of Rome*, book 32 and 33, which describes Hispania as two different provinces. The influence of geography on political and municipal organizations was too great for one man to govern, as mentioned before. At the same time, without provincial boundaries for administrative purposes the entire region governed as one enormous province would become an administrative abyss. So, in 198 BC the *comitia centuriata* elected two men for the praetorship of Hispania with the decree that the newly elected praetors should determine the boundaries of their *provinciae* to better administer Hispania.[100] The titles given to these new provinces were Hispania Ulterior (Farther Hispania) and Hispania Citerior (Nearer Hispania). These terms referred to how close these provinces were to Rome.

The newly formed Roman province consisted of: **Hispania Ulterior**, a region of Baetica roughly located in the Guadalquivir Valley of modern Spain and extending to all of Lusitania (present day Portugal south of the Minho River), Gallaecia, Asturias (presently Northern Portugal and Galicia (Spain)), Cantabria and the Basque Country; and **Hispania Citerior**, a region encompassing the southeastern and northeastern coasts of Hispania including the Ebro River Valley of modern Spain.

This division, which occurred in 197 BC, was not only created for conducting administrative business but also to have an area of operation so praetors would be able to control the constant fighting against the Iberians along the Ebro River Valley, as well as the Iberians and Gauls from the Pyrenees and the Iberians to the south, who seem to have attacked or raided Roman settlements in spurts throughout this period. Though little is known about how much fighting went on, we can assume the reason for this split was that it would be easier for the praetors to control their respective areas with military operations to quell native rebellions, instead of chasing Iberians all over the countryside. According to Richardson's research on the subject of Rome's early administrative development much is still unknown, so it must be assumed that the governing patterns set by the Scipios continued.[101] What can be stated for sure is that a basic administrative arrangement was installed to pay, feed and supply the army, but once the coastal Iberian population had been somewhat pacified other administrative institutions were established and later modified.The difference between the pre and post 197 BC regime in Spain was that at first it was an ad hoc government due to the war being fought against Carthage and the uncertainty of duration of Rome's occupation of the peninsula, but after the defeat of the Carthaginians and the discovery of the vast wealth in fertile land and minerals, Rome decided to alter its commitment in Hispania from temporary to permanent.[102] Thus the two Hispanias were created.

Roman Occuption of Hispania

The decade that followed Scipio's departure from Hispania in 206 BC was a period in which the developments of the previous years finally began to blossom. The crucial decision during those early years was whether or not to remain in Spain, and once the decision was made to stay, it simply remained for those entrusted with the task of governing the Spanish province to continue to maintain law and order, ensure the upkeep of the military forces under their command and extend Roman control throughout the entire peninsula. At first this was achieved by the continuation of the ad hoc methods of governing, employed by the three Scipios, but as time went on, modifications were added on until a permanent system of government was in place.

Within this newly established province and the beginnings of a stable government the Romans managed to install the *ager publicus*.[103] With this law they could found colonies and set the status quo of conquered cities and towns. The Romans also continued to integrate the *stipendium*. Also implemented were obligations to provide local products and provisions in the event Roman legionnaires went on military campaigns, including supplies for auxiliary troops. Mining towns were allowed to mint coinage of bronze and silver to facilitate payments of tribute, the acquisition of food, and salaries for the military.[104] Concerning the Iberian tribes, the Romans found it impossible to deal with the leaders of each tribe, even though the tribes had a highly personal system of allegiances among themselves. To deal with them, the Romans developed a loose non-formal series of arrangements and alliances that would serve them adequately during this period.

In 198 BC, two new men were elected. These newly elected praetors were given senatorial power to govern the province, but overall management of the provinces was supervised by the Senate.[105] The two men were C. Sempronius Tuditanus for Hispania Citerior and M. Helvius for Hispania Ulterior.[106] Arriving in Hispania in 197 BC, each praetor brought with him 8,000 infantry and 400 cavalry, to replace the army that had been serving in Hispania prior to their arrival.[107] On orders from the Senate, these two men had the task of demarcating the borders between the two provinces. According to Schulten, the division was established between Carthago-Nova and Baria (modern Villaricos), and would move northeast towards Gaul (modern France), northwest to the far reaches of the Ebro River and southwest along the Spanish coast toward Gibraltar.[108]

Though these praetors had senatorial arrangements, their ability to pursue their own policies to get the Iberians to produce more grain, clothing and money began to enrage many of the tribes. The indigenous peoples of both provinces independently yet simultaneously rebelled against the Roman government. The heads of these rebellions were two tribal kings: Culchas, a former Roman ally of the Punic Wars from Baetica (today Andalusia), and Luxinus, ruler of two towns in the northwestern sector of the Guadalquivir Valley in the south.[109]

Late in the year 197 BC, a letter arrived in Rome from Praetor M. Helvius in Ulterior, reporting that large-scale fighting between Roman forces and the two tribal kings had broken out. According to the dispatch, fifteen to seventeen fortified towns had taken sides with Culchas, while Luxinius had strong support from the cities of Carmo (modern-day Carmona) and Bardo (location unknown).[110] To make matters worse the Malacini and Sexetani tribes from the southeast coast of Hispania and several other southern tribes within Baetica decided to join the cause.The rebellion overtook the entire eastern and southern region.[111] It seemed that the rebellion would spread further inland and that even the Phoenicians on the central southern coast of Hispania and the inhabitants of the region between the Guadalquivir and Guadiana rivers were going to join in.[112]

Although fighting had been going on for some time, the rebellion was not considered by the Senate as a full-scale war. The praetors went on campaign and both earned an *ovatio* when they returned to Rome after their governships.[113] Rome's success was also reaffirmed when Helvius, who had a successful campaign against the Iberians, returned to Rome with a considerable amount of loot: 12,675 pounds of silver and 17,023 Spanish denarii,[114] while L. Stertinius brought with him 50,000 pounds of silver.[115]

But the end of 197 BC, another letter arrived in Rome stating that the forces of the governor of Citerior, C. Sempronius Tuditanus, had been defeated and the proconsul mortally wounded.[116] With the news of the Roman defeat and the death of a praetor (which may have been due to the small reduction of troops that had been forced upon the arrival of these governors and the Senate's refusal to send reinforcements due to military operational needs), the situation changed. [117]

In 196 BC two new praetors were elected, Q. Fabius Buteo (Ulterior) and Q. Minucius Thermus.[118] Arriving in Hispania, they quickly recognized the difficult plight the army faced, and requested the Senate deploy an additional Roman legion to each province. The consuls were ordered to furnish the two praetors with one legion each from the four new legions recently raised, alongside 4,000 allied infantry and 300 cavalry.[119] When these two men arrived in Hispania, Minucius quickly went into action against two Iberian chiefs, Budar and Baesadines of the Turboletae tribe.[120] Though he had some success, the Romans did not triumph straight away. With the arrival of Roman reinforcements, the two Iberian chiefs were defeated at Turda, when 12,000 Iberian warriors were killed and Budar was captured.[120]

Before the year drew to a close, however, the Celtiberians began mustering a new army. This army was so massive in size that it became apparent that it would take more than the two governors' legions to deal with them. So at the beginning of 195 BC, when the annual allocations for the provinces came before the Senate, it decided that because the rebellion in Spain seemed to have escalated into a full-scale war, it was necessary to send reinforcements commanded by an experienced consular general.[121] The consul who was elected and given *consular imperium* to 'govern' Spain took with him two legions, 15,000 allied infantry, 800 cavalry and twenty warships to assist in ending this war. And so the entire operation as well as command over the two praetors fell to M. Porcius Cato, who was tasked with resolving the Iberian problem.[122]

Along with Cato, the newly elected praetors P. Manlius (Citerior) and Ap. Claudius Nero (Ulterior) arrived in Hispania. The Senate was worried that Cato's army was not large enough to subdue the Iberians and sent an additional force of 2,000 infantry and 200 cavalry to reinforce it.[123] Having sailed with a fleet of twenty warships from Portus Lunae, north of Pisa,[124] Cato moved south by sea towards Emporion (modern-day Ampurias), eliminating on his way an Iberian stronghold that dominated the Massiliote port of Rhoda (modern-day Rosas).[125]

He disembarked and quickly set up several camps outside Emporion, with the intention of ending the insurrection as quickly as possible.[126] Livy's work seems to suggest that Cato chose Emporion because the city comprised of Greek settlers and pro-Roman Iberians and a seaport. The Greeks and Iberians welcomed the Romans for within Emporion's population there was an element of Roman colonists that helped influence the locals.[127] Once his army had made camp, Cato occupied his time with gathering intelligence on the enemy's strength and position as well as conducting a number of forced marches and tactical training exercises around his base at Emporion. He also conducted several raids into the countryside to provide food and supply for his troops. So successful were these raids that he was able to dismiss the *redemptores* (Roman merchants who followed the army), sending them back to Rome with the remark, 'War feeds itself.'[128]

During his short stay at Emporion, Cato was approached by three envoys from Bilistages, the chief of the Ilergetes, one being the chief's son.[129] They reported that they were under heavy hostile pressure from a neighbouring tribe who had recently attacked one of their settlements. Without Roman assistance they could not hold out much longer and with the help of 3,000 Roman legionnaires they could dislodge the enemy.[130] Unwilling to divide his army and having information that an enemy force was close by, Cato devised an elaborate ruse. He announced to the ambassadors that despite his own difficulties he would help them, and issued the order to prepare the ships so that a force of 3,000 men would deploy. Satisfied on seeing the Roman soldiers boarding the ship, the ambassadors left to report to their king that the Romans were coming to their rescue. But as soon as the Ilergetes were gone, Cato ordered his men to disembark and marched them into winter quarters 3 miles (5 km) from Emporion.[131] The intention of this ruse, according to Frontinus, was to discourage the Ilergetes' enemies from further conducting their operations. At the same time it boosted the morale of the Ilergetes to hold out a little longer.[132]

This deception was quickly followed by a military encounter soon after the *castra hiberna* (winter quarters) was set up. Cato marched his army from Emporion, laying fields and towns to waste with fire and sword, spreading terror as his army plundered the surrounding towns, and scattering the local inhabitants in all directions.[133] According to Livy, in contrast to other Roman generals, Cato generally marched at night in order to cover as much ground as possible. These night marches were also perhaps a way to avoid giving away their location, and to take the enemy by surprise when contact was made. This kind of manoeuvre was at first a training exercise for the new soldiers, but during one such exercise an enemy force was encountered, which led to the capture of numerous prisoners and caused the enemy to cease venturing outside their fort's defences at night.[134]

On another such night march, Livy writes that Cato brought his army upon an enemy camp. After positioning his troops he waited to make his move at daybreak, when he launched one legion against the Iberians. Alerted, the Iberians drew up men to fight the Romans. The Roman cavalry, which held the flanks, was the first into action. Charging head on into the enemy's ranks, it immediately ran into trouble. The cavalrymen that held the right wing of the charge were quickly repulsed and their hasty retirement created alarm and panic among the Roman infantry moving towards the enemy's battle formation. Seeing this, Cato resorted to psychological warfare, ordering two cohorts to be taken around the enemy's right and show themselves at the enemy's rear before the infantry became engaged. This menacing Roman presence to the enemy's rear made the battle even, for the enemy now had to worry about being attacked from behind; still, the Roman right wing had become so demoralized that many of the men panicked and took flight, making it difficult for the Romans to hold the line. The left wing, on the other hand, was pressing back the barbarians' frontline, and the Roman cohorts to the barbarians' rear were creating panic among them. After hard hand-to-hand fighting, the Iberians were forced back into their camp, at which point Cato sent in his reserve legion to storm their fortifications. Surveying the enemy's position for a weak point, Cato discovered that the defenders were vulnerable at the left gate of their camp, so he directed the *hastate* and *principes* of his second legion to concentrate their attack on that position. The defenders holding the gate could not withstand the attack any longer and abandoned it, leaving an opening for the Romans. All further attempts to retain the camp were discarded and after some fighting the Iberians flung away their arms and standards and surrendered.[135] Livy states that many were killed, particularly Iberians, for on seeing that they were facing defeat they crowded together at the narrow spaces of the gates in an attempt to enter their camp, while Roman soldiers cut them down from behind.

After the battle, the Romans plundered the camp and harried the local fields in search of supplies until the signal was given to stop. After allowing several hours for rest, Cato decided to move his victorious army to Tarraco. Advancing uninterrupted along the coast due south, Cato's plunderous march through enemy territory scattered tribesmen over a wide extent of the country, causing many inhabitants in the area to submit to his rule. As they did not fight against Cato's army, he addressed them in kind terms and dismissed them to their homes. As he continued his advance, delegates from various communities met with him, only to surrender. By the time he reached Tarraco the whole north side of the Ebro River had been subjugated and the Roman soldiers who had been made prisoners through various mishaps were brought by the natives as a gift to the consul.[136]

This was seen as an amazing victory, for Livy writes, 'He is considered to have done three things on that day which deserve praise.'[137] He says the reason for the victory was Cato's having led his army into hostile territory, placing his army in a dangerous position far from his ships, supplies and his own camp, where the only thing his men could trust were themselves, their courage and skills to survive such a perilous campaign. The second reason was his strategic manoeuvre against the Iberian encampment, when he decided to throw his reserve cohorts to the enemy's rear. Thirdly, his order for a second legion to advance in battle formation right up to the camp's gate, while the rest of his troops were scattered in pursuit of the retreating enemy, led to success.[138] Overall this seems to have been a successful campaign, for by the end of it, according to Plutarch, Cato claimed he had subdued over 300 Iberian towns.[139]

While he was encamped at Tarraco, rumours soon spread among the

Iberians that Cato intended to invade Turdetania in the south and march against the Bergistani.[140] Due to these false rumours, seven fortified cities belonging to the Bergistani decided to revolt, but the rebellion was suppressed as quickly as it started without any serious fighting. Yet no sooner than Cato had returned to his base at Tarraco, and before he made any further plans to advance south into Turdetani, these same people for some unknown reason (not mentioned in the ancient texts) revolted again and were subdued again, but this time not treated so leniently — Cato sold a large portion of them into slavery to discourage any repetition of revolt.[141]

Cato's campaign in and around Emporion and the Ebro River Valley has received several different evaluations from scholars. Those favourable to Cato assume that he was in the right in conducting a military operation in the area to quell the troublesome Iberians, for the area was supposedly the heartland of the rebellion that had beset the province for two years prior to his arrival. But there is little reason to believe this. If these people had been in open conflict with the Romans before Cato's arrival, it is extraordinary that they took no action against him when he first reached Emporion, and that he was allowed to place his troops in a series of small encampments outside that city.[142] Richardson claims that although the first signs of hostility came from the local tribes, the Romans were at fault due to the repeated plundering expeditions and raids on friendly Iberian villages mounted by Cato for the purpose of training and provisioning his army. If Cato had not inflamed the local tribes, rebellions in the areas under Roman control would have not occurred. But it seems that the self-appraising Cato wanted a magnificent victory, so he chose where to fight and whom to triumph over, even if they were Rome's allies. Not only was it important to be a successful commander and consul in the provinces, but his success had to be recognized by Rome if he was to advance his military and political career.

While Cato was putting down the Bergistani rebellion, he ordered praetor P. Manlius to gather an army and march inland towards Turdetania to take control of the rebellious Turdetani.[143] This begs the question of what Manlius was doing in Ulterior, as he was praetor of Citerior. Although the answer, according to the ancient texts, is not so clear, it seems it is partly explained by Turdetania's location. In Roman geography, Turdetania was in the Baetis Valley, and although most of that region was in Ulterior, a part of its northern lands was situated in Citerior's southern part. With this said, it does seem that Manlius pushed the war across the provincial boundary.

The second part of the answer is perhaps that Praetor Appius Claudius Nero may have requested Manlius' assistance to crush the rebellion. But according to Livy, Nero is mentioned only three times in connection with the events in Spain during 195 BC.[144] The absence of any mention of him in the report of the fighting against the Turdetani seems to confirm that Nero had left the province to fulfil another assignment. It is difficult to imagine that he would allow someone else to command his troops and conduct a campaign in the province assigned to him.[145] Perhaps it can be said that Nero left the province a few months after he arrived, giving command to Manlius, taking another position elsewhere in the Empire.[146]

Initially Manlius had no difficulty with the Turdetani, who were considered the least warlike of all the Iberian tribes.[147] But trusting their advantage in numbers, the Turdetani did venture to oppose the Romans. When the armies met, the Romans began the battle with a cavalry charge that threw the Turdetani into disorder. This was followed by an infantry attack against the Turdetani line. The Romans decimated them, for the Turdetani warriors were hardly a contest for seasoned Roman troops, who were familiar with the enemy's tactics.[148] Still, that battle did not end the rebellion, for the Turdetani hired a force of 10,000 Celtiberian mercenaries prepared to carry on hostilities.[149]

Cato, perturbed by the Bergistani uprisings and receiving news of what Manlius was up against, began to be convinced that all Iberian tribes would do the same whenever they had the chance. So he decided to disarm the entire Iberian population north of the Ebro River. This step aroused such bitter feeling that many Iberians, according to Livy, supposedly committed suicide because they believed that life was not worth living without the right to possess arms.[150] On hearing this news, Cato summoned all the tribal chiefs and informed them that it was not in the interest of Rome to see the Iberians suffer, and that it would be in their best interest to abstain from hostilities. After giving them a few days for deliberation, they were summoned to a second conference, which produced no answer. Angered by their response, Cato announced that he would level their city walls in a single day. Suddenly, some tribal chiefs gave in, but others did not. Those who were noncompliant suffered the consequences, had their walls torn down and soon surrendered, with the exception of the wealthy Iberian city of Segestica (a ruined city near Zaragoza), which was taken by storm.[151]

The Celtiberian mercenaries employed by the Turdetani further added difficulties to Praetor Manlius' campaign. Manlius wrote to Cato for assistance and the consul marched his legions into the region. He found on arrival that the Celtiberians and the Turdetani were occupying separate camps. Encountering Turdetani patrols, skirmishes commenced at once and the Romans came off victorious, however desultory the fighting was.[152] The Celtiberians were treated differently, being respected for their fighting skills.[153] Cato sent a military tribune to them with three choices: join the Romans; receive double the pay that they were to get from the Turdetani and go home under a guarantee from the Roman government that they would not suffer for having joined the enemy; or, if they were in any case bent on war, fix a time and place where they could decide the matter by arms. The Celtiberian leader asked for a day's grace for consultation. When the Celtiberian war council met, no decision was made because of indecisiveness. While the question of war or peace was still in suspense at the council meeting, the Romans brought up provisions from the fields and Turdetani fortified villages to their own encampment. Cato could not induce the enemy to fight during this lull, for he had made a bargain with them, but he secretly sent some lightly-armed cohorts on a plundering expedition into Celtiberian country which had not yet suffered from Roman encroachment. At the same time he clandestinely marched to Segontia (modern day Sigüenza, Spain) with plans of attacking it, for he had received information that a large amount of supplies belonging to the Celtiberian mercenaries had been left there for safekeeping.[154] On Cato's return from his secret raid, he discovered that the situation with the Celtiberians had not changed, and ended the campaign season by paying the army with the captured plunder.

The following spring, he set out with seven cohorts for another expedition north of the Ebro River, leaving four legions under Manlius' command as a show of force.[155] Cato marched north into the Ebro River Valley to conduct separate campaigns against the Sedetani, Ausetani, Lacetani and the Suessetani.[156] After fighting the Sedetani, Ausetani, and Suessetani near the Ebro River, a number of Iberian towns surrendered to Cato. Of the four tribes that Cato went up against the Lacetani, a remote forest tribe, remained in arms, partly through their love of fighting and their fear of retribution from tribes friendly to Rome that they had raided while Cato was occupied with the Turdetani.[157] It was for this reason— their raiding — that he attacked them. Cato halted his men a little less than half a mile from an unnamed Lacetani town. Leaving a cohort to guard his camp with strict orders not to move until he returned, he led the rest of his force around to the other side of the town. His auxiliaries, mostly Suessetani (now allies), were ordered to advance to the city's walls for the assault. As soon as the Lacetani recognized the Suessetani arms and standards and remembering how they often raided their fields with impunity, they flung open the city gates and rushed out to attack them.

Cato, seeing what was happening and having expected it, quickly galloped to the city walls to see if he would be seen by the enemy. Successful, he signalled to his men to come forward. Along the city's wall and through the open gate they went, as the defenders had forgotten to close it when they rushed out in a mad rage in pursuit of the Suessetani. Before the Lacetani realized what was happening the town had passed quietly into Cato's hands. On seeing the diabolical ruse the Romans had inflicted upon them, they could do nothing but surrender.[158]

These accounts show Cato's ability to deceive friend and foe to gain maximum effect with minimum effort. His actions in these reports can be seen as propaganda for his career advancement, for they show that his tactical skills were not merely used to suppress rebellions, but to make resurgence impossible and to save manpower. It was easier to deceive an enemy than to spill blood. One might therefore see Cato as an ambitious militaristic politician, but there are some accounts of how he also acted with compassion, such as when he rescued the town of Vergium from an army of brigands.

According to Livy, Cato led his army against Vergium (modern-day Berga, Spain), a fortified town that served as a haunt and shelter for brigands who were in the habit of raiding the peaceable districts of the province. Vergestanus, the town's chief, went to Cato to ask for his help. Once Cato had come up with a plan, he instructed Vergestanus to return home. When the bandits returned from a raiding expedition and settled down, Cato made his move. On seeing the Romans approaching the town walls, they went into a frenzy and readied themselves for battle. When the Romans reached the city's walls, with his sympathizers Vergestanus carried out Cato's instructions to seize the citadel and open the main gate. By the time the brigands realized what was happening they found themselves caught in the middle. On the one side, the brigands faced Romans scaling the walls, and on the other the townspeople had begun to arm themselves, joining the fighting and opening the main gate to allow the Romans in. When the consul had gained possession of the town he gave orders that those who had held the citadel be set free and retain their property; the townsfolk who had sided with the brigands were sold into slavery and the surviving bandits summarily executed.[159]

The subjugation of the Iberian people was slightly more difficult for Cato than it had been for those generals who had served in Spain before him. Prior to the Second Punic War, the Carthaginians treated the Iberians as second-class citizens, but when the Romans came many tribes saw them as liberators and allies; thus many sided with the Romans. But after the war, the Romans were exploiting the Iberians and so their attitudes changed. By the time Cato arrived in Hispania the Iberians had had enough: some 40,000 tribesmen were up in arms.[160] Had it not been for Cato's arrival, their powers of resistance would have perhaps exhausted Rome's involvement in Hispania. But Cato was a man of such force, energy and ambition, taking up and executing single-handedly the greatest and smallest tasks alike, that he likely changed the outcome.

Cato's time in Hispania is of importance in examining why the native populace came to detest Rome's presence in their beloved land, because of the abundance of information on it in the writing of Livy, Appian and Cato. An analysis of the historical accounts suggests that the people Cato fought were not actively opposed to the Romans until he arrived and savagely plundered and ravaged their territories in order to supply his coffers and equip, feed and pay his army. There is no doubt that Cato was a successful commander, but whether his campaigns were necessary and to what extent it helped pacify Hispania is questionable. They do provide invaluable information, however.

The ample sources make it possible to see how Cato governed the provinces. They show that his style of government was harsh on the locals, and this is one reason why the Iberians disliked the Romans. As with everything else in the administration of Hispania at this time, relations with the Iberian tribes lacked the formal legal structures that would later become a feature in the life of the province. What made matters worse for the praetors who followed Cato, and even those before him, is that they showed apparent disregard for the alliances made by former commanders. But in some cases instead of using a *foedus* (treaty) to make an alliance official, the Romans at first built a *societas* (a partnership/alliance) with a tribe, even though they could not be fully trusted when the Romans needed them to come to their aid. Although there were several existing treaties, such as with Saguntum and Gades, the use of the full-scale *foedus* was not implemented.[161] Although there had been new alliances — which in reality were shaky —this still signalled to the Iberians that Rome's word was not to be trusted. The results of these unsteady treaties, which were satisfactory for Cato, however, were unlikely to gratify Rome's allies or awe her enemies. Though Cato claimed that Hispania was pacified by the time he left in 194 BC, the province over the next fifty years was more rebellious than before.[162]

On the other hand, Cato's presence saw the establishment of some new basic financial arrangements that would improve the futures of both Rome and Hispania.[163] The coastal territory along with the Ebro River Valley had been finally subdued, and a systematic policy of economic exploration, especially in mining, had been emplaced by Cato.[164] As for the administrative functions of the provinces, Cato made few or no alterations except regularizing tribute (*stipendium*) and instituting income from the silver and iron mines.[165] Also, throughout the ancient accounts Cato's desire to not overspend his budget is demonstrated by his refusal to buy food and supplies for the army; instead he seized it from the locals.[166]According to Livy, in his speech for consulship Cato proclaimed that he was able to cut expenses due to the quantity of booty he had taken.[167] This evidence also shows that he introduced measures that brought large sums of money from the iron and silver mines throughout the provinces.[168] Although Hispania was governed by an ad hoc government, it was an economically successful business, all be it blended with violence and opportunism at times; after all Cato did not come to Hispania to reorganize the administration of the province, but to fight a 'war' and win victories to advance his career.[169]

By the end of his tenure in Hispania, Cato claimed that the province was at peace. On his return to Rome, the Senate, in recognition of this, voted him a three-day *supplication* and a triumph.[170] It also decided to withdraw two of the four legions to celebrate Cato's triumph and show the Roman population that Hispania had been pacified.[171] However, as the following years demonstrated, the Senate was wrong in believing Cato's proclamation.

In 194 BC, in the aftermath of Cato's campaigns and Manlius' praetorship, two new praetors were sent to Hispania. P. Cornelius Scipio Nasica (son of Cn Scipio, who had been killed while on campaign in Hispania in 211 BC) was sent to Ulterior and Sextus Digitius (who had fought alongside Scipio Africanius during the Second Punic War) to Citerior.[172] In the aftermath of Cato's controversial 'victories', the newly elected governors had to face the enemy with forces less than half of their predecessor. Because of Cato's ruthless campaign these men had to deal with several rebellions that began to erupt all over the country, especially the Celtiberians, Lusitanians and several other tribes whose main objective was to defend their rich and productive lands.[173]

During the first few months of Digitius' governorship a large-scale rebellion quickly broke out. So large was the rebellion that Digitius could not contain it and was defeated. His defeat took him somewhere north of the Ebro River to lick his wounds and better prepare his army for another campaign against the skilled warriors of the Celtiberians. Utterly demoralized, the remnants of Digitius' army stayed within the compounds of their camp until more reinforcements could arrive; the Celtiberians had won this rebellion.[174]

Digitius' governorship was saved only by the assistance of Nasica. Livy writes that had it not been for Nasica's victory over the Lusitanians, all of Hispania may have been lost.[175] His campaign against the Lusitanians, a tribe feared among all Iberian tribes, seems to have ended the thought or continuation of the general uprising that was occurring throughout Hispania.

In an ambush during Nasica's campaign, his small army attacked a large Lusitanian army of bandits who had plundered Roman southern Spain and were on their way home with the booty. Eventually the Lusitanians broke and fled, suffering thousands of losses.[176] Nasica allowed the inhabitants of a city that had been sacked to reclaim what the Lusitanians had taken from them, and the rest of the booty was sold and the proceeds distributed among his soldiers.[177] With this large-scale defeat of the most feared tribe in Hispania, the Iberian tribes stopped rebelling and fifty towns, according to Livy, surrendered to the Romans.[178] Although this battle stopped the Lusitanians and Celtiberians from further rebelling, it showed that Cato's statement hid an instability that he had left behind.

Cato's departure from Hispania transformed many tribal groups that lived within the Roman realm from a nomadic and pastoral lifestyle to a sedentary and agricultural one. The Roman occupation of their lands harmed the way of life and social classes of many tribes, and in particular the young men who were the tribes' future. Lacking a warrior's lifestyle many youths become mercenaries, Roman auxiliaries, bandits or rebels in order to follow their forefathers' way of life. Outside Roman occupied territory, fear and rumours of Rome's hand reaching further inland incited other tribes to rebel against the oncoming Roman occupation, such as the aforementioned Celtiberians and Lusitanians, who lived in the interior and western coast of the peninsula. The continuation of warfare in areas allegedly pacified by Cato demonstrated again the effects of the misinformation that reached Rome due to its distance from Hispania. The information that had reached the Senate through Cato about the state of affairs was very different from the reality of Roman control in the provinces.[179] This can be seen more clearly during the years 193 and 192 BC.

After the battle near Ilipa there were no further problems with any other tribes, for Nasica astonished the tribes in the southern and central part of Hispania by a series of victories due to his generalship and veteran soldiers. The only tribe that constantly caused problems during his governorship was the Lusitanians, who although they had just been defeated continued to cause devastation in the southwestern part of Hispania.

It is also interesting to see that during the praetorship of Nasica and Ditigius we find Nasica, governor of Ulterior, fighting in the northern Meseta, while his colleague from Citerior was campaigning in the south. From Livy's writings on the locations of the campaigns, it seems that interprovincial boundaries were confined to the coast, while inland a commander was free to engage any tribe when an opportunity or provocation presented itself.[180]

Given the uncoordinated nature of these campaigns it shows that there was no grand design for the eventual conquest of the Iberian Peninsula.

With the onset of the year 193 BC two new praetors were elected to take over Hispania. Gaius Flaminius went to Citerior and M. Fulvius Nobilior was allotted Ulterior.[181] On hearing talk of the poor state of affairs in Hispania, before leaving Rome Flaminius tried to induce the Senate to assign him one of the city's legions. They refused because senior members of the Senate said their decisions must not depend upon rumours stated by private individuals in the interest of particular magistrates, and that no importance should be attached to anything but dispatches from praetors and the reports their officers brought home.[182] If there was a sudden uprising in Spain that needed more men, the praetor had the power from the Senate to raise emergency troops outside Italy. What is not clear in the Senate's statement is where these soldiers would come from. What it probably had in mind when setting this policy was that troops would be raised in Spain. But that was problematic, because the Roman population in Spain around that time could not have been very large and many of the Iberians once friendly to Rome were now enemies.

Livy goes on to say that just before Flaminius left Rome, Senator Valerius Antias said he should go to Sicily to enlist men.[183] With this, the Senate gave him the power to enlist men into his army. As a consequence, when on his way to Spain he was suddenly carried by a storm to Africa, he immediately decided to administer the military oath to veteran soldiers who had once belonged to Scipio Africanus' African Army, which settled had in North Africa after the Second Punic War. From Africa he was able to conscript an army of 6,200 infantry and 300 cavalrymen, and with that legion — for there was not much to be expected from Digitius' army — Livy said he managed very well.[184]

With the remoteness of Hispania and the limitation of the Senate's source of information, one can clearly see the difficulties it experienced in keeping a close watch on events in the province and on the activities of the proconsuls.

Arriving in Hispania, the rumours of war that Flaminius had proclaimed turned out to be less of a threat than he had feared, but believing that it would come, he initiated a pre-emptive campaign. His first target was the Oretani tribe, who lived on the southern side of the Sierra Morena, which bordered his province.[185] Though the Oretani lived in the province of Ulterior, Flaminius ignored provincial boundaries and crossed over. Within a few months of setting out onto the Sierra Monena, Flaminius captured the Oretani's main city of Inlucia.[186] While Flaminius was busy campaigning against the Oretani, Nobilior became engaged in a campaign against a confederation of tribes made up of Vaccaei, Vettones and Celtiberians, who came from the northern part of the peninsula near the border of Citerior. In hot pursuit of them, Nobilior climbed out of the Guadalquivir River Valley and marched to the Sierra Morena, just passing Flaminius, and fought the confederation near the city of Toletum.[187] By the time Nobilior took the city of Toletum (modern-day Toledo) he had marched his men some 125 miles (200 km).[188]

The following year these two praetors faced the same tribes again. Flaminius laid siege to and captured the wealthy and well-fortified Vaccaei city of Licabrum (today it is part of modern-day Córdoba) and defeated their leader, Corribilo.[189] Meanwhile Nobilior fought two successful actions against the Oretani and captured their fortified towns of Vescelia (modern-day Vilches) and Helo (location unknown), while several other towns surrendered voluntarily. Campaigning against the Oretani, he seized two major Carpetani towns: Noliba and Cusibis (locations unknown), and advanced east as far as the source of the Tagus River.[190] While Nobilior was attacking the small but strongly fortified city of Toletum, the Vettones sent a large army to relieve it.[191] Like Flaminius, he defeated them in a pitched battle, and after routing them he took their city. Unlike Flaminius, Nobilior invested time in 'Romanizing' the city, further extending the Roman provincial border. 192 BC was a successful year for the Romans in both provinces. Because of Nobilior's accomplishments in Hispania, he entered Rome in ovation with over 10,000 pounds of silver, 13,000 silver denarii and 127 pounds of gold.[192]

Although provincial borders existed, they were disregarded because the enemy's constant movement across borders forced praetors to conduct many cross-border raids onto each other's territory. Though these men crossed each other's borders there was no clear pattern of set strategies on how they or future praetors were to conduct solo operations or combined military operations. If a warring tribe was within one praetor's province he would try to contain it, but if the tribe withdrew across the border back to its territory or into the neighbouring province the praetor transferred his attention there by pursuing his enemy. It was in the best interest of the Romans to take out the enemy as quickly as possible rather than waiting for permission from the other praetor, because of difficult and slow communications. Though the provinces were created for administrative purposes, militarily it was a different story, for the Romans regarded the land they occupied as hostile.

In 191 BC it was decreed that L. Aemilius Paulus take over the governorship. Along with taking command of Nobilior's army, he was also allowed to raise 3,000 fresh infantry soldiers and 300 cavalrymen for service in Hispania Ulterior; the end result was that his new legion was made up of two-thirds allied troops, with the rest Roman.[193] A force of reinforcements of the same strength was sent with C. Flaminius, who was to govern Citerior.[194] These two praetors were stationed in Hispania for two years because the war against Antiochus in Greece had begun.[195] Nothing more is heard of Flaminius after 192 – 191 BC until 187 BC.[196]

As soon as Paulus set foot in Hispania he began campaigning against the Bastetani and Lusitanians, two tribes that lived in the eastern part of the newly extended province.[197] These two campaigns were marred by gloom, for 6,000 Roman soldiers fell. A worse defeat occurred against the Lusitanians near the town of Lyco (modern-day Pinos Puente); the survivors fled to their camp, which they had difficulty defending. Finally they retreated by forced march, fleeing from the enemy into friendly territory.[198] Once he had reorganized his legions, Paulus immediately set out again and besieged the Bastetani city of Hasta (an ancient town near Jerez de la Frontera). Facing stiff resistance, Paulus was compelled to issue an edict that freed the slaves belonging to the inhabitants of Hasta, and decreed that these newly freed people would hold and possess the land that at that moment they toiled over. The news of the edict spread across the city like wildfire and within a few days the slave population revolted, the city surrendered and Paulus kept his promise. This information comes from a bronze tablet found near the town of Alcala de los Gazules, 50 miles (80 km) east of Cadiz.[199] Once he had pacified the Bastetani, he set his sights on the stubborn Lusitanians, which he managed to defeat before his governorship ended in 189 BC. According to Livy this campaign had a demoralizing effect on the Iberian tribes that had continued to rebel. The Romans inflicted on the Lusitanians 18,000 casualties and captured 2,300 men, who were later sold into slavery.[200] This report of Paulus' victory was heard across the peninsula and Rome, which in turn made matters quieter in Spain, but only temporarily.

According to Livy, P. Iunius Brutus quickly replaced L. Baebius Dives who died at Massilia (modern-day Marseille, France) on his way to Hispania.[201] Ready for action, Brutus was surprised to find Ulterior peaceful on his arrival. The Senate had sent 1,000 Roman infantry and 500 cavalry, as well as 6,000 allied infantry and 200 cavalrymen.[202] Flaminius' replacement, L. Plautius Hypsaeus, found the same situation as Brutus upon his arrival in Hispania. It seems that Paulus' victory over the Lusitanians had quieted the Iberian tribes' will to fight.[203] On his return to Rome he received a triumph.[204]

In 188 BC L. Manlius Acidinus (Citerior) and C. Atinius (Ulterior) were elected praetors. With them, the Senate allotted more troops; this time 3,000 foot soldiers and 200 cavalry were added to each provincial legion stationed in Hispania.[205] Their arrival in Hispania was peaceful, but by 187 BC the Celtiberians and Lusitanians were up in arms again and ravaging the lands of tribes friendly to Rome. The Senate left the new magistrates to deal with the situation.[206]

In late 187, C. Atinius, who was into his second year as praetor, fought a pitched battle with the Lusitanians near Hasta. Despite killing 6,000 of the enemy and taking the city, he died after being struck by an arrow.[207] When Atinius' death was announced in Rome, the Senate quickly elected C. Calpurnius Piso for the job as praetor of Ulterior.[208] With the Senate's advice to hasten his departure, he rapidly sailed out from the port of Luna in northern Italy, so that the province might not be left without an administrator for long.[209]

In Citerior, rebellion broke out; Acidinus ended up fighting an indecisive battle with the Celtiberians. A few days later the Celtiberians, having collected a larger force, attacked the Romans near the town of Calagurris (modern-day Calahorra). There is no explanation as to why, though their numbers were increased, they proved to be the weaker side. Livy says that 12,000 were killed, 2,000 made prisoner, and the Romans gained possession of their camp and booty.[210] With Piso already in Hispania and the arrival of Acidinus' successor L. Quinctius Crispinus, the two men decided that at the outset of the new year (186 BC) they would combine forces and lead a victorious campaign against the Celtiberians and Lusitanians. The praetors took both their armies into winter quarters.[211] Together they commanded the largest army in Hispania since Cato. Along with the two legions permanently based there, an additional 3,000 Roman legionnaires and 20,000 allied infantry, as well as 200 Roman and 1,300 allied cavalrymen, were sent to Hispania to bring up Roman military presence from two to four legions.[212] Unfortunately Livy does not give details for the levying and distribution of armies of that year.

As soon as each army left their winter quarters, Piso and Crispinus marched into Baeturia towards Carpetania. They joined forces in preparation for carrying out concerted operations against an enemy encampment in Carpetania. According to Livy, the first battle began at an unknown spot not far from the cities of Dipo (modern-day Elvas, in northeast Portugal), followed by another at Toletum (Toledo) between foraging parties, who were soon reinforced from both camps, and gradually the whole of the two armies were drawn out into battle.[213] Because of the enemy's knowledge of the countryside and tactics, the Romans were routed and driven back to base camp. Roman losses amounted to 5,000, while the enemy's were light.[214] Fearing that the camp might be attacked, both commanders withdrew their legions during the night, and the Lusitanians appropriated what had been left behind.[215] After this incident, according to Livy, the Iberians remained inactive for several days and returned to their villages (see Map 8).

To recuperate their troop losses the two praetors spent time drawing Iberian mercenaries and auxiliary troops from friendly cities and restoring the courage of their men, which had been shaken in battle. Having regained their courage, the soldiers began to petition their leaders to meet the enemy and wipe out their disgrace.[216] On seeing their motivation, the two praetors decided to move forward with a new campaign. Marching onto the Meseta, the Romans fixed camp at a spot 12 miles from the Tagus River. Then, taking up their standards, they formed into a closed square and marched at night to the banks of the river. At daybreak they saw an enemy hilltop fort on the other side. Finding two places where the river was fordable, the army split in two and crossed — Piso on the right and Crispinus on the left. Spotted, the Lusitanians and Celtiberians stirred for action. The Romans, meanwhile, transported their baggage across and began to set up a new camp. But seeing the enemy in motion from the hilltop fort, the Romans deployed into battle formation.[217]

The Iberians, full of spirit after their recent victories against the Romans at Dipo and Toletum, fought fiercely. The Romans, still smarting from their humiliating defeat, fought like wild men. During the battle, the Roman centre, made up of two of the bravest cohorts, fought so gallantly that the Iberians found themselves unable to dislodge them at first. But they soon formed themselves into a wedge formation and began to cut through the Roman centre. When he saw that his line was in trouble, Piso sent two of his staff officers, T. Quinctilius Varus and L. Juventius Thalna, to the centre to stimulate their men's courage and warn them that all hopes of victory and of keeping their hold on Spain rested with them; if they gave way, not a man would ever see the other side of the Tagus, let alone return to Italy.[218] Piso, along with the cavalry, made a short detour and charged into the flank of the enemy's wedge as it was pressing back the centre. Crispinus delivered a similar charge on the other flank. The cavalry under Piso fought with great tenacity. Livy claims that Piso was the first to strike down an enemy, and rode so far into the hostile ranks that it was difficult to recognize to which side he belonged.[219] The praetor's conspicuous courage fired up the cavalry so much that their charge ignited the infantry to fight harder. Motivated, the Romans bore down and began to sweep away their foe.

The cavalry pursued the fugitives up to their camp, and plowed through the crowded enemy as they tried to escape the Roman onslaught.[220] Here a fresh battle began with those left behind to guard the Iberian camp. The Roman cavalry was obliged to dismount and fight on foot, according to Livy, while the reserve infantrymen were called up to help the cavalry take the camp.[221] The Iberians were cut down; it is said that not more than 4,000 escaped into the countryside from an enemy that had numbered more than 35,000.[222] Of the Romans and their allies little more than 600 fell, and of the native auxiliaries about 150.[223] Exhausted from fighting, Piso and Crispinus ordered the men to remain in the enemy's camp. The next day both praetors addressed the men and awarded the soldiers.[224] It is remarkable to see these two independent commanders, who had been assigned separate provinces, working together as they did. Perhaps their success can be attributed to their ability to ignore egos, attitudes, ambition, and protocols.

This experiment of cooperation was not repeated by the next two praetors, A. Terentius Varro (Citerior) and P. Sempronius Longus (Ulterior). It is said that Ulterior was quiet during Longus' tenure (184 BC and 183 BC) because of the successful campaign of Piso and Crispinius the year before. Unfortunately during his second year as praetor, Longus was incapacitated by illness, which he died from before returning home.[225]

In Citerior, Varro arrived and immediately took his army on campaign against the Suessetani, who lived north of the Ebro River. After winning several victories against them, he took the Suessetani's main city of Corbio. From this point on Varro's province was quiet.[226] The following year, 183 BC, he campaigned against the Ausetani, who lived in the coastal areas south of the Pyrenees, and against the Celtiberians.[227] Unfortunately, this is the only information Livy gives us until book 40, in which Varro enters Rome in an *ovation*, bringing with him 9,320 pounds of silver, 82 pounds of gold and seven golden crowns weighing 60 pounds each.[228]

Chapter 2
First Celtiberian War

During the early part of 182 BC, two new praetors were elected and quickly sent to Hispania, for the Senate had received news from Varro that the Iberians, especially the Celtiberians, were up in arms in both Hispania Citerior and Hispania Ulterior, owing to the long illness and death of the previous praetor, which led to the lapse of military discipline as well as the Romans impeding on Celtiberian lands.[1] P. Manlius was elected to command Ulterior, which he had administered before, and Q. Fulvius Flaccus went to Citerior.[2] Manlius, who had been Cato's second-in-command in 195 BC, arrived in Ulterior and quickly began to organize the province's affairs and reassemble the army, which had scattered after Longus' death. But when Flaccus arrived in Citerior he immediately went on the offensive and attacked the town of Urbicua.[3] During the siege of Urbicua, the Celtiberians counter-attacked Flaccus' rear. A fierce battle took place and the Romans suffered heavy losses. But no display of force could draw Flaccus away from the siege, and his perseverance finally won out. The Celtiberians, exhausted by so many minor battles, withdrew and left the city a few days later. This enabled the Romans to take the city and sack it. Flaccus gave the large amount of booty that was captured to his soldiers.[4] Beyond this event, Livy says, Flaccus did nothing worth recording in 182 BC.

But Appian says Flaccus did. In Appian's work, besides combating the Celtiberians, Flaccus had an encounter with a small nomadic tribe called the Lusones who supposedly lived on the Ebro River along with several other small Iberian tribes who had very little land.[5] According to Appian, Flaccus fought and defeated the Lusones. With this defeat most Iberians dispersed to their towns, but those who were lacking in land and lived a nomadic existence fled to Complega.[6] Basing themselves within the city's walls, they demanded Flaccus compensate them with a *sagos* (a Celtic word for cloak), a horse and sword for every family with a man who had been killed by a Roman during the battle, and that the Romans leave Hispania before things got worse for them. As an act of intimidation, Flaccus set up camp in front of the city's gate and promised that he would bring them their demands.

Despite the Iberians' threats and demands, they did not trust the Romans and abandoned the city.[7]

The following year, a large-scale rebellion broke out in Citerior. The Celtiberians were able to round up as many as 35,000 men.[8] On hearing that the Celtiberians were arming themselves, Flaccus began to draw auxiliary troops from friendly tribes, but was only able to gather a small number. At the onset of spring in 181 BC, he led his army into Carpetania and set up camp near the town of Aebura (modern-day Talavera de la Reina), while a small detachment was sent to occupy the town.[9] A few days later, the Celtiberi were encamped at the foot of a hill about 2 miles away from the Romans. When the praetor became aware of their proximity, he sent his brother Marcus Flaccus with two squadrons of native cavalry to reconnoitre the enemy's camp. His instructions were to approach as closely as possible to the camp's rampart to get some idea of the camp's size, but if the enemy's cavalry was spotted on the move, he was to pull back without fighting.[10]

For several days the cavalry squadrons probed around the enemy's camp. Each time the Celtiberians saw them, their cavalry emerged from the camp in an attack formation. But the Romans would not fight, and withdrew into the countryside. At last the Celtiberian leader ordered his entire army to form a battle line midway between the two camps, but not to attack the Romans. Each morning for the next four days the Celtiberian army formed up to antagonize the Romans into coming out and fight, but the Roman general kept his men within the ramparts of his fort. Seeing that the Romans were not moving, the Celtiberians gave up antagonizing the Romans and returned to their camp.[11]

For the next several days both armies sent out cavalry units on patrol in case of any movement on the part of their enemy. While each army watched their fronts, both sides went out to collect supplies and wood at the rear of their camps, neither side interfering with the other. After many days of inactivity, Flaccus decide to initiate an attack and ordered L. Acilius to take a cohort of allied troops and 6,000 native auxiliaries to make a circuit around the mountain which was behind the enemy's camp. When he heard the sounds of battle he was to charge down on the enemy's camp.[12]

The Romans started their march in the middle of the night to escape observation. At daybreak Acilius sent C. Scribonius, the commander of the allied troops, with his cavalry up to the enemy's camp rampart. When the Celtiberians saw the Romans approaching, their cavalry streamed out to intercept. The signal was given for the Roman infantry to ready themselves. No sooner than Scribonius heard the clatter of the advancing enemy cavalry followed by several infantry units, he turned his men and made for their camp. As soon as Acilius considered the Celtiberians sufficiently drawn off from guarding their camp, his army sallied forth from their camp in three separate groups. Without delay the Romans charged down the hill and into the enemy's camp. When the camp was captured Acilius set a signal fire to show Flaccus that the Romans had taken the fort.[13]

The Celtiberians at the rear of the fort were the first to catch sight of the flames; this was followed by a rumour through the entire Celtiberian battle line that the fort had fallen. Dismayed, the Celtiberians were uncertain what to do, for there was no shelter to return to if they were defeated. Their only hope lay in keeping up the struggle, so they decided to continue to fight.[14] As the battle raged for several hours, the Celtiberian centre began to weaken, while its right flank pressed hard against the Roman left flank. The Roman left flank would have been repulsed had it not been for the arrival of reinforcements. Romans who had been left to hold the Celtiberian town of Aebura appeared in the middle of the battle. Between Acilius and these soldiers from Aebura, the Celtiberi were cut to pieces; the survivors fled in all directions. The Roman cavalry was sent after them and slaughtered many who tried to escape. According to Livy, as many as 23,000 men were killed that day and 4,700 made prisoner; 500 horses and 88 military standards were captured.[15] Of the two legions that fought, more than 200 Roman soldiers, 830 Latin allies, and 2,400 native auxiliaries were killed.[16] The praetor led his victorious army back to camp, while ordering his second in command, L. Acilius, to remain at the enemy camp that had just been taken. The following day the spoils were collected, and those who had shown conspicuous bravery were rewarded in the presence of the entire army.[17]

Aebura was turned into a military outpost and hospital for the wounded to be attended to. Once the town was modified into a Roman outpost, Flaccus marched his legions through Carpetania to Contrebia (modern day Albarracin).[18] When Contrebia was about to be besieged, the townspeople sent an envoy to the Celtiberians for assistance. After several weeks, despairing that any help from their countrymen would arrive, the inhabitants surrendered. The delay was not through any reluctance on the part of the Celtiberians, but due to harsh winter weather which rendered roads impassable and river crossing difficult as incessant rain had caused floods.[19] Flaccus found himself compelled by the terrible storms to move his entire army into the city. When spring arrived, the Celtiberians moved against the Romans, ignorant of the city's surrender. After they succeeded at last in crossing the rivers, they arrived before Contrebia. To their bewilderment, they saw no Roman camp outside the walls, and concluded that it had been transferred elsewhere, or the enemy had withdrawn. So they decided to approach the town without taking precautions or keeping proper formation. Suddenly, the Romans made a sortie from its two gates, attacking and routing them. This surprise attack amounted to 12,000 killed and more than 5,000 captured; 400 horses and sixty-two standards were also taken. According to Livy, this second major defeat prompted the locals to dispense any further planned attacks against the Romans and rather bolster the defence of their forts and villages.[20]

Leaving Contrebia, Flaccus led his legions through the Celtiberian countryside, ravaging the land as he marched. He stormed many of their forts until the greater part of the Celtiberian nation surrendered, increasing the Roman Empire further west. In Ulterior, praetor Manlius fought several successful actions against the Lusitanians.[21]After these campaigns, both provinces remained quiet.

Shaping the Province

In 180 BC, two new praetors, T. Sempronius Gracchus (Citerior) and L. Postumius Albinus (Ulterior), were elected to take over Hispania. During the election, L. Minucius, a staff officer, and two military tribunes, T. Maenius and L. Terentius Massiliota, who had come from Flaccus' command, arrived in Rome and reported to the Senate their great news about Flaccus' victorious campaign, the Celtiberian surrender, and the establishment of order throughout the province. In addition, they told the Senate that there was no need of the subsidy which was usually sent to supply the army for the following year because the province was now able to sustain itself.[22] They then requested that homage be paid to the gods for these successes and that Flaccus be allowed to bring back on his departure from Spain the army whose courage had served him well.[23] According to Livy, this was a must, for the soldiers were in such a determined mood that it appeared impossible to keep them any longer in the province, and they were prepared to leave without orders, so this decision was necessary to avoid mutiny.[24] Gracchus, who was to succeed Flaccus, strongly objected to this proposal, arguing that he would be robbed of a veteran army and be forced to control an unsettled and rebellious province with raw recruits.[25]

The question of the army for Gracchus was settled and in defence of the veterans, the debate ended with a compromise. Gracchus was ordered to enlist a fresh legion of 6,200 infantry and 450 cavalry along with 7,000 allied infantry and 300 allied cavalry.[26] Veterans who had been stationed in Hispania for several years or were close to retirement were allowed to go home. Flaccus received permission to bring away with him as he saw fit those soldiers, whether Roman citizens or allies, who had been transferred to Hispania prior to 186 BC, while those who arrived after 186 BC would stay on and honour their contract with Gracchus.[27] Flaccus was also at liberty to bring all those whose bravery had served him well during his two successful campaigns against the Celtiberians.[28]

While the Gracchus debate went on in Rome, Flaccus led his army out from winter quarters and initiated a third campaign against the Celtiberians that had not surrendered. Irritated more than intimidated, the Celtiberians had been secretly building an army and planning a strategy to strike at the Romans at Manlian Pass, which they were certain the Romans would march through.[29]

In the meantime, while Gracchus was building his army, he instructed his colleague L. Postumius Albinus, who was on his way to Ulterior, to inform Flaccus that he was to bring his army to Tarraco (modern-day Tarragona), where Gracchus intended to disband the old legion, incorporate the new legion with some of the veterans into various corps, and reorganize the entire army.[30] This information compelled Flaccus to abandon his operation and withdraw his army hastily from Celtiberia.[31]

The barbarians, ignorant of Flaccus' real reason for withdrawing, believed he had become aware of their uprising and turned yellow and fled. With this thinking, the natives invested more time in setting up their trap at Manlian Pass. When the Roman column entered the pass, the enemy ambushed them from both sides. As soon as Flaccus saw this, he gave the order for every man to stand and fight and hold their ground. The Roman packs and baggage animals were piled up in the middle. Readying his men for battle, Flaccus told them they were dealing with uncivilized barbarians who had twice submitted to Rome's power but who are compelled to fight by treachery and not by true courage. He told the soldiers that they would not return home without distinguishing themselves, for at this moment the enemy had given them the chance of a glorious and memorable triumphal homecoming in which they would march through Rome with their swords reddened and dripping with the blood of their foes, and every man would be a rich man from the spoils of war. Time did not allow him to say more for the enemy had reached the formation.[32]

The battle was fierce and desperate. The Roman legionnaires and the allied troops fought splendidly, but the native auxiliaries could not hold their ground as the Celtiberians realized they were no match for the Romans, and instead bore down upon the auxiliaries in wedge-formations. This manoeuvre gave the barbarians much needed advantage in whatever direction they carried out their attack. The Celtiberians fought so hard that they threw the legion's ranks into disorder.[33]

Seeing this, Flaccus galloped up to the cavalry and shouted: 'Unless you can come to the rescue it will be all over for this army!' Its commander shouted in reply, 'What would you have us do? For we shall not slack in carrying out your orders.' He replied: 'Close up your cavalry squadrons and let your horses go where the enemy wedge is pressing our men. Your charge will have all the greater force if you make it on unbitted horses.'[34] They removed the horses' bits and charged into the wedge from two directions, inflicting great slaughter upon the enemy. With the wedge broken, the Celtiberians completely lost heart and began to look for a means of escape. When the auxiliary cavalry saw the Roman cavalry's notable feat, they too spurred their horses against the enemy, who were now thoroughly shaken and began to flee in all directions. This proved a decisive move.[35]

As Flaccus watched them run, he vowed to build a temple to Fortuna Equestris and celebrate insolemn Games to Jupiter Optimus Maximus.[36] As the Celtiberians scattered, the Romans regrouped and began cutting them to pieces all throughout the pass. It is asserted that 17,000 enemy were killed on that day, and more than 4,000 taken alive, together with 277 military standards and nearly 600 horses. The victory was not without loss, for the Romans lost 472 Roman soldiers, 1,019 allied soldiers and 3,000 native auxiliaries.[37]

For the rest of the day the victorious Roman army remained encamped just outside of the pass. With its former glory renewed, it marched to Tarraco the next day. Tiberius Sempronius Gracchus, who had landed two days before, went to meet Flaccus and congratulated him upon his successful conduct. The next day the two men went among the soldiers to decide who should be released from military service in Hispania and who would be retained. After releasing the time-expired men from their military service, Flaccus returned to Italy with his veterans, while Gracchus led his legions back into Celtiberia.[38]

Once in command, Gracchus immediately went into action. Appian tells us that the city of Caravis (Magallón),which was in allegiance with Rome, was being besieged by 20,000 Celtiberians.[39] Receiving news that the city would fall in the next few days if it was not rescued, as there was no means of secretly communicating to the town to alert them of his presence, Cominius, a commander of a cavalry squadron, came up with an idea and presented his plan to Gracchus. That night Cominius donned a Spanish *sagum* (a military type cloak) and mingled with the enemy. Once he gained entrance to their camp as an Iberian, he attempted to make his way into Caravis. Finding an entrance through the city's wall, he told the people that Gracchus was at the city's outskirts, so they should hold out a bit longer. Three days later, Gracchus attacked the besiegers, who fled into the countryside.[40]

Several weeks later, some 20,000 'inhabitants' of the Celtiberian city of Complega (site unknown) came to Gracchus' camp in the guise of petitioners for peace by bearing olive branches. When they had entered the camp the signal went out for the Iberians to attack. The attack threw the Romans into disarray. Gracchus quickly and cleverly abandoned his camp to the enemy and simulated a false retreat; he then suddenly turned around and fell upon the unsuspecting Iberians while they were plundering the camp, killing most of them. He then went onto capture Complega and the surrounding countryside and towns.[41] Once everything had settled, he divided the land among the poor of Caravis and Complega and settled them on it, and made carefully defined treaties with all the surrounding tribes, binding them to be friends of Rome.[42]

After the winter of 180-179 BC, the praetors (Gracchus and Albinus) agreed upon a joint plan of operation. Albinus, whose province had been quiet since his arrival, was to march through Lusitania against the Vaccaei, and if he encountered stiff resistance he was to return to base camp. Gracchus was to penetrate further into Celtiberia. But for some unknown reason he changed plan and marched south toward Turdetania, bypassing Carpetania and Oretania, and concentrating his troops on the high Guadalquivir Plateau, which borders both Oretania and Turdetania.

Making his way south, Gracchus began conquering the city of Munda, taking it in one nocturnal attack.[43] After taking hostages and placing a garrison to hold the place, he marched on through the Genil River and Seirra Nevada until he reached the southern coast, pillaging several fortified towns and villages and burning their crops until he came to another city of exceptional strength called by the natives Cértima (modern-day Cartama), northeast of Munda.[44] While Gracchus prepared to bring up siege engines against the city's walls, a delegation arrived from the town. Their words betrayed a primitive simplicity: they made no concealment of their intention to continue the struggle against Rome, for they requested permission to visit other Celtiberian towns and ask for help; if it were refused they would then take counsel among themselves to either fight or surrender. Gracchus gave them permission, and in a few days they returned, bringing with them ten more envoys.[45]

According to Livy:

> The delegates ate and drank. Then the oldest amongst them spoke by asking Gracchus on how and with what army he would combat against the Celtiberian nation. Gracchus told them that he relied upon his

splendid army, and if they wanted to see it for themselves so that they might carry back an account of it, he would give them the opportunity of doing so.[46]

He goes on to write:

So Gracchus then sent word to the military tribunes to order the entire army to equip themselves and practice their manoeuvres under arms. After this exhibition the envoys were sent home, and they dissuaded their countrymen from sending any succour to the besieged city.[47] At Certima, on hearing about the Roman army's strength and that their only hope of assistance had failed, they surrendered. At day's end a war indemnity of 2,400,000 sesterces was levied upon the Celtiberians and they had to give up forty noble youths to serve in the Roman army, as a pledge of the loyalty to the Romans.[48]

Gracchus then marched into the Carpetania region to take the city of Alce (modern Ciudad Real). For some days he confined himself to annoying the enemy by sending skirmishers against their advanced posts, but every day he sent them out in stronger numbers in order to draw the full strength of the enemy outside its walls. When he saw that he had gained their attention, Gracchus ordered the commanders of the native auxiliary units to offer slight resistance and then turn back to camp in hasty retreat, as though they had been overwhelmed by the enemy's numbers. He in the meantime would position his men behind every gate of his fortified camp. Gracchus soon saw his men running back towards the camp with the enemy following in disorderly pursuit. As the Celtiberians came within close range of the Roman camp's wall, a battle-shout was raised and the Romans burst forth simultaneously from all the camp's gates. The enemy could not stand against this unexpected formation and were routed. Nine thousand Iberians were killed that day, 320 taken prisoner, while 112 horses and thirty-seven military standards were captured. From the Roman army 109 fell.[49]

Gracchus then led his legions away from the city and deep into Celtiberian territory, which he ravaged and plundered. When the natives saw him carrying off their property and driving away their cattle, some tribes voluntarily bowed their heads to the Roman yoke, and within a few days Gracchus accepted the surrender of a 103 towns, while securing an enormous amount of booty.[50] He then marched back towards Alce and commenced besieging the city. At first the townsmen withstood the assaults, but when they found themselves attacked by siege-engines, they lost confidence in the protection of their walls and retired to their citadel. Finally they sent envoys to place their people and all their property at the disposal of the Romans. The

Romans agreed and received a large amount of booty and many townspeople were taken to be sold into slavery. Among them were the two sons and the daughter of Thurru, the chief of the Celtiberian tribes. On hearing of the Alce's surrender, Thurru asked for safe conduct to visit Gracchus at his camp. When he arrived his first question was whether he and his family would be allowed to live. The praetor replied that his life and family would be spared. Thurru then asked if he would be allowed to fight on the side of the Romans. Gracchus granted his request and released his family; from that time on he followed the Romans, and his gallantry and faithful service was helpful on many occasions.[51]

Ergavica, another powerful and influential Celtiberian city, became alarmed by the defeats that had befallen its neighbours.[52] When it was reported that the Romans were on their way, they opened the city's gates to them. Livy says that although many cities had surrendered, the surrenders were not made in good faith by the Celtiberians, for whenever Gracchus withdrew his legions from these areas, hostilities were renewed.[53] It seems that the reason for this statement from Livy is because soon after Ergavica surrendered, Gracchus fought a major battle with the Celtiberians near Mons Chaunus (probably referring to Mount Moncayo). It lasted from dawn until midday.[54] Three days later a bigger battle was fought and the Celtiberians suffered a striking defeat that cost them 22,000 casualties, while more than 300 were taken prisoner, along with the same number of horses and seventy-two military standards.[55] The defeat was so decisive that it ended the First Celtiberian War.[56] According to Livy, it seems that this battle finally made the Celtiberians assess their situation and sincerely commit to real peace. Gracchus had now become a celebrated hero both in Spain and Rome, and was awarded a splendid triumph.[57]

Once the First Celtiberian War was over and the treaties signed, he founded the city of Gracchurris (modern-day Alfaro), in the Upper Ebro Valley. Although the majority of Iberian towns had full Roman rights by the time of Caesar Augustus, at their establishment they were no more than outposts with no legal rights or status of any kind.[58] The establishment of Gracchurris marked the beginning of Roman influence in the central northern part of Hispania. For a long time it was believed that Gracchus had founded only one city, but during the late 1950s an inscription was discovered near Mengibar on the banks of the Guadalquivir (the ancient Baetica) showing us that he founded another. This stone marker records a dedication to Gracchus: *'Ti. Sempronio Graccho deductori populus Iliturgitanus.'*[59] Iliturgi was a mining town and a military frontier outpost.[60] If Gracchus was active in this region he was establishing communities not only in his province but outside it. With the further annexation of Celtiberian lands, the Romans began to consolidate this territory to effectively explore and exploit it more intensely for economic gains. To accomplish this, Gracchus first had to establish an extension of the provincial border by stationing frontier garrisons and persuading a major portion of the tribes within his realm to sue for peace and build an alliance with Rome.

In view of the time available for Gracchus to campaign amid his reorganization and settlement of the province it is unlikely that the First Celtiberian War was a full-scale war. According to Polybius and other ancient historians, Gracchus had become renowned for the large number of villages, town and cities that he had captured; many of these had actually surrendered instead of suffering his wrath in siege.[61] There is further evidence that Gracchus' arrangements were accepted by the Celtiberians.[62] According to Appian, Gracchus made some progress towards peace in the peninsula after years of fighting by having many Iberian tribes sign treaties, thus making them 'friends' of the Romans.[63] In contrast with most praetors in Hispania, Gracchus spent time negotiating with Celtiberian ambassadors and delegates and had personal contact with tribal leaders, reminiscent of the friendly relationships established by Scipio Africanus during the Second Punic War.[64] His alliances with the Celtiberians and Vascones would facilitate Roman domination of Celtiberia. Along with these treaties, Gracchus imposed the following stipulations on the tribes: pay taxes and render men for military service as auxiliary troops.[65] Along with these stipulations, the *vicensima*, a requisition of five per cent of the grain harvest, was established.[66] This annual quota represented a more efficient system of provisioning Roman and allied soldiers than hiring contractors from Italy or Cato's 'live off the land' policy. A final provision to *pax Gracchana* was that the Celtiberians could fortify existing cities but not establish new ones.[67] There is also some evidence of the introduction of civilian administrative organizations (i.e. issuing rights for mining to minting currency) and public works (i.e. roads). Besides being a war hero, Gracchus is also remembered for his administrative arrangements, which ensured peace within the conquered territory for the next quarter century.[68]

During the First Celtiberian War, Albinus conducted a successful campaign against the Vaccaei in the wilds of central southern Spain, supposedly killing 35,000 enemy warriors and collecting a large amount of booty.[69] Unfortunately there is practically no information on Albinus' activities to support this statement from Livy. Although he campaigned against the Vaccaei, the campaign may not have been long enough to cause such damage, for he arrived in his province too late in the summer to undertake a campaign as large-scale as Gracchus'. Also Livy seems confused about the time of Albinus' arrival in Hispania, initially saying that he was in Hispania before Gracchus, but the following year denying that he could have won victories against the Vaccaei because he arrived too late in the province to launch any type of campaign.[70] We can only assume that perhaps Livy was right in saying that Albinus arrived in Hispania with enough time to take control of his province, but was sent as a messenger to contact Flaccus, rather than a military commander, as he had arrived in his province too late in the season to conduct a full-scale campaign. Perhaps he did conduct small-scale raids and attacks to keep the populace in check and to plunder booty, food and supplies for his army. He probably fought one pitched battle against an angry mob of barbarians.

At the end of their governorship in 178 BC, these two praetors celebrated their triumph; first, Sempronius Gracchus for his victory over the Celtiberians and their allies, and on the following day L. Postumius Albinius over the Vaccaei and Lusitanians. Unfortunately there is no account of the campaign against the Lusitanians or further details about the events of 178 BC. The account of the Lusitanian campaign seems to have been lost and is only mentioned in Livy's epitome.

The Pacification of Hispania Continues

The general picture that emerges from the writings of Appian and Livy is one of continuous and unsystematic fighting. In terms of Roman territorial gains or treaties established between the Romans and Iberians, little stability was achieved in the peninsula because of the constant breaking of treaties and raiding of each other's lands. Prior to Gracchus and Albinus, there was no grand design for the conquest of the peninsula because the Romans and the Iberians were in a constant state of war. But after the victories of Gracchus and Albinus a period of peace existed.Unfortunately Livy and Appian, our two main sources about Hispania, wrote less about this backwater province during that time, focussing their attention elsewhere.

History shows us that during the scarce periods of peace in Hispania, immigration from other provinces and Italy helped the province increase its status through the introduction of Roman culture, which contributed to the economic and social transformation of the eastern and southern areas of the peninsula. Immigrants bringing Roman culture to Hispania were initially administrators, educators, soldiers, merchants, technicians and craftsmen. Sons of upper class Iberians were assimilated by being sent to Rome for their education.[71] But with new immigrants appearing at this time, many unscrupulous and shady businessmen, tax collectors and even government administrators also arrived, and in time this behaviour gave the Iberians a reason to renew rebellions with consequent interventions by the Senate or praetors, thus making pacification more difficult to achieve.

Of all the praetors who went to Hispania during the 170s BC, almost nothing except their names is known. In Livy's Book 41, it begins at the end of 178 BC; unfortunately there is no mention of what went on in the province except that the praetors were M. Titinius Curvus (Citerior) and T. Fonteius Capito (Ulterior) who were both proconsuls that took governorship of Hispania from 178 BC to 176 BC.[72] As praetors, they received a *supplementa* of troops — 3,000 Roman citizens and 200 cavalry, with 5,000 infantry and 300 cavalry from their allies.[73] Besides this information, it seems that Curvus was the only one involved in some sort of fighting and that the size of his army was reduced from two to one legions during his governorship.[74] Perhaps the reason that these men were not mentioned is because after the Celtiberian defeat and their submission to Gracchus, the province remained quiet. After the return of Gracchus and Albinus to Rome in 178 BC, warfare in the two provinces became less intense. Apart from the names in Livy's work and several minor events that occurred between 178 – 171 BC, very little is known.

The *sortitio* (casting of ballots) of 175 BC has also been lost from Livy's text but at least the praetor of Citerior is known to have been Appius Claudius Cento. On his arrival to Citerior, the Celtiberians broke Gracchus' treaty and resumed hostilities by attacking a Roman fort. The day had hardly started when Roman sentries on the ramparts and at the gates caught sight of an enemy advance in the distance. After the alarm was sounded, Appius Claudius quickly addressed the men with a few words, after which the soldiers then made a simultaneous exit from the fort's three gates.[75] The Celtiberians met them as they emerged and for a short time the fighting was equal on both sides, but because of the tight space of the gates, the Romans were having a hard time getting out and into action. But as soon as they got clear of the gates, the men formed up and deployed their line formation. They then made a sudden charge which the Celtiberians could not withstand. In less than two hours the Celtiberians were defeated; 15,000 were either killed or taken prisoner, and thirty-two standards were captured. The Celtiberian camp was stormed later the same day and the survivors from the battle dispersed to their various towns; this ended the uprising on the same day.[76] After that they submitted quietly to the authority of Rome. This is the only information Livy gives about Claudius' praetorship of 175 BC to 174 BC, except that at the end of book 41, Claudius returns to Rome and celebrates anovation for his victory over the Celtiberians, bringing with him 10,000 pounds of silver and 5,000 pounds of gold.[77]

As for the person who took over for Fonteius, according to Richardson a man using the cognomen Centho, found in the 'Fasti Triumphales', may have served as praetor of Ulterior. There is no surviving record of his activity in Hispania.[78]

In 174 BC P. Furius Philus went to Citerior, while Cn. Servilius Caepio went on to govern Ulterior. Each brought with him 3,000 Roman infantry and 150 cavalry and 5,000 allied infantry and 300 cavalry.[79] In 173 BC, two new praetors were elected and allowed to take 3,000 Roman infantry and 200 cavalry to reinforce the army in Hispania.[80] Of the two only M. Matienus arrived and took control of his assigned province, Ulterior; his colleague, N. Fabius Buteo, died at Massilia (today Marseilles, France). On receiving the information of his death, the Senate decreed that one of the two returning praetors, P. Furius and Cn. Servilius, would have to have his governorship extended for another year. It fell to P Furius Philus.[81] The following year, 172 BC, M. Iunius Pennus (Citerior) and Sp. Lucretius (Ulterior) were chosen to go to Hispania.[82] During their first few months in office, these two men asked for a *supplementa* of soldiers, but were refused. But when it was reported that hostilities would soon break out, the Senate provided the praetors with the standard number of required soldiers to keep the legions up to strength.[83] The *supplementa* consisted of 3,000 Roman infantry and 150 cavalry and 5,000 allied infantry and 300 cavalry.[84]

We see from the texts that these praetors' terms after 175 BC were only one year instead of the usual two. According to some scholars the increase of praetorships to two years came about with the creation of the law *lex Baebia de praetoribus* in 179 BC in conjunction with *lex Baebia de ambitu* of 180 BC. *Lex Baebia*, according to Mommsen, originated from the need for praetors in Hispania to spend two years there before returning to Rome to become candidates for consulship. But we see from the texts that these praetors' terms after 175 BC were only one year instead of two. The reason praetorship in Hispania was reduced from two years back to one is unknown, but it has been suggested that the senatorial class preferred to have a larger number of magistracies to compete for office rather than a smaller group when it came for consulship candidacy.[87]

In 171 BC, in the midst of the war against Perseus, king of Macedon,[88] the two provinces were combined into one.[88] L. Canuleius Dives was sent to Hispania for two years. During Dives' governorship two incidents occurred, according to Livy.[89] The first occurred before he left for Hispania, when a delegation of natives from both provinces was given a Senate audience in

Rome. The delegates complained of the rapacity and oppression of several Roman magistrates. Falling on their knees, they begged the Senate not to oppress Rome's allies any longer. Though there were other indignities that they complained of, the evidence bore chiefly upon the illegal seizure of money. Dives was instructed by the Senate to appoint four senatorial counsels (*recuperators*) who had previously served in Hispania, and to try each of the individuals from whom the Spaniards demanded redress; and the emissaries were allowed to pick counsellors who had also served in Hispania to represent their case. Several days later the delegation was called into the Senate house, the decree was read to them, and they were told to nominate their counsel. They named four — M. Porcius Cato, P. Cornelius Scipio, L. Aemilius Paulus, and C. Sulpicius Gallus. The *recuperatores* then commenced with the cases of M. Titinius Curvus, P. Furius Philus and M. Matienus. These former praetors of Hispania had been charged with very serious offences.[90]

The first case involved litigations from both provinces against M. Titinius, who was acquitted after two adjournments. After the trial a disagreement arose between the emissaries and as a result the *patroni* (patrons) split. Those from Citerior chose M. Cato and P. Scipio as their counsel, those from Ulterior, L. Paullus and Sulpicius Gallus.[91]

The second trial began soon after, with each party having its own trial. The representatives from Citerior brought their case against P. Furius Philus, while those from Ulterior brought their case against M. Matienius.[92] After the first adjournment, both accused men went into voluntary exile. Philus went Praeneste (modern Palestrina, Italy), while Matienius went to Tibur (modern Tivoli, Italy).

It is unclear what satisfaction the Iberians gained from the court proceedings, but according to Livy there was a rumour that although the Iberians had complaints against these men their counsels were prevented from summoning members of the Roman nobility and men of influence who had served in Hispania, which perhaps shows that the counsellors had been prevented by powerful forces within the Senate from making the accused suffer the punishments they deserved.[93]

These courtroom events have attracted some scholarly attention, for they constituted the first occasion in which complaints from provincials were dealt with by a quasi-judicial procedure.[94] The use of *recuperatore* and the reference to '*pecuniae captae*' (charge of extortion) suggests that these trials were the precursor of those later conducted by the '*quaestio de repetundis*' under the law developed by C. Gracchus.[95] Richardson writes that Gracchus' law and the Senate decree stated that no Roman magistrate should be permitted to impose their own price value on the corn Iberian farmers were required to supply, thereby increasing the amount of money he would receive from the local communities should he permit them to pay cash rather than handing over the grain.[96] The same decree forbade a Roman magistrate to force the Iberians to sell off the half-tithe or one-twentieth of the crop that was apparently due to the Romans or impose his own officers on the communities in order to extract money from them by force.[97] These decrees would stabilize the market from magistrates attempting to profit from the sale of corn to Rome. Iberian farmers would, furthermore, receive cash payments from magistrates instead of handing over the grain or corn on credit. It is clear that by 171 the Senate was dealing with abuses of the taxation system, which were causing problems for local populations all across the Roman Empire. Though the Senate and praetors tried to fix these problems by emplacing a fixed tax, known as a *stipendium*, tax problems still continued.

Leaving the trials early, Dives levied troops and went off to Hispania to prevent more Iberians from complaining or accusing Roman citizens of crimes. But prior to his arrival in Hispania, a second incident occurred. A delegation arrived in Rome representing a new 'race' of men (in fact, more like a new generation). They declared themselves to be born of Roman soldiers and Iberian women who were not legally married.[98] There were over 4,000 of them, and they hoped that the Senate would give them their own town and Roman citizenship. The Senate decreed that they should send in their names, and they should be settled on the coast at Carteia (San Roque, Spain), and as a bonus, any Carteian who wished to remain there should be allowed to join the Roman colonists and receive an allotment of land. But as for citizenship, Livy makes no mention of it. This place became a Latin colony called the 'Colony of the Libertini'.[99]

A third and final event can be found in Publius Annius Florus' writing. During Dives' second year in Hispania trouble brewed when a messianic figure named Olonicus ran around the province brandishing a silver spear he claimed was sent from heaven. It was said to be a sign from the gods, who would give the Iberians the power to defeat the Romans if they followed him. But the revolt soon burned out following his untimely death.[100]

In 169 BC, M. Claudius Marcellus took over the praetorship of the entire province and brought with him a *supplementa* of 3,300 men to reinforce the existing legions in the province.[101] On his arrival to Hispania he had ordered the draft of 4,000 Iberian infantry and 300 cavalry. During his governorship Livy writes that he captured one town, called Marcolica (modern-day Marjaliza). The following year, 168 BC, he was replaced by P. Fonteius Balbas, of whom nothing is known.[102]

The lack of information about the 170s BC was due to the affairs of

Hispania being less at the forefront because much of the news was the same and important events were happening elsewhere, such as the war in Macedonia. Also during this period, many career-minded Roman military officers and consuls began to believe that serving in Hispania was disadvantageous to their careers. This negative outlook can be seen in 176 BC, when two praetors of the six elected to serve in various provinces claimed that for religious reasons they were unable to leave Rome and proceed to their designated overseas province. The two, as it so happens, had been assigned to take over Hispania.[103]

The sudden decline in the popularity of serving in Hispania is noted on several occasions, such as an account by Livy from 173 BC after praetor N. Fabius Buteo died on his way to Hispania Citerior. The Senate required a new praetor and asked the two returning governors to cast lots to see who would stay another term. This was an odd procedure, since it was obvious the man who had previously governed Citerior should have stayed behind to rule in Buteo's place. But perhaps, so as not to stir any hard feelings or sentiment, the Senate thought it would be safer to leave the decision to chance.

Prior to 177 BC, warfare in Hispania made or broke men's military and political careers, but after the Gracchan settlements and treaties the likelihood of such success lessened. After 166 BC it declined even further. The *Fasti Triumphales*, the triumphal arch in Rome which records all the triumphs and ovations awarded since the earliest times, are extant for the period from 166 BC to 155 BC and does not record a single celebration by a magistrate returning from Hispania.[104]

With a Roman victory ending the Third Macedonian War in 167 BC, the Senate decided to revert Hispania to its former provincial pattern of having two provinces instead of just one.[105] In the same year, Cn. Fulvius was sent to Citerior and C. Licinius Nerva went to Ulterior.[106] The following year two new praetors were elected, A. Licinius Nerva and P. Rutilius Calvus. Livy does not mention to which province each was assigned.[107]

There are long gaps and fragmented documentation in Livy's work, but Appian continues to describe what went on in the Iberian Peninsula after 155 BC. There is little content between the years after the First Celtiberian War in 179 BC and onset of the Lusitanian War in 155 BC, however. The little information that exists is from vague accounts of skirmishes with Celtiberians in 170 and 174 BC[108] and with Lusitanians in 163 BC.[109] Though minor revolts broke out, the military successes of Albinus and Gracchus and the peace treaties that came about from these campaigns ushered in a period of relative calm in Hispania that lasted until 155 BC. This semi-peaceful period was marked by a reduction in military strength in the province and an absence of triumphs and ovations for returning governors.[110] But the days of the Gracchan peace were numbered, as we shall see in Chapter 5.

The Senate's Involvement in Hispania from 205 to 160 BC

Although much of this chapter has concentrated on the governorship of the province and covered many military campaigns and battles, one cannot ignore the Senate's involvement in Hispania. During the Second Punic War and after, the Senate played an important part in forming the province by placing policies, making arrangements for sending men to govern the provinces, sending provisions to the troops and allowing praetors to enlist new recruits into the army.

Once the Carthaginians had been vanquished in Hispania in 205 BC, the Senate began to elect and send praetors to Hispania as governors on a yearly basis. During Rome's occupation of the peninsula, the Senate initiated the practice of sending two praetors to rule over a large piece of territory, dividing it into two sub-provinces in 197 BC. But there were times, during a national emergency such as war, that the Senate would abandon the method and have one ruler govern the entire province or extend each praetors' tenure from one to two years and sometimes three years. The governors that had served in Hispania during a time of national crisis all served three years except C. Flaminius (Citerior), the only one on record to have served four years.[111]

At times the Senate would also combine the two *provinciae* into one to make it more economical to the praetor who was sent there. This move freed up one praetor to serve elsewhere and gave the army extra manpower to fight in the warzone. One such example was in 171 BC, during the Third Macedonian War (172-168 BC). War had broken out in earnest and in order to leave a commander free to be at the combat zone, the Senate saw it fit to reduce the number of praetors sent to Hispania to one.[112]

Though Hispania was under military rule due to continuous fighting, senatorial power from Rome came into force between 178 BC and167 BC. At first there was a lack of interest by the Senate in the internal management of the area or on how the praetors conducted their military operations and campaigns. The only time the Senate was involved was in the debate over how a praetor returning from Hispania could qualify for a triumph.[113] For praetors to be rewarded with a Senate-approved triumph, it was decided that they must have led a successful military campaign rather than expand or stabilize a territory. This attitude shows that it was aggression and not imperialist expansion that they encouraged.[114]

But after 178 BC the Senate became more involved in the affairs of

Hispania, for example dealing with lawful acts. One such example recorded by Livy is the hearings of several former praetors that were charged with extortion.[115]After the trial the Senate decreed that it would have a bit more control over Hispania's affairs and its officials.[116]

As for establishing settlements, it was usually done on a praetor's own initiative and there is no sign of prior approval by the Senate in the founding of cities. Though the Senate had the power to override the praetor's decision later on, it never did for the basic reason that distance made using its veto power difficult. By the time the Senate's veto arrived in the praetor's hand, it would have been months too late and the town would have already grown roots.

Though there is no record of the Senate using its veto power over the establishment of Roman towns, there is historical evidence and much scholarly research confirming that there was a difference between towns founded by local commanders and those that the Senate established. Gracchurris (established by Gracchus), Corduba (established by Marcellus) and several other towns were not recognized by the Senate and so did not receive the status of '*colonia civium Romanorum*' until the time of Julius Caesar and Augustus.[117] As mentioned earlier, one settlement, the town of Carteia, which is documented as having been established by a direct appeal to the Senate from the offspring of Roman soldiers and Iberian women who had no right of *conubium*.[118]Although these people had a moral claim on the Roman state for assistance, they were still seen as foreigners (*peregrine*), but because they directly appealed to the Senate they acquired a status within the Roman system.[119]

Another recorded incident involved an alteration to the tribute payments and troop levies laid down by Gracchus in 179 BC. At first they were imposed only on Celtiberian tribes, but were later widely imposed on other Iberian tribes. In 154 BC, in the course of negotiations with the Senate, the Celtiberian tribes of Belli and Titthi argued that they had been released from their obligations to Rome according to the treaty they had signed with Gracchus. In Appian's writing, the Belli and Titthi tribes' argument was brought forth to the Senate, which granted both tribes an exemption, but added that they should continue to serve Rome for the betterment of their people.[120] It seems that when the Senate was directly approached by provincial delegates presenting their cases, it showed no reluctance to act on their requests or demands. But when it came time to implement the provincial delegates' requests there is little indication that it took any initiative in the internal affairs of the provinces, which was in the hands of the praetors. Even though the Senate granted the tribes an exemption, it was only temporary.

With all this in mind, it is perhaps safe to say that the attitude taken by both Roman praetors and the Iberian people towards treaties and other relations, or the establishment of settlements, indicates that the power of decision making was mainly in the hands of the praetors, whether or not the Senate attempted to enforce its policy. This independence is not surprising considering the power entrusted to a praetor, who held '*imperium.*' Rapid decision making was required in an area sporadically in a state of war, and because of distance and poor communications between Hispania to Rome it was vital for the survival of the empire that these men make on-the-spot decisions. But on the praetor's return to Rome, the Senate was bound to scrutinize his activities, including his military failures as well as successes. If a provincial delegate complained about a praetor's misdeeds, the Senate acted by reprimanding or correcting the praetor's mistake.[121] Thus debate in the Senate about Hispania focused mainly on the praetor's military record, which area or how much more land had been added to the empire, and whether he should receive a triumph or not.

Although Rome played a part in the affairs of Hispania it was the praetors who in reality brought Hispania to Rome or vice-a-versa regarding its policies. Though the Iberian Peninsula was constantly at war, from the end of the Second Punic War to the middle of Gracchus' governorship, various civil institutions were beginning to develop. These 'civilian' arrangements grew out of military functions: for example, taxation of the locals began as a levy of grain and corn to feed the troops. But the most notable changes occurred during T. Sempronius Gracchus and L. Postumius Albinus' praetorship between 180 BC and 178 BC. After much fighting the two men, particularly Gracchus, were able to set up peace agreements between the Romans and various tribes, dictating the policies that the Senate had been trying to implement since the end of the Second Punic War. Livy records the negotiations between Gracchus and the Celtiberians, but we do not have the details of the treaty for the last chapters of Book 40 and the beginning of Book 41 may have been lost. Appian is the only source to describe these arrangements, but does so without much detail.[122] Unfortunately his brief description is not much help when attempting to determine the extent of Gracchus' arrangements. They were, however, the basis for relations between the Romans and those tribes that would later be involved in the Third Celtiberian War, also known as the Numantine War.[123] In the end the practices, institutions, polices and cultural influences that were to shape the area into provinces of the Roman Empire came from Roman military commanders and not from the Senate.

Chapter 3
Lusitanian Warfare and Weapons

If we look closely at the history of the Iberian Peninsula, especially the western part between the years 155-138 BC (the campaigns of Viriathus), we cannot help but be amazed at how several dispersed tribes without cohesion, discipline, espirit de corps or military training were able to humiliate and defeat in battle after battle the most fantastic war machine ever: the Roman army. It is estimated that during this period the Lusitanians killed over 25,000 Roman legionnaires, and injured many others so seriously that they were unable to return to the Roman rank and file.

In order to understand the dimensions of the conflict and the reasons for the success of the Lusitanian army we must examine the tribal military formations and weapons of the people living in the territory the Romans called Lusitania. Although each operated independently, these disorganized tribes were obliged at times to ally themselves to combat a common enemy. Through my research, I have been able to build up a picture of the dimensions and reality of the conflict that pitted these people in a ten-year war against an organized, disciplined and experienced Roman army.

Before we begin the study of the war, to understand Lusitanian military tactics we must look at the lives of Lusitanian warriors, their ideals and combat techniques, character, armament, influences and contacts.

The Warrior

To understand the behaviour of Lusitanians in the battlefield and the measure of their weapons, we must try to assume the shape of the combatant. Though the Lusitanian army had men from the warrior class, the majority were non-professional soldiers. Its citizen soldiers came from all professions, such as craftsmen, farmers and shepherds. Although most Lusitanian men were not from the warrior or noble class, they were used to constant tribal warfare and, as such, became skilled and resolute citizen soldiers. In addition, many had also been mercenaries or bandits at one time or another.

Despite being citizen soldiers, Lusitanian warriors' soldiering skills were so top notch that according to the classical texts they were agile, cunning, ferocious, versatile, indefatigable, and brave — but still somewhat inferior to the Roman legionnaires because they lacked unit cohesion and professionalism. The 'Iberian' fighting skills and their system of warfare are far more apparent in historical accounts than what these people did on an everyday basis. The aggressive nature of Iberians, especially the Lusitanians, was due not only to an innate warlike disposition but also because poverty and unequal distribution of wealth turned those without material property into outlaws.[1]

Lusitanians had a basic attitude about life and regarded warfare as a part of it, as did many societies of this type throughout the ancient world. War was considered part of their background and was a rite that all young men had to participate in to pass from adolescence to manhood. Diodorus reports that it was characteristic of the Iberian people, particularly the Lusitanians, that when a boy reached adulthood he would, in order to show his courage and newly gained skills with weapons, be sent into the mountains and left there for some time.[2] This process would show which youths were the fittest and strongest, enabling them to progress into mature warriors. In some other cultures, weaker youths and the physically uncoordinated might not survive. They would often be cast out of the tribe and perished when left to fend for themselves. This brutal method occurred among various peoples, including the Spartans, for it ensured that the tribe remained strong and healthy. The style of training and the constant practice these young men were put through was intended to build a formidable fighting man capable of facing and evading all types of situations, no matter how tough. To the Romans, attached to the old methods of fighting as a unit, these barbaric guerrilla tactics constituted a huge surprise. Life was hard in a hostile environment of harsh mountain living, and everyday hazards were a large part of Lusitanians' daily lives. One can say that the mountains, hills and plains were their home and wars against other tribes were a form of ultimate survival.

For the Lusitanians, weaker youths were not outcasts. Those who showed a high degree of intelligence were placed under the care of priests who would nurture and encourage their talents for the good of the tribe, while others became apprentices under craftsmen. It was through these people that new techniques and advances would come. Others who did not possess the physical build to be a warrior, nor the intelligence or talent to become a craftsman, would become farmers and food gatherers. There was at least one way each member could contribute to the tribe.

With young men's baptisms into adulthood they may have received tattoos. The Romans recorded tattooing in cultures they considered barbaric and came to think of the practice as a barbarian trait. It was thus deemed unseemly for Romans to get tattoos, so they primarily used them to mark slaves and condemned criminals. But this does not mean ordinary Romans did not tattoo themselves — many did, especially during military service.[3] However once certain individuals, such as noblemen, began to move up in the social ranks of Roman society, they often found it wise to consult the services of a physician to have their tattoos removed. The written records the Romans left behind show there was a booming business in tattoo removal, attesting to the fact that Roman citizens got tattoos — no matter how 'barbarian' the practice was considered.[4] Unfortunately, for the Iberian cultures there is no proof of tattoos except the assumption that pre-Christian Germanic, Celtic and other central and northern European tribes were often heavily tattooed, according to surviving accounts.[5] Many scholars speculate that with all the Celtic cultural influences on Iberians, they also assimilated the desire to have tattoos in their culture.[6]

In prehistory, the dance initiated hunting ceremonies that were surrounded by a halo of magic. In time hunting dances were transferred to the hunt of humans (i.e. the war dance). The war dance involved mock combat performed as a ritual connection with endemic warfare. Warriors preceded war dances and songs with magical rites; Lusitanian culture always sacrificed a male goat, horse or human to Cariocecus, the god of war. The hypothesis is that such dances and songs formulated a magical spell perhaps used to recall ancestors' warlike audacity and to ask them for blessing and success in either battle or raid.[7]

Upon the death of a warrior, funerary rites were performed. Several ancient texts mention various funerary practices among the Iberian peoples, especially the Lusitanians. The best example of Lusitanian funeral rites is that of Viriathus' own.[8] His body, attired in his best raiment with his weapon at his side, was burnt on a tall pyre. Warriors began a frenzied dance around the pyre, while a squadron of horsemen executed funerary marches and bards sang about the glorious deeds of the dead hero. Once the flames died down there were funerary games, involving 200 contestants, above his remains. This account was of the type of funerary rite that only took place for great warriors or tribal chiefs, while funeral ceremonies for lesser men were probably of a simpler nature.

After the funeral pyre had cooled down, the warrior's ashes were placed in an urn and buried in a small grave with his *falcata* (a Lusitanian curved sword) and all of his other weapons and personal belongings, while funerary games were celebrated.[9] The celebration of these games was perhaps a reminder of the famous '*devotio iberica*' practiced by the Lusitanians. Even in death the oath of loyalty, taken between warriors and their leaders, held until the warriors committed to accompany their leader to the other world themselves died in combat.

The Horse

To understand properly the importance of the horse in Lusitanian culture, we must look back to the sixth century BC when the Celtic tribes of Central Europe emigrated west in the direction of the Iberian Peninsula. These tribes, despite minority status, were technically more advanced than the local inhabitants. For example they used iron while the majority of Iberian tribes still used bronze. Along with these technical advances, the Celts also had magnificent horses.

They had a type of horse from Central Europe that was a scale above the Western European horse. Though very robust, its mobility and speed were reduced and its handling somewhat difficult. But when Celts arrived in the Iberian Peninsula, they quickly noticed the equine population that roamed the land. In the mountainous buttresses of the northwest, the Garranos dominated the landscape. Despite the fact that these horses were small and rustic, they had great mobility and an incredible capacity to survive a harsh land, no matter how inhospitable. In the area around the rivers of Mondego, Tagus and Sado, the region was dominated by the Sorraias, a race considerably larger and heavier than the Garranos, but also rustic with great mobility. In time these people created a gene pool that became known as the current Lusitano horse.

The crossbreeding of the Central European horse with peninsular horses gave birth to a breed that came to be celebrated by Pliny, Possidonius and Silio Italicus. The almost divine character fo the Lusitano was expressed by the Iberians in their passion, respect and esteem for it.

The horse enjoyed such great importance in the social and military activities of the Iberian people that it was honoured and considered as a divinity as well as warrior. In some places, such as at Mula (modern-day Murcia), sanctuaries and temples praising Ares Lusitani (the god of horses) were built to honour these magnificent animals. Another source that provides evidence of the horse's role in a warrior's life is the numerous action poses painted on vases, statues and votary figurines found throughout the peninsula. Finally there are the horse burial sites that contribute to our knowledge about the horse in Lusitanian culture.[10] On worshipping Ares Lusitani, the Lusitanians sacrificed a goat and a horse, which perhaps portrayed a very strong symbolic significance — the horse being the very representation of the warrior's spirit rising to the heavens in hope for sacrifice and triumph.

By the time the Lusitanian War began, the cavalry and not the infantry was the backbone of the Lusitanian Army. In order to understand properly the impact that the horse had in the victorious campaigns of Viriathus, we must take a look at its training and equipment.

The robust Central European horse that the Celts utilized was somewhat difficult to handle. The Celts, who had become skilful with iron, had managed to create devices for the horse's mouth and harnesses to handle them better. These Celtic inventions (halter, bridle bit and reins) made it very easy for the rider to control the new Iberian breed. A vast number of horse bits have been discovered in Iberian sites and they are snaffles, acting on the flesh by pressure from front to rear. They are simple wings that prevented sideways movement and did not put pressure on the palate.[11]

Iberian wild horses, as described in many Roman texts, were very fast, of great beauty and of moderate size. They were also praised for their stamina and strength, as they were usually ridden by two men over long distances.[12] Recently discovered fragments of vases and painted stucco, confirm that two horsemen often rode a single horse. Even though the horseman's effectiveness depended on his riding ability, a large part depended on the use of saddles. At this time, actual saddles were not used, but saddle pads made out of wool, linen, weaved vegetable material, animal pelts or leather hides secured by a broad leather girth.[13] Sometimes the padding was extended to cover the horse's neck in order to protect it from the reins and trappings. Usually the rider had to manage the reins with one hand and hold his weapon with the other. Nevertheless, some cases exist where the neck-guard became a rein-control to enable the horseman to use both hands to handle weapons.[14] Riders undoubtedly rode astride, but there are vases that depict a rider mounted side-saddle — though a possibility, this effect is probably due to the artist's inability to apply true perspective to artistic rendering. As well as makeshift saddles and bridles, spurs can be seen in many Iberian vase paintings and statues. Stirrups cannot though, which perhaps implies that they were not used in Iberia.

Among Celtic scholars today there is some controversy as to who invented the horseshoe, which became an important contribution to the art of cavalry warfare. It is alleged that the Celtiberians may have introduced it in the fourth century BC.[15] This idea was boldly asserted by author Rafael Martinez, who discovered some of the oldest known examples found in burials sites in central Spain.[16] But the theory is questionable because early Asian horsemen used horse booties made from leather and plants and in time introduced them to the eastern European tribes who then emigrated west.[17] Another hypothesis claims the Celts had invented the horseshoe.[18] But no matter who came up with it, this invention greatly increased the military potential of the Iberian/Lusitanian cavalry and influenced the reorganization of their enemy's forces and the latter's use of Celtic technology.

The type of 'superhorse' the Celts had bred and the equipment they used increased the mobility of the Lusitanian cavalry, becoming the very essence of their army. It is estimated that cavalry made up twenty to twenty-five per cent of the Lusitanian total force, compared with fourteen per cent of the Romans'.[19] Also with these horses the Lusitanians developed a tactic of speed and surprise in which each horse carried two men: the horseman and auxiliary.[20] On the battlefield, the auxiliary dismounted and would go into battle on foot while the rider stayed on horseback. After the battle or if they needed to quickly withdraw, the auxiliary would remount and rapidly move out beyond the battle line or field.

The training of Lusitanian horses and horsemen was intense, but care was taken to not injure the horse. It was trained to kneel and wait in silence until a signal was given by the rider to stand up and walk towards him. It was also taught to climb and run on rough terrain, and to stand still during combat.[21] In open combat on the battlefield, when the cavalrymen fought on foot, they would leave their horses behind the battle line and the horses would not move until their masters returned (if the horseman did not return the auxiliary would take it).[22]

To demonstrate the affection and respect they had for their beloved horses, horsemen extravagantly decorated them with lavish headdresses, decorated parasols, a wide variety of prominent frontal ornaments attached to the brow, decorative chest plates, colourful wool caparisons, bells hanging from a throat-lash, and sometimes even chain mail.[23] Even the wings of bridle bits were decorated with metal rings, crescents and other shaped metal decorations. In the Iberian Peninsula the custom of dressing up horses still exists, and many anthropologists have traced this tradition back to the ancient Iberians.

But in war all decorations were withdrawn and only essential items used. Beside essential equipment, each horse had fixed on its halter a bell, rattle or headpiece so the rider could recognize his horse by the sound of the rattle's tinkle or headpiece design in the middle of all the chaos of battle.[24] These small decorations must have played an important part in combat, for there are representations of them in paintings of Iberian horses that I have had the opportunity to see. There have also been some archaeological finds of picket pins. Attached to the reins, they were perhaps used during battle. When caught in the melee of battle, horsemen would dismount and tether their horses, and as the horses were treasured by the warriors they would perhaps form a circle to protect them while fighting off the enemy at the same time.[25]

Compared to Lusitanian cavalrymen, the Romans were by nature poor horsemen. From archeological data about saddles, it seems that a Roman cavalryman straddled the horse on its kidneys instead of closer to the front. This was because it meant the horse's reins were longer, limiting the animal's mobility.[26] Equitation was restricted to the aristocracy who trained in the many schools throughout Roman Italy; thus the horse was not taken seriously as a weapon of war.[27]

The Lusitanian Army

In Roman literary works, the Lusitanian warrior was usually described as a mercenary incorporated into Hannibal's army during the Second Punic War.[28] Men under Hannibal became skilful in the art of war, and in their fight against Rome the Lusitanians applied what they had learned about war during their time with the Carthaginians. According to Livy, these Iberian tribes were incited to fight Rome by Hannibal's blistering speeches.[29] From this incitement the Iberian tribes sustained 200 years of fighting, without truces, for their independence (218-18 BC).

At the onset of Rome's conquest of the Iberian Peninsula, it was relatively easy for the Romans to occupy Iberian lands for they encountered friendly or submissive tribes. However, the further they marched into the peninsula, the more resistance they met. Of all the tribes they encountered the Lusitanians were the most challenging, due to their warlike mentality. According to Livy, the Lusitanians were warlike because of their appearance and their love for raiding and fighting, but when not raiding they were quite peaceful.[30] However, when their way of life was threatened by the Romans, they went on the warpath.

With this said, one has to look at why the Lusitanians were warlike and why the Romans attempted to pacify them. For starters the Romans had a belief that if one was not Roman one was a barbarian, and so there was a reason why Roman culture was forcefuly imposed upon the Iberians, bringing the peninsula under their domination. What's more, the Lusitanians lived a way of life (as mercenaries and bandits) that was considered by the Romans to be disgraceful.[31] Thirdly, although the Lusitanians were a proud and independent tribe, the Romans disliked this because if it was independent from the Roman yoke of power the tribes under Roman control would also want to be free and independent. Thus it became important that Rome control the western part of the peninsula.

With Romans encroaching on their territory and threatening their way of life, the Lusitanians began causing trouble for them after the First Celtiberian War. The Lusitanians initially launched border incursions, later followed by systematic raids into the rich southern cities of Rome's newly established ally, the Turdetanians. Between 193 and 180 BC there were a number of military dispatches and reports from Roman governors about the Lusitanians.[32] The Romans thus classified the Lusitanians as barbarians, mercenaries and bandits, because they devoted themselves to theft, fighting and dragging to their borders the spoils of war that had been accrued from countless raids. From a Roman point of view, they had to be put in their place to prevent their behaviour becoming infectious to the other Iberian tribes.

As the Iberian Peninsula suffered under the yoke of Roman imperialism, the violence the Romans committed against the Iberian tribes caused many of them to rebel. Rome had made enemies of the Iberians due to its policies and hypocritical political tactics. One example was an occasion in the Second Punic War, when the Romans persuaded the Iberians that they had declared war on Carthaginian oppression and tyranny, by boasting that Rome fought under the flag of pacifism, which in reality was false. Due to such Roman deceit, the Lusitanians launched a guerrilla war that successfully held off the Romans in various legendary scrimmages. From Punicus to Viriathus, the Lusitanians defeated several Roman legions. The war lasted from 193 to 138 BC, and only when the Romans successfully bribed three trusted Lusitanian officials to kill Viriathus did the Lusitanians fall and the war end.

One must remember the state of affairs in some of Lusitania's poorer areas. Poverty incited men to become armed robbers and mercenaries, which later proved important practice for guerrilla tactics against the Romans and their allies during the Lusitanian War. Perhaps, when the war began, the campaign against the Romans was seen by the Lusitanians as a hunt, raid or robbery acted on an impulse or organized on the fly rather than a military operation. But as time went on, the war escalated, and Viriathus was elected leader, he built an army of undisciplined highwaymen into one of warriors, with views about what they were fighting.

Among the able and skilled warriors in the newly formed army, some veterans were dedicated to Virathus' cause and able to assume positions in his army as captains, seen as a more permanent role similar to chieftain. As in similar armies, these men who had shown exemplary conduct or heroism were perhaps granted land or cattle as reward for their services. But in battle the ultimate prize for a Celt was not the victory, but the taking of a human head from the enemy. If a warrior took a head from an enemy, he believed he took on the heroic qualities of his victim.[33] Heads were kept as trophies and the removal of an opponent's head by a youth was seen as automatic qualification for manhood and acceptance as a full member of his tribe. It is believed that the Lusitanians and Iberians may have participated in the practice of head hunting.

To build and organize his army it was important for Viriathus to garner the fidelity of his soldiers. His soldiers were not just Lusitanians but also men from other Iberian tribes, integrated into a multi-ethnic army.[34] L. Perez Vilatela says Viriathus' army consisted of mostly Lusitanians, Callaecians, Celts, Vettones, Turdetanians, Bastetanians, Conii and Vaccaei.[35]

In spite of ethnic diversity, Viriathus seems to have given excellent military training and logistical preparation for his upcoming guerrilla operations. Showing great leadership skills, he was able to build a base with strong discipline and appropriate training. According to several classical texts and the research conducted by Muñoz and Schulten, Viriathus gained his combat experience by leading bandit incursions and raids into central and southern Spain and from participating in tribal warfare as a young man.[36] He probably had some organizational skills that led to the formation of his army into combat militia units instead of a ragtag army of marauding barbarians. In time the Lusitanians expanded their campaign across central and southern Hispania and some times recruited other allies, thus improving his numbers.

As for training his army, Viriathus had them continue doing what any tribal warrior would do when they were not out raiding. As a pastime, warriors were continuously fine-tuning their skills by conducting 'gladiatorial' combat (this ranged from friendly contests to fights to the death to settle serious differences between warriors), weapons training, boxing, combat simulations, and hunting and raiding expeditions on neighbouring tribes allied to Rome, which served as preparation and training for the soldiers that would become his army.[37] This army was now prepared for offensive guerrilla warfare and the weapons they had were well adapted for their military needs.

The Lusitanian army was composed of two bodies: infantry and cavalry. These military branches were perfect for Lusitanian hit-and-run tactics, for they carried light armour and weapons. In comparison to the Roman army, the Lusitanians lacked engineers (i.e. for siege warfare) and artillery (catapults and ballistas), as well as elephants. It seems the Romans used elephants against the Celtiberian and Vaccaei, but we have no specific information that indicates that they were ever utilized against the Lusitanians.[38]

The Lusitanian army relied heavily on ambushes, so it was important to have mobile infantry. Most of the infantry units wore light armour and carried javelins, shields and swords. These warbands were the lightest armed and among the most 'annoying' when harassing Roman troops. They would cause many Roman casualties throughout the day before withdrawing into the night. They would hide out in the surrounding hills or forests, only to attack again the following day. Besides using guerrilla tactics, the Lusitanians at times copied Roman military formations and tactics to defeat a Roman legion at their own game.

Through Iberian vase paintings and sketchy information from classical authors, several historians have come up with theories on how the Lusitanians may have conducted themselves while on campaign.[39] The infantryman is believed to have carried several javelins with bronze or iron metal tips, or '*sude*', wooden javelins sharpened and fire-hardened on both ends, along with a *scutati* (a long oval shield) for protection and a sword for close-quarter fighting. Along with these weapons some Lusitanians were experts with a sling and carried an assortment of different sizes for various distances. Each soldier took three javelins, two as offensive weapons and the third as a defensive one if needed. In an open pitched battle they would form a loose shield wall and from a distance throw two javelins towards their objective, while the third javelin served as a defensive weapon for an oncoming attack from the enemy's light infantry and skirmishers or regular cavalry charges. This did put them at a disadvantage against trained heavy assault infantry. Although ineffective against heavily armoured Roman soldiers, they played havoc on lightly armoured or unarmoured men and horses.

To incite the Romans to attack, the Lusitanians would prematurely organize themselves on the battlefield into an unorganized battle formation in front of the Romans' main battle line. They would then release volleys of slingshots and javelins until the Romans gave the order to attack. When the Romans began to move the Lusitanians would retreat behind their main battle line, which was waiting in ambush. The aim of this type of skirmishing was to disrupt enemy formations by causing casualties before the main battle, and to tempt the opposing infantry into attacking prematurely, throwing their organization into disarray. Once the preliminary skirmishing was done, the skirmishers would participate in the main battle as reserve troops or as warriors participating in the melee. Due to their mobility, skirmishers were also valuable in guerrilla warfare, for they would instigate an ambush by harassing the Roman column in the hopes that the Romans would give chase and follow them into the ambush's kill zone.

The Iberians were skilled riders who made widespread use of cavalry in all their campaigns, not only on Spanish soil but overseas during mercenary service. From these experiences, especially under Hannibal, they not only fulfilled the tradition of light cavalry as a force to distract the enemy but also proved capable of defeating Roman cavalry formations in battle.[40] The Lusitanians were skilful horsemen who rode surefooted, agile and resilient Iberian horses that were excellent for a country with rough terrain. Altogether they had the ability to fight on the battlefield, they could only battle for a limited duration due to lack of armour, so were used as shock troopers against infantry.

During Viriathus' generalship he used the cavalry as a stealthy, mobile guerrilla force that would harass and cut down unwary enemy formations before disappearing back into the hills instead of being wasted in costly pitched battles. This was possible due to one of the surprising characteristics of Iberian armies: their peculiar training of horses.[41] This meant many of the deceptive ambushes performed by the Lusitanians were surprising to an incautious enemy. The skilful training of Iberian horses combined with hit-and-run surprise tactics caused Romans to wonder why they could not beat an uncivilized rag-tag band of warriors.

Though the cavalry was not often used in pitched battles, there were times when they were called upon to inflict a decisive blow to the Romans. These horsemen were used to great effect against Roman infantry. But most of the time the cavalry played the role of dragoons, dismounting to fight on foot alongside the hard-pressed infantrymen.[42] As dragoons, these men would charge into the battle and form a protective ring around their beloved animals to keep them from harm's way or leave them behind several yards away.[43] Though they wore light armour and were armed with several small javelins (labelled by the Romans as *veruti*), the Iberian sword (the *falcata*) and a small rounded shield (the *caetrati*), which could be a disadvantage to less hardy horsemen, their ferocity, martial arts skills and thirst for freedom took precedence. As mentioned, the cavalry was excellent for skirmishing tactics as they were able to carry many short light throwing spears and hurl them at enemy formations while staying out of reach. Their javelins spent, they would enter the melee, if needed. They were armed and fast enough to stand up to most light and medium cavalry and medium infantry, but would get cut to pieces by heavier infantry or cavalry if they fought them in pitched battle. So at all costs these types of battles were avoided.

Via the ancient texts, it has been presumed that Viriathus may have had an elite cavalry troop made up of men who had proved their worth and dedication to their chieftain in the heat of battle.[44] While their backgrounds might have varied, they all had in common a religious oath of fealty. As these men were considered elite, they perhaps protected themselves with light armour of quilted linen under a composite of leather and esparto fibers attached to another layer of quilted linen and thin metal plates that absorbed cutting blows. Their weaponry was the *falcata* and *caetrati*. Although not numerous, these cavalrymen were fundamentally used as scouts and bodyguards. Being an experienced combat veteran and leader, Viriathus probably utilized these men as reconnaissance troops due to their mobility.[45]

As discussed earlier, the Lusitanian army was not entirely Lusitanian but intermixed with warriors from other tribes that had allied themselves under Viriathus' banner. These fierce men were used to a constant state of warfare, having served on countless raids and attacks on neighbouring tribes, probably having even served as mercenaries at some point, which afforded them their equipment and battlefield experience. Lusitanian warriors, according to Livy, seem to have been the most feared soldiers the Romans faced.[46] Their ability to hide in tall grass and seemingly appear out of nowhere, attack quickly and suddenly disappear worried and demoralized their opponents, who lost battle after battle against these hardy men. When properly supported these men were able to cut off retreats, harass supply lines and lower the enemy's morale to the point of making them take winter quarters before the campaigning season was over. Contributing to Viriathus' success in conducting guerrilla warfare against the Romans were the following four factors: his army's agility and flexibility on the battlefield, the use of the javelin, Iberian ferocity, superb swordsmanship and superb horsemanship.

Strategy and Tactics

To set the stage for this war we must take a look at Lusitanian military strategy. Viriathus' army won its victories over Rome's legions due to its intelligence network, deception, surprise attacks and ambushes, the black spirit of revenge and the thirst to remain free. In general, this form of guerrilla warfare was used by all the tribes that inhabited Hispania. This shepherd-soldier's strategy was being used before the Romans arrived on the peninsula. The need for men to train in the art of war is evident: robbery and raiding neighbouring people demanded that men also become 'soldiers' and not only bandits.[47] Exercising their skills as outlaws and their knowledge of how to use the surrounding terrain to their advantage turned these bandits into guerrilla fighters, for they began turning their skills as highwaymen into military tactics of surprise, forecast, ambush and false escape. This style of warfare was used at first as a defensive strategy, but under Viriathus it became a terrible offensive strategy that put fear into Romans.[48]

The political-military objective of Viriathus was for his homeland to remain independent in relation to Rome's imperial expansion into the rich southern regions (Beturia, Carpetania and Baetica), which was threatening Lusitania. So instead of waiting and allowing the Roman war machine to come onto his land he went on the offensive, either to liberate the territories under the Roman yoke or to keep out the Romans from his homeland. Though Viriathus and his army fought and defeated the Romans outside their territory, he never turned the conquered territories into Lusitanian possessions, preferring to heighten his victory by increasing his men's booty through raids and attacks on the Romans and their allies and allowing the tribes to live out their lives as they saw fit. For an occupation to take place, the Lusitanians would need manpower and material means and, above all else, an organized and administrative capacity that they did not have at their disposal. This dilatory, wear and tear strategy on occasions led to mortal tactical blows to the Roman army.

The dilatory strategy of skirmishes instead of battling on open fields was preferred because the Lusitanians were not able to maintain the necessary perseverance for a lingering campaign. So the tactics used by Viriathus varied according to the circumstances. At times the Lusitanians attempted to tire the opponent by disturbing them and impeding their provisions; at other times they sought to eliminate them through surprise ambushes or raids. Along with guerrilla tactics, the Lusitanians used the natural terrain and any land formations that offered abundant natural defences. But for these tactics to work, speed and surprise were the essential. The use of the horse was thus a determining factor. Each horse, as mentioned, carried two fully equipped warriors onto the battlefield; one man would fight on foot, the other on horseback. On withdrawing from the battle the rider and his partner would quickly remount and leave the scene.

Viriathus' mobile strategy required that his army be constantly on the move so as not to give the Romans any chance or reason to capture or destroy it. But when operating far outside the borders of Lusitania, his soldiers would need to rest and resupply themselves. On these few occasions his men occupied a friendly fortress, city or the hills of nearby towns as temporary bases of operations. Two such places have been recorded: Tucci (modern-day Martos, Spain) and Mons Veneris (Sierra of San Vicente in the province of Toledo, Spain).[49]

Besides relying on mobility and outside 'allies', one of the tactics constantly used by Viriathus was the hit-and-run ambush, according to the ancient texts. This guerrilla tactic was usually employed with speed and surprise within a mountain pass, a valley, in a narrow passage of a heavily forested area or anywhere enemy soldiers were obligated to march in long and narrow columns or tight formations. In an open or wooded area, Viriathus would try to annihilate Roman legions with attempts to disperse the Romans by conducting simultaneous surprise attacks using infantry soldiers and cavalrymen. He would then concentrate his forces on Roman formations, that had broken off from the main body. Once the Roman unit was devastated the Lusitanians would quickly disappear using their 'inhuman' ability to hide in the grass and thick hard terrain.

When Viriathus wanted to completely withdraw from battle and mislead the enemy, he used the following tactic: he would choose a group of soldiers and launch an unexpected attack at a different place along the Roman line, and while the Romans reacted to this new attack the main Lusitanian formation had time to flee and hide. He would also at times withdraw his troops from battle by simultaneously dispersing his army into small groups and reuniting it at a pre-determined spot.[50]

The one tactic that the Lusitanians rarely used was an open battlefield formation. When the Lusitanians did fight the Romans on open ground they usually used deception. The reasons for not fighting them in the open was due to their shortage of warriors, weapons, provisions and the lack of disciplined warriors to fight in organized military formations as the Romans did. Like the samurai of Japan, Lusitanian warriors had their own sense of the warrior spirit and individual glory, for these elements played an important part in their ethos. Knowing the negative characteristics of his army, Viriathus took advantage of them and transformed them into weapons. The Lusitanian/Celtiberian warriors went to war not only for individual glory but for the thrill of the assault, robbery and raid.[51]

But when the Romans and the Lusitanians did meet on the battlefield, mobility, deception and assault were crucial for victory. Throwing weapons were more important than the sword when it came to mobility. While the fundamental line of Viriathus' battle plan was the assault, deception played an important role in disorienting the Romans into making mistakes that cost them dearly. It is precisely this new modality of guerrilla war, along with a daring person who had an offensive spirit, that distinguishes the Lusitanian War from the other wars that took place on the peninsula. The First Celtiberian War and the Numancia War, for example, were defensive.

The deceitful tactic used by Viriathus was the attacking retreat. On the battlefield, the Lusitanian formations inspired awe and fear among the well-disciplined Roman legions partly because the Lusitanians, as most Celtic warriors, wore face paint of a blue dye made from a substance called *pastel de tintureios*. Before the fighting commenced the Iberian warriors would use tremendously loud war cries which the Roman soldiers called *barritus*.[52]

Issued by thousands of warriors, this war cry may have frozen the blood of many bold legionnaires.

After a great deal of preparatory chanting and ritual dancing on an open battlefield, trumpets blared out giving the signal to attack. Viriathus' warriors would attack in a disorganized mass formation. At a pre-arranged signal given by the trumpets, the fighting was halted and the warriors would retreat giving the appearance of a defeat.[53] Once the Lusitanians began to retreat the Romans chased them. With each 'withdrawal' the Romans most of the time mounted a pursuit, while maintaining their formation. After several attacks of this kind, the Romans would sometimes lose their discipline and break formation to pursue the retreating warriors. At this point a pre-arranged signal was given and the warriors would quickly regroup and mount a counter-attack which would frequently decimate the disorderly and heavily armoured Roman ranks, who were less agile in individual combat.[54]

At times, this Lusitanian manoeuvre would continue for several days, forcing the Roman legions to pursue the Lusitanians. But it was difficult to maintain such a pursuit for occasionally Roman military discipline would turn into bloodlust, and losing their military discipline in an area unknown to them cost the Romans dearly. Fighting against masters of guerrilla warfare in this manner cost Roman lives and material. After several manoeuvres of this type, the Romans would perhaps begin to lose their nerve and patience and withdraw from the pursuit. Then the Lusitanians signalled their predetermined signals, regrouped and counter-attacked the Romans, massacring and dispersing the demoralized Roman legion, who were exhausted and slow due to their heavy equipment.

This sort of military manoeuvring was known by Romans as *concursare*, described by historians as a simple absence of tactics, but this belief has been misconstrued.[55] For the Lusitanians to have held off the Romans for ten years there had to be some kind of coordination that allowed these ambushes, advances and retreats to occur simultaneously in the heat of battle without leaving groups of warriors outnumbered or isolated. It is clear that this model of combat was not developed at random but masterfully well designed and magisterially implemented.

In judging Viriathus' strategy, which has received many complimentary remarks from classical Latin authors and modern-day historians, it is also necessary to point out that Viriathus drove the Lusitanians to war because of circumstance and not for personal ambition or glory.

Weapons

Throughout museums of Portugal and Spain there are various Iberian statues in which we can see clearly the similarity of the clothes and armaments which the warriors wore throughout the peninsula.[56] These statues give us an idea of the type of tunics they wore and the various types of shields, daggers, axes, spears, slings and swords they used. Many warriors in Hispania used the combination of javelin, spear and sword to fight. Although lightly equipped, they were badly armoured compared to the Romans; their only protection was either a bare quilted tunic or a quilted tunic with thin metal plates, a breastplate or chain mail, and either a helmet or leather cap.

As with most warriors throughout history, weapons were a matter of individual preference and fighting style. Lusitanian warriors' preferences included combinations such as the *falcata* and *caetrati* (small shield), the spear and *gladius* with a large oval shield, or the spear and the *falcata* with a small shield or long shield. Others preferred carrying axes instead of swords, but although axes were mentioned in some classical texts, they do not appear to have been much favoured in Hispania.[57] Their martial arts skills of sword and buckler combined with their unpredictability and ferocity made Lusitanians excellent in single combat and they were often able to surprise and kill Roman soldiers in this manner.

SWORDS

Of all the weapons the Lusitanians bore, the sword stands out the most. Within their hodgepodge of weaponry the swords used by all Iberians tribes fell into two simple classifications: the straight (*gladius hispaniensis* and atrophied antenna sword) and the curved (*falcata*).

In the last few decades it has been possible to identify the prototype of the Iberian straight sword. The original influence can be found in the Greek *xiphos*,[58] *makhaira* and *kopis* swords introduced to the peninsula through Greek commercial endeavours or Iberians taking up mercenary service with the Greeks.[59] This sword design was then imitated by the natives. But the actual Greek sword was short-lived: with the arrival of the Celts in Spain around the tenth to the sixth century BC, the Celtic long sword began to be locally adopted.[60] It has been suggested that the first model of Iberian sword was not of a Greek design but derived from the Celtic sword, which had a long, straight blade.[61] Perhaps by the fourth century BC, it had been adapted by the entire region, giving origin to the Iberian-styled atrophied antenna sword. These swords had a flat iron double-edged blade and were shorter, topped by two small horizontal balls or discs. Compared to the early Roman sword that was a little longer and thinner than the standard Greek *xiphos*, the Iberian sword was sharpened on both edges with a sharp stabbing point, making what the Romans called the '*gladius hispaniensis*' ideal for encounters with foes with longer weapons, enabling the swordsman to swing, cut and slice from side to side.[62] Using a buckler or small shield to block or parry his enemy's longer spear or sword, the wielder of the double-edged *gladius* would then step inside the swing of the longer weapon and slash side to side and pierce the opponent at close range with staggeringly brutal efficiency and force.[63] The transformation of the Celtic model into an Iberian version made the sword lethally effective.

References to the *gladius hispaniensis* are abundant in classical texts. During Rome's Iberian campaign, the Romans experienced firsthand the effectiveness of the *gladius hispaniensis*.[64] In the beginning of the Roman presence on the peninsula during the Second Punic War, Roman legions came into contact with Iberian mercenaries, impressed with the technical and operational level of their swords. They quickly adopted and began using Iberian swords.[65]

Being very pragmatic people, the Romans never hesitated to adopt for their own benefit the technology and practices of other cultures they brought within the empire. The adaptation of the short sword was one such example that the Romans took from Hispania. But there has been some controversy over this subject — several scholars believe that the Romans did not get their idea for their famous short sword from the Iberians but from the Greek *xiphos*.

It has also been generally thought that the later Mainz type swords were similar to the Iberian *gladius*, but some scholars think this is not the case. For some, the Iberian *gladius* is the mother sword of all other Roman sword designs.[66] In the opinion of myself and others, it seems that these early blades follow the same Celtic pattern, with the difference being in a longer and narrower blade. I believe that in time the *gladius* changed to a blade that was thicker and shorter, which can be seen in the later *gladii*, now known as the Mainz, Fulham and Pompei types.[67] As mentioned before there are many references in the classical texts to the 'Spanish sword' and not the Greek sword.[68] A majority of scholars believe that the *gladius hispaniensis* derived from an early Iberian sword commonly known as the atrophied antenna sword. If we look closely at this weapon, we quickly realize that there are two separate types: antennae swords that originated from Central European models during the La Tene periods I and II, and atrophied antennae swords from the Iberian Peninsula.[69]

Aside from all the controversy and speculation about what sword the Romans adopted, the fact is that the design of the Iberian sword at that time was considered ideal for the people the Romans referred to as barbarians and for the new tactics the Romans encountered.

Prior to the *gladius hispaniensis*, the Romans used the Greek design, a sword unaltered since the Bronze Age. It was designed to stab and gorge an opponent with its thick and heavy blade. As a weapon made for stabbing rather than slicing or cutting, the point of balance and centre of percussion were not important in the manufacturing of Greek swords, so it was naturally an unbalanced weapon.[70] As such, much force was required in its handling, which naturally decreased its combat effectiveness and tired soldiers quickly.

But analyses of the Iberian swords verify that their point of balance coincides exactly with the union of the blade and the handle, making the sword more malleable to its handler.[71] Given this extraordinary malleability, it guaranteed much greater balance, making the sword more efficient. Used in close combat, it made the combatant a highly effective fighter. It was ideal for cutting and stabbing.

Lusitanian blacksmiths were extremely skilful and zealously hid their specifications, which were transmitted in great secrecy from generation to generation. Therefore the degree of perfection in the manufacturing of weapons throughout the peninsula was enormous. Diodorus reports that the Iberians practiced a peculiar habit before fashioning their swords.[72] Uncertain of the quality of the steel, they had a habit of burying their iron because soft iron rusts more quickly than steel.[73] After a period of time in the ground, rust would eat the weak iron and what was left was forged into excellent swords. The weapons that were fashioned were so magnificent that Polybius writes that they were considered good for both cutting and thrusting and would cut through anything which got in their way.[74]

The sword was manufactured by pattern welding, a process that was very popular and widely used until the eighth century AD.[75] The blade was composed of three parts: two tempered and highly resistant lateral metal strips and one metal strip that was the central nucleus of the blade. It was done by a process of composing several thin strips of steel that were less tempered to guarantee flexibility to the blade. When these three metal plates were put into the hearth, they were kept there until the outside of the metal had a slight glow. The reason for this was that while the outside of the blade was hot, the central nucleus remained 'soft' to preserve the sword's flexibility upon completion. When the sword blade was taken out of the hearth it was slightly cooled down and hammered on both sides while continuing to cool off. This process would be repeated two to three times.

The sword was then polished by a wooden wheel with pig fat and fine sand and immediately afterwards with talcum powder, leaving it as brilliant as a mirror. To demonstrate the quality of the product and the purity of the steel, Philon tells us that the sword-maker would pick up the sword horizontally over his head and, with one hand on the sword hilt and the other at the tip of blade, he would bend it. The sword bowed with both ends touching his shoulders. He would then let go of the blade and if it straightened itself out without any distortion it was ready for use.[76]

It was due to the technical superiority of this Celt-Iberian weapon that after the Second Punic War the Romans abandoned their old sword, modelled on Greek design, and adopted the Iberian sword. But they only took the design, not the manufacturing technology and techniques of the sword's secrets. Without a doubt Lusitanian swords were technically much better constructed and much more balanced, therefore making them more effective than any sword around at that time.

With the type of sword created for the Lusitanian warrior's way of life and later used to fight a lightning war against Rome, a special scabbard was developed to deal with how the sword was transported. The *gladius* was placed inside a leather sleeve reinforced with two metal bars on each side attached to three or four rings. At the end of the scabbard the two metal bars were welded together, forming a stud. As for the metal rings, the front rings protruded outward forming a bulge in the centre of the scabbard to be used to place a small knife and spear heads. When travelling through the countryside the scabbard was suspended on a leather belt on the right or left side of the waist, or carried by a leather strap suspended from either shoulder.

FALCATA

The third Iberian sword, which has not been mentioned yet, was the famed curved saber or *falcata*. The *falcata* was the most emblematic and effective weapon in the Lusitanian arsenal and brought terror to the toughest Roman legionnaire.[77] It was without a doubt the weapon of choice for all Iberian warriors over several centuries. This can be said due to the large amounts of these swords found on excavation sites throughout Spain and Portugal.

Its origin is unknown but there are three schools of thought on the subject. The first is based on the theory that the sword evolved from the curved 'Halstatt' knife of Central Europe, which had spread to Italy, Greece and later Spain.[78] The second claims that the *falcata* was a direct copy of the Greek *makhaira* or *kopis* swords that were introduced byGreek merchants or by Iberian mercenaries recruited by the Greeks around the fifth or sixth century BC.[79] The third theory holds that the *falcata* was of an indigenous creation, but many historians give little credence to this idea, for Greek influence was rampant throughout the Mediterranean.[80]

The term *falcata* is not ancient. The Romans had a habit of calling all Iberian swords *gladius hispaniensis* except the *falcata*, which they named *machaera hispaniensis*.[81] Unfortunately we do not know what the Lusitanians called it.

But the name *falcata* seems to have been coined by Fernando Fulgosio in 1872, on the model of the Latin expression *ensis falcatus* or 'sickle-shaped sword'.[82] He presumably went with *falcata* rather than *falcatus* because the Spanish word for sword, *espada*, is feminine. Although there are other theories, this one seems to be the most popular and logical as it follows the grammatical rule of the language. The name caught on very quickly, and is now firmly entrenched in scholarly literature.

The *falcata* has a peculiar shape, for it is a one-edged blade that pitches forward towards its pointed end, with the sword edge concave on the lower part of the sword, but convex on top.[83] The sword's design characteristic is an unnaturally large curved blade with a point of balance near the tip of the blade, making the weapon basically unbalanced and delivering a very lethal blow because its weight is near the tip of the blade.[84] Its blade shape distributed the weight in such a way that the *falcata* was capable of delivering a blow with the momentum of an axe, while maintaining the cutting edge of a sword. So, while the Roman legionnaires used the *gladius* to stab, the *falcata* was used to stab, slice and cut. The Lusitanians, being a warlike tribe, constantly fought in agglomerated formations, so a short weapon brought enormous advantages in malleability and effectiveness. Thus the length of the sword was very important. The usual length of the Iberian *falcata* was 60 to 70cm (23 to 27 inches), but the length of the Lusitanian *falcata* was much smaller — from 40 to 50cm (15 to 20 inches). Although it was normally a single-edged weapon, double-edged *falcatas* have been found.

Though mostly used for combat, the sword could also be ornamented. This hilt was usually adorned with a frieze of plaited or interlaced scrolls and took the shape of an animal's body. The pommel usually ended with a head of an animal, such as a horse, wolf, bird or feline, sometimes inlaid with precious stones for eyes. Besides combat swords, there were also ritual swords that were highly decorated.[85]

In many statues of armed warriors, the *falcata* is encased in the same type of metal-framed leather scabbard used for the Iberian *gladius*, as mentioned in the previous section. The *falcata* was hung by a leather strap from the shoulder across the body to the opposite hip, the strap being attached by metal rings on the scabbard and strung across either shoulder by a leather strap across the back. According to the classical texts the *falcata* used in the Iberian Peninsula was manufactured to perfection.[86] Like the samurai of Japan, Lusitanian warriors maintained a spiritual connection to their swords and when they died their swords were buried with them.

As the Lusitanians were master swordsmen, using a fast-moving style that required light equipment and quick handling weapons, one wonders what type of shields they used to protect themselves. They used two types: the *caetra*, a small circular shield used by *caetrati* or light infantry, and the *scutum*, modelled after the long shield of Celtic origin used by *scutati* or heavy infantry.[87] The *scutum*, despite its popularity in south and central Hispania, was never much appreciated among the Lusitanians, because it impeded the warrior's sword fighting movements and mobility.

Many statues and vase drawings, seem to confirm that the *caetra* was preferred. Also known as the buckler, this 30 to 60cm (1ft to 2ft) diameter light round shield was constructed from wood sections attached by two metal bars of bronze, copper or iron; it was then covered with leather. Although the buckler was commonly rounded, it took on many shapes and sizes. Size varied from 60cm (2ft) across to perhaps 30cm (1ft) in diameter. All shields had metal fittings and ornaments on the face with an iron boss in the middle, added to deflect sword blows as well as arrows and spears.

In combat, the shield was not only effective at blocking, but as an extremely proficient secondary weapon. Iberian troops used the boss to punch opponents. When on the move these compact bucklers could be hung on a belt or across the back by a strap, so as not to be burdensome to the soldier on the march or forging for food, but still handy for when the enemy was close.[88] Cavalrymen would usually carry the buckler so as to not over-encumber their mounts or limit their horsemanship.[89] This small shield survived throughout the Middle Ages into the Renaissance. One reason for the buckler's long life was probably its convenience.

The *scutum* was the classical long shield of Celtic origin. Like the Celts, the Lusitanian's version was flat, unlike the Roman curved version. As with the Roman and Celtic examples, the Iberian *scutum* had a large spindle-shaped boss that could be used to punch opponents during combat. During marches it would be hung over one's back like a backpack.

Ancient Iberian warriors were heavy users of javelins. In ancient Iberia, the spear was used by all Iberian tribes and was described by many different terms, perhaps indicating that there was a wide variety of models. They would cast this ranged weapon in volleys to disorganize the enemy formation before advancing into close combat with swords. The spear, which was used with deadly accuracy, was part of their armament. From modern archaeological research within the confines of the Iberian Peninsula there seems to have been an assortment of spears which have been classified into three groups: traditional and conventional spears of wooden shafts and metal heads, the all-iron type called *soliferrum* by the Romans, and lances.

Regarding the traditional spear, there are three subgroups according to the length of the blade. First were blades with a length of 30cm (11inches) or more. The number of large blades that existed are considered to have been used by heavy combat infantry. Second were blades of approximately 20cm to 30cm (7 to 11 inches). This suggests that they were popular and used on an everyday basis in hunting and combat. Livy called this type of Iberian spear *phalarica*. The third type of blade measured 20cm (7 inches) or less. This type was used by the cavalry. Horsemen rode with the blades at their waists or attached to their sword sheaths, so as not to impede their movements. Near the battlefield the horsemen would cut a wooden stem from a tree branch and put on the blade. If it was not used it was returned to its original place.

The conventional spear or javelin, according to vase painting, seems to have been the weapon of choice. It was light and every individual warrior carried a bundle of javelins into battle to throw before the enemy charged their formation, and at times the spears were used in hand-to-hand combat.[90] From archaeological excavations, spears heads ranged in sizes from 20cm (7 inches) to 60cm (23 inches). Longer spear heads suggest that they were used to penetrate armour, while the shorter spear heads were probably thrown from horseback and at close range. Of all the conventional spears and javelins the Iberian people used, the *falarica* was the most dreaded. In some texts the *falarica* is indicated as a Roman weapon, although its origin seems to be the Iberian Peninsula, for Livy makes a reference to it when mentioning that the *falarica* was used by the Iberians against the Carthaginians near Saguntum.[91]

The *falarica* was a javelin with a long iron pointed rod of about 90cm (35 inches) in length with a short wooden handle. Although the iron spearhead was a thin rod, a section was thick, giving the weapon weight to further improve its ability to penetrate and making it an armour-piercing weapon. Several vase paintings show the use of javelin thongs, wound round the shaft to impart a stabilizing spin and additional thrust when it was thrown.[92] This weapon was so feared that when it stuck into a shield without entering the body, it terrified the enemy.[93] As well as being a throwing spear, it was also used as a ranged incendiary device: bundles of grass or packs filled with a combustible substance were bound to it and ignited.[94] During sieges the burning *falarica* was thrown against wooden palisades and thatched roofs to start fires and cause havoc. When the Iberians were besieged they hurled flaming *falaricas* at the besiegers' siege engines. As an incendiary device it had an enormous psychological effect, helping to spread fear among enemy troops.

The *soliferrum* was an Iberian ranged pole weapon made entirely of iron. It was forged from a single piece of iron usually measuring between 1.5 to 2 meters in length and around 1cm in diameter. Though slim, the central part was usually thickened to facilitate a hand's grip. Sometimes there were mouldings of about 10cm wide in the middle of the weapon to further improve grip and to prevent it from slipping because of sweaty hands. The *soliferrum* was an extremely effective heavy javelin. The weight and the density of its iron shaft, its small diameter and its narrow tip made the *soliferrum* an excellent armour-piercing weapon when it was thrown at close range, enabling it to further penetrate heavy shields and armour. Unlike the *falarica*, the *soliferrum* remained in use in the Iberian Peninsula under Roman rule until the end of the third century AD.

Another weapon that was used was the pike. The pike was a long two-handed thrusting spear used extensively by the infantry as a counter-measure against cavalry assaults. The pike was extremely long, usually 3 to 4 meters (10 to 14 ft). It had a wooden shaft with a sharp fire-hardened wooden tip. Near the head of the pike, the shaft was often reinforced with a wooden crosspiece, probably to stop the horse from continuing to run itself through. This sort of pike can still be seen among the cattlemen of Andalusia who use it to control their herd of cattle. The extreme length of such weapons required a strong piece of wood such as well-seasoned ash, which was tapered towards the point to prevent the pike from sagging at the ends. The pike's length allowed a great concentration of sharpened points to be presented to the enemy, with their wielders at a greater distance when combating cavalry.

In the collection at the Archaeological Museum of Zaragoza there is another type of throwing weapon which is rarely found, known as a *tragula*. The tip of this barbed spear came in several different forms. Usually it had only a sharpened tip with two or more small protruding spikes. This hybrid spear was something of a dart or arrow which was thrown from a long leather thong by which it was then recovered if possible.[95] It proved to be dangerous to its user and deadly to its victim, for the barbed dart required to be cut out of its victim. Some minted Roman-Iberian coins bore on their reverse sides a military motif of a rider armed with a *tragula*.

SIDE ARMS

While the sword and the spear were primary weapons, many warriors also carried daggers and knives. The *gladius* was not the only weapon the Roman legionnaires used that came from Iberia. The *pugio*, a light dagger worn by

Roman troops, was of Iberian origin. Measuring roughly between 31 to 45cm (12 to 17 inches) long, the *pugio* was made of iron and had a sharp double-edged triangular blade. At the hilt, the blade was between 7 to 15cm (2 to 5 inches) wide. From statues we can see that Iberian warriors wore the *pugio* on the opposite side to the *falcata* or *espada*. In combat it was used as a back-up weapon. A small utility knife was also used as a last ditch weapon, a smaller version of the *falcata*. Roughly 20 to 25cm (8 to 10 inches) long, it had the same shaped blade as the *falcata* and was usually carried in a sheath attached to the *falcata* scabbard.

The sling is the only long-ranged missile weapon to have been found on the Iberian Peninsula during Viriathus' time.[96] Many men were armed with a sling and leather pouch of shots along with their sword and buckler. During peacetime these men relied on its range and they used rounded rocks that they found in their day-to-day life. But shot could be moulded from lead, which was mined throughout the area, and these smooth, well-rounded projectiles performed better in battle than misshapen stones. So ubiquitous was the sling that its ammunition remains today one of the most common finds in military contexts.

The Lusitanians manufactured their slings in accordance with the height and length of their arms.[97] The best slings were generally made from the stems of the black sedge (*Shoenus nigricans*) intertwined with tendons from a bull's or horse's neck along with hair from a horse's tail.[98] Each warrior carried three slings of different lengths that were used for various distances. It has been proposed that they carried the slings by tying the short size sling around the forehead, with the other two around the waist.[99] The idea for the length of the slings comes from the types of projectiles found on excavations. The lead or hardened clay projectiles were small-scale but it seems their various sizes dictated the type of sling that was used. For heavier projectiles, smooth stones slightly larger than the lead or clay versions were chosen. As for the lead and clay projectiles, they are oval and approximately 5cm in length. From some archaeological excavations within the *castros* (fortified Iberian villages), it appears that these projectiles were moulded in large quantities in groups of six to eight on soapstone moulds.[100]

There is one last weapon in the arsenal — poison. Strabo mentions that it was common for Iberians to carry a small receptacle containing a quick-acting poison, which they did not hesitate to take rather than be captured and sold into slavery.[101] The poison was extracted from the root of the *Ranunculus sceleratus* or *Ranunculus sardonia*. It produced a contraction of the lower jaw, giving the victim a sinister 'sardonic' smile. This was terrifying to Roman legionnaires, who thought dead men were defying them from beyond the grave.[102]

Armour

Lusitanian body protection was basically similar to that of other tribes in the peninsula, but showed some of their own design characteristics in the way they used fabric, leather, natural material and metal in making their armour.

Tunics and thick cloaks gave a degree of protection. We assume they were made of coarse wool or linen and dyed with earth tones, allowing them to blend into their environment. Over their tunics, Lusitanian warriors wore body armour made from an assortment of materials from light quilted linen-leather armour to iron breastplates. Though they wore an assortment of armour, it was usually light and made of leather combined with a small bronze breastplate.[103] Their light armour was made of a composite of leather and esparto fibres connected to metal chain links, perhaps added to absorb cutting blows. After the tanning and drying process was complete, this light armour was sewn together and then soaked in a vinegar and salt solution to stiffen it. It was then reinforced with tightly wound padding made of flax or esparto. Once the leather had hardened it was coated with lard or sheep tallow for waterproofing.

The second type of armour that can be seen on Iberian statues was made out of metal which usually came in two styles: small metallic plates and chain mail. The Lusitanians inherited the Celtic technique of manufacturing knitted iron (i.e. chain mail). The chain mail shirt consisted of about 25,000 metal links, all riveted and tempered by hand, which could take approximately one year to make.[104] The battle effectiveness of chain mail in deflecting sword blows was so amazing that many warriors made their own chain mail shirts or tunics because it was much cheaper than making armour out of metal plates and did not require an expert blacksmith. Renowned for its lightness and resistance to sword blows, Lusitanian armour was quickly incorporated into Roman legionnaires' protective gear, until the end of the second century AD.[105]

As for the scaled armour seen on Iberian sculptures, it was made of small iron plates cut into 5cm in length and 1mm thick.[106] The scales were generally set in layered tiles and attached to a tanned leather vest that had been cooked in animal intestines.[107] These metal-plated vests were fixed to the combatant's upper body via leather straps that hung from the shoulders and tied from the back.

A third type was simple metal breastplates, which were used by many cultures in ancient times. Lusitanian breastplates varied in different shapes and sizes from round to square, and were sometimes elaborately decorated with raised images. Generally the *pectorals* were worn using a set of three straps, one going over each shoulder and another around the man's torso. Roman *pectorals* were also used by Iberian/Lusitanian warriors, who plundered them off Roman corpses.

Mixed armour, consisting of all the above material put together, was what most horsemen used. The suit of armour was made of leather-backed metal scales for the chest area and chain mail links for the bottom part. It has been suggested that this design was created so as not to impede a horseman's mobility and agility.[108] This type of armour can be seen on Iberian vases found at Liria, Spain, which also corresponds to the type Lusitanian horsemen might have worn.

Some Lusitanians also protected their legs. Thick wool leggings were worn, but probably more for protection against the cold than from weapon blows.[109] But according to Strabo and from the few sculptures that have been discovered, certain warriors actually wore metallic greaves for leg protection.[110]

The major preoccupation of a Lusitanian warrior besides protecting his body was shielding his head. We know that a majority of head gear was made of leather or animal tendons, which unfortunately means none have survived due to the biodegradability of the material.[111] The main headgear was a sinew hat that came in two different styles: the hood and the skullcap. The hood was made of leather or chain mail, which hung down to the soldier's shoulders, protecting his head, neck and shoulders. The skullcap, on the other hand, was smaller and fitted around the man's crown, nape and temples. Those who did not use some type of headgear let their hair fall free, and when on a military campaign wore a strip of leather or cloth around their head.[112]

As for the few metal helmets that have survived in the Iberian Peninsula, they seemed to have been used between the fourth century BC and second century AD. Of all the helmets of that period found in the peninsula, they have been classified as Montefortino. These helmets were mass produced and used during the First and Second Punic Wars, the Celtiberian Wars, the Lusitanian War and in the Civil War between Caesar and Pompeii.

Montefortino helmets[113] were believed to have originated in the Celtic occupied lands of northern Italy and soon became very common throughout the entire western Mediterranean, being mass-produced and used by the Carthaginians and early Roman Republic.[114] The helmets were constructed by overlaying three 2-3mm bronze plates at the edges and hammering down to form a fold, which was then heated up and tempered to strengthen it against sword blows.[115] This type of head protection not only safeguarded the entire head but the back of the neck and face, for on both sides two face guards were added to protect the face from slashes. These anatomical articulated face plates were made of either metal or leather clamped together under the support of the rearguard, at the back of the helmet, for there were two rings on each side of the helmet to which the face plates were fastened by hooks, then tied under the chin as a chin strap.

This concept for a helmet was so well thought of and at the time so advanced that it has been supposed that the Romans rapidly adopted it into their army after the Second Punic War and maintained its design until the end of the Roman Empire. Unlike the Celtiberian and Roman models, the Lusitanian models only protected the cranial section of the head. Curiously, the Lusitanians seem to have not worn face guards (metal or leather) perhaps because they blocked peripheral vision or just got in the way during combat. Finally, at the summit of the helmet sits a button or mount of variable height with a hole in the middle. The soldier would place a mane of dyed horse hair of various colours in it, perhaps to identify which tribe or military unit he belonged to or to signify rank, like a Roman centurion worn to indicate status within the Roman military formation. Overall the durability of these helmets proves that the technique and the care put into the manufacturing of them was a sign of quality workmanship.

Campaign Life

According to all the texts written about the Lusitanian War, the Roman campaign season took place during the spring and summer months, but the Lusitanians campaigned all year round. During spring and summer, when the Romans were out of their forts either conducting training or military operations, the Lusitanians were hard at work subjecting them to ambushes, raids and surprise attacks. When autumn came around, the Romans usually began to wind down their campaign season and search for a place to establish a fort or secure a city or town for winter quarters, while the Lusitanians continued to conduct military operations, but on a smaller scale — harassing and raiding Roman convoys and Roman allied towns in search of provisions. By winter the Lusitanians were spending their time 'indoors' preparing for another campaign season, but at times they would attempt to sack a Roman friendly outpost or town.[116]

For the warriors, campaign life was difficult and subject to various dangers. From the few ancient texts, we can see that the Lusitanians were constantly on the march and on the offensive, so it was necessary for Viriathus' army to survive off the land by hunting and foraging to obtain the minimal ration of food which they ate and drank whenever possible. When the men camped at night they slept on the ground wrapped in their woollen *sagos* (long capes).

Spoils of War

The most outstanding aspect of ancient Iberian warfare was the appropriation and distribution of spoils. Ancient warfare, just like modern warfare, was a complex mechanism that granted political prestige, social promotion and economic dividends to either a country or persons. During the Iberian wars the great beneficiaries of this type of warfare were the warrior tribal chiefs. The territories they raided and at times conquered would bestow upon them fame and fortune, followed by the control of goods and spoils once the victorious military leader had commandeered the tribal chief's authority.

Among the Lusitanians it was different; instead of the tribal chief reaping the benefits, the entire tribe shared in the spoils of war and booty appropriated by robbing and raiding Rome's army and allies. Generally, captured products and spoils arriving in a community were distributed by hierarchy from a central point. Tribal chiefs would distribute the goods among family heads. Then the spoils were redistributed among family members. This model, adopted by the groups in power, meant spoils were distributed in the form of gifts in exchange for support and services. This was a way to regulate social ties with other clans as well. But as in all societies, there were signs of inequality evident in some classical texts.[117]

The sharing of spoils gave prestige to the tribal leader and his authority. But to gain more support and more power, he not only had to win battles but also maximize his booty to offer his constituents larger gifts and offerings. Eduardo Sanchez Moreno argues that a great part of Viriathus' alliances with other tribes were established not only by diplomatic negotiations but with the exchange of gifts in political-religious ceremonies.[118]

On a personal level, mutual offering was an important instrument to create social relations and personal bonds. Personal offerings were considered as a commitment among individuals and were therefore a precious element of social bonding. The key to this type of offering and gift giving was the creation of a personal *devotii* (devotion), making a man obligated to another or men obligated to each other in a special Iberian military custom.[119]At Viriathus' wedding the powerful Astolpas offered his guests exquisite delicacies, jewels and luxurious dresses.[119]Although the ancient sources say Viriathus despised Astoplas for his greed and wealth, he recognized the use of Astolpas' gift giving in gaining allies — offering presents in return for their *devotii*.[120]

Finally there was the distribution of booty among the military. The spoils that were acquired were also used to gain the loyalty and support of the army. According to Diodorus, rewards were based on merit and loyalty. He states that Viriathus awarded those who had distinguished themselves in battle with special gifts, and because of this reward system along with his fair treatment, the Lusitanians followed him willingly.[121] Following the Celtic way of life and their influence upon Lusitanian society, rewarding warriors was done by giving them gifts and throwing a banquet or celebration to recognize their merit.[122] Portuguese and Spanish historians believe that Viriathus rewarded his warriors as he did as a deliberate attempt to destroy the social ranking that divided the aristocrats from the rest. By rewarding simple men who possessed the true value of what men should be rather than just being born into privilege, he was establishing a social competitiveness among the newly established 'men of value and honour' against the old elite.

The attitude of Viriathus in sharing the spoils of war among his people has not really been studied by historical investigation even though it was thoroughly referred to in classical texts.[123] The Hellenistic and historiographic view of the ancient writers from Posidonus through Diodorus saw Viriathus as an equal and a generous man, turning the Lusitanian leader into the prototype of 'the good savage' derived from the Cynical and Stoic doctrines of that time.[124] Because of this socio-economic mechanism of redistribution of goods and rewards in Lusitanian society, the classical sources portrayed this shepherd, thief and warrior as a proto-historic 'Robin Hood'.

Chapter 4
Viriathus the Man

Though there is little information on the illustrious life of Viriathus, several classical authors decided to touch on some aspects of it due to his leadership skills and his actions that caused much terror among the soldiers of Rome. At times he was referred to as the 'scourge of the Hispania'.

The two key sources for the study of Viriathus are Appian and Diodorus Siculus. Book 6 of Appian's 24-volume history on Rome is dedicated to the Iberian Peninsula. One of his main sources was Posidonius, a Greek polymath who wrote about the peninsula in the middle of the second century BC. Appian also bases his work on Polybius, a contemporary Greek historian who recounts the facts about Rome's presence in Hispania. He wrote his history in forty books, but a good part has been lost. Diodorus was a contemporary historian during Julius Caesar and Caesar Augustus' time. He wrote 'Bibliotheca' in forty volumes, many of which are now lost, but in the books that have survived he collected much information on the Celtiberian and Lusitanian Wars.

Both Appian's and Diodorus' descriptions rely on the direct knowledge of the subject that Posidonius and Polybius had, and are therefore of great value. But classical authors followed various routes when writing their works. For example, the Greek historian Strabo's writings used Polybius because he had detailed descriptions of the terrain, people and customs, while Posidonius' work was used by Diodorus who offers us a more idealized view of Viriathus, along with his observations and commentaries of Rome's endeavour in the Iberian Peninsula.

What is interesting about Polybius is that he was cognizant of his opponent's military strategy as well as Rome's, and was therefore objective about indicating Rome's bad management of the war and giving credit and value to Viriathus' military skills. Posidonius distorts the narrative in favour of Rome. For example, he blames Viriathus' assassination on the assassins, removing Quintus Servilius Caepio as the mastermind behind the plot.

But the official Roman version of the Lusitanian War is seen in the annals of the work of Titus Livius (better known as Livy). In his collection of 142 books bestknown as 'The History of Rome' (unfortunately only 35 have been discovered), there are many extracts detailing what occurred on the Iberian Peninsula. Along with what survives of this profound literary work, Livy's writing was also compiled in a fourth century AD summary called 'Periochae' which also mentions several events that occurred in the peninsula.

We also have access to an independent version from Cassius Dio, who wrote a collection of eighty books titled 'Roman History' in the middle of the second century AD. Unfortunately of the eighty books only fragments of the first thirty-six have survived. The Lusitanian War is mentioned in fragments of Book 22.[1]

Finally there are some isolated mentions from other classical authors such as Florus, Orosius, Justinius, Eutropius, Veleius Paterculus, Cicero, Aurelius Victor, Gaius Lucilius and Frontinus. They show Viriathus as an extraordinary enemy of Rome.

Thus for the study of Viriathus as a historical figure we only have Roman or Romanized-Greek sources. As for the oral tradition used by the Lusitanians, Viriathus was larger than life, and if any written works did exist in the Iberian language, they have been lost in time. If an ancient history of Viriathus did exist it would have likely been drawn up, modified and manipulated by the Romans so as to prevent the Lusitanian population from making a hero and martyr of him and to discourage any attempts at independence. As the old saying goes, '*Victori spolia ire*' (to the victor goes the spoils).

The Name

Leite de Vasconcelos writes that Viriathus is not a proper name but a root word that stems from the Celtic word *viriola* (bracelets), *viria* being the abbreviation.[2] Bracelets were used abundantly by the Iberian people and perhaps as classical writers knew very few Celtic words, it is not surprising that they documented evidence without any proper names of certain men or peoples.

The name Viriathus, however, is more Celtic than Iberian, as demonstrated by Celtic inscriptions that have emerged from throughout historical Celtic lands, such as the Danube region, Germania and Gaul. It has been assumed that the name 'Viria-tus' means 'the bearer of bracelets'.[3] Although the word has the same Celtic root, it does not have the same meaning in Latin. The Latin *vir* signifies 'man' or 'rod'.[4] Though some grammarians defend this Latin claim, there is no proof of this word usage for Viriathus' name.

Historian Victor de Tusculano disagrees with de Vasconcelos. He writes that Lusitanian tradition and the eloquent testimonies of Roman historians along with archeological findings demonstrate that Viriathus is a proper name within the Lusitanian anthroponomy.[5]

Birthplace

There has been much debate over where exactly Viriathus' birthplace is. Various districts in Portugal have claimed it — Gouveia, Linhares, Folgosinho, Valesim and Póvoa Velha. The debate began in the 1920s when Schulten, the German archaeologist and historian, spent a portion of his life studying the Lusitanians and Celtiberians in depth. He came to believe that Viriathus was born somewhere in the region of Serra da Estrela, the former Mons Herminius, which lies between the Tagus and Douro Rivers.[6] His justification was that Viriathus was a Lusitanian shepherd and bandit who roamed the hills and mountains of Lusitania — so why not choose the highest sierra in Portugal as a perfect site for his birthplace!

But the basis for his argument is sketchy; pastoral life and banditry were not exclusive to the hills and mountains of Lusitania and could occur anywhere within the Iberian Peninsula from the plains of Andalusia to the Meseta Plateau, or to the coastal waters of Portugal. Furthermore, if Viriathus was born in Sierra da Estrela, in the western part of Lusitania, he was born near mountains or hills. But according to Diodorus, Viriathus descended from Lusitanians living along the ocean, in the occidental part of Lusitania.[7] Perhaps Diodorus' statement was misread or misinterpreted, or a mistake was made when his work was being translated from Latin, but the Sierra da Estrela, although on the eastern side of Portugal, is nowhere near the sea. So was Schulten wrong?

After many years of debate and discussion, there has been some agreement on where Viriathus might have been born. At the forefront of this new thinking is L Garcia Moreno. In his work 'Infância, Juventude e Primeiras Aventuras de Viriato' (Childhood, Adolescence and First Adventures of Viriathus), he analyzes all the data in the ancient sources on Viriathus and declares that there are two possible places where he may have been born.[8] The first agrees with Diodorus' claim that he was born in Lusitania near the coast, while the second supposes that he came from the slopes of the sub-Meseta of the Baetica Cordillera. The same idea also comes from Luciano Perez Vilatela, who has dealt with the study of the Lusitanian people on a major scale.[9]

Both Garcia Moreno and Vilatela suggest that Schulten invented the Serra da Estrela theory due to Viriathus' status within the tribe, the activities he conducted in the area during the war, and his Lusitanian descent. They both explain why Schulten and his followers, mainly Portuguese and Spanish historians, are incorrect about this, but each has his own hypothesis.

Garcia Moreno claims that the Roman name for the Serra da Estrela, Mons Herminius, does not appear in any of the ancient sources in reference to Viriathus. The ancient sources seem to make mention of a place called Aeminius instead, which is the name of a river and an *oppidum* (city) in the province of Lusitania, or in one case a tribe called the Aeminianenses, according to Pliny.[10] This is supposedly his birthplace. While Moreno has Pliny to back his theory, Vilatela's hypothesis is backed by Diodorus and Varro. Vilatela writes that Viriathus was not born exactly in Serra da Estrela but in another sierra in the same Sistema Central, yet much closer to the ocean.[11] But other classical works show that he may have been born around the area of Mons Tagrus in the area of Sintra, which is in close proximity to the Atlantic Ocean.[12] Though Viriathus' birthplace remains a mystery, these ideas provide more logical connections and consistency with the classical texts than Schulten's theory.

Although all the ancient sources and some modern sources accept Viriathus' origins as Lusitanian, some historians think he was born in other regions of Hispania. At the end of the nineteenth century and the onset of the twentieth century, historians Joaquín Costa and Anselmo Arenas Lopez defended their hypothesis that Viriathus was not of the Lusitanians but of the Luso, a small tribe within the Celtiberian realm that inhabited the area around Teruel in central eastern Spain.[13] Even though the two covered Viriathus within the context of the Celtiberian and Lusitanian Wars, they emphasized that Viriathus was Celtiberian and not Lusitanian. Another author, M. Peris, takes Viriathus' birthplace to the lands near Valencia in southeastern Spain, transforming Viriathus into an 'Ibero-Valencian'.[14] This is hard to believe, for Valencia was established after the war.

In recent years there has been a theory that places Viriathus' homeland south of Lusitania, not between the Tagus and Douro Rivers but in the city of Arsa, located in Celtic Beturia (modern Andalusia). According to the ancient texts, after the peace treaty of 140 BC was signed by Q. Fabius Maximus Servilianus and Viriathus, Viriathus seems to have established a second home at Arsa.[15] The Arsa theory supposedly suggests that because he set up camp there it might as well have been his birthplace. But this theory is hard to swallow and many historians disagree, feeling that it was simply his second home, for it was where he started to establish his 'dynasty' and he perhaps planned to make it the centre of his power over all the land he had taken from the Romans.

In Portugal there have been claims that he was born in Loriga, which was actually a Lusitanian stronghold called Lobriga. During the Lusitanian War, the Romans named this fortified city Lorica, which means 'warlike harness' or 'armour' in Latin. The Romans named it such because of its strategic importance in the mountain range, and to its protagonist attitude during the war (*Lorica Lusitanorum Castrum est*). Its name has remained unchanged for the past 2,000 years and its significance in antiquity played a part in the historical blazon, creating a theory that Viriathus was from this area. Though it is situated in the Sierra da Estrela, this theory should be treated as mere fantasy, for there is no mention of the city in the classical texts when referring to Viriathus. It has been assumed that this city was picked because of its location and because in the classical text they continuously mention that Viriathus was from the mountains.[16]

An additional theory arose in the 1990s. According to writer and journalist João Aguiar, perhaps Viriathus was born in the locality of Aritius Vetium (present-day Alvega), a city that stands on the left bank of the River Tagus in the Sierra da Estrela.[17] Unfortunately, there is no proof of this theory, nor detailed explanation, so it too is thought of as mere speculation.

Lastly, there is a theory formulated by Paulo Alberto Farmhouse, who writes that according to the geographic location of the territory Viriathus roamed, there seems to be a connection to the region of Turdetania that should not be overlooked.[18] According to his research, during the war this area was much frequented; Viriathus' wife was from this region; his assassins, who were his lieutenants, were from Urso, an important Turdetanian city. Although there are many indicators that point to this possibility, it still demonstrates the difficulty of positioning with precision the provenance of his story.

Of all these theories, the one that has stuck with us most was from Schulten: the hills of Mons Hermínius. His theory was taken to another level and turned into exact history in the 1930s by fascist propaganda of the Estado Nova (New State) led by dictatorial president António de Oliveira Salazar, who spread this theory as mainstream history about the origins of Portugal. But in state theory the 'historical' location of his birthplace was later changed to Santa Comba Dão, which in reality was the birthplace of Salazar. Though the population did not believe the second theory, they did the first, and it has lasted into the twenty-first century.

Though these theories try to legitimize Viriathus' birthplace, all have a nationalistic flavour and deep localism seeking to claim land as the home of the national hero. In reality Viriathus was neither Portuguese nor Spanish, but a member of a people called the Lusitanians who inhabited an area of the peninsula that extended from the coast of Portugal, north to the Douro River and south just past the Tagus River and towards the west to Toledo and Seville in Spain.

It seems clear that Viriathus was from Lusitania and lived among the Lusitanians along the Atlantic Ocean, as deduced from the ancient texts. It is even clearer that he resided in the southern part of Lusitania for many of the texts refer to Viriathus' campaigns as being mostly conducted there, with limited military operations in Central Hispania. In the end, whether Viriathus was born in Sierra da Estrela or not will continue to be an enigma.

Besides not knowing exactly where Viriathus was born, we also do not know the exact year of his birth. One hypothesis that has been thrown around claims he was born between 179 BC and 170 BC, which would make him between 20 and 30 years old at the time of the massacre of the Lusitanians by Praetor Servius Sulpicius Galba in 150 BC. The reason historians pick this timeframe was because 150 BC was also the year that the Viriathian War began, after Galba, as we shall see, massacred 9,000 Lusitanians and enslaved 20,000 in one day. Of the 1,000 that escaped, Viriathus was one. So if we accept this historical reference and place Viriathus in his twenties, a mature young man adept at leading men into combat and conducting military operations on a major scale.

Still, other historians state that Viriathus was born prior to 179 BC; some even go as far as suggesting 190 BC. This theory means Viriathus was in his forties at the time he started his guerrilla war. But it seems unlikely that he would have led men into battle in his fifties. Being born in 190 BC may be a bit far-fetched for very few people lived that long during that time.

Personality

Though it is difficult to pinpoint the date and place of Viriathus' birth, we know he was of humble origins, as this was repeatedly mentioned in the ancient sources. However, this should not be taken as absolute truth, since it deals with a traditional formula of showing a poor man rising to the top, exclusively due to his personal values and morals. Ancient writers seem to treat Viriathus as the ideal hero whose character was forged in his youth due to the environment in which he grew up in. Viriathus arises in history with a strong and fascinating persona, as did other barbarian military chiefs and leaders, such as Vercengitorix, Clovis, Boudicca, Alaric and several others.

Viriathus is presented in ancient passages as a man whose strength and virtue came from his experience as a juvenile in the wilds of Lusitania. The ancient texts referred to Viriathus as a Lusitanian from an obscure lineage, a man who had been labelled a shepherd (which, by the way, is questionable), an outlaw and a bandit leader (*latronum dux*), and soon after a general and a tribal leader who became famous for his achievements and deeds as a warrior chief. His natural attributes, agility, physical strength and skills in hand-to-hand combat are well documented.[19] It is also written that he spent most of his life living in a hostile environment, living off the land with minimal food and drink, and slept in beds of whatever nature offered him, for he had contempt for all the riches and luxuries of civilized life.[20] The ancient texts also document that he was a man who went straight to the point when he spoke his mind; to the Romans this was a sign of an untutored and unspoiled man.[21] He was therefore, for the Romans, a wild man who was introverted and solitary.

Viriathus was physically and spiritually a son of the mountains. His body, vigorous since birth, was strengthened each day by the rude pastoral life he lived under the open sky. Fighting wild beasts and human enemies as a shepherd, hunter, bandit and warrior, and surviving in the wilds of ancient Lusitania year after year, he was able to achieve complete domination of body and spirit. The Romans were amazed at his endurance, for he was a man who never fatigued, never suffered from hunger, and knew how to take advantage of unfavourable circumstances. Cassius Dio said it best about Viriathus' physical strength and endurance:

> Starting with a natural aptitude and building on this with his training, he was swift in flight, and he had great stamina in hand-to-hand fighting. He was happy with whatever food he could get his hands on, and was satisfied to bed down in the wild. Consequently, he was above suffering from heat and cold, and was untroubled by hunger or any other hardship; as content with whatever was on hand as he was with the very best.[22]

When he became general and leader of the Lusitanians, Viriathus was viewed as a man who fought for liberty, justice and equality, according to some of the Roman texts. Only on rare occasions did the Iberian tribes accept or submit to the orders of one man. But because of his personality, intellect and logic he maintained the entire time not only the title of chief but also 'king', which was later recognized by the Romans. As a military commander he sought loyalty and obedience. As a leader, he possessed an intelligence that was of enormous value in making decisions during the war.[23] In short, he was not ambitious or power hungry, but bellicose, cognizant of the military arts and schooled in the understanding of practical affairs. Using diplomacy and strict discipline, it seems he found the equilibrium between the authority that he thought was right to exercise and the extreme equality that his compatriots required. During his leadership there were no mutinies, rebellions, uprisings, riots nor desertions or defections, which could have caused internal crises. Once again we revert to Dio on Viriathus' mental capacity:

> He could quickly plan and execute whatever needed to be done — and he had always a clear idea of what that was. Furthermore, he knew exactly when to do it. He could pretend ignorance of the most obvious facts and just as cleverly hid his knowledge of the most hidden secrets. In everything he did, he was not only the general but his own second-in-command as well.[24]

With this said Viriathus seemed to have never flaunted his power, continuing to live as he had done before among the Lusitanians. Even though he was superior to his fellow countrymen in his political ethos and patriotic sentiment, he made the lower social class his equal. Above all else, he led his people to believe that they possessed the gift to foresee the future, winning their respect and confidence to lead them to victory. Though he had an amazing personality and qualities, he had a message about man's greatness in general. But with this, he had a great naivety due to his profound trust in others, which in the end was his demise.

Infancy and Youth

We do not know for sure who Viriathus' parents were, but according to legend his father was named Cominio and was chief of a small tribe situated somewhere within the realm of Lusitania.[25] When Viriathus was five years old, his father, leaving for war against another Iberian tribe or the Romans, left the family under the protection of the Igeditans, with whom the Lusitanians were allied.[26] As legend goes, his father died in combat and Viriathus grew up among the Igedium warriors and with them learned the art of war.[27] According to Lusitanian customs, the first born was usually the heir of the family and so Viriathus, being the third child (the second was a sister), was forced, as many other young people were, to choose a different life. Usually this led them to move elsewhere to make a name for themselves or live a quiet life.[28]

As the story goes, by the time he was 16 years old, tanned by the sun's rays and weathered by the wind, walking the mountains and living among the highlanders as a hunter and herder of sheep and goats, he had become a man. Having physical prowess at this early age, he joined a group of bandits and soon began to stand out for his qualities and amazing capacity to lead men; in time he began to lead the life of a bandit leader with his own raiders.[29]

Though the story of his youth is based on legend, it is not all pure fiction. While nothing is mentioned in the literary sources to indicate his humble origins or the circumstances of his infancy and childhood, we do have several references about his youth from Diodorus, Florus, Dio Cassius, Orosius and Eutropius that present him first as a shepherd and hunter, then as bandit and later a bandit chief, and finally a guerrilla leader and tribal chief.[30]

Marriage

The marriage of Viriathus in 141 BC deserves attention for it plays an important role in what he stood for in Iberian culture. A. Garcia y Bellido and H.G. Gundel interprets this episode as evidence of a serious class disequilibrium in Lusitanian society during the epoch of Rome's conquest of the Iberian Peninsula.[31] In agreement, J. Maluquer de Montes notes that the rich nobles were proprietors of the mineral rich agricultural plains, while the poor controlled the mountain wilds by herding livestock and by reverting to banditry.[32] In this context, Viriathus' marriage to a woman of a wealthy land owning family was an alliance or union between the two social classes, showing that a poor man can raise himself to the top — although there still was some animosity from the upper class.

Legend has it that Viriathus was passionately in love since a young age with Astolpas' sister or daughter, whose name is believed to have been Tongina.[33] But he was from a lower noble class and Astolpas wanted to marry Tongina off to a man with greater economic means. As things changed for Viriathus, Astolpas had to accept the marriage even if he did not have a good relationship with him. This is evident from Viriathus' attitude on his wedding day, when he rejected the food offered to him and criticized his host's vast wealth.[34]

The story of Viriathus' wedding in Diodorus Book 33 deserves in-depth consideration, for it encompasses a discourse about Lusitanian social structure.[35] In his passage about Viriathus' scorn for Astolpas' wealth, Diodorus states that during the wedding celebrations great quantities of gold and silver were displayed, along with many different precious stones and all sorts of embroidered robes. On seeing this, Viriathus rose from his seat, leaned on his spear, and showed contempt and disdain instead of admiration or surprise.[36] Diodorus says that during the wedding banquet Viriathus, in a single remark, spoke volumes of good sense and showed ingratitude toward his benefactors.[37] Diodorous states, 'that much touted wealth of his "father or brother-in-law" was itself subject to the man who held the spear; furthermore, he owed him [Viriathus] a greater debt than others, yet offered him, the true master of it all, no personal gift.'[38]

In other words, although the proud Astolpas had all the gold and silver in the world, he still bowed 'to the man who held the spear' — he was still a pawn of Rome. Or one could interpret it that instead of being under Rome's yoke, Astolpas was under the power of Viriathus, for he held the spear (power) and held the people under his influence. Diodorus puts words of wisdom about power in Viriathus' mouth.

In another paragraph, Diodorus writes:

> When many valuable articles were exhibited, Viriathus after lingering at these precious objects asks Astolpas, 'How is it that the Romans, who have seen all these riches at this banquet, have kept their hands off these valuables despite the power to wrest from you?' Astolpas replied that no one had ever moved to seize or ask for them though many knew of the existence of his vast wealth. Viriathus then asks, 'Then why in the world, if the authorities granted you immunity and the security for you to enjoy these things, did you desert them and choose to ally yourself with my nomadic life and my humble company?'[39]

This was a good question. Once again Diodorus makes Viriathus out to be a wise and cultured barbarian who knows about politics, especially when it comes to the subject of political alliances. What kind of relationship could exist between the rich Astolpas, lover of wealth, and the 'miserable' Viriathus, a frugal and crude person? Viriathus seems to be amazed that the rich Astolpas preferred to hold a dangerous alliance with him and simultaneously ally with Rome instead of choosing one or the other, but unfortunately no response from Astolpas is recorded. One can only point out that the wealthy Astoplas called for a peace to be made between Viriathus and Rome, which in the eyes of Viriathus was a sign of submission to Rome. But for Astoplas it was no doubt a guarantee that his tribe would survive Rome's oppression. So Viriathus saw him as a weak leader.

These passages can also serve to confirm Viriathus' humility. J. Lens Tuero and Marco V. Garcia Quintela consider them an example of Hellenic Cynical and Stoic doctrines, with the objective of painting Viriathus as the 'good savage', who was moral and stood up for what he believed in.[40] In this sense, it is perhaps safe to say that the ancient writers, besides telling a story, were also morally edifying their decadent Greek and Roman readers, promoting the idea that though the Iberian people were considered by the majority of Romans as barbarians, they were somewhat civilized. The fragments about the life of Viriathus that were collected by ancient historians allowed his character to be employed in parables, allegories and moral examples.

Garcia Quintela concludes that Diodorus' writing, besides containing historical facts on a person, is the base for a sort of a 'captialist ideology'. This would mean that Astolpas'wealth represents the imbalances in the distribution of wealth. But some scholars argue that it actually reflects the subordination of *ploutos* (wealth) to *kratós* (force, will) in a civilization predominantly based on a warrioristic ideology.[41]

According to Muñoz, the fact that the ancient passages emphasize the physical and moral superiority of Viriathus over Astolpas is not surprising because in ancient times the warrior's values, skills and courage took precedence over a character solely distinguished by wealth.[42] The two characters also represent two different social classes in Lusitanian society — the rich and the poor. Thus Viriathus is a proud, self-confident and self-sufficient man who did not believe in material wealth but in spiritual freedom and liberty.

Along with presenting the words between the two men, Diodorus says Viriathus refused to take part in the banquet and ate a little bit of bread and meat only after he had given some to his men. He then made a small sacrifice to the gods and ordered one of his men to fetch his bride, whereupon the two mounted a horse and disappeared into the mountain wilds.[43]

The ancient texts give us a look at the lifestyle these men lived, a hard life of washing in cold water and eating one meal a day, and show that one does not need much material wealth to be self-sustaining. But on a deeper level these writings exemplify Viriathus' lack of social graces, yet show him as a humble man who put his soldiers before himself — a true sign of a great leader. These passages about Viriathus'gestures are part of a collection that can be likened to a Hellenic motif and theme on the subject of appropriate morals and a humble life. They also illustrate thatViriathus' behaviour at the banquet was perhaps a manifestation of his institutional position as a leader of warriors within Lusitanian society. As for the small sacrifice, it perhaps signifies that Viriathus was not asking for any consent from Astolpas, declaring that his only liability was before the gods. This would have been a kick in the face to tradition because a traditional Iberian marriage required explicit consent from the family. This was not to happen here.

Diodorus praises Viriathus' direct manner of speaking, which is derived from his lack of education.This quality is demonstrated too through the accounts of how Viriathus rebuked the people of Tucca for constantly changing sides between him and the Romans. The traditional fable Diodorus chose as an analogy for this rebuke was one found in the works of the Roman fabulist, Phaedrus.[44] During the Lusitanian War the problems of forming alliances gained complexity. The political centre of power in southwest Iberian Peninsula was in Baeturia. The people and territory over which Viriathus extended his power were not just primitive tribal groupings — they were more civilized than most Iberian tribes to the north and west of the peninsula. There were cities that had been in existence for longer than most Roman towns and cities, and they had a social organization and a very complex political system that was absent in the rest of the tribes. With the Roman occupation of southern Spain, two parties existed in these cities, one that favoured the Romans and one that favoured the Lusitanian War effort. Guided by the events and politics of the day, Iberian tribes had a bad habit of constant flip-flopping regarding whose side they were on. Viriathus expressed a scornful attitude towards these tribes and their leaders, much as he did with Astolpas.

According to Muñoz, Astolpas' indecisive behaviour created such strong tensions between him, Viriathus and the Baeturian people that it may have culminated in Astolpas' execution by Viriathus a year later. You may ask yourself, 'Was the tension between these two individuals really so bad that one had the other executed?' The answer is complex. Even if they did not like each other, as the ancient passages claim, Viriathus would not have executed Astolpas just because he did not see eye to eye with his politics.Both were wise and intelligent tribal leaders and Viriathus had married into the family.

Then why the execution? History has three stories about Astoplas' death. The first is that sometime before Viriathus' own assassination (a year later after Astoplas' death), he attempted to negotiate a peace treaty with the consul of Citerior, Marcus Popilius Laenas, as the Lusitanians were becoming war weary (see Chapter 7). During the negotiations, Laenas demanded Viriathus give up all Roman deserters that had joined the Lusitanian cause and some hostages, who would either be sold into slavery, imprisoned, executed or forced to commit suicide. It is believed that on hearing that Astolpas was one of the men on Laenas' list who had been picked to commit suicide, Viriathus killed Astolpas, on the one hand to save him from the dishonour of committing suicide, and on the other to show Rome that he could be a loyal ally if need be. On hearing news of what Viriathus had done, Laenas became upset, perhaps sensing that Viriathus was not as trustworthy as he said he was. Angered by what Viriathus had done, Laenas decided to cut off the right hand of every Lusitanian hostage and told Viriathus that he had to unconditionally surrender and then relinquish all weapons in Lusitanian hands for there to be peace.[45]

The second story begins with the same idea: Viriathus desperately wanted peace for his war-weary people, but as he had become the scourge of Rome, Laenas ordered him to execute Astolpas to show his loyalty. To appease Laenas and to have peace, Viriathus gave in. He made the gesture to show the Romans that he had submitted himself to the will of Rome.[46] Bitterly, he too accepted the politics of his time, which in the end cost him his life.

The last story is part Portuguese legend and part factual history. Viriathus' marriage to Tongina, Astolpas' daughter or sister, was initially seen as a good idea. Perhaps it would calm Viriathus' vengeful rage against the Romans, increase Astolpas' area of power and his influence among the Iberians and Romans, increase trade relations with the Romans, and better Rome's foreign policies in Hispania. At the wedding feast, it is known that several high-ranking Roman representatives were present. But on seeing that the marriage to Tongina did not curbViriathus' hate for Rome — for he spoke out against the Romans — Astolpas, to save face, committed suicide because he was not able to constrain him.[47] Leanas then perhaps used Astolpas' suicide against Viriathus, saying it was his fault and that there would be no peace, which helped turn his compatriots against Viriathus, who they perhaps saw as ambitious, power hungry and a danger to the welfare of the southern tribes of Baetica, home to the three assassins.

This intra-family conflict, more than any other event, gives the reader the notion that Viriathus was, without a doubt, a leader of a nation. He had obtained the most overwhelming victories in the history of Lusitanian resistance against Rome, and the exchange of words between him and Astolpas shows us that Viriathus saw Astolpas as a Roman pawn who had subjugated his people to the will of Rome. After Astolpas'death, his fighters belied the alliances with Rome and joined Viriathus' army with the idea of total liberty for their people.

Finally, the status of Astolpas within his family should be discussed. This question was first asked by Garcia Quintela, who brought into light the exact interpretation of the Greek term *synkedestés*.[48] For many years it was believed that Astolpas was the father of the bride, but through intense examination of ancient Greek and Latin texts on the subject there has been a correction: he was Viriathus' brother-in-law and not father-in-law as previously believed. Traditionally the father gave a bride away, but in this society a bride was able to choose her own husband, and a sister chose a wife for her brother. Match-making was apparently not done by the parents but by siblings. So in the end Astolpas seems to have been Tongina's brother.

Trifunctional Hypothesis of Viriathus' Life

According to M.V. Garcia and B. Sergent, if we look more closely at these different moments that were composed in the reporting of the marriage and Viriathus' life, there are elements of a tripartite structure. They claim that there is a tripartite ideology within the marriage text that distinguishes between several Iberian religious and cultural particularities.[49] They claim that the three forms of Georges Dumézil's controversial 'trifunctional hypothesis' are in the text about Viriathus' marriage. The hypothesis states that Indo-European societies and religions divided everything into three. In this section the trifunctional theory will be analyzed.[50]

The hypothesis is derived from the Indo-European theme that postulates a tripartite ideology (*idéologie tripartite*) reflected in the existence of three classes or castes — priests, warriors and commoners (farmers or tradesmen) — corresponding respectively to the three functions of the sacral, the martial and the economic. This thesis is especially associated with the late French mythographer Georges Dumézil. According to Dumézil, Proto-Indo-European society comprised three main groups corresponding to three distinct functions: sovereignty, the military, and productivity. Sovereignty fell into two distinct and complementary sub-parts, one formal, juridical and priestly but worldly, the other powerful, unpredictable and also priestly, but rooted in the supernatural world. The second main division was connected with force, the military and war, while the role of the third, ruled by the other two, was productivity, herding, farming and crafts.[50] Mythology was divided in the same way: each social group had its own god or family of gods to represent it and the function of the god or gods matched the function of the group. The trifunctional ideology in Lusitanian culture is present in numerous manifestations of social life, including the organization of its pantheon of gods, its hierarchy, matrimony, and in the position of individuals in society.[52] It is organized around three general principles or hierarchal functions.

Garcia Quintela writes:

> The first function, which we will call (F1), groups together themes concerning the magical and cosmological aspects of the world order and the manifestations of this order among humans (agreements, pledges, etc); in social terms, it is formed by the priests and the king, who is chosen from among the warrior caste. The second function, referred to here as (F2), is organized around strength and protection and is represented socially by warriors. The third function, here designated as (F3), is connected with the reproduction of society in all of its facets, from sexual unions to the preservation and production of harvests and herds of animals, and in general to abundance and important quantities; socially, this is the activity of the producers.[53]

The theory begins by exploring the texts that present Viriathus passing through three different phases throughout his life.[54] It starts with Viriathus' youth as a shepherd and the austerity that made him physically strong (a denigrated version of motif F3). It then goes on to show how he fought animals, wild beasts and men until a great crowd chose him as their chieftain, and he immediately surrounded himself with a band of thieves (F2), showing himself to be an honourable and competent military commander. Finally, he proclaimed himself the legitimate chieftain, renouncing his position as the head of the group of thieves, and set out to wage war against the Romans (F1, the transition from warrior to king).[55]

Garcia Quintela goes on to say that a similar trifunctional order appears in Cassius Dio's description of Viriathus. He states:

> The opening formula sums up the text of Diodorus mentioned above (and the same in Florus, I, 33, 15), with the sequence of a trifunctional life. An explanation is then offered of Viriathus' qualities as a warrior (F2), his austerity (F3 denigrated) and his intelligence (F1).[56] The text ends with an evocation of the 'three sins of a warrior' that Viriathus avoided.[57]

The 'three sins of a warrior' mentioned by Diodorus and Cassius Dio are the thirst for wealth, dynastic ambitions and excess rage. Cassius Dio ends one of his passages with a description of Viriathus the warrior as 'without any desire for wealth, dynastic ambition and without rage...instead with a love of fighting and combat'.[58]

Diodorus and Dio say that the three failings of the Indo-European warrior had been erased from Viriathus' personality.[59] This is reiterated by Diodorus when he affirms that Viriathus was outstanding for his sobriety (*autarkeia*), which according to Garcia Quintela's theory makes him independent of the servitude of F3; his preference for liberty (*eleuthéria*), which was a radical affirmation of sovereignty (F1); and his bravery (*andreía*) (F2).[60] These texts situate Viriathus in a category of royalty defined according to Indo-European principles.

Furthermore, in the texts of Diodorus, Cassius Dio and Florus, we find a biography that is a moral portrait of Viriathus in accordance with the rules of the theory. According to Garcia Quintela's research, this structure coincides with many biographies of other great leaders of Indo-European tribes and royal houses, such as the Persian king Cyrus the Great, or Romulus, one of the founders of Rome.[61] The text of Cassius Dio is equivalent, in the way it structures the trifunctional series, to the portrait of the 'good king' or to the Roman concept of a 'noble savage'.

Viriathus' wedding, as told by Diodorus, is an episode narrated as a marriage rite that was purely Lusitanian and not Greek or Roman. (Strabo incorrectly likens the Lusitanian wedding to a Greek one, perhaps because the narrative was transmitted via Hellenic language and expressions.) In general terms, within the Indo-European ideology there are three types of marriage. Besides its special religious importance, one type was required to have the acceptance of the guardian parents of the bride (F1); another type involved the capture of the bride, or from the mutual consent of the couple to be married (F2); the third type occurred with a circulation of goods, or with a representation of the bride being purchased (F3).[62]

As for the usage of the trifunctional hypothesis in Viriathus' wedding, firstly, Viriathus complains that Astolpas had not offered him any kind of gift (F3). Secondly, tensions arise at the banquet, but the wedding continues even though Viriathus orders his companions to bring him his wife, as if she were being captured (F2). Finally, Viriathus carries out religious ceremonies and takes his wife to share in his residence which consummates the marriage (F1).[63] Each step of the marriage defined a precise and distinct ideological focus, and Dumézil compares Viriathus' wedding to a similar structure between the union of young Romans and Sabine women.[64] Dumézil considers this to be an exceptional case for there are other myths that invoked the trifunctional ideology of marriage by presenting a hero who married three different women according to the correct manners for each function.[65]

The trifunctionalism in Viriathus' wedding was necessary for those young Iberians who aspired to become royalty, or for the young bachelors of early Rome, for without marriage, the social order could not be maintained. As for Viriathus, although he does well without material wealth he needs the fecundity to establish his own royal bloodline.

Trifunctionalism explains the most significant episodes of Viriathus' life as transmitted by classical sources to reflect an ideology associated with royalty with Indo-European roots. Yet we would have to twist the facts to limit ourselves to this conclusion without recognizing that the clearest, most significant and articulated parallels come from Celtic mythology.[66] The only plausible explanation in reading these tales is that they are based on Celtic adaptations of a more general Indo-European theme, the conception of royalty as a synthesis of the three functions described above.[67] Since this theory arose in the late 1970s and early 1980s there has been a mixed scholarly debate over it. Many believe that it is incorrect and overstates certain elements in the texts to reach an objective that has no evidence, while others disagree on certain aspects of the theory. But on the other hand there are stern supporters of this theory.

Other Theories about Viriathus' Marriage

Some scholars think that the trifunctional hypothesis is not plausible here, but, having dug deep into the ancient texts, use this hypothesis as a base to add or conjure up new theories on the marriage's significance for Viriathus' personality and feelings towards the Romans. Several new theories have been constructed, such as one that says Viriathus did not offer any gifts or dowry because he did not respect Astolpas who had allied himself with the Romans; another suggests tensions persisted during the feast, but the marriage was still celebrated; and a third that has Viriathus rejecting Astolpas' formal delivery of the bride to him, instead ordering one of his men to bring her to him, very similar to an abduction (like the rape of the Sabine women).

Regarding the first theory, according to traditional cultural mores, Viriathus should have offered some type of gift or bride price for his bride, but he did not.[68] From a traditional bride price point of view, the groom gave the woman's family some type of gift, whether money or material items; but from ancient texts, it seems Iberian men did not offer gifts to a bride's family. The ancient testimonies, as pointed out by J.C. Bermejo Barrera, correspond to a situation in which the bride's brother gave his sister gifts rather than her parents.[69]At the same time, the newly married couple was also granted a dowry that would form part of their future hearth. In the case of Viriathus the text is incomplete, so we can assume that he followed traditional mores, but it must take into consideration the possibility that he did not. He may not have had received a dowry because Astolpas' family may have disagreed with this marriage and as Lusitanian women were able to chose their own husbands, she followed her heart. Unfortunately we will never know why or if Viriathus did not receive a dowry, but one can only assume from his personality that he was not into wealth compared to freedom and power.

Regarding the second theory, it postulates that Astolpas (who represents Rome) came to terms with the wedding as an amicable agreement to end the war, but in Lusitania it was rejected since peace would have been a sign of submission to Roman terms. This signified that in the end he did not voluntarily lower himself to Rome by making himself take his wife and riding out to his secret mountain camp. In the global sense of the account, neither party (Rome and Lusitania) would give in to the other so easily.[70]

As for the third theory, Viriathus' bride plays a passive role in the scene and does not participate in any of Viriathus' decisions. This is unlike Lusitanian women, and Celtic women in general, for they played a proportionate role in Celtic society, but since women played a semi-passive role in Roman and Greek culture it would not appear correct to show a strong leader like Viriathus dependent on a woman. Observing the lines of Hellenic tradition for women, the fact is that the protagonist is the representative of the bride. Also Viriathus' abduction of his bride falls into agreement with the ancient and modern-day practice of bride kidnapping. In the Indo-European marriage model it seems that the autonomy of women was often taken by force, as represented in mythology and history by the tribe of Benjamin in the Bible; by the Greek hero Paris stealing the beautiful Helen of Troy from her husband Menelaus, thus triggering the Trojan War; by the rape of the Sabine women by Romulus, the founder of Rome; and by the fact that it was a common marriage practice in Sparta.[71] The presence of the three matrimonial functions (if one utilizes the trifunctional theory), this union is very similarly presented to the legend of the Roman abduction of the Sabine women.[72] Once again one must not forget who wrote these texts!

These interpretations of Viriathus' marriage permit us as readers or scholars, to perceive relationships between these episodes of Viriathus' life with an Indo-European trifunctional ideology and the Lusitanian and Roman point of view. They even perhaps explain specific ethnographic circumstances about the region or culture.

Viriathus' Generalship

Throughout Europe each nation has its popular barbarian hero who squared off with Rome, either before and after Viriathus' claim to fame within the historical context. But of all the barbarians that fought Rome, Viriathus is one of the most well known, for according to Roman texts he was unusually intrepid and the most tenacious that Rome ever saw. Viriathus' military skills and leadership put him in the ranks of other illustrious barbarian military leaders of the ancient world such as Ariovistus, Vercingetorix, Arminius, Tacfarinas and Decebalius. He has been viewed as a pragmatic man who had exceptional command skills. Like that of the other Iberian tribes, the warlike tradition of the Lusitanians, in a pure military sense of strategy, was not a surprise to the Romans. They had already encountered other warrior chiefs such as Punicus and Cesarus, who had proved worthy adversaries, but their fights were short-lived due to the amazing strength and technology of the Roman war machine. Viriathus, who had some combat experience, delivered to the Romans a war so intense that it lasted eight years and was recorded in several chapters by Roman writers. To some ancient as well as modern historians he was a political and military genius who introduced a new military initiative: guerrilla warfare.

We do not know exactly what his admirable qualities as a warrior were, nor his exact strategy, his civic virtues and morals, his conception of unity and national cohesion, but he was able to convince the chiefs of other tribes to join his cause. Elected from among other Lusitanian chiefs, Viriathus was able to bring together Iberian tribes who had fought each other and against the Romans, in time managing to merge the entire western Iberia under his command. Viriathus' victories against Rome did not create jealousy, envy or rivalry from other chiefs but great prestige as a combatant and as a leader. Besides being an amazing military commander, he was influential and a great communicator at tribal meetings, and seems to have been ardently patriotic in fighting for his freedom as well as for his countrymen. Because he possessed these qualities he established a single command and voluntary compliance that all followed blindly, and because he was so respected there was neither defection nor desertion within his ranks. Each tribal chief acted as a subaltern deployed with a guerrilla band to conduct some sort of task in the theatre of operation.

In the aftermath of Galba's massacre of the Lusitanians in 151 BC, Viriathus was elected a leader and organized an incredible army.[73] With more than 20,000 men he led an amazing guerrilla campaign against the Romans, which they dubbed the 'Thieves' War' or 'Fiery War'.[74] With his vivacity, spirit, strong will, generosity and realist views, Viriathus displayed all the qualities of a skilful leader. His experiences as a bandit leader during his youth enabled him to form an army of guerrilla fighters and with his knowledge of paths, villages, caves, water sources and terrain, he showed his talent as a military leader and tactician. For Viriathus to have been a successful leader, it seems he led his men from the front so that his soldiers would recognize him as a true leader and warrior. Furthermore he never took more of the spoils than the share that he allotted to each of his comrades. Soldiers and civilians alike also respected him for his striking wit, and he surpassed every one of his men in temperance as well as in toil, he constantly slept in full armour, and he was always on the alert and ready for battle. Theodor Mommsen said of him, 'It seemed as if, in that thoroughly prosaic age, one of the Homeric heroes had reappeared: The name of Viriathus resounded far and wide through Spain; and the brave nation conceived that in him it had at length found the man who was destined to break the fetters of alien domination.'[75]

It is doubtful that he was a simple shepherd who lived in the mountains of Mons Herminius, as legend has it. It is more believable that he was educated in the ways of other tribes and had access to military teachings and training that allowed him to transform his tribes of shepherds and bandits into a solid army and conduct a guerrilla war based on strategic elements and tactics that were extremely sophisticated for the time. In addition it is perhaps plausible to say that he may have had some knowledge of the Latin language, making him capable of diplomacy, for the ancient texts mention that the Romans appointed Viriathus *amicus populi Romani*, a title given to tribal chiefs and kings who allied themselves or made peace with Rome. By the end of his life, Viriathus' fame reached such a height that for a long time he was a symbol of the warlike spirit of Lusitania.

Map 2: Pre-Roman Populi of Portugal

Chapter 5
The Lusitanian War with Rome Begins

The next series of events on the Iberian Peninsula were so substantial that literary remarks were left by several classical authors, particularly Appian. The Lusitanian War, called *Purinos Polemos* (Fiery War), was a war of resistance fought between the advancing legions of the Roman Republic and the Lusitanian tribes from 155 to 139 BC.[1] In 154 BC, another long war in Hispania Citerior began, known as the Numantine War. It was fought by the Celtiberians and lasted until 133 BC. The efforts of the Romans in pacifying Lusitania and the western part of Hispania were largely undone by the revolts of the years 155 to 133 BC. The Lusitianian War and the even bloodier Numantine War in Citerior marked a turning point in the history of Roman Hispania.

It is difficult to know exactly how many years the Celtiberian Wars lasted. Unfortunately the data available to us via the classical authors is conflicting. Appian, who collected his information from Rufus Avienus Festus and Publius Sempronius Asellius' writings, says the Lusitanian War lasted seventeen years (155 to 139 BC); Velleius Paterculus, Justinus, and Pompeius Trogus say it was ten; Doidorus eleven years; while Livy, Florius, Orosius and Eutropius put it at fourteen years.

Schulten and various other studies on the subject fix the years at seventeen, in agreement with Appian. However, the Lusitanian War did not last seventeen years consecutively, but was fought on two separate occasions. The first lasted four years: 155 to 151 BC. It started when the Lusitanians and Vettones began to conduct large-scale raids into Roman occupied territory. The Romans reacted by sending an army to teach the two tribes a lesson, but they were defeated and an all-out war broke out. But the Lusitanian War under the leadership of Viriathus began in 147 to 146 BC and ended in 139 BC. This fearsome war was started by Roman greed and escalated into the massacre under the leadership of praetor Servius Sulpicius Galba and the proconsul Lucius Licinius Lucullus. It is impossible to explain the time frame of the war because it seems each author used different figures as starting points — thus 153 or 152 might count as the outbreak point of major warfare throughout western Hispania, while 150 or 149 when Galba broke the Luso-Roman peace treaty could also be seen as a major starting point for the war.

When discussing the Lusitanian War it is impossible to ignore the illustrious cavalier, the sober and glorious Viriathus. He represents the true war against Rome, the ferocious fiery war, without truces, with a character of more defined violence that ever before. Starting in 219 BC, when the first Roman troops invaded the Iberian Peninsula during the Punic Wars, it would take 200 years to Romanize the entire peninsula, and of all the tribes that inhabited it, the Lusitanians were the hardest to conquer because of their love of freedom, independence and fighting.

The Politics of Roman Imperialism in Hispania

The politics of Roman imperialism in the Iberian Peninsula began with an early trading treaty with the Carthaginians dating from around 348 BC.[2] The treaty forbade Roman vessels to trade beyond Mastia (present day Cartagena) in southern Spain. Although the Carthaginians had been a major influence upon Hispania, progress was slow, but, immediately after the First Punic War with Rome, the Carthaginian General Hamilcar Barcas, filled with bitterness at the loss of Sicily and Sardinia, set out to permanently establish Punic power in Spain.

There is no doubt that his intention was to secure control of a sturdy population for the reemergence of a new Punic army to take on Rome rather than revenue for the treasury, for his prime motive was to bring a war of revenge against Rome after the defeats he had suffered.[3] He met with striking success, for his generalship was superb and his rule firm, but not oppressive. When he fell in battle in 229 BC, Hasdrubal, Hamilcar's older son, succeeded and carried on the work of winning over the Iberian tribes at a more rapid pace than his father had. The Massiliots[4] as well as the Romans realized that these Carthaginian victories would soon deprive them of all their Spanish trade — for no other nation could trade where the Punic standard was planted. There is little doubt that it was trade affairs between Hispania and Massilia that drew Rome's attention to Spain.[5]

The Massiliots had gradually lost a large part of their Iberian trade routes and within a year or two their flourishing colonies of Emporias and Rhodae would doubtless go under. If Rome cared little about the question of open ports in Hispania, the Massiliots had other ways of arousing Rome's interest. They reported to Rome that a Punic attack upon Emporias was imminent for Carthage had supposedly declared war against Massilia, which would involve Rome because of their alliance. At the same time, representatives of

Massilia began spreading rumours throughout the Roman government that the ultimate purpose of the Barcids in Hispania was to muster a large army to wage a war of revenge upon Rome. In the end their 'diplomacy' was effective.

Rome became thoroughly concerned about Punic advances in Hispania, and sent envoys to Hasdrubal in 226 BC with requests for a treaty stipulating that 'the Carthaginians should not cross the River Iber (Ebro River) in arms'. Rome obtained what it desired and in pursuit of the same policy of anticipating Carthaginian military aggression, entered into a defensive alliance with Saguntum, an independent Iberian city of considerable strength, 100 miles south of the river.[6]

Thus matters stood when in 221 BC, Hannibal, Hamilcar's young son, succeeded in taking command of Hispania. He at once subdued the whole peninsula as far as the Iber River, with the exception of Saguntum, and then, at the head of a splendidly trained army, in accordance with the plan and purpose that his father had taught him from youth, he made ready to bring on a war with Rome.[7] Saguntum, as it happened, offered a plausible excuse for the Carthaginians to besiege the city, for it had committed some hostile acts against a Spanish tribe allied to Carthage. By picking up this quarrel, Hannibal perhaps hoped to force a declaration of war from Rome. If that happened, Carthage would be forced to support Hannibal's operation in Hispania (but not an invasion of Italy, which he did on his own initiative, for the Punic aristocracy lived by trade and not by war, so they strongly favoured peace with Rome). The capture of Saguntum would wipe out the last unfriendly people in his rear, enabling him to close the harbour to the Roman navy and secure booty with which — according to Polybius — he hoped to mollify the home government and equip his army for the long march into Italy. He accordingly attacked Saguntum in 219 BC when the Roman consuls were busy in Illyricum.[8] After an eight-month siege, Saguntum fell. The Romans sent envoys to Carthage, demanding the punishment of Hannibal and, upon the refusal of their request, war was declared.[9]

So the main reason for the Roman presence in the Iberian Peninsula was to obstruct Carthaginian expansionism rather than the desire for world conquest.[10] Rome at first did not plan to conquer the area but only to control the Carthaginians. During this time Rome did not see itself as imperialistic but acted on impulse of self preservation. However, the desire to take advantage of the area later formulated into an imperialistic agenda after the Second Punic War. The Carthaginian exploitation of the Iberian economy and human resources of the peninsula offered the motivation for Rome to decide, set and explore those resources for its own interests.

Though Rome came out of the struggle victorious, it suffered many irreparable losses, and her gains would prove a burden. The Roman oligarchy's main interest after the Second Punic War was in expansionism, and the conquest of new lands drew the Romans to the idea that expansion was very lucrative, even if a burden at first. For conquering this new land would later provide Rome with a multitude of slaves, a necessary labour force, a canvass of taxes for the state, and new resources of minerals and food products, so as to ensure the success of the Roman economic system. This all points to the economic content of Roman imperialism combined with other political, military, social and cultural factors.

The invasion of Hispania had been a political necessity during the war, since it alone could furnish the enemy with new recruits and its retention afterwards was, of course, the only conceivable course. But for the next two centuries this new province would cost the Roman state more than it yielded.[11] Furthermore, the Spanish tribes were far from ripe for political responsibilities and they had no love for an orderly regime. Roman negotiations with each 'sovereign' tribal leader were countered with constant difficulties owing to the fact that the people were divided into innumerable tribal groups. No sooner had a Roman general sworn a treaty with a tribe than it would reshape itself into a newly formed tribe and disclaim participation in the preceding agreement. The policing of Hispania degenerated into undignified and costly guerrilla warfare, disgraced by schemes and stratagems. Roman generals learned to deal with the trickery dealt to them. Nowhere did Roman warfare and diplomacy descend to such devious ways as in Hispania. But we shall come to this again. Suffice to say that at various times during the following century, the Roman Senate would have been relieved to hear that the whole peninsula had disappeared underwater. In the end the Romans stayed in the Iberian Peninsula, leading them to a repressive upheaval of the indigenous people.

But what we call imperialism is something very different from the European imperialism of the nineteenth century. According to Theodor Mommsen, Roman imperialistic expansionism was hardly of an imperialistic character compared to the modern age — rather a series of defensive measures adopted during a war Rome considered preventive.[12]

As preventive as their policies may have been, the methods the Romans implemented of exploiting the land and people led to the irremediable evils of the plantation system, with its concomitant evils of slave labour, which prevented the healthy development of more productive farming when Rome's population was increasing.[13] And yet how could the government know that Rome's population would soon reach abnormal proportions and it would be difficult to recover leased lands for colonization, and also that the landlord system, once firmly entrenched, would become so impregnable that it permanently excluded the small farm? Nor did the Senate foresee that Rome would one day govern a score of foreign provinces whose armies would have to draw their strength from the Italian countryside and foreigners if the state was to survive. Rome did its best to meet the situation using past experience, but the problems it created through war and its hunger for expansion became too complicated, and Rome's stubbornness, along with corrupt emperors and a lack of experienced leaders, was inadequate to rule over such a large land mass over time.

The Second Punic War wrought few changes to the newly acquired province of Hispania, which had readily fallen into the form of government shaped for Sicily.[14] The federation in Italy had stood the endurance test better than could have been anticipated, and the Senate saw no reason for introducing any innovations there. In fact, because of the general satisfaction, the Senate even grew negligent about making several well-deserved promotions towards citizenship. At the same time, the old city-state government of Rome had proved itself versatile enough to meet the exigencies of the Second Punic War, but the early losses on the field had been appalling, and it is usual asserted that these heavy losses were due to an oligarchical system that placed annual civil magistrates at the head of the army causing the political situation in Hispania to be somewhat chaotic.[15]

The Politics of Roman Imperialism upon Lusitania

One cannot fully endorse the idea that the Roman campaigns to conquer Lusitania were exclusively economical, because on looking closely at why Rome would conquer Lusitania, one can see essential political and military factors. As mentioned in Chapter One and the previous section, which discusses the control of the entire peninsula, after the Second Punic War invading Lusitania was not only a defensive measure to protect Roman gains, citizens and allies against Lusitanian incursion and raids, but was also complemented by economic reasons. As mentioned, the beginning of Roman occupation of Hispania was a necessary operation if Rome's strategy for the Second Punic War was to succeed and there is no end of practical reasons why the Romans could not immediately evacuate the territory after they had gained and lost so much.

However, Roman intervention in the affairs of the Iberian population disturbed the relationships between the indigenous communities, which placed the Romans at a disadvantage. Roman dominion over southern and eastern Iberia was not fully ensured, for some of the communities continually offered strong resistance. To get rid of Roman oppression the indigenous population had to make some offensive and defensive actions. The Romans reacted quickly by putting down these rebellions. At first Lusitania did not seem to have been important to the Roman initiative of extending deeper into the peninsula, for the Romans were busy consolidating and putting down rebellions in the eastern part. The aim was to satisfy the Senate with an effective control of the eastern and southern parts, to ensure excellent profits in the future. While the Romans consolidated former Carthaginian lands, the Lusitanians took advantage of a confusing situation and began to cross over into Roman territory, devastating the newly gained territory. Because of the horror of Lusitanian incursion, the Romans reacted quickly and sent several legions to patrol the territory between the Guadalquivir and Guadiana Rivers.[16] For the next several years, however, the Lusitanians continued their incursions into Roman-held territory and this began to draw the attention of the Senate. The Lusitanian attacks did not cease until Caius Atinius, praetor of Ulterior, set out against them in 186 BC.

After being defeated by Atinius, the Lusitanians seem not to have launched any cross-border incursions between 178 and 156 BC except a few skirmishes here and there along the Luso-Roman border of Baetica. But shortly afterwards the situation changed rapidly. As we will see in the next section, commanded by Punicus, the Lusitanians attacked cities that had allied themselves to Rome. After Punicus' death the Lusitanians continued to fight under Cesarus, who attacked one of Rome's allies, the Conii, taking their city, Conistorgis. But the victory was short-lived, for, after the capture of Conistorgis, Cesarus was killed in battle and his army defeated by the Romans. The defeat prompted the Romans to begin the process of subduing the local population of southwest Hispania. In time this subjugation turned violent and became the prelude to the great Lusitanian insurrection under Viriathus.

During the Lusitanian War, Roman military operations intended to prevent further Lusitanian incursions into Roman occupied territory. Even though Rome could not tolerate these incursions any longer, it had great potential at any given time to completely change the situation via peaceful means, by giving the Lusitanians land or commercial rights. But believing in its great military prowess, the Roman Senate assumed that through continuous suppression of the Lusitanians and Vetones, it would be sufficient to finish off these 'primitive people'. How wrong the Senate was!

Rome's actions against the Lusitanians and Vettones showed a weakness in its strategy. The mountainous defensive *castro* system (walled villages), which had a vertebral column along the Guadalquivir and Guadiana rivers as well as further up towards the Douro River, left a wide zone of land with no space to restrain them. Rome was confident that its cultural movement and commercial contacts in that part of the territory would produce, in the short term, the stability and pacification of the Lusitanian territory and neighbouring peoples. At the same time, a strong military presence in the surrounding area was thought to instil fear in these people, but it instead agitated and aggravated many of the tribes.

In any case when the Romans reached Lusitania they realized that they had bitten off more than they could chew. But until the Lusitanians were completely dominated the Iberian Peninsula would be unstable, because they were a strong and warlike nation. These people were so defiant that they gave hope to other tribes, inspiring them to continue, restart or start new rebellions against the Roman yoke of imperialism. Once the Lusitanians had been quelled, the task of pacification would be easily facilitated, but it would take until 19 BC to completely pacify Lusitania.

With the aid of some documentary sources, the Luso-Celtiberian Wars are presented in a large part of Roman historiography as a conflict between imperialist domination and indigenous communities'spirit of independence, which have been seen as two antagonistic ideologies. But in reality, it seems that it was the disproportionate greedy ambition of a few individuals that made Rome's consolidation of Hispania difficult and led to these conflicts.In the end the Celtiberian Wars reached such magnitude that they forced the Roman Senate to introduce institutional changes in the province and reorganize and strengthen the Roman army in Hispania.

The Fire is Ignited

The year 197 BC was a year of particular significance for Hispania, with the conclusion of the division of the conquered territory. Hispania was split into two Roman provinces: Hispania Citerior and Hispania Ulterior.[17] This administrative reform of Hispania identifies a clear political process of conquest that would affect the Lusitanians.

The Senate deployed qualified praetors or consuls with one or two legions alongside auxiliary troops. Though these magistrates had in their hands all the administrative, judicial and military power, their management was supervised by the Senate. Representing Rome, the governors required that taxes be paid and that each tribe pay a tribute, as aid to Rome, by having their young men serve as auxiliaries in the Roman army. Also, governors were given imperial power to issue edicts and proclamations, collect taxes, regulate the politics of newly subjugated peoples and the right to life and death, both for the citizenry, army and the indigenous population, as well as changing the status of conquered cities by having already Romanized cities print more currency and send it to them.

Unfortunately for the Romans, strict political and military supervision, aggravated by the endless spoliation and greed of Roman magistrates who sought personal fortunes, rapidly caused the emergence of Iberian insurrections, strife and rebellions. The worst rebellions were always provoked by the excesses of the Roman authorities, as was the case in the First Celtiberian War. But on the other hand there were several tribes who were not under the Roman yoke of imperialism and pretty much did what they wanted to do as long it did not affect the Romans. At times these tribes went a bit too far and raided Roman occupied towns, which the Romans did not tolerate, as we shall see.

The Lusitanians were the first to create problems for Rome with their incursions and systematic raids on the rich cities and towns of occupied Roman territories east and south of Lusitania. Since 193 BC, the Lusitanians had been fighting the Romans on and off. During the second half of the second century BC, they were the only people of the Iberian Peninsula that continued to resist the Roman Empire.

The first time the Lusitanians were cited as enemies of Rome was around 194 BC when they entered Hispania Ulterior and sacked several cities in the Guadalquivir Valley.[18] Praetor P. Cornelius Scipio Nasica, cousin of Scipio Africanus and son of Gnaeus Scipio who was killed in Hispania at the Battle of Ilipa (Alcalá del Rio) during the Second Punic War, attacked and defeated the Lusitanians at Ilipa, as they were returning to Lusitania loaded with riches. Intoxicated with loot and returning to their homeland, they were ambushed by an inferior Roman force. The battle lasted, according to Livy, for a good part of the day. Though the Romans were outnumbered, their ambush was successful because they were in a close and serried formation, while the long column of Lusitanians became hampered by many herds of cattle and was weary from a long march across the country. At first the Lusitanians threw the Romans into some disorder, but soon the fighting became even. During the struggle, Nasica vowed that he would celebrate Games to Jupiter if he routed and destroyed the enemy. At length the Roman attack became more insistent and the Lusitanians began to give ground. Finally they broke and fled, and in the hot pursuit that followed up to 12,000 enemy warriors were killed, 540 prisoners taken, and 134 standards captured.[19] Roman losses amounted to seventy-three. Enriched with the spoils of war taken from the enemy, Nasica led his victorious army to the city of Ilipa, one of the cities ransacked by the Lusitanians. Upon arriving within the city's walls he laid out his captured booty in front of the city's inhabitants and allowed them to reclaim their property. The unclaimed booty was handed over to the quaestor to be sold and the proceeds distributed among the soldiers.[20]

It is important to highlight the fact that after this the Romans saw the Lusitanians and other neighbouring populations that were not under their control as uncivilized bandits and robbers of their fertile and rich lands of Baetica.

In the years 191 to 190 BC, Lusitanian incursions became such a burden for Rome, that praetor Lucius Aemilius Paulus Macedonicus had to wage a harsh campaign against them.[21] The Lusitanians, according to Livy and Orosius, penetrated deep into Bastetania and defeated a Roman garrison in the vicinity of the city of Lyco.[22] The Romans are said to have suffered more than 6,000 casualties. At the end of the winter of 190 BC, Paulus hastily formed a new legion in conjunction with a collection of allied soldiers and managed to defeat the Lusitanians somewhere in Baetica. Trusting in their previous victory, the Lusitanians had neglected to maintain their defensive and offensive stances and instead devoted themselves to plundering. As a result they were routed and put to flight: 18,000 were killed, 3,300 captured to be sold as slaves, and their camp stormed.[23] This battle contributed much to the tranquility that followed in Hispania. With such a large victory, Paullus returned to Rome with a multitude of gold, but for political reasons he did not obtain a triumph or the ovation. Before leaving Hispania he founded the town of Turris Lascutana which was considered as a *colonia latina libertinorum* thanks to the local support he had against the Lusitanians.[24]

In 188 and 186 BC, Lusitanian and Celtiberian incursions against Baetica began again.[25] These must have been so alarming that the praetors, L. Manlius Acidinus of Hispania Citerior and C. Atinius of Ulterior, sent disturbing reports to Rome and requested reinforcements. Despite these reports saying that the Celtiberians and Lusitanians were united in war and beginning to ravage the territories of their allies, the Senate left the new magistrates to deal with the situation on their own.[26] This attitude would have dire consequences. By 186 BC, the Lusitanians had crossed the Guadalquivir and taken the city of Hasta (Mesas de Asta, close to Cadiz) and forced its inhabitants to declare that the Romans were hostile.

Soon after the first dispatches reached Rome others arrived as well. Where the originals went unheeded, the Senate now listened, but it was too late. According to Livy, Atinius fought a battle with the Lusitanians in the neighbourhood of Hasta. He claims that as many as 6,000 enemy were killed; the rest were routed and driven out of their camp.[27] Atinius then led his legions to attack the fortified town of Hasta, which he captured with little difficulty. But while he was approaching the walls somewhat incautiously, he was struck by a missile and a few days later he died of his wound. The Senate quickly elected C. Calpurnius as a new praetor.[28]

A year later, further clashes are recorded when a combined Roman force commanded by L. Quinctius Crispinus and C. Calpurnius Piso were routed by a large native force made up of Lusitanians, Celtiberians and Vaccaei close to Toletum (modern Toledo) and Dipo (modern Elvas).[29] According to Livy, the Iberian victory was helped by their knowledge of the terrain and the nature of their fighting style.[30] The two Roman armies were routed and driven back to their camp. Luckily for the Romans, the Iberians did not press on their attack. This allowed the demoralized Romans to lick their wounds, but fearing that their camp might be stormed the next day, both commanders decided to withdraw their armies during the middle of the night.

At dawn the Iberians formed up and marched up to the camp's rampart; surprised at finding the camp empty, they entered it and appropriated what had been left behind in the confusion of the night. They then returned to their own camp and remained inactive for several days. The losses of the Romans and their allies in the battle amounted to 5,000; Iberian losses are unknown.[31] But, soon afterwards, on crossing the Tagus River, it was the turn of the two Roman praetors to defeat the Iberians, who suffered huge losses in a long and hard-fought battle.[32] After this campaign, Hispania was quiet throughout the winter. When the praetors returned to Rome, each was unanimously decreed by the Senate a triumph.[33]

In 181 BC, Livy refers to several small pitched battles between the Lusitanians and praetor P. Manlius, but does not give information about the battles nor describe their locations.[34] In 180 BC, under the praetorship of L. Postumius Albinus and T. Sempronius Gracchus, the Roman army was able to consolidate its defensive line along the Tagus River, advancing the province of Baetica's border further north.[35] Due to their continuous incursions, Albinus set out against the Lusitanians and managed to pacify them by force. Gracchus then worked at attempting to Romanize the area via the establishment of colonies, and by the end of 179 BC, the Romans had succeeded in pacifying the central regions of Hispania and bringing them under their control.

On returning to Rome both men received a triumph, implying that they had conducted a successful campaign against these two tribes.[36] But the measures taken by the two praetors were not sufficient and caused a wave of new revolts, for incoming greedy praetors failed to follow Gracchus' policies. Instead of building on what the two previous had established, they began violent and arbitrary campaigns against certain Iberian tribes, leading native emissaries to address the Senate with their protests, but to no avail.

Livy ends his writing about the Iberian Peninsula at 181 BC with the exception of a few minor mentions of skirmishes against the Lusitanians in 163 BC.[36] In 163 and 162 BC, under the consulate of P. Cornelius Scipio Nasica Corculum and C. Marcius Figulus, the Lusitanians again rebelled, only to be defeated — unfortunately we do not know the details.[37] After this period, there is no more news of Lusitanian incursions.

Perhaps the reason Livy and Appian omitted the 170s, 160s and part of the 150s BC was the policies and treaties introduced by T. Sempronius Gracchus. These policies brought relative peace between the Hispanic populations and the Romans. Another reason was that Rome had become involved in the Third Macedonian War, making Hispania a minor concern. However, this did not cease the struggle against the Romans, nor did the Lusitanians withdraw from their incursions and looting within the Guadalquivir Valley. The next time one reads about Roman involvement in Hispania, it is in Appian's book on the Iberian Peninsula with the outbreak of the Celtiberian War in 153 BC and the Lusitanian Wars.[38]

The First Lusitanian War

In 155 BC the political and military situation in the Iberian Peninsula had radically changed again, to a point that it created enormous concern in Rome. During this period of turmoil, the following episode came to be an important symbol of Iberian resistance, for it motivated future Iberian leaders to resist Roman imperialism while showing the Romans that the conquest of the Iberian Peninsula would be tougher than they thought.

Lusitanian incursions were systematic and well organized to the extent that one must assume that these actions were part of a resistance struggle against Rome for Lusitanian and Celtiberian independence rather than simple robberies. The numerous defeats to the Lusitanians and Celtiberians must have deeply discouraged the Roman citizenry in Rome, as reported in the classical texts, for they could not understand why they were suffering so many defeats against primitive tribes.

The first Roman episode in this new war with the Lusitanians occurred in 154 BC. The account comes from Appian, who took his information from Polybius, who had personally participated in both Celtiberian Wars (the first from 181 to 179 BC and the second from 154 to 153 BC). Appian writes that the praetor of Hispania Ulterior, M. Manlius, was defeated by a Vettone and Lusitanian alliance under the command of a Lusitanian warrior chief named Punicus, who undertook to pillaging populations that had submitted

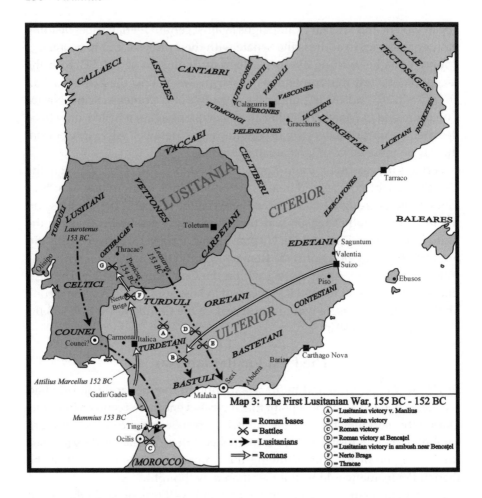

Map 3: The First Lusitanian War, 155 BC - 152 BC

themselves to Rome.[39] Punicus' forces were so determined to show the Romans that they meant business that they even defeated praetor L. Calpurnius Piso.[40] Of the 15,000 Roman soldiers that were stationed in the area, 6,000 men were killed along with the army's commander Terentius Varro.[41] Punicus quickly took advantage of the victory and marched cross the entire Guadalquivir Plain until he reached the Mediterranean coast, where he sacked many other cities. Alarmed by Punicus' campaign, many Romanized cities begged for Rome to send more troops as well as forming new Iberian auxiliary units. But his campaign was short-lived for during an attack on one of these allied cities, Punicus was killed by a stone to the head.[42]

A new chief was soon chosen by the Lusitanians. Ceasarus was his name. The following year (153 BC) he led incursions as far as the city of Sexi (Almuñécar, Granada) sacking many cities along littoral Andalusia. At the same time, elections were held in Rome to elect two new praetors to Hispania. The praetor designated for Hispania Citerior was Quintus Nobilior Fulvius, while Hispania Ulterior was entrusted to Lucius Mummius. Along with these two newly elected officials, it was also decided that a strong army be sent to Hispania to remove the Celtiberian and Lusitanian threat; the Roman army totalled approximately 30,000 men between the consular troops and Spanish auxiliary allies. On arriving in Hispania, Nobilior quickly set out to pacify the Celtiberians. Once they were located, he managed to defeat an army of Celtibarians, Vettones and Vaccaei near Toledo and took their leader, Hilerno, prisoner.[43]

At the start of 153 BC the Lusitanians fought and repelled Roman soldiers from their border. Caesarus pursued them but was obliged to withdraw in the face of Mummius' large army of auxiliary legions. This defeat after several victories, especially at Bencatel (Vila Viçosa), phased Caesarus' confidence and he decided to take another route and attempted to continue his campaign.[44] The Romans went on to pursue Caesarus in a disorderly fashion, but when Rome received intelligence reports of Mummius' movements, they were handed bad news, for his army had been ambushed resulting in about 6,000 Roman deaths.[45] Ceasarus' army recaptured the booty that had been taken from his men as well as the Roman camp, seizing weapons, much-needed supplies and Roman standards, which they paraded throughout Celtiberia in mockery of the Romans.[46] The victory rejuvenated the Lusitanian and Celtiberian spirit to continue the fight against the invaders.

Mummius withdrew from the campaign and took his remaining 5,000 troops for training at an unknown location.[47] In the meantime, he sent a dispatch to Nobilior asking for support in his campaign to annihilate Ceasarus' army. In response, Nobilior sent considerable reinforcements. Mummius kept watch to see if Ceasarus and his men would enter or exit the province, planning to ambush them, kill many in the process and take their booty.[48] According to legend, during a Lusitanian incursion Ceasarus was killed in an ambush at the spot where the chapel of São Tiago (Saint James) is today in the district of Bragança, the municipality of Vimioso. The legend says it was built on top of the ruin of a Roman temple that Mummius erected in compliance with a vote from his soldiers who had fought in the campaign.[49]

Soon after another Lusitanian leader rose up: Caucaenus.[50] He quickly formed an army and marched south to attack the Conii, taking their largest city, Conistorgis.[51] The Conii were targeted because they had allied themselves with the Romans. Caucaenus' troops then marched into Andalusia and crossed the Mediterranean from the Strait of Gibraltar by boat.

Appian writes that landing somewhere between Morocco and Libya, Caucaenus' force was split into two: one ravaged Libya while the other laid siege to Ocilis (modern Arzila, Morocco).[52] Mummius, however, pursued them with 9,000 infantry and 500 cavalry.[53] They soon encountered one of Caucaenus' forces and a battle ensued in which the rebels suffered 15,000 casualties and the siege of Ocilis was raised.[54] Mummius distributed as much Lusitanian bootyas his men could carry to his army, and burnt the remainder in honour of the gods of war.[55]

The following year, 152 BC, two new praetors, Marcus Attilius (Ulterior) and M. Claudius Marcellus (Citerior), were assigned to Hispania. In Rome, Mummius received the honour of a triumph for his victory over the Lusitanians, which had raised the morale of Roman citizens — many had been preoccupied with the pessimistic news that was coming from Hispania. As for the two newly appointed praetors, they quickly lashed out at the troublemaking Lusitanians and Celtiberians. Luck was on the side of the Romans, for Marcellus, after winning several victories near Nertóbriga (which is perhaps Fregenal de la Sierra, Badajoz) made a pact with the Celtiberians. This treaty was refused by the Roman Senate, however, forcing each side to continue the war.[56] But as winter was setting in Marcellus went into winter quarters at Cordova, where he provided his auxiliary troops to Attilius in his campaign against the stubborn Lusitanians. With Marcellus' reinforcements M. Attilius penetrated Lusitania and took the city of Oxthracae (location unknown).[57] Taking the city of Oxthracae along with 700 Lusitanians, Attilius so terrified all those that lived in the vicinity that the inhabitants called for peace.[58]

This peace meant nothing to the rest of the Lusitanians. When Attilius went into winter quarters, Lusitanians from other areas went on a rampage and besieged several Romanized cities.[59] Armed Lusitanian incursion continued to blight the Baetician regions and be a thorn in the Roman legions' side. Shortly after, Marcellus once again approached the Roman Senate with his peace proposal. Under pressure from the citizenry, the Senate agreed to the terms, which created a brief period of tranquility in Hispania (from 151 to 143 BC).

In 151 BC Claudius Marcellus was replaced with Consul Lucius Licinius Lucullus,who shared governorship of Hispania with the now infamous Praetor Servius Sulpicius Galba — these two characters are regarded as the most despicable in the conquest of the Iberian Peninsula. In the eyes of most Iberian historians these two well-established political and military men came to Hispania to enrich themselves rather than attempt to stabilize the provinces for the benefit of the empire. Their greed destabilized certain areas and caused several tribes to rebel.

Galba's Massacre and the Rise of Viriathus

Praetor Servius Sulpicius Galba and Proconsul Lucius Licinius Lucullus arrived in 151 BC. Upon reaching Hispania, both men immediately began campaigning against the Iberian tribes. Lucullus was disappointed to find that the Celtiberians had made peace; so he decided to launch his own campaign against the Vaccaei and Caucaei, massacring the second tribe after having made an agreement with them.[60] He would later be involved along with Galba in Viriathus' rise to power. As for Galba, he continued Attilius' campaign against the Lusitanians.

As mentioned in the last section, the Lusitanians from the vicinity of Oxthracae signed a peace accord with Marcus Attilius that forced the submission of several Lusitanians and Vettones tribes. But this treaty was not accepted byLusitanians from other areas. These tribes, either breaking or ignoring the treaty, again began to ransack the Roman occupied countryside.

Receiving reports that the Lusitanians were up in arms and sacking Roman settlements, Galba rapidly organized his army and marched towards Lusitania to relieve his Roman subjects, who were being hard-pressed by the Lusitanians. Having travelled 500 *stadia* (90 km) in twenty-four hours, his exhausted troops were immediately formed up and sent straight into battle against a large Lusitanian force that had stationed itself on the northern outskirts of Carmo (modern-day Carmona).[61] Galba succeeded in putting the enemy to flight, but made the mistake of pursuing them. Exhausted, disorganized and scattered, his army pursued the Lusitanians incautiously. On seeing this weak and disorderly pursuit, the Lusitanians counter-attacked and a fierce contest ensued, in which 7,000 of the 15,000 Romans fell.[62] After this devastating defeat, Galba managed to collect the remnants of his army and quickly took shelter in Carmo, situated a few miles away from the battlefield. Once he had reassembled, he marched out and took up winter quarters at Conistorgis.[63] While wintering there (151 to 150 BC) Galba assembled about 20,000 allied troops for a new campaign when spring arrived.[64]

In Hispania Citerior L. Licinius Lucullus, who had conducted his own private campaign against the Vaccaei, was wintering in Turdetania. On learning that three separate Lusitanian armies were crossing into his territory, he sent his best commander against the northern group which resulted in 4,000 Lusitanian casualties.[65] Meanwhile he organized his remaining legions and marched out of Turdetania heading south to Baetica in search of wealth and the other two groups. During his minor campaign in southern Spain he ran into one of the groups, a medium sized Lusitanian force. During the battle he killed 1,500 bandit-warriors as they were preparing to cross the Strait of Gibraltar into North Africa.[66] The rest of the rebels fled onto a hill, which Lucullus encircled, capturing them to sell into slavery.

With the arrival of spring in 150 BC, both governors decided on a joint strategy of pillage and destruction in an attempt to put an end to the persistent raids by the Lusitanians in Roman territory.[67] They set out in a pincer movement; Lucullus turned east towards Lusitania, while Galba left Conistorgis and marched north into Lusitania. The two forces advanced deep into Lusitania, pillaging and destroying towns. Though this strategy failed to bring to battle the bulk of the enemy's forces, it had the desired effect of forcing the Lusitanians to agree to a truce.

The Lusitanians sent an emissary, declaring that they repented for having violated the treaty which they had concluded with Atilius, and promised henceforth to observe it faithfully.[68] Galba received the envoys and made a truce and pretended to sympathize with them. Lucullus by now had joined forces with Galba and they planned to use the same treasonous scheme that Lucullus had used with the Caucaei.

The way in which Galba acted on this occasion is one of the most infamous and atrocious acts of treachery and cruelty that occur in Iberian history. Galba received the ambassadors kindly and lamented their circumstances, especially the poverty of their country that had induced them to continuously indulge in banditry, break agreements and revolt against Rome. According to Appian, Galba told the envoys: 'For it is the poor quality of the soil and lack of resources that compels you to do the things you do. As an act of kindness I will give my poor friends good land and settle them in rich country, dividing them into three sections.' He proposed to resettle them on three fertile plains under the protection of Rome. To subdue them without violence, he induced them to leave their homes and assemble into three hosts, with their women and children, to be sent to designated ares in which he would later allow each host to settle.[69]

The Lusitanians celebrated this new alliance by sacrificing a man (a prisoner caught in one of their raids) and a horse. Months later, more than 30,000 Lusitanians had gathered to wait for that promise to come true.[70] On an agreed date in 150 BC they congregated at the arranged location. Galba then divided them into three sections and showed each group a stretch of open land, ordering them to stay in the area until he could provide them with a town.[71] But there was to be no distribution of lands, just death and slavery. Turning back to the first group, Galba addressed them as friends, asking them to give up their arms, for surrendering their weapons was a sign of peace and it was superfluous for an agrarian way of life. When they had done so, Galba had his men surround the Lusitanians and ordered his soldiers to kill every able-bodied man.[72] He hurried on and treated the second and third group in the same manner, each group being ignorant of what was happening to the other groups.[73]

In the aftermath of the massacre 9,000 lay dead and as many as 20,000 were taken prisoner. Most of the survivors were either forced into slave labour or sold into slavery.[74] Those that did not give in were massacred. However, a number of Lusitanians managed to escape from the bloody scene; one was Viriathus, destined one day to avenge the wrong done to his countrymen.

Appian and several other authors state that Galba, although already very wealthy, was extremely stingy and greedy.[75] Of all the loot produced, Appian says that the praetor carefully allocated only a small part to his soldiers, another small part to his friends and kept the remainder for himself.[76]

After these actions, Lucullus and Galba returned to Rome in 149 BC, richer and more powerful than before. Expecting to be honoured with a triumph, instead the two were accused of committing heinous acts that went against the newly instituted *Lexde rebus repetundis*, proposed by L. Calpurnius Piso in the earlier part of 149 BC. This law basically stated that if non-Romans from the provinces complained about Roman magistrates and pro-magistrates who used their power wrongly to acquire personal wealth, Rome would be compelled to make restitutions, thus protecting non-Romans from violence and extortion.[77] Outraged about the incident, several Roman tribunes lead by Lucius Escribonius Libo (a plebeian) and M. Porcius Cato instituted proceedings against Galba and Lucullus by introducing a bill (*rogation*) to release all those Lusitanians that had surrendered and been sold into slavery in Gaul, while a constitutional tribunal was ordered to investigate the praetors' behaviour.[78] On hearing this, several former praetors, such as Q. Fulvius Nobilior, who were against the *rogation* defended Galba's actions.[79]

Lucullus, who was a bit more politically cunning than Galba, bribed the senators and was freed from all charges; in return he had to build a temple to the goddess Felicitas, a forced religious act to the goddess for forgiveness of his past transgressions.[80] Galba, on the other hand, decided to stand his ground and became involved in a serious judicial battle, even rejecting Cato's *rogation*. Galba, the most celebrated orator of his generation according to Cicero, defended himself. To achieve the compassion and pity of the senators, he appeared in front of the Senate with his children and ward, asking the Roman people to protect them if he was found guilty and sentenced to death. In principle, the Senate denied absolving him of his crimes, but when he decided to deliver a large part of the booty that he had stolen in Hispania into Rome's coffers and the Senators' pockets, the Senate acquitted him.[81] Money brought more compassion than words did, and as Galba was one of the richest men in Rome he had no problem buying it. It is probable that Galba was never actually brought before a court, for he may have faced condemnation if he had. So strong was the power of money that five years later he was elected Senate consul.

What is more significant is that one of the few survivors of Galba's slaughter was Viriathus. Roman historiography links Galba's cruel and unscrupulous episode with Viriathus'ascension to become one of Rome's most challenging adversaries for the next eight years. He was the protagonist of the Lusitanian War and his name was repeatedly echoed in senatorial election speeches throughout Rome.

From this point on the Lusitanians did not raid Baetica just out of desire for treasures and profit but to maintain their cattle, farming and the overall survival of their people, due to the poor quality of soil in Lusitania.[82] In the highlands there was much poverty and a lack of vegetation, so goats and sheep were the only thing that could transform into wealth and survivability.[83] In the end, the Lusitanians just wanted pastures of their own.

In conclusion the twenty-five years of peace initiated by Sempronius Gracchus was broken. Though Galba incited the Lusitanians, who had by now reached a desperate situation due to the behaviour of several Roman governors, they were also to blame for the war. Both sides were responsible, but in defence of the Lusitanians, their reason for initiating the war was justified for they needed land to solve their economic problems and Rome did not offer them land but deceived them as Galba had. Galba's terror and excessive cruelty against the Lusitanians had ruined Rome's hopes and the only chance at pacifying the Lusitanians and their desire of getting pastures and better farmland. The Lusitanians were in an unbearable situation which left them no other solution than to fight Rome. It is perhaps safe to say that the massacre was the reason for the major revolts that broke out throughout the whole of Hispania between 147 and 133 BC. As for the Lusitanian War, Galba's betrayal and massacre of the Lusitanians in 150 BC ended the first phase and began a new phase of rebellion that would spread like wildfire throughout Hispania.

Chapter 6
The Viriathan War
(The Second Lusitanian War)

Classical authors, primarily Polybius, Livy, Appian and Diodorus, highlight that the Iberian Wars the Romans undertook in Hispania against the native populace were the most difficult and cruelest of all those Rome had engaged in so far. The Roman soldier had to face not only a dangerous enemy but also

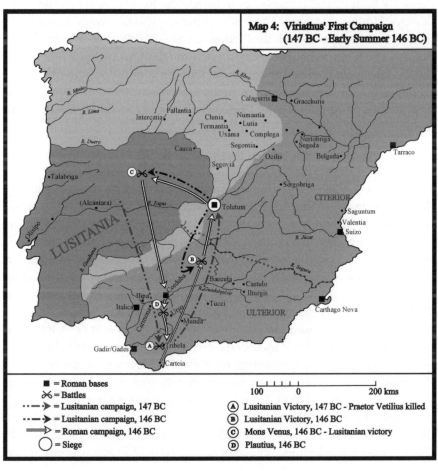

Map 4: Viriathus' First Campaign (147 BC - Early Summer 146 BC)

■ = Roman bases
✗ = Battles
·–·–▷ = Lusitanian campaign, 147 BC
·–·–▷ = Lusitanian campaign, 146 BC
⟹ = Roman campaign, 146 BC
◯ = Siege

Ⓐ Lusitanian Victory, 147 BC - Praetor Vetilius killed
Ⓑ Lusitanian Victory, 146 BC
Ⓒ Mons Venus, 146 BC - Lusitanian victory
Ⓓ Plautius, 146 BC

100   0   200 kms

a hostile environment. It was not in vain that Polybius, an exceptional witness of the facts and a friend and advisor to Publius Cornelius Scipio Aemilianus Africanus Numantinus, classified this entire period of more than twenty years of warfare as the 'fiery war'.[1]

Slavery, murder, treason, breaches of treaties, brutal executions, massacres of both Romans and Lusitanians alike and ethnic cleansing were tactics that became part of the new style of war called 'guerrilla warfare'. With the inability of Rome's military power to defeat a 'barbarous' people, it came to be seen by many Romans as a costly war with no end in sight, and with little in return (i.e. profits). In time, this war would begin to exhaust the patience of the Roman Senate so much that they decided to stop Iberian resistance by any means necessary. Also, Rome's praetors were urged not to look to Rome for material resources, aside from manpower, to continue the war effort. The fighting would become horribly inhumane. Death, pillaging, rape, and even genocide became the common practice for the Roman generals that were deployed to this war zone. The war became so vicious because Rome never wanted to accept peace with the Iberians on an equal footing, in spite of their defeats. The Romans believed they were better than the barbaric Iberians, so the Iberians were required to surrender without conditions, something they would never do. The Lusitanians preferred to die rather than accept these new treaties on Roman terms. Therefore they defended their liberty to the death.

Viriathus Strikes Back

Three years (150 BC to 147 BC) had passed since Galba's massacre and the Romans were beginning to get accustomed to the splendourous peaceful haven the peninsula had become. Of course this was only an illusion, for Galba and Lucullus' massacre had left not only profound and bitter marks in the Lusitanian psyche but a resistance movement capable of making war against the Romans. While the Romans were enjoying the peace, among the Lusitanians the survivor Viriathus was taking leadership of his people and planning to severely damage Roman rule in Lusitania and beyond.

Although a new, 'Homeric' hero was emerging, there was no news of any rebellious activity in Lusitania. Perhaps the Lusitanians were licking their wounds and preparing themselves for a wrath of revenge. In the meantime Rome became involved in new commitments, such as fighting the Third Punic War (149 BC to 146 BC).[2] The Aegean also needed Roman attention, in particular the insurrections in Macedonia, which had only recently come under Roman control (in 148 BC) with the elimination of King Andriscus by Quintus Caecilius Metellus. Whatever happened in Hispania was minor until

147 BC when the Lusitanian War created a new dimension in warfare.

In Appian's writings, Viriathus would be elected head of his tribe sometime between 150 BC and 147 BC and would soon begin to outline his plan and organize a small army to terrorize the Romans.[3] Unfortunately there is no record of what went on among the Lusitanians during these years, but we know that by the end of 147 BC or the beginning of 146 BC the Lusitanians had assembled an army of 10,000 men under a nameless tribal leader and invaded the pacified area of Turdetania.[4]

Reaching the Guadalquivir Valley, the Lusitanians were intercepted near Urso (Osuna) by a Roman legion belonging to the newly elected praetor of Hispania Ulterior, Gaius Vetilius, who had recently arrived from Rome with a new army on top of the army awaiting him in Ulterior. On receiving news that the Lusitanians were in his territory, Vetilius quickly marched against them from his winter quarters in Córdoba with his entire army of 10,000 men.[5] He fell upon the Lusitanians while they were foraging for supplies, killing many of them and forcing the rest into an unnamed place where, if they stayed, according to Appian, they were in danger of famine, and if they came out they would fall into the hands of the Romans.[6] The Lusitanians' situation had become desperate. Being in this unknown place, surrounded and without provisions, they sent messengers to Vetilius with olive-branches (a sign of peace) asking for good land to settle on, and saying that thereafter they would obey the Romans in all matters.[7]

Vetilius promised to give them land if they surrendered their weapons, but when an agreement was nearly made to that effect, Viriathus, who had escaped the perfidy of Galba and who was among them as a junior chieftain, suddenly reminded them of the Romans' unreliability and bad faith, often swearing oaths only to break them soon after. To make matters worse Viriathus pointed out that entire Roman legions and their leader had escaped from the perjuries of the Roman Senate, but the Lusitanians had not. He told the warriors that if they swore allegiance to him he would show them a safe retreat from the place.[8] On this basis, negotiations with Vetilius were suspended.

Moved by his eloquent speech and excited by the new hopes he inspired in them, the Lusitanians nominated Viriathus on the spot as their supreme commander. He quickly proposed a plan of action to break the siege.[9] In Appian's report on the matter, Viriathus drew the warriors up into a battle line formation as if they were ready to fight, but gave them orders to divide themselves up into many small groups and when he gave the signal, which was his mounting his horse, they would then scatter in all directions, break through enemy lines and make their way by different routes to the city of Tribola (a city south of Urso) and wait for him there for reassembly.[10]

While the men prepared themselves for their escape, he asked for 1,000 of the best warrior-riders to stay behind with him to keep Vetelius busy.[11] With these arrangements made, the Lusitanians began to flee in many different directions as soon as Viriathus mounted his horse. Vetelius, afraid and confused about what was happening and realizing that it was impossible to pursue so many groups, ordered his men to stand down against those who had scattered in different directions, and instead turned towards Viriathus and his 1,000 warriors, all on horseback and standing on the horizon, apparently as if they were waiting for an attack. The Romans charged towards them and a battle ensued. Having very swift horses, Viriathus and his men put their plan into effect: harassing the Romans by attacking, then retreating, standing still and again attacking and retreating.[12] This manoeuvre consumed the entire day and the next for he continuously had the Romans running around in circles on the same field.[13]

The bold plan worked and the Lusitanians had escaped. After two days of toying with the Romans, Viriathus and his men disappeared from the battlefield like ghosts. When he reckoned that his army had safely made their escape, while the Romans were bivouacked for the night his men set out for Tribola via unmarked and devious paths on very agile steeds.[14] Thus Viriathus, in an unexpected way, rescued his army from a desperate situation. Once known by other tribes in the vicinity, this feat brought him fame and many reinforcements from different quarters, enabling him to wage war against the Romans for the next eight years.[15]

The Battle of Tribola

Vetilius soon realized what had happened, and wanting to avenge his embarrassment, he slowly began searching for the Lusitanians, but the Romans were not able to follow at an equal pace or search fast enough due to the weight of his men's heavy armour, their ignorance of the roads and terrain, and the inferiority of their horses. On receiving intelligence that the slow-moving Romans were in the vicinity, Viriathus quickly reorganized his small army and prepared for a large-scale ambush (see Map 4).[16] Ready for war, he posted a greater part of his army in the thickets along the pass of the Sierra de Ronda, in the Barbesula River Valley (today called Guadiaro).[17]

Confident that his superiority in numbers would ensure victory, Vetilius pursued Viriathus until he came upon Tribola. Viriathus instigated a skirmish and quickly retreated through the pass in an attempt to lure Vetilius into a trap. The Romans again underestimated their enemy. Vetilius, failing to send out an effective scouting party, fell for Viriathus' diversionary tactic and gave chase into the pass. When the Roman army entered the pass, Viriathus suddenly turned and charged head on into the Roman ranks, while those laid in waiting in the wooded slope sprang the ambush. Viriathus had led Vetilius into a lethal trap. The Lusitanians swarmed the Romans like locusts from all sides, killing as many of them as they could. At the end of the battle, several hundred soldiers had survived and were taken prisoner, including Vetilius himself. According to Appian, the man who captured him didn't realize who he was and, considering him worthless because he was old and fat, killed him.[18] But Diodorus has a different version, in which Viriathus condemns him to death. The result was disastrous for the Romans; of the 10,000 soldiers over 4,000 were killed including Vetilius, while some 6,000 survivors made their way with difficulty to the city of Carpessus on the Mediterranean.[19] The Romans had been introduced to a new face of war; the hit and run tactic and alternating attack and retreat. After the incident the Romans named this type of warfare, the *concursare*.[20]

Badly demoralized and incapable of counter-attack, the remaining Romans headed towards Carpessus under the leadership of Vetilius' quaestor, who stationed the men within the town's walls. He requisitioned 5,000 allied Belli and Titthi warriors living in the area of the Jalón Valley, Spain, and sent them against Viriathus, who slew them all to make an example of what would happen to any Iberian tribe that sided with Rome. After that incident, Vetilius' quaestor remained quietly in the town waiting for assistance from Rome.[21]

After the battle of Tribola, Appian writes, with this newfound encouragement and leadership Viriathus invaded the prosperous and fruitful region of Carpetania, plundering it freely until Gaius Plautius arrived from Rome with another army of 13,000 soldiers.[22]

In the aftermath of the battle, the Roman Senate saw Viriathus as a threat to the stability of the entire peninsula, but was only able to send reinforcements to make up the losses already suffered in the rebellion. Unfortunately for the Romans they did not have sufficient forces in Hispania to put an end to Viriathus. This was because Rome was still engaged in the Third Punic War, committing its main efforts to compete with its long-standing rival Carthage for hegemony of the western Mediterranean Sea.[23] All the Senate could do was attempt to contain Viriathus as best as it could.

On the other hand, Roman military leaders viewed him as a popular warlord and an able enemy general. To handle this new menace they had to change their tactics. The Roman commanders stationed in Hispania came up with a strategy of dividing up their forces and attempted to surround Viriathus' small army, in an effort to surprise him at every turn so as to weaken his army before the final hammer blow. According to Tusculano, fresh new Roman legions were deployed to protect the southern part of Hispania, but unfortunately for them they did not manage to engage Viriathus in southern Lusitania, but in the Meseta Central and in the south of Spain. Though the Romans had stationed the nucleus of its army in the south, Roman military commanders found it difficult to employ and engage their legions in Lusitania due to the rugged terrain. Without the conquest of the central region, Roman legions could not advance north and west without jeopardizing their overall security.[24] Perhaps the Romans would have been able to conquer Lusitania quickly through a three pronged attack, one from the sea on the Atlantic coast and two from inland, avoiding crossing the Serra da Estrela by going around it. With this strategy the Romans could have dominated Lusitania and the entire peninsula. But the lack of a sound military strategy resulted in a fight that caused major bleeding to the Roman forces. Viriathus exploited the situation by negotiating alliances with the Celtiberians and other tribes of the Meseta Central. The Romans tried their best to deal with Viriathus, but it was not good enough and they continued losing men in large numbers.

Theatre of Operations

The entire northwest of Hispania was involved, in different levels, in the Lusitanian War. But, furthermore, the war had great implications on the areas of the Meseta, Asturias, Andalusia and Cantabria. In some instances, there was a connection between Viriathus' guerrilla campaign and the Second Celtiberian War. For example, Viriathus incited the Vaccaei and the Numantians against Rome as well as the Galaicians, Vaccaei, Belli, Titthi, Cantabrians, and Arevaci.[25]

Even if the theatre of operation was actually within the border of modern-day central Portugal and outskirts of Lusitania, it was in this large area called the Beiras and Extremadura, Spain, that the Romans found it difficult to operate. Due to its thick forests and the country's high and inaccessible sierras along with the cold, rough and arid mountains of the inhospitable Meseta Central, which did not offer many possibilities for a successful Roman military campaign, this wild country caused many problems in Rome's attempt at pacification. This difficult terrain made it a safe haven for the many Lusitanian villages and fortified *castros*. But the eventual conquest of these territories was inevitable as the Romans needed to protect and defend their allies and Baetican possessions against Lusitanians attacks.

Rome would press Lusitania with all the weight of its military power, stationing its legions near Lusitania's borders in a show of force to maintain a policy of 'peace'. During these years, Rome also began to send a different type of governor to Hispania, one that was morally on the level and different from Galba, for Rome wanted to forget the cruel greed that Galba and the overly ambitious Lucullus had exhibited as governors. This policy did not work, however, for the Lusitanians had been emotionally and spiritually scarred by so many Roman injustices that they were now blinded by rage and wanted Roman blood.

Viriathus' Guerrilla Campaign

Viriathus' victory at Tribola enabled him to roam all of Baetica without opposition. The news had reached all corners of Hispania,which vibrated with patriotic enthusiasm. It raised the morale of the Lusitanians and inspired widespread resistance against Rome throughout the land. Viriathus became

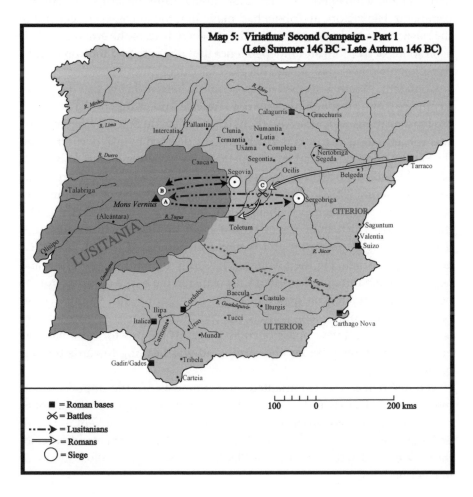

the chief instigator of other tribal rebellions that arose throughout Hispania during an eight year period, becoming the 'terror of Rome'. With his experience, wit and unorthodox tactics, Viriathus' army dominated and plundered the lands of Beturia and the entire fertile Guadalquivir Valley. His victory did not bring large numbers of soldiers to his cause at first. At the start of the war, only a limited number of neighbouring tribal chiefs joined his cause, such as Brigeu, clan chief from another Lusitanian tribe.[26] This would later change.

These alliances with Brigeu and other tribal leaders marked the beginning of a united front against the Romans, that if successful would ruin Rome's plans for the peninsula. Before the war various Iberian, Celtiberian and Lusitanian tribes fought the Romans seperately, with each tribe operating in complete independence from the others, but now Viriathus' thirst for revenge had somehow enabled him to unite many different tribes under his command. His victory at Tribola had made him the uncontested general of the Lusitanians and a beloved chief they obeyed, because he embodied their aspirations of freedom and independence. But it was hatred for Rome and a thirst for vengeance that started his glorious career.

Confident, Viriathus seemed to have come to believe that he had the power to oppose Rome, through his superior strategy, knowledge of the land and the bravery of his warriors. And though he was aware that the Roman army was concentrating its forces in Turdetania, he decided to turn north through the Sierra Morena and head into Carpetania, the richest and most fertile area of the Meseta. Unopposed, he continued his campaign into Carpetania towards Toletum (Toledo). According to the late Teófilo Braga, Viriathus had somehow made a defensive alliance with the Vettones and Vacceus, under the terms of which their forces would meet in Toletum to plunder it.[27] Viriathus arrived promptly at Toletum and plundered it with his allies, according to Braga. He then enlarged his army by adding new allies and began to march through the rest of Carpetania in the hopes of luring out the next Roman praetor or general, as he had done with Vetilius. After plundering the countryside still unopposed, Viriathus returned to Toletum and prepared for a new phase of combat against the praetor, who had just arrived from Rome with another army and was heading towards him for battle.

Vetilius' defeat was commented on in Rome as of little importance; as mentioned previously they were too involved in two major conflicts. But as they had only one governor to run the entire province since Vetilius' death and were somewhat worried that the Lusitanian War might get out of hand, the Senate decided to elected Gaius Plautius Hypsaeus as Vetilius' successor in Ulterior.

A few months later, sometime during the spring of 146 BC, Plautius arrived in the province with another small army of 10,000 infantry and 1,300 cavalry (see Map 5).[28] Perhaps the reason more could not be deployed was that Rome was heavily committed to its third war with Carthage. As praetor, he quickly imposed a high state of alert in his province and asked for aid from the governor of Citerior, Claudius Unimanus. At the same time Plautius sent between 4,000 and 5,000 Roman soldiers to relieve Vetilius' defeated army at Carpessus (today San Roque, Spain) and to aid Rome's allies, the Belli and Titthi. During their march, this Roman legion ran into Viriathus' army and was cut to pieces.[29] Unfortunately, there are no details of the battle. But at this point, Plautius sent out the remainder of his army and began his search for Viriathus.

Plautius discovered Viriathus' whereabouts in Carpetania and attacked, but Viriathus — instead of fighting Plautius the conventional way — reverted to hit-and-run guerrilla tactics. Worried that his small army would be outnumbered, Viriathus quit Carpetania and withdrew into Lusitania. Plautius quickly instructed one of his generals, Quintus, to take a legion and follow Viriathus, while he took another in an attempt to flank Viriathus' army from the south, whereupon reaching a certain point both Roman armies would attack Viriathus simultaneously. While pursuing Viriathus' retreating army, Plautius received the dreadful report that Quintus' legion had been wiped out as it reached its rendezvous point, which has been identified as Ebora (Evora).[30] Viriathus, utilizing his signature 'feigned flight' tactic, turned on his pursuers and routed them, killing most in the process.[31]

With the outbreak of the Lusitanian War in 147 BC and Viriathus' invasion of Carpetania, Plautius seems to have decided to transfer the command centre of his military operations against the Lusitanians to the centre of the peninsula, which was outside of Roman control. I believe he left Ulterior and marched deep into Celtiberian territory because he felt threatened by Viriathus' deep incursion into Roman dominated southern lands — perhaps he thought that if Viriathus launched raids into southern held territory nothing would stop him advancing eastward into Citerior, inciting rebellion among the 'pacified' Iberian tribes. Thus it was very important to place a Roman presence in that area. By 133 BC Carpetania had definitively become incorporated into the Roman dominion.

However victorious, Viriathus withdrew his forces into his home ground by crossing the Tagus River and setting up camp somewhere in the hilly area the Romans called Mons Veneris (the Hill of Venus).[32] Despite his recent defeat, the determined Plautius and the rest of his forces made haste and crossed the Tagus in pursuit of the Lusitanians. Finally catching up to

Viriathus and keen to redeem his prior defeat, he attacked. Plautius sustained another defeat with so much slaughter that he and his survivors fled in a disorderly fashion. Plautius was so shocked by his losses that he withdrew early from the campaign season and took the rest of his army into the security of winter quarters in Baetica in the middle of the summer, refusing to venture out against Viriathus for the rest of his term as governor. According to Diodorus, Plautius was condemned upon his recall to Rome, charged with *minuta maiestas* (little treason), and sent into exile.[33]

Viriathus' victory at the Battle of Mons Veneris left him with the initiative to exploit his victory in a series of attacks on Roman garrisons and towns in central Hispania, which caused much damage, not least to Roman morale. Now unopposed, he went on a rampage through central Hispania confiscating and destroying crops and pillaging towns that had allied themselves with Rome, in particular the Celtiberian city of Segobriga. Those towns or cities that supported Viriathus were untouched and crops were paid for in booty.[34]

After defeating Plautius, Viriathus strategically based himself on Mons Veneris, from which he could launch raids into all the neighbouring regions and continue his incursions along the Tagus River. The choice of this location as the centre of his operations proves again that Viriathus was a great strategist. He also extended his influence north to Sierra da Guadarrama, in the Sistema Central, moving hastily through this territory and forcing the habitants to respect his orders.[35] Also around this time he seems to have carried out an expedition against the Roman allied city of Segovia, which was situated in Vaccaei territory; unfortunately for the Lusitanians it was not as lucrative as Toletum.[36] He made his next advance near the end of 146 BC, moving towards another Roman allied city, Segobriga (actual Cabeza de Griego near Cuenca).[37] Viriathus managed to surprise its inhabitants and conquer the city by using the same tactic of ambushes, false withdrawals and surprise attacks he had used against Vetilius and Plautius. The destruction of the Segobrigan army was recorded by Frontinus. He writes that Viriathus sent men to carry off their flocks of livestock. When the Segobrigan soldiers saw this, they rushed out of their fortress in great numbers. The marauders pretended to flee and drew the Segobrigans into an ambush where they were cut to pieces.[38] From a certain point of view, the defeat of these Romans cities acted as building block for Viriathus'reputation as a leader and his ability to persuade other tribes, especially the Celtiberians, to ally themselves with him.

Alarmed that Viriathus was running rampant through the Hispanic countryside and worried that he might cause trouble in his province, Claudius Unimanus, the Governor of Citerior, deployed his troops against him, presumably near the end of the campaigning season (autumn) of 146 BC (see Map 5). But like the previous praetors, according to Orosius and Florus, he was defeated in battle.[39] The battle was a disaster for Unimanus, who lost a legion and its standards, which were taken as trophies and later publicly displayed throughout the mountain countryside on Viriathus' orders. The morale of the Roman legions fell even further after this event.

Viriathus' generalship in this campaign brought him further prestige and fame, for he had showed all Iberians that it was possible to defeat Rome. With these victories many warriors from all over the Iberian Peninsula began flocking to his standard. But with the war against Carthage finally concluded, Rome was free to solve the Iberian problem and concentrate on defeating the Lusitanians.

But before I continue with Viriathus' campaign, another individual that needs to be mentioned in this drama is Caius Nigidius. Though he is only mentioned by Roman historian Sextus Aurelius Victor and several modern Portuguese and Spanish historians, Nigidius was praetor of Citerior when Unimanus was praetor of Ulterior. Richardson and Professor E. Kornemann are the only two authors who try to explain and place him in the chronological sequence of the Lusitanian War. According to Richardson, Victor suggests that Nigidius was a praetor who was soon defeated after Unimanus.[40] But this is questionable: Kornemann suggests that Nigidius was the unnamed lieutenant of Fabius Aemilianus, who was left in charge when the latter went to Gades (Cadiz) in late 145 BC (see below) and was defeated by Viriathus.[41] If so, he was not a praetor. Richardson, however, says there is a chance he was praetor of Citerior in 144 BC because a Roman defeat is recorded, and it would have been more justifiable to have then sent Quintus Caecilius Metellus Macedonicus, the hero of the Macedonian War, after such a disaster, rather than after a victory by Laelius and Aemilianus in 144 BC.[42] But confusion arises when one looks into the classical texts, for instead of mentioning Nigidius as praetor of Citerior, they cite Laelius. So perhaps the arrival of Metellus in 143 BC was the result of Laelius' defeat. The lack of information about both Nagidius and this episode has caused great confusion about what occurred in Citerior during 145 and 144 BC.

Having mentioned Nigidius, I should also mention a battle that he may have been involved in as praetor, which is not well documented or known in the annals of history but well known in Portuguese legend and folklore. The story of this battle has been passed down from generation to generation and documented by several Portuguese authors such as Braga and Tusculano, whom I have used as references (of these two authors, I use Braga's account of the battle, which is the better of the two).There is also information on a

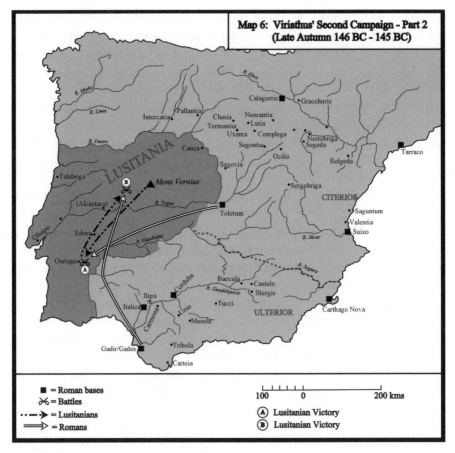

Map 6: Viriathus' Second Campaign - Part 2
(Late Autumn 146 BC - 145 BC)

stone tablet at the Cenáculo Museum in Evora, which was discovered during the early part of the twentieth century. It mentions Unimanus and a C. Minicius, perhaps Unimanus' legion commanderat the time of the battle. Braga believes that this unidentified battle was fought at Ourique in the present-day Alentejo region of southern Portugal.

As the story goes, Viriathus found himself in the Alentejo region near Ebora when the newly arrived preators, Unimanus and Nigidius, set forth on their urgent campaign to repress the Lusitanians and erase their prior defeats. On receiving intelligence from their spy network, the praetors planned to attack in a pincer movement: Unimanus from the south through the mountains of Ourique, and Nigidius, who had been operating in Vaccei territory, from the north toward Ebora, the Lusitanian capital.[43] They believed that caught between two legions Viriathus would certainly be defeated and they would be then able to occupy the entire region.

On reaching Lusitania the two generals set their plan into motion.

Meanwhile, Viriathus heard of the plan through his vast and dedicated spy network and decided to smash one of the legions as quickly as possible so as not to get caught between both. To do that he needed to choose the battlefield and herd them in, one legion at a time. After much cat and mouse manoeuvring, Viriathus decided to attack Unimanus first near Ourique, for Nigidius was still days away from his position. A battle ensued, but unfortunately there is no information beside a mention from Dio Cassius, who wrote this passage, perhaps to show the tenacity of the Lusitanians:

> In a narrow pass 300 Lusitanians faced two cohorts of 1,000 Romans. As a result of the action the Lusitani lost 70 while the Romans lost 320 men. When the victorious Lusitanians retired, one of the warriors became separated and was surrounded by a detachment of cavalry. The lone warrior quickly stabbed the horse of one of the riders with his spear, and with a blow of his sword cut the rider's head clean off, causing such terror among the other Romans that they prudently withdrew under the warrior's arrogant and contemptuous gaze.[44]

Besides showing the low morale of the Romans it also details the determination of the Lusitanians. From Braga's research, it looks like perhaps this minor battle took place at Serra d'Ossa, which is about 160 km (100 miles) from Ourique, but again due to the lack of information one cannot be sure if this is the exact place.[45]

Ultimately, Viriathus completely defeated Unimanus. Unimanus withdrew from the campaign so as to avoid greater bloodshed, but fearing persecution from Rome, he sent a messenger to ask his colleague Nigidius to halt his march and attack the Lusitanians wherever he encountered them. Nigidius agreed, changing course to march north, where he stopped in the Beira region of Portugal. Upon arrival he set up a camp at Viseu and began military operations.[46]

Viriathus, through his spy network, received information about the bivouac site at Viseu. He immediately moved into the Beira region and attacked Nigidius, who was no match for Viriathus. Defeated, Nigidius quickly packed up and withdrew to an unnamed or forgotten fortified city, which Viriathus quickly besieged. Nigidius, lacking provisions and fearing that the city would fall to the Lusitanians, abandoned it in the dead of night. But Viriathus' spies informed him of this movement and he quietly followed Nigidius, who was thus obliged to fight as he fled, further reducing Roman manpower and morale. Though there is little information on Nigidius' praetorship in Hispania there is some evidence from stone tablets and markers that have been discovered in the area, such as the ones found in the Riba-Côa region, that he existed.[47]

When news of the latest developments in Hispania reached Rome, the Senate deemed the situation threatening enough that it immediately sent replacements to Plautius along with a consular army. Consul Quintus Fabius Maximus Aemilianus, the adopted son of Lucius Aemilius Paulus, conqueror of Macedonia, was given Ulterior as his province.[48] At long last Rome had a competent veteran general in Hispania. Furthermore, Aemilianus, through connections in the Senate, was able to get Gaius Laelius Sapiens, a good friend of his, elected as praetor of Citerior to replace the demoralized Unimanus. These two men were chosen as praetors because the Scipio faction (Aemilianus was also the adopted son of Publius Cornelius Scipio, the eldest son of the famous Publius Cornelius Scipio Africanus) held much power in the Senate and intended to concentrate a large number of troops in Spain in order to carry out their agenda of political and administrative reforms, as well as revising the old treaties and alliances started by Scipio Africanus after the Second Punic War.

But because Rome was involved in other conflicts in Greece and Africa, it did not have an army large enough to carry out their plan in Hispania, though it had qualified persons to do the job. With the ending of the wars in Greece and Africa, a larger army could be transferred to Hispania. But in an effort to spare the worn-out veterans of the Punic, Greek and Macedonian wars, Aemilianus levied a small field army of new recruits: 15,000 legionnaires and 2,000 cavalrymen.[49]

While Aemilianus remained in Italy organizing another army, Laelius, who was more given to peace than war, arrived in Citerior. According to Tusculano, perhaps his leanings toward peace were a good thing for he had inherited a beaten and demoralized army. During his tenure as governor, he was more of an ambassador than a general, attempting to demonstrate that he meant to make peace with the Lusitanians by promising that the Senate would give them land.[50]

The Lusitanians, who also wished to establish peace, were constantly reminded by those who had survived Galba's massacre not to trust the Romans, and so they continued to be suspicious of all Roman praetors. The Lusitanians had ceased to believe Rome's promises and answered with continuous fighting, for there would only be peace when the invaders abandoned their homeland.

At first Laelius did not leave the safety of his encampment until he reorganized what was left of the army, but as with all armies around the world, whether ancient or modern, a show of force was necessary, so patrols had to be conducted. Laelius attempted to avoid fully-fledged open battles, but his patrols were constantly involved in skirmishes and ambushes. Laelius became convinced that the Lusitanians would never comply or accept another peace proposal from Rome. Henceforth, his troops lived in a constant state of alert, because the guerrillas never rested and had spies everywhere. According to the Viriathus legend, there was another battle, the Battle of Carteia. This battle is not well documented in the classical texts, but again, in Portuguese lore it is well known. As legend has it, Viriathus realized how cautious Laelius was and decided to take the city of Carteia.[51] He advanced towards it and surprised the Romans, who had set up camp in the area. The Lusitanian attack was ferocious, but the Romans responded magnificently, surprising Viriathus. After a prolonged battle, Viriathus was able to thwart them. Though it was another resounding victory, the battle obliged him to withdraw from his plans to take Carteia, for it was bloody and costly. As for the Romans, the loss of soldiers had become sensitive for their numbers were beginning to fall and, not knowing when to expect reinforcements, they lived in a state of anxiety, leaving Viriathus to roam around the countryside freely. This status quo was maintained until Aemilianus' arrival.[52]

The Arrival of Aemilianus

Aemilianus and his army finally arrived in Beatica near the end of the summer or early fall of 145 BC, indicating that they perhaps made their way by sea instead of overland through Gaul and had had to wait for the sailing season to commence.[53] The ships disembarked soldier after soldier in the vicinity of Cartagena.[54] The waterborne landing operation and their march east to Urso were so lengthy that Viriathus had time to prepare for another campaign. With his network of spies, Viriathus came to know the strengths and weaknesses of this new army, and soon he would strike the Romans at every turn.

Aemilianus quickly went searching for Viriathus, marching his men east to Urso (Osuna). On receiving vital information from his spy network, Viriathus quickly moved his men into the vicinity of Urso, prepared an ambush, and defeated Aemilianus' troops.[55] The Roman army was inexperienced in combat and was not adequately prepared to deal with such powerful Lusitanian forces. The Battle of Urso, though disappointing to the Romans, did not preoccupy Aemilianus, who kept on marching to Urso.

With the arrival of winter 145 to 144 BC, Aemilianus took his army into Urso (Osuna), fortified the city's square and spent an entire year (mid-145 BC to mid-144 BC) training his raw recruits and securing local cooperation. He also refused to be provoked into action prematurely by the guerrilla tactics

Map 7: Viriathus' Third Campaign - Part 1
(Winter 145 BC - Spring 144 BC)

■ = Roman bases
✕ = Battles
··—➤ = Lusitanians
⟹ = Romans
◯ = Siege

100   0   200 kms

Ⓐ Lusitanian Victory
Ⓑ Lusitanian Victory

used by the Lusitanians.[56] While training his men, he was able to muster some allied forces from Urso. Not wanting to face Viriathus until his inexperienced army had been sufficiently drilled, he left it in the care of his legate and went to Gades to offer a sacrifice to Hercules at the famous Temple of Melqart, so that he and his army would be blessed with strength to conduct another campaign against Viriathus.[57]

During Aemilianus' absence Viriathus attacked a cohort of Roman foragers, who were caught by surprise. Many were killing and the others were terrified.[58] The legate was lured out to fight Viriathus and was swiftly defeated for his poor judgment, enabling Viriathus to capture standards and booty. The Lusitanians also launched an attack on the town of Corduba.[58] Although he besieged the city, he did not attack it, for it was a Roman stronghold and an attack would have been costly to the Lusitanians. When Aemilianus returned, Viriathus consistently attempted to draw the Romans out onto the battlefield, but Aemilianus was never tempted. He continued to exercise his troops, only sending them out on patrols to come into contact with the enemy and conduct minor skirmishes in an effort to strengthen his men's resolve, test the enemy's strength and give his soldiers much needed experience. When he sent out foraging parties, he always surrounded his lightly armed forgers with heavily armed men, while he and his cavalry roamed the countryside using the same manoeuvres he had seen his father use in Macedonia.[59]

At the end of winter, Aemilianus and Laelius were ordered by the Senate to continue their praetorships. With the onset of the campaign season (spring 144 BC) Aemilianus deemed his army sufficiently ready to fight. Aemilianus and Laelius joined forces and attacked Viriathus. They were miraculously able to hide their movements and Aemilianus successfully launched a surprise attack on the Lusitanian encampment near Beja, inflicting appreciable losses and forcing them to withdraw.[60] Viriathus regained his men's composure and counter-attacked the Romans with his now famous

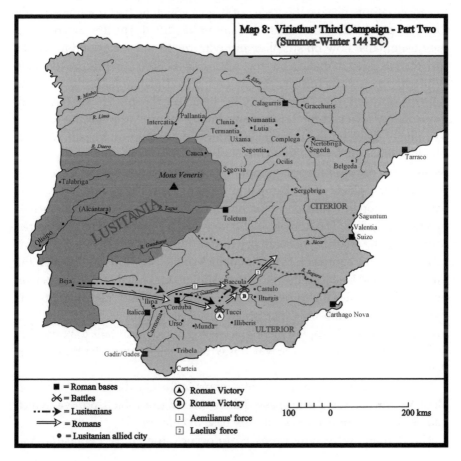

Map 8: Viriathus' Third Campaign - Part Two (Summer-Winter 144 BC)

feint retreat tactic. He attacked with such impetus that Aemilianus ordered a withdrawal, leaving behind numerous casualties and supplies. After the battle Viriathus chased the fleeing Romans. Once again Viriathus proved to the Romans that he was the better general.

Over the course of 144 BC, the Romans actually began to succeed in putting Viriathus' forces to flight but only after numerous valiant struggles (see Map 22). Some historians say Viriathus began to suffer defeats because the Roman leadership began to think and act like him, but that is not the real reason, though it probably helped. The reason the tables had turned was very simple, Viriathus was beginning to feel the loss of his men as well as the lack of supplies, for he had been constantly campaigning and not giving time to his men to rest and replenish their provisions. Regardless, Viriathus was now on the run and the Romans succeeded in recapturing two of Viriathus' allied towns. One was plundered and the other burnt down.[61] Historians believe that one of these unnamed cities was Tucci (Martos, Jaén), and that its fall forced Viriathus to leave the valley of Baetis, which he had dominated for a four year period. The second city remains unidentified. The Romans pursued the Lusitanians. Low on supplies and with the Romans close on his heels, Viriathus decided to make a pit stop at Baecula (Bailén). But this proved fatal. While his men gathered provisions and rested just outside the city, the Romans showed up. Despite having been on the march all day, they immediately attacked the Lusitanians, killing many. Although the Romans had finally defeated the Lusitanians, they did not destroy Viriathus' army. The Romans quit while they were ahead because of the incoming winter weather, according to Appian, moving into winter quarters at Corduba.[62] After the first phase of the campaign it seems Aemilianus ordered Laelius back to Citerior with his troops, for the classical texts do not make any further mention of Laelius. The Romans had finally won a victory, giving them a brief respite and the recovery of some key towns.

There is some confusion regarding which of the two Romans defeated the Lusitanians and besieged the two cities. Appian does not mention the person by name but implies it was Aemilianus. Roman writer and statesman Marcus Tullius Cicero is the only person to say that Laelius actually defeated Viriathus that year.[63] Appian mentions Laelius' victory but fails to notice that he had omitted Laelius, so the way it is written makes the reader think it was Aemilianus.[64]

Virathus had lost all his points of support in the Guadalquivir Valley and all of Andalusia. Aemilianus passed the winter in Corduba (Cordova) which had been turned into a major military base in Ulterior.

The Romans were now prepared to occupy the entire peninsula, and

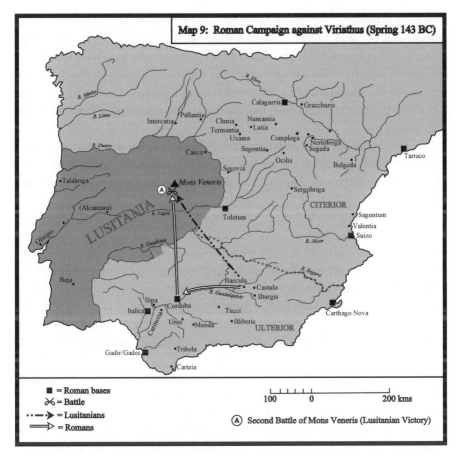

Map 9: Roman Campaign against Viriathus (Spring 143 BC)

■ = Roman bases
✕ = Battle
∙∙∙─▶ = Lusitanians
═▶ = Romans

100   0   200 kms

Ⓐ Second Battle of Mons Veneris (Lusitanian Victory)

ceased to worry about losing the entire region to a bunch of uncivilized people. Still the situation in Hispania was considered severe and Rome decided to dispatch to Ulterior a praetor who had military as well as political experience. As the other wars Rome was involved in had recently ended, they planned to increase military presence on the peninsula and prolong the consular command to two years instead of one. This exceptional measure gives us an idea of the importance the Roman Senate gave to the issue about Viriathus. Regardless of Aemilianus'successes, Viriathus' campaign against the Romans had inspired many Celtiberian tribes to follow his example. In fact by 143 BC Celtiberia had broken out in an open insurrection that would later be known as the Numantine War. This more than neutralized Rome's current good fortune against Viriathus.

Indeed, this Roman success was not of a great importance apart from the fact that it was the first time the Romans had overcome the Lusitanians in ten years of fighting. Alas, these victories were temporary, for after

Aemilianus departedfor Rome the Romans were defeated in battle after battle during 143 BC and 142 BC. Furthermore, Viriathus had persuaded, since Baecula, the Arevaci, Belli and Titthi to break their alliances with Rome and join forces with him. Yet a large part of the Celtiberian tribes began their own war in 143 BC, the Numantine War, which would last ten years.[65] During these same years, Viriathus renewed his offensive and recaptured Baetican lands once again.

The next praetors after Aemilianus and Laelius to try their mettle against Viriathus were Quintus Pompeius (Ulterior) and Q. Caecilius Metellus Macedonicus (Citerior). During 143 BC and 142 BC Pompeius caused the Romans to lose what they had recently gained. On taking command of Ulterior, he immediately began campaigning against Viriathus. Their first encounter benefited the Lusitanians. Viriathus followed his usual pattern the minute he came under attack and retreated north of the Tagus River, towards the famed Mons Veneris.[66] On occupying the hill, Viriathus immediately turned on his pursuers, killed over 1,000 Romans and captured many standards and much supply. Quintus Pompeius was driven back to his camp.[68]

After the Second Battle of Mons Veneris, Viriathus decided that his army's summer excursion would be to ravage the area around the Guadalquivir and retake Tucci, which had been lost to the Romans the previous year. Once he managed to drive out the garrison from Tucci, Viriathus occupied it and created a stronghold that supported his offensive operations and raids throughout the valley of Guadalquivir and Bastetania.[68] While Viriathus plundered the territory, Quintus Pompeius was paralyzed, as Appian says, by his 'cowardice and inexperience'. Ultimately, Quintus Pompeius went into winter quarters in the middle of autumn, leaving Baetica's defence in the hands of an Iberian from the city of Italica named Gaius Marcius. His fight with Viriathus ended without positive results.[69] The year 143 BC was full of Lusitanian successes. Viriathus built himself a small 'empire' that extended from the Atlantic Ocean in the west to Meseta Central in the east, as well as Andalusia to the south.

In Citerior, Quintus Caecilius Metellus Macedonicus began to feel the repercussions of the Lusitanian War, as it had caused the Celtiberians to begin the Numantine War. Dispatches made the Roman Senate aware of the severity of the situation, and it immediately deployed to Citerior an army of 30,000 infantry and 2,000 cavalry.[70] Appian does not provide any news for the year 142 BC, but Livy makes a minor note that Metellus in some capacity fought the Lusitanians.[71] One must conclude that the situation stayed the same and few or no military operations occurred.

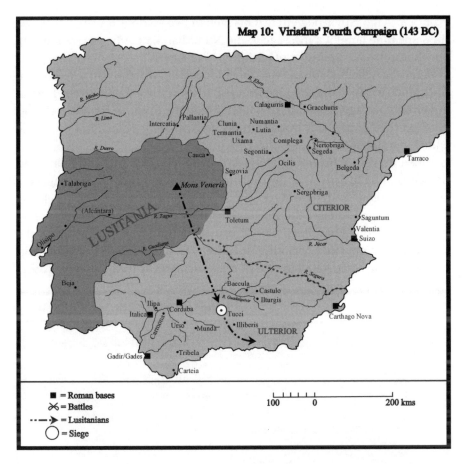

Map 10: Viriathus' Fourth Campaign (143 BC)

By 141 BC the situation in Hispania had become intolerable for Rome because of the effect of Viriathus' achievements and growing fame on the Celtiberians. His influence, however, was not sufficient to achieve a union of all the Iberian people against Rome, due to excessive individualism among chiefs and tribal integrity. Thus the Iberians never managed to completely trump the Romans.

In Rome, the Iberian situation deeply disturbed the Senate and its citizens so much that the war was becoming unpopular. The Senate rapidly decided to resolve the matter by sending new legions to Hispania with the intention of putting an end to the Lusitanian and Celtiberian Wars, as well as sending two new praetors. The task was not easy, however. Several classical authors provide data on the following events.

During the early part of 141 BC, Quintus Fabius Maximus Servilianus, the brother of Quintus Fabius Maximus Aemilianus, succeeded the inept Quintus Pompeius. He brought with him an army of 18,000 infantry and 1,600 cavalry.

From Carthago Nova, he marched his men in two sections towards Tucci. At the same time he sent a message to the Numidian king, Micipsa, requesting ten elephants and a number of additional horsemen.[72]

Before Servilianus' forces were joined together, Viriathus attacked one of the legions with 6,000 warriors; this was his first contest with the new Roman governor. During this small, unnamed battle the Romans fought well and repelled the Lusitanians, but according to Appian, it seems that the battle ended in a stalemate.[73]

When the rest of his force, which now included elephants and Numidian horsemen, finally arrived at the outskirts of Tucci, Servilianus constructed a large base camp and advanced against Viriathus. After several weeks he finally managed to eject the Lusitanians from Tucci, which Viriathus had recaptured from Pompeius. The Romans' initial success in routing the Lusitanians compelled Viriathus to retreat to Lusitania. Servilianus had managed to achieve his objective of retaking Tucci as well as several other

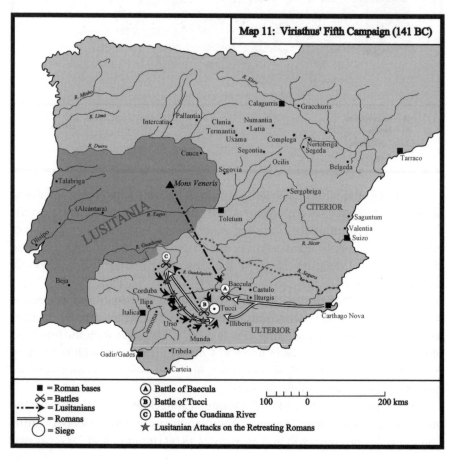

Map 11: Viriathus' Fifth Campaign (141 BC)

■ = Roman bases   Ⓐ Battle of Baecula
✕ = Battles   Ⓑ Battle of Tucci
···▷ = Lusitanians   Ⓒ Battle of the Guadiana River
⟹ = Romans
○ = Siege   ★ Lusitanian Attacks on the Retreating Romans

100   0   200 kms

Romanized cities in Baeturia that had fallen into Lusitanian hands;[74] this allowed him to plan his conquest of the Algarve, southern Lusitania and the Tagus River Valley in Central Spain.[75] In the course of his flight north from the Romans, Viriathus noticed that their pursuit had become disorderly, so he rallied his men and turned on the Romans, killing some 3,000 and driving the rest back to their camp near Tucci. During the Roman retreat, Viriathus constantly harassed them using frequent hit-and-run tactics at night and during the heat of the day, making use of any moment the Romans might not expect it, thus destroying their morale. The Lusitanians continuously attacked the Romans until they reached their camp. Though they had quickly set up a perimeter defence and even put up a gallant fight, they were driven out of their camp and back towards Tucci.[76]

After this battle, Viriathus realized he was in a desperate situation. Due to constant fighting and campaigning, his army had dwindled in numbers and was beginning to suffer a shortage of food supplies, so he decided to retire to the Lusitanian heartland to rebuild his army. Under cover of night and after setting up a diversion by burning down his camp, he departed Baetica.[77] Failing to defeat and capture Viriathus, Servilianus made a decision that his army, for the rest of the year, would plunder and retake Baeturian towns that had allied themselves with Viriathus' cause. Servilianus' campaign was successful. He marched against five unnamed Baetican towns that had collaborated with Viriathus. After plundering Baeturia he turned southwest and marched against the Cunei (a group of people that inhabited southern Portugal).[78]

But prior to Servilianus' campaign into southern Portugal, he headed south from Baeturia into Turdetania, were he captured and plundered the towns of Eiskadia, Gemmella and Obulcula, which at one point or another had been garrisoned by Viriathus' army. The smaller towns that were taken were pardoned, Appian writes.[79] But from all the towns taken, Servilianus took about 10,000 prisoners that were eventually sold into slavery, apart from 500 who were beheaded. The 500 men that were executed were the village and town leaders. The Iberians were not the only ones to be punished. Roman subjects that had supported Viriathus' cause had their right hands cut off, while army deserters that had been captured either hiding in towns or fighting alongside the Lusitanians were executed.[80] This was not a war waged with gentility and chivalry.

After the reoccupation of Turdetania, Servilianus marched west into the Algarve region of southern Portugal. Unfortunately Appian has no information except that Servilianus conducted a military campaign of some sort against the Cunei and Conii. Appian says he then turned north and invaded Lusitania in an attempt to bring out Viriathus from hiding.[81]As he was on his way north, two bandit chieftains, Curius and Apuleius, attacked the Romans with a guerrilla army of 10,000 men.[82] The Latin names of these chieftains suggest they were Iberians who formerly served in the Roman army as native auxiliaries and upon being discharged took on Roman names and citizenship, or on the other hand that they had deserted it and kept their Latin names. Either way, they attacked the Romans. The classical sources give no information on the battle, such as whether the bandit army was Lusitanian, a mixed band of Lusitanians, Conii and Celtici who where in league with Viriathus, or neither. But according to Appian this army was more interested in plunder than in defeating Servilianus, since it took a considerable amount of booty from the Romans and perhaps even from the Lusitanians and other Iberian tribes.[83] The Romans eventually rallied around their commander and were able to vanquish the guerillas and recover their booty; in the process Curius was killed in battle.[83]

Appian also makes a reference to another bandit chief, Connoba, who was set free by Servilianus after he had cut off the warrior's right hand. After this humiliating act, there seems to have been increased guerrilla activity in southern Hispania and southern Lusitania.[84] Viriathus may have had problems persuading these tribes to agree to help him in his war of liberation. The Iberians' lack of unity compared to before began to weaken the resistance movement, which may explain why Viriathus made peace with the Romans the following year.

On his way back from Lusitania, after the failed attempt to force Viriathus into open battle, Servilianus decided to besiege the town of Erisane (location unknown), for it had been loyal to Viriathus.[85] Servilianus encircled the town and began to build a trench around it. Viriathus rushed to its defence and successfully smuggled himself and a large contingent inside the town walls under the cover of darkness. At dawn his men and the town's garrison made a successful sally against the Roman sappers working on the circumvallation trenches. Servilianus quickly marshalled the rest of his army for a fight. Shortly afterwards, Viriathus attacked the bulk of consular army and defeated them. The Romans retreated in complete disorder, hounded by Viriathus' cavalry and with the infantry hot on their heels. The Lusitanians managed to herd the Romans into a precipitous place from which they could not escape.[86] The Romans' defeat was inevitable. The running battle came to an end when Viriathus surrounded and trapped the Romans in a narrow valley pass with high slopes. The Romans had no choice but to surrender unconditionally.[87]

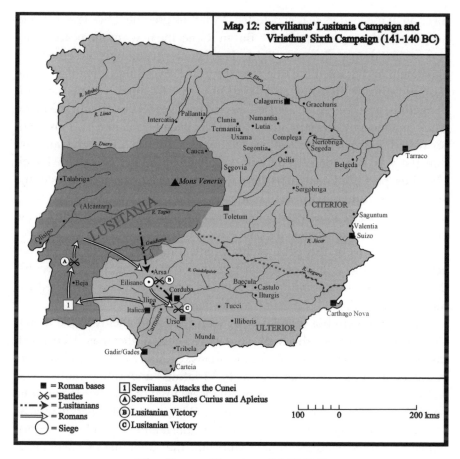

Map 12: Servilianus' Lusitania Campaign and Viriathus' Sixth Campaign (141-140 BC)

The Peace Treaty of 140 BC

Having placed the Romans in such an unfavourable situation and tired of so many years of war while other tribes left his alliance to conduct their own campaigns, Viriathus was willing to make peace. The terms he offered Servilianus were of the mildest handed to a defeated enemy; he asked for a withdrawal of all Roman soldiers from Lusitania and that its borders be respected and recognized as a sovereign independent nation. He also said the Lusitanians must be granted the status of *amici populi Romani* (friends of the Roman people), and Viriathus would become Rome's ally. To his surprise and delight, Servilianus accepted and negotiated the peace agreement.[88] The treaty was signed, as Livy writes, with *aequis condicionibus* (equal conditions), but some historians think the terms were nevertheless favourable to Rome, for it had only to withdraw from Lusitania and the northwestern portion of the Baetica region, which had supported Viriathus' endeavours.[89] Once the meeting of the leaders was concluded, Viriathus presented the agreement to his people who in turn ratified it. But in Rome, the news of the peace treaty was received in a different light. The Senate grudgingly accepted the agreement and granted the title *amicus populi Romani*, indicating that Rome now recognized Viriathus as a 'king'. Despite this they felt he was still dangerous, and the Senate advised incoming governors to disrupt the peace using any means necessary, since Rome had been humiliated by a group of uncivilized barbarians and lost rich territories in Baetica.[90] Though it appears that the war had come to an end, resolved by an act of generosity on Viriathus' part, the Lusitanians were still very problematic in the eyes of the Senate. Unfortunately for the Lusitanians, the peace would not last long. Meanwhile, Servilianus remained in Hispania Ulterior as magistrate for the year 140 BC so as to oversee the peace accord.

Viriathus was at the peak of his political-military career for he had achieved — after a long period of fighting — the recognition his people deserved. From this point on, the Romans and Lusitanians respected the limits and boundaries established by the peace treaty.

One cannot help but wonder why, with the hated enemy at his mercy, Viriathus let them off the hook so easily. The question has been much discussed and debated without the historians reaching a consensus, but there is a general agreement that crucial to Viriathus' underlying motive was *realpolitik*. He finally saw that his people were tired of war, but to end it he needed a massive victory over the Romans. With the defeat of Servilianus he saw an opportunity to end the war and establish an independent territory, which prompted Flourus to later dub him the 'Romulus of Hispania'.[91] Carried by this newfound pride of independence, the Lusitanians sought an allied status and the delimitation of borders independent from Roman authority. As already mentioned, as far as we know the Lusitanians up to this point were a set of tribes without a national identity. But as the Lusitanian War progressed, their tribal mindset began to change into one of nationalism. This was a chance for Viriathus to make things right.

But as conditions of the treaty between Viriathus and Servilianus were simplistic, this motive is perhaps problematic. Schulten has pointed out best in his writing about Viriathus, 'we are facing an enigma for it is impossible that we can find in Viriathus the explanation for his clemency, because no one had ever been more forewarned against the perfidy of Rome than him.' Thus the question remains: why was he easy on the Romans?

Though the classical texts say nothing about it, some modern interpretations see the peace in the framework of a nationalistic tendency. Nineteenth century Roman and Greek historian and author U.J.H. Becker was the first person to study the treaty of 140 BC. He writes this statement with a nineteenth century perspective:

> He knew (Viriathus), taught by many years of experience that he was capable of shattering the impetus of Roman warriors with defeats. With a defeated enemy he expected to make old enemies into friends and for himself, give his people something (land), via the generosity of a noble act.[92]

The Portuguese nationalistic interpretationbrings into play the nineteenth century concept of revolution and makes Viriathus capable of a 'noble and great act' due to his 'faith in his work and his people'. But it is absolutely anachronistic to think that — Viriathus fought for freedom and nothing more.The circumstances in Hispania during the second century BC did not closely resemble what was seen in nineteenth century Europe. The Lusitanians tended to pursue objectives that were based on self-preservation since the subject matter of life at that time was rather more harsh and complicated than national identity. But historians want to see Viriathus in a political sense: becoming king of an independent Lusitania, an ally of Rome rather than a crazed barbarian bent on seeking revenge until he was caught or killed. On the other side of the spectrum, some historians make references to a personal agenda of beginning his own royal bloodline.[93]

Viriathus may have had a change of heart and proposed peace because the Lusitanians were tired of constantly being at war with the Romans, and having taken the rich lands of southern Hispania, he now sought an agreement that would give them peace, freedom from paying taxes to Rome, and the ability to trade with Rome, since his countrymen possessed the mineral wealth of Beatica. P. Bosch Gimpera and P. Aguado Bleye in R. Menéndez Pidal's book, *História de Espanha*, say Viriathus' unusual act of signing the peace treaty was simply due to the fact that the Lusitanians were war weary and exhausted.[94]

Gundel disagrees, however, saying it is not logical that a nation of warriors would get fatigued from constant warfare, especially when they were ahead of the game — Servilianus' army was encircled and a Lusitanian triumph was ensured.[95]

But many historians have come to believe that Viriathus knew the internal tensions of the Lusitanians and that his 'military' was exhausted and that, little by little, weariness from war was becoming evident among his tribal companions. He calculated that he could not maintain the war against Rome much longer as his warriors were becoming scarce and allies could not be obtained because they had become involved in their own rebellions.

Accordingly, it was concluded that the annihilation of another Roman army would not favour Viriathus' political objectives and the war would continue, and possibly be even more violent than before. This concrete reflection on all that had happened to this point must have led Viriathus to engage in peace negotiations with the Romans.

These theories seem very logical, for had Viriathus put another Roman army to the sword Rome would never forget or forgive. However long it took, it would be a war to the death, and as the Lusitanians were getting short on manpower and provisions and getting war weary, this was their best bet to end the war.

We can safely assume that both sides did not spend much time negotiating the peace terms for Viriathus saw a chance to get what he wanted and Servilianus saw a chance to live another day. A rapid resolution was needed. On seeing that he had the Romans in the palm of his hand, Viriathus saw the chance to get what he wanted: peace and land for his people. Viriathus had led the war against Rome with an offensive and defensive strategy for some time, fighting for the independence of his people until that right moment during the battle when he realized that this was his chance to guarantee the consolidation of his conquest through a treaty.[96] Without a doubt the acquisition of lands, according to Muñoz, was his political objective. The desire for land had always played an essential role in all negotiations between the Romans and the Lusitanians. The Romans used the knowledge that the Lusitanians wanted land to their advantage, as when Galba promised land as a way to reach peace, but broke his pledge and slaughtered them. As we have seen, this was the principal reason for the Second Lusitanian War.

Negotiations with Vetilius were based on the promise of land, but had a different outcome for the Lusitanians were bent on revenge and wise to not fall for the same trick twice (if it was a trick, for Vetilius may have been honest about his proposal), declaring war by completely destroying Vetilius' legion. But after eight years of war the Lusitanians wanted peace. So when Viriathus attacked Servilianus' army with the intention of destroying the Romans, he had a change of heart, realizing he could not continue fighting forever and that if he wanted something for his people he had to, in a way, Romanize himself to gain the respect of his enemy. With respect in place, the Romans would now perhaps grant his people the land that they had already occupied in Beturia.[97]

In terms of Viriathus' own personal agenda, some historians believe that his motives for this surprising treaty were based on difficulties in his family affairs. At his marriage, a year prior to the peace treaty, his father or brother-in-law, Astolpas, had invited the Romans to the wedding.[98] It seems that

Viriathus and Astolpas were not on the best of terms, Viriathus despising his vain, ostentatious displays of wealth and criticizing his friendship with the Romans. This hostility would extend to other noble Lusitanian families, friends and anyone who supported Astolpas and the Romans or did not have the sense to realize what the Romans were about. These internal disagreements between the rebel leaders and the neutral noble Lusitanian families may have hindered Viriathus' military power to the point that he was willing to make peace with the Romans. Fortunately for Viriathus, these tensions were not so serious as to reach extremes. Though he was forced into this unexpected political situation of making peace with Rome, Viriathus did not feel the influence of the rich Lusitanian families, or trust them.

Considering the Romans' point of view, from his evaluation of the 140 BC treaty Gundel tells us that it did not happen as a result of the Romans' previous encounters with Viriathus, but due to other events occurring that same year (i.e. the Numantine War). And if Rome did not accept the Lusitanian peace treaty, there may have been a possibility of joint action with Celtiberians, who had been fighting the Romans since 143 BC with much success.[99] Fighting a two front war was something Rome wanted to avoid, so it was important to Rome that they sign a peace treaty with the Lusitanians.

But this peace would not last, for the Romans would break the treaty, continue the war and kill Viriathus. After Viriathus' death, as we shall see in the next chapter, the remainder of his army yielded to the Romans, delivering the lands back into Roman hands. This clearly shows that the fertile lands of southern Hispania were never fully in Lusitania hands. They were not able to administer, organize and maintain their gains, mostly because, many historians believe, unlike the Romans the Lusitanian leaders had a tribal mindset, so making a peace treaty was just a way for the Lusitanians to stop fighting and a means of making Roman pacification more effective.

Viriathus must have considered the possibility that the treaty would be annulled, for although Servilianus had surrendered and agreed to the treaty, he did not actually represent the general opinion of the Senate. However, Viriathus seems to have been convinced that the treaty would be honoured by Rome, granting him independence, but the following year the treaty was broken. But for now success was total, as expected; the treaty was ratified by the Senate.

Rome's Attitude Towards the Treaty

Rome's attitude towards the ratification of the peace treaty was two-faced. They smiled and let the barbarians have their day in the sun, but deep down they had another idea. As related by Appian, in Rome the treaty had become controversial, for the *comitia centuriata* had ratified the treaty in the knowledge that it was signed by Servilianus under duress and in a humiliating circumstance with a barbarian race on equal terms.[100] To the Romans, Livy states, it was a 'shameful peace', being technically a *foedus aequum* that put both parties as equals.[101] It was considered offensive to Roman dignity to be equal with a barbarian race.

Naturally, Rome would interpose a political military action that would be totally effective in the following year. As we will see in the next chapter, this was not a sign of a broad political vision, but a risk that Rome believed would make this 'newly established small state' fold. Within the scheme of political relations, smaller states will always have to be dependent on greater powers to some extent, while the larger state will in the end impose its law unless it faces a political situation internally or externally that could undermine its endeavours. The small state's only possibility of breaking away from the power yoke of the larger state was to take whatever opportunities arose to obtain the best dividend for self-sustainment and sovereignty.That is what Viriathus thought would happen at the end of the war: that Rome would see Lusitania as an equal power.

If Viriathus had not signed the treaty with Rome in 140 BC after the victory over Servilianus' army, the Lusitanians perhaps would not have lasted another year, as Gundel wrote, 'precisely because Viriathus was not the adventurer whose only objective was to fight ... which against a large potent force ... [in time] would lead to inevitable disaster.'[102]

Chapter 7
The End of
the Viriathan War

Inevitably, the peace did not last long. The defeats and humiliation Viriathus had inflicted on the might of Rome for so long could not be allowed to go unpunished. In 139 BC, the Senate had elected Servilianus' brother, Quintus Servilius Caepio. The Senate saw the it as a 'shameful peace' (*deformem pacem*) and Rome did not lack voices that spoke out against the treaty and considered the peace worthless. The extent of this grudge became apparent when the next governor arrived in the province.

Servilius Caepio Breaks the Peace

The situation in Hispania change radically with the arrival of Caepio in Hispania Ulterior in 139 BC. On analysis of the ancient texts about this time, it seems that Caepio arrived in Hispania with a hawkish attitude. He regarded the war as unfinished business because he wanted to avenge the family honour, and he saw Hispania as a place for military glory and still ripe for plundering. Appian writes that Caepio hated the treaty so much that he continuously spoke out against it and wrote a letter claiming that the treaty was highly dishonourable and disgraceful to the Romans.[1] One can only guess at what Caepio wrote, but it seems he may have requested authorization from the Senate to become involved in some type of action against Viriathus, for Appian writes that the Senate secretly encouraged Caepio at first to annoy Viriathus in whatever way he saw fit.[2] With the consent of the Senate, he acted quickly to initiate hostilities against the Lusitanians. Knowing how the Roman mind worked, Viriathus refused to be provoked; and when Viriathus invoked the treaty's terms, the Senate would rein in Caepio. Yet despite the amity of the recent peace, it is possible that eventually some of Viriathus' more hot-headed clansmen took matters into their own hands, especially now that they felt that they could defeat the Romans at will. This perhaps gave the Romans the excuse they needed to break the peace. After Caepio's fussing over the Lusitanian matter and continual letter-sending to several prominent Roman senators, the Senate voted to ditch the resolution of the previous year, giving Caepio the order to resume open warfare on the Lusitanians. At the same time, Marcus Popilus Lenas, Governor of Citerior, was given permission to break the peace treaty with the Numantinans, a Celtiberian tribe located in Central Hispania.[3]

Cassius Dio writes that as a leader Caepio was an unscrupulous and harsh man. He says Caepio had a habit of putting his men in harm's way for he was self-centred and cruel.[4] At first it seemed that the bad blood between the Roman general and his men would do the Lusitanians' work of getting rid of Caepio. Unfortunately for Viriathus and his people, however, this did not happen. Even though the Roman army in Hispania lacked morale at this point, it was still large and dangerous.

In 139 BC, Caepio began a series of calculated provocations to test Viriathus' patience. Viriathus' resolve to keep the peace broke and he retaliated with his usual guerrilla tactics of hit-and-run attacks, false withdrawals and surprise counter-attacks on the aggressive enemy. Though he had reluctantly returned to arms, he still felt that a peace deal was possible.

Desperately wishing to recover certain southern regions of Ulterior from Lusitanian control, from his large camp at Castra Servilia, near Cáceres, Caepio began a series of military operations designed to provoke a Lusitanian reaction. Caepio was the first Roman to march deep into Lusitania. He arrived near the Sesim tribal capital of Cempsibriga (modern day Sesimbra, just south of Lisbon), established an encampment, Castra Caepiana, and began building a road(which has been recently discovered) to connect his two camps. This route would later be part of the Via da Prata ('silver highway').[5] According to Professor Jorge de Alarcão, the base at Castra Caepiana appears to have become a secondary operational headquarters, used to either keep the Celtici at peace or to attack Lusitania from the south.[6]

In addition, seeing that Celiberian and Lusitanian attacks had rendered it difficult for Roman troop movements coming from the east into the western part of the country, Caepio carefully sought to bring troops from North Africa directly into western Hispania instead of marching them across the entire peninsula from Carthago Nova on the eastern side of Hispania. Thus the consolidation of Atlantic ports such as Castra Caepiana, near the Sado River estuary, was part of a new policy: the establishment of *castella* in Lusitania. These would not only protect new Roman gains in the area but also defend the future route of the Via de Prata until Norba Caesarina (Cáceres).[7] The founding of Roman encampments and new towns along this newly established Roman road ensured the successful movement of soldiers, civilians and goods, as well as allowing the Romans to control the area

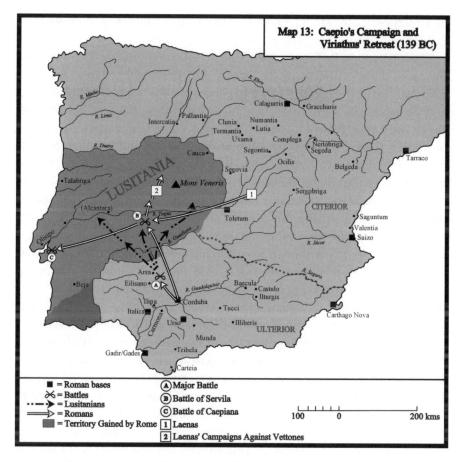

Map 13: Caepio's Campaign and
Viriathus' Retreat (139 BC)

between the Guadiana and Tagus Rivers, thus blocking the Lusitanians from further incursion into Baetica.

Without means of a strong defensive position in Baeturia,within southern Hispania Ulterior, Viriathus was forced to withdraw his men and support from several cities, such as Arsa and Erisane, before the superiority of the Romans, who were marching from Carpetania recapturing and destroying Iberian property along the way.[8] Reckoning that he did not have sufficient men to engage the Romans, Viriathus once again employed the guerrilla tactics that had been successful since the battle of Tribola. To successfully withdraw his remaining army from Baeturia, he instructed the greater part to slip away through hidden ravines and passes, while he himself drew up the remainder of his forces on an unnamed hill to give the impression that he was willing to fight.[9] Upon receiving reports of Viriathus' location Caepio qickly marched to the area. But Viriathus managed to get away by executing several swift surprise hit-and-run attacks. When he concluded that his army had reached their safe haven in Lusitania, he withdrew and crossed the Lusitanian border.[10]

The Lusitanians having escaped, Caepio followed their tracks by crossing the mountains of the Serra da Estrela. But once in Lusitania, for some unknown reason he turned north and penetrated the territory of the Vettones and Gallaeci who were Lusitanian allies inhabiting the area between the Tagus and Douro Rivers. Lusitania had again come under attack. According to Appian, Caepio attacked the Vettones and Callaici and laid their fields to waste.[11] Unfortunately, Appian once again does not give any information on this campaign. But this is the first mention by a classical author of Romans conducting military operations north of the Tagus River and close to the Atlantic coast.[12] I believe this was an attempt to destroy and discourage Viriathus' allies and other tribes that may have had the notion of coming to his rescue when called upon. It may also have been a show of force to instil fear and dampen rebellious fervour within these tribes. In the meantime, exhausted by several years of constant war and perhaps sensing defeat in their midst, some Lusitanian tribal leaders may have demanded that Viriathus re-open negotiations with the Romans, as we shall soon see.

Exploiting a period of relative calm in his war against the Celtiberians, Popilius Laenas joined forces with Caepio to attack the Lusitanians, forming another front. According to Muñoz, Laenas seems to have invaded Lusitania by marching through the Douro River Valley.[13] This theory is reinforced by several recently discovered ruins that suggest Laenas built a series of military base camps to support his penetration into the heart of Lusitania.

With the Romans breaking the peace treaty and the military invasion of Lusitania by two large Roman armies, Viriathus was unable to continue fighting and was forced to seek peace from Laenas.[14] One might ask why Viriathus chose Laenas instead of Caepio, for it was Caepio who had been chasing after Viriathus the entire time. Historians have concluded that Viriathus contacted Laenas instead of Caepio because Caepio's march into Lusitania was postponed due to a mutiny among his cavalry, provoked by his harsh treatment of his men.[15] This theory derives from a description Cassius Dio wrote in his *History of Rome*. Because of the mutiny, it seems that Laenas advanced further into Lusitania than Caepio.

The meeting between Viriathus and Laenas seems to have taken place in Laenas' camp. During the encounter, Laenas required as a preliminary condition to set the stage for peace negotiations that Viriathus deliver his most influential and brave comrades in arms. This may well have included Astolpas.[16] Viriathus agreed, and the first term of the Viriathus and Laenas meeting was satisfied. Dio writes that Viriathus had killed a part of those he had delivered, and gave the rest to Laenas.[17] Strabo states that among the prominent Lusitanians handed over there were Roman deserters. Once they were in Roman hands, they had their right hands cut off immediately, so that they would never again strike Rome. This Roman act of cutting off hands was introduced by the Lusitanians.[18] But according to Muñoz one wanted man was missing: Astolpas, who is believed to have been assassinated by Viriathus' own hand, an event of which Cassius Dio makes the only mention, and by family status not by name.[19] Again, one wonders why Astolpas was murdered. Taking into consideration all the angles, we come to the same conclusion: Astolpas was the richest land owner in the southern region who was useless for the Lusitanian struggle and played politics with both Romans and Iberians; Viriathus, to get in the good graces of the Romans, did their bidding and allowed them to control a newly acquired region. Some might interpret this as perhaps Viriathus selling himself out to the Romans for land and peace. Others may think he had his own agenda, such as establishing his own kingdom by taking over his in-law's lands once the Romans had finally recognized him as a king.

As the story goes, this was not enough for the Roman consul, so he imposed more conditions upon the Lusitanians, including disarmament. The Lusitanians were ready to commit to all the Roman demands but refused to surrender their weapons, which would have been the worst affront that could be made to the Lusitanian people.[20] Viriathus, realizing that it would be impossible for a new pact to materialize with the consul, ceased negotiations and withdrew into the mountains. Laenas continued his campaign across the Lusitanian province.

Pressured by his countrymen to make peace, it did not take long before Viriathus came into contact with Caepio, who had finally quelled his mutiny. Although Viriathus could have resisted a bit longer, his people were war weary and demanded peace, so he attempt to negotiate another treaty. Viriathus sent out messengers to lure Caepio to the negotiating table. Within weeks contact was made and Caepio arrived near Mons Veneris, Viriathus' base camp.

Treason and the Death of Viriathus

The negotiation and treachery that occurred between Viriathus and Caepio is well known, as reported by Appian, Diodorus, Livy and several other classical writers.[21] Most sources see Caepio as the one who ended the Lusitanian War, for he was the true organizer of the plot to destroy Viriathus.

History tells us that Caepio decided to attack Viriathus, who was still camped on the forested hill of Mons Veneris, which had been his base camp throughout the war. But, given the temper of his men due to the recent mutiny, Caepio knew the risks of battle with Viriathus, both for his soldiers and particularly for himself. Therefore he tried another tactic; he attempted to negotiate. On the other side of the battle line, as mentioned, Viriathus had been forced into seeking peace with the Romans. Unfortunately it is not known who made the first move, but whoever it was, it resulted in an agreement that the two men would meet.

According to Appian, as emissaries of peace Viriathus sent three of his most trusted allies, who perhaps by his standards were more intelligent and prudent than the rest of his companions. They were three of his lieutenants: Audax, Ditalco and Minurus.[22] Diodorus used the Hellenized forms of their names; Aulaces, Ditalkon and Nicoronte.[23] With their supposed knowledge of the Latin language, Viriathus entrusted them to go to Caepio's camp to negotiate the terms and conditions for a new peace treaty. According to Diodorus these three men, seeing that Viriathus was eager to end the war, volunteered to meet the Romans with the promise that they would persuade Caepio to make peace if Viriathus would send them as envoys to arrange a cessation of hostilities.[24]

Arriving at the Roman camp, the emissaries presented Viriathus' terms to Caepio. The exact terms and conditions of the treaty were not recorded, but what is known is that Caepio wanted to stop dealing with the likes of Viriathus and that the emissaries were treated like royalty during their visit. Caepio showered them with lavish gifts and promises of personal wealth and they were overwhelmed by the sumptuousness of his camp in the field.[25] It was not difficult for Caepio to lead them down the road of corruption and murder.

Caepio, after several days but without difficulty, managed to bribe them and talk them into helping him end the war. Caepio assured them that the standard of living they saw and much more could be theirs; all they needed to do was to kill Viriathus. After receiving personal guarantees on the promise of future wealth and their personal security, the three men agreed. They left the camp and speedily returned to their own encampment.

That is Appian's version, but Diodorus writes something slightly different. Diodorus states that the three men were from Urso, which seems to play an important part in the story.[26] He writes that these close comrades, seeing that Viriathus' prestige was beginning to suffer and eager to end the war, began to be apprehensive about their own necks (as they knew what happened to Roman subjects caught fighting alongside the enemy).[27] Deciding to claim that they had oratory skills and knowledge of Latin, they were able to convince Viriathus that they could persuade the Romans into a peace treaty.[28]

With his three lieutenants gone, Viriathus and his war council were riddled with anxiety, for they expected the three emissaries to return within a day or two with an answer from Caepio. Viriathus and his council kept a constant vigil and only separated to rest when convinced that the emissaries would not arrive before the day was done. As for the emissaries, it is said that they must have returned to the vicinity of their encampment during the dead of night a few days later via impenetrable paths, only to lurk, stalk and watch for the right time to implement their heinous act.[29]

Appian writes that Viriathus slept very little due to his anxieties and hard work and always rested in full armour, so that on waking he would immediately be ready for anything.[30] So it can perhaps be concluded that the Lusitanians received frequent night alarms and that Viriathus constantly received information from his spies, messengers and lieutenants at all hours of the day and night. When his delegates returned in the middle of the night, they were immediately admitted to Viriathus' tent without question. Appian comments, 'this was the reason his friends were able to come and meet him during the night.'[31] Diodorus also mentions that the three men made their way to Viriathus' tent that fateful night.[32]

Diodorus says the emmissaries claimed to have won the consent of the Romans to write up a new peace treaty. This aroused high hopes in Viriathus, but the reality was of course very different.[34] This bit of 'good news' was a way to distract Viriathus as much as possible from any suspicion of the truth.[35] Appian goes on: 'relying on his lack of sleep, Audax [as he is mentioned again in Appian's text, we must assume he was the ringleader] and the other two men watched him and, just as sleep came upon him, taking advantage of the trust and friendship that Viriathus had in them, they entered his tent as though there was some pressing news and quickly attacked him, stabbing him in the throat, as that was the only vital area of his body that was unprotected.'[36] Viriathus had found death at the hands of his compatriots instead of Caepio's. Because they were trusted men, nothing was noticed and they easily fled into the night, walked through trackless mountain country, crossed the Roman picket and entered Caepio's camp before the murder was discovered the next morning.[37] They met with Caepio and immediately sought their compensation, but he had other plans. Caepio said they would soon have what they wanted, and sent them to Rome. He let them keep what they had received in advance; as for the rest he supposedly passed on their demands and requests to Rome.[38] What happened to the three men after that is not known.

In Eutropius' version, when Viriathus' assassins arrived at Caepio's emcampment to tell him of the implementation of the crime and ask for their payment, he answered, *'est numquam Romanis placuisse imperatores a suis militibus interfici.'* ('It was never pleasing to the Romans that a general should be killed by his own soldiers.')[39] Caepio coolly assured the assassins that they had misunderstood his meaning and that he would never have encouraged men to kill their own commander. The killers were then turned out of the Roman camp without a penny for their deed.[40] In this version, Iberian treachery met Roman treachery.

In yet another version, more common in Portuguese lore, Caepio told the assassins 'Rome does not pay traitors who kill their chief', a response worthy of a veritable Caepio, but too noble for a general whom upon his return to Rome in 106 BC was tried by a tribune of the plebs, Gaius Norbanus, for the loss of his entire army (80,000 men) at the Battle of Arausio.[41] Caepio was convicted and given the harshest sentence allowable: he was stripped of his citizenship, forbidden fire and water within 800 miles of Rome, nominally fined 15,000 talents (about 825,000 lb) of gold, and forbidden to see or speak to his friends or family until he had left for exile. (The huge fine — which greatly exceeded the treasury of Rome — was never collected.) Caepio spent the rest of his life in exile in Smyrna (today known as İzmir, Turkey) in Asia Minor.

The well known phrase 'Rome does not pay traitors' is no more than an invention, but it perfectly portrays the feelings of the traditional version, which we know from Appian, Eutropius and Orosius: that the view of Rome was that it had never approved that a chief, leader or king be killed at the hands of their soldiers. It is possible that this version was put into circulation years after the event took place, in an effort to conceal the shame Caepio brought upon Rome of being responsible for enticing others, especially enemies of Rome, to do their dirty work.

As mentioned, Viriathus' three so-called friends, according to Diodorus, were from Urso (Osuna), a Turdetanian city south of Cartagena in the province of Baetica. This city was once a Roman controlled city that had switched to Viriathus' side when the war began.[42] Besides being Roman freedmen, these three may have had been heads of Baetian tribes who had joined Viriathus' rank and file, and because of their status in Iberian society later came to be considered close associates, so were given leadership positions as lieutenants or captains. In addition, their names were not of Celtic origin: according to Tusculano, Audax or Aulace's name is of Phoenician or Persian origin; Ditalco/Ditalkon was of Greek descent or Iberian Greek (but his name also implies that he may have been of Cretan birth), and Minuro is said to have been a Carthaginian name.[43] So Viriathus' chosen emissaries were not Lusitanian. The question of why he chose three individuals that were not Lusitanian has become an enigma. In their defence, it is likely that Caepio threatened to destroy their home if they did not cooperate with him. Thus these men may have had no choice but to do what they did. I believe that any one of Viriathus' companions, whether Lusitanian or not, would sooner or later have done the same deed.

As for Servilius Caepio's deceitfulness, he was no stranger to those sorts of tactics. It has been said that Gaius Servilius Structus Ahala, an ancestor of Caepio, served as his model in saving Roman interests in Hispania against the Lusitanians.[44] As the story goes, related by Livy and others, while Ahala served as *magister equitum* in 439 BC, Roman dictator Lucius Quinctius Cincinnatus faced a conspiracy plotted by consul Spurius Maelius, one of Rome's most wealthiest landowners at the time, who supposedly planned to overthrow Cincinnatus and crown himself king. When the plot was discovered, Maelius was summoned before the aged Cincinnatus but refused to appear and set the conspiracy into motion. The following morning, when Maelius and his supports assembled in the forum, Ahala once again summoned Maelius to appear before the dictator for a trial, but Maelius took refuge in the crowd, at which point Ahala rushed into the throng and killed him. So Viriathus' death has been compared to that of the killing of Spurius Maelius. While Ahala's act was perpetrated to please Cincinnatus and save Rome, the other Servilius' attempt to save Rome by killing Viriathus, a newly established barbarian king, was to please not a dictator but the Roman Senate, who saw this man as a threat to their interests in Hispania.[45] Whether he used underhand means or not, Caepio seems to have released Rome from committing itself further against a dangerous enemy.

In Rome, the rumour that Caepio had a hand in Viriathus' murder was considered as an unworthy act by the Senate and the oligarchy.[46] This unscrupulous act committed by one of its elite upper class compatriots was seen as an act of moral decadence that misrepresented the fundamental ideas of the Republic. Thus in 139 BC when Caepio's governorship had ended and he returned to Rome, he was denied a triumph by the Senate even though he had succeeded in ending the Lusitanian War by defeating Viriathus and his successor, Tautalus.

Back at the Lusitanian camp, the surprising discovery of Viriathus' body by his attendants at daybreak raised much commotion throughout the Lusitanian army. They immediately felt sorrow and grief and were overcome with fear, considering the dangers that threatened now their great leader had been killed.[47]Along with the dread they felt at the death of Viriathus, they were very grieved and angry that they could not find his murderers.[48] The death of their beloved Viriathus was devastating to their psyches, for he was the power that seems to have made the Lusitanians feel invincible. Viriathus' countrymen must have doubted that they could survive without him.

In conclusion, the demise of Viriathus was simply due to political and personal circumstances, greed, self-preservation and a desire for peace (which Viriathus resisted). These elements had made the situation favourable to the Romans. With Viriathus' death, the war for Lusitanian independence also died.

The Funeral

Viriathus' funeral must have been an extraordinary sight, for the classical texts state that he received the best honours the Lusitanians could afford. His body was dressed in a magnificent garment and cremated on a high pyre while many sacrifices were made to the gods on his behalf.[49]

The entire army was present at the burial, Appian writes; squadrons of infantry and cavalry ran around him in full armour in the 'barbarian fashion' reciting praises and songs in tribute while dancing around the fire. They then sat down in silence around his burning body until the pyre burnt out. Once the flames were out, immersed in deep emotional pain, the Lusitanians watched as his ashes were collected into an urn. Once the funeral rites had ended, 200 pairs of gladiators conducted mock gladiatorial games of combat in front of his grave in dedication to his courage and warrior spirit.[50]

Unfortunately, no Roman historian indicates the place where the crime was perpetrated or where Viriathus' grave is located. In addition, the Lusitanians seem to not have made any type of pilgrimage to his gravesite, for many of his followers and supporters were forced to hide from persecution for several years after his death. So the location of his grave has been forgotten. Since the 1500s AD or perhaps even earlier, many historians and early to modern archaeologists have attempted to locate it but to no avail. The earliest recorded so-called discovery of Viriathus'grave was by João de Barros, who has been called 'the Portuguese Livy', for he is one of the first great Portuguese historians, famous for his *Décadas da Ásia* (Decades of Asia), a history of the Portuguese in India and Asia. According to Barros, he supposedly found the grave on a farmstead marked by a gravestone or funerary marker with a Latin inscription about Viriathus. Brás Garcia de Mascarenhas — poet, historian and military hero of the Portuguese War of Restoration (1640-1668) and author of the epic poem *Viriato Trágico* — believes that Viriathus' final resting place was in the ancient city of Saguntum, located near Valencia, Spain. According to legend when Caepio relocated many of Viriathus' warriors and their families they took his remains with them and reburied them there. Nineteenth century historian Augusto Soares de

Azevedo Barbosa Pinho Leal wrote that Viriathus is perhaps buried in Numão, a town erected by the survivors of the siege of Numancia in 133 BC.[51] Most writers since then, however, have come to a speculative agreement that perhaps Viriathus' ashes are buried somewhere around Cava de Viriato, in Viseu, Portugal.[52] But these are speculations, for no hard evidence has been found to date.

The popular belief that he may be buried at Cava de Viriato is unsound, for it was a Roman military camp created after Viriathus' death. According to Alarcão, the encampment has been traditionally considered a Roman army base built by Sextus Iunius Brutus during his governorship (137 to 136 BC) and was used throughout the entire Roman occupation of Lusitania. After the Romans left the Iberian Peninsula, it fell to the Islamic occupation, for there is evidence that the Arabs modified the base during the wars against the peninsula's Christian kingdoms in the 990s AD.[53] As for the Lusitanians occupying the area, it is only speculation, as mentioned before: to date no Lusitanian artifacts have been discovered in the area.

Tautalus and the End of the Lusitanian War

The death of Viriathus signified the end of Lusitanian resistance against Roman expansion in western Hispania. Though the Lusitanians were devastated by Viriathus' death and their army had become increasingly small, they still had the desire to continue the fight against the Romans. As soon as Viriathus was buried, a successor was quickly elected: a man named Tautalus (by Appian) or Tautamus (by Diodorus). According to the ancient texts he was 'not of the same quality as Viriathus.'[54]

Tautalus wanted to finish what Viriathus had started, so he reorganized the army and launched a 'military' expedition to the east towards Saguntum on the eastern coast of Spain, in an attempt to retake southern Hispania.[55] The campaign began with incursions into the fertile lands of Baetica in Hispania Ulterior, continuing until he reached the mineral rich land of Bastetania, near Carthago Nova. Instead of advancing towards Saguntum, he decided to attack Carthago Nova. Far from their homeland and fatigued from being constantly on the move, Tautalus' army was defeated and driven away by a Roman legion that protected the region around Carthago Nova. Realizing that he would not be able to complete Viriathus' dream of defeating the Romans and establishing a free Lusitania, he turned back.[56] Without Viriathus' skills and tactical leadership in war, they were unable to resist for much longer.

While Tautalus ran rampant across Ulterior, Caepio prepared his army to move against him. At the Betis River (Guadalquivir), Caepio met Tautalus for the first and only time. As Tautalus' army crossed the river, Caepio spotted them and quickly ordered his men to attack, but unfortunately not one classical writer wrote about the battle, except that it happened and the outcome was a Lusitanian defeat and Tautalus' surrender.[57] Although the Lusitanians elected a new leader committed to continuing the war, the heart had gone out of their cause. Thus the Lusitanian War had come to an end.[58]

Caepio had easily obtained the victory that had evaded his predecessors for so long, and the Lusitanians were now obliged to sue for peace without conditions. Fortunately for the Lusitanians, they did not suffer again the cruelties of a Galba or Laenas. With great benevolence, Caepio did just as Galba had promised before the massacre in 150 BC: he allocated them enough land and even threw in a city. A decade of war had depopulated much of the country and Caepio could now deliver the Roman promise to settle the Lusitanians on lands fertile enough that they could live without resorting to brigandage.[59] Because of the respect that the Romans had for their fighting prowess, the Lusitanians were subsequently treated with leniency compared to other Iberian tribes. With the war over, Rome would now be able to extend its empire further west and northwest. What honourable generals had failed to do in years of open warfare, a duplicitous bully had accomplished by treachery in a short single campaign. But it would take another century for the Romans to feel secure in Lusitania. After that we hear no more of victorious Lusitanian campaigns or of charismatic native chiefs.

Viriathus' death began the integration of the Lusitanian territory into the Roman Empire, yet total pacification of Lusitania was only achieved under Augustus. J.J. Sayas put it best when he wrote, 'The betrayal of Viriathus accelerated the end of the Lusitanian resistance, but if he had lived, he would have prolonged the war, but he would still not have been able to impede Roman military expansion into Lusitania.'[60] The Romans had learned several valuable lessons that would later help them further expand their empire against barbarian tribes in Gaul and Germania as well as in the east.

Chapter 8
Campaigns of Lusitanian Pacification

After Viriathus' death, the unconditional surrender of Tautalus, and Decimus Iunius Brutus' Lusitanian campaign, the situation in the region changed radically. The Lusitanians would become Romanized, acquiring Roman culture, language, laws and technology, and even marrying Romans. In time the Lusitanian way of life and the local language, integrated with Latin, locally evolved into what would become the Portuguese people and language. By the time Lusitania was pacified there was no need for pacts nor peace treaties for the Romanized Lusitanians now had the same advantages Roman citizens had. The truth is that the Romans sought to improve the conditions of the places they occupied, but at the same time they had a tendency to exploit or confiscate everything that produced wealth. They forced new subjects to pay taxes, and sold rebellious locals into slavery. What could be seen as pacification could also be seen as exploitation.

After the Lusitanian and Celtiberian wars, many of the local inhabitants became subjugated and some became the slaves of rich land proprietors throughout the empire. By the second century BC, the number of slaves was well beyond that of freemen. Historians, I believe, nourish a particular admiration for the Roman Empire. There is a naturally a seductive aspect to a primitive tribe becoming an advanced empire, but sometimes we, as historians, forget how bloody the creation of the empire was, through its many armed conflicts and the displacement, enslavement and even annihilation of many native and foreign tribes and peoples.

Though Viriathus' Lusitanian War had ended, there was still much campaigning to be done against the last strongholds of his army, which consisted of the northern Lusitanian tribes and Viriathus' former allies. If the Romans wanted to control the entire western section of the peninsula, they first had to pacify Lusitania and Galica. To do this they had to set out on a campaign of punishment and persecution, as we shall see in this next section.

Brutus' Campaign of Pacification

In 138 BC, following Caepio, the governor of Ulterior was Decimus Iunius Brutus, who was an illustrious speaker, a man of great culture and a literary patron of his friend the poet Lucius Accius.[1] Upon taking office, he immediately set out to quell the remaining Lusitanians and other northern Iberian tribes for they had monopolized the fighting against Rome during this period. Although some tribes collaborated, we can say that this war was never jointly organized, and it ended quickly.

Brutus' first action prior to his campaign was the fortification of Olisipo (Lisbon) and the building of a base of operations close to Moron (location unknown), a Lusitanian city on the banks of the Tagus River.[2] This military base was 500 *stades* from the sea. Its exact location is uncertain but Iberian archaeologists believe it may be around the vicinity of Santarém or Alpiarça. According to Alarcão, however, the site is perhaps somewhere north of Santarém, according to artifacts found in the area of Chões de Alpompé in Vale de Figueira.[3] Still other archaeologists believe Brutus' camp to have beenat Alto de Castilla in Alpiarça.[4]

Brutus may have fortified Olisipo because of the rise of Iberian guerrilla activity in and around Lusitania. It was necessary for the Romans to launch a military campaign against the central and northern tribes, otherwise the flame of rebellion could have reignited and spread across the country like wildfire, and Rome could have lost everything it had accomplished so far. On a personal level, it was also necessary for Brutus to lead a campaign to promote his military and political career, as well as for the simple covetousness of integrating new lands into the Roman dominion.With the unexpected defeats the Roman army suffered in central Hispania during the Iberian wars and the Lusitanian War, Brutus decided to arrive by ship to Olisipo's shores instead of marching across southern Hispania into Lusitania. At Olisipo, he quickly ordered his army to fortify the city and build a port. This was to ensure that the Romans had a foothold in the western part of the Iberian Peninsula that would enable them to navigate into the interior of the country via its rivers. This would allow them to deliver food and supplies to a western port instead of making the long overland journey across the peninsula from an eastern Spanish port.[5] Sailing through the Strait of Gibraltar and right into Olisipo was much easier than marching across an area that was unknown and dangerous. We can only guess that Brutus may have conducted some sort of minor military operations in the vicinity of Tagus prior to his march north, but unfortunately Roman historians do not provide details.

During 138 and 137 BC, from his Olisipo base camp, Brutus advanced north along an existing Atlantic coastal road from Olisipo (Lisbon) to a fortified Callaici and Bracarii city that would later be renamed Bracara (Braga).[6] Brutus conducted his campaign in a very different way from previous praetors. Though he was sent out to deal with the Lusitianians and their allies, he gave up the idea of chasing them throughout the entire territory that bordered the following rivers: the Tagus, the Durius (Douro), the Lethes (Lima), and the Baenis (Minho), all of which were navigable rivers that would later be used to transport supply and provisions. Considering it difficult to catch up with these warriors who knew how to move around the countryside rapidly, he decided to turn against their towns and *castros*.[7] According to Appian, Brutus had the idea of turning on the *castros* and towns to punish the Iberian population for rebelling against Roman authority and to disintegrate the Lusitanian army, as the warriors would return to their homelands to protect their loved ones from the onslaught, thus disbanding the troublesome rebel army.[8] At the same time he and his army would make a profit by taking booty from these towns and return to Rome rich men.

Brutus covered the journey from Olisipo to Cales (Oporto), until he reached the mouth of the Douro River.[9] He was the first Roman to have led any type of expeditionary army this far north, but he did not stop here. From several classical texts that mention his campaign, it seems he was determined to cross the famous River Lima — believed to be the River of Forgetfulness — further north of Cales, then penetrate deep into the unknown and towards the point of the land known as *terrae finis*, 'the end of the earth'. Faithful to his strategy of sticking close to the sea and lowlands, he disregarded the highlands so as not to be surrounded or trapped by a guerrilla army and to have easy access to Iberian towns from the coast, whose villages, towns and cities could be taken easily without too many Roman casualties. But though this was a great strategy, his army suffered a setback on a spiritual level for the Roman soldiers were religious and superstitious. Believing in the spirit world and the underworld, an entire imaginary realm of myths, legends and dangers lay ahead within these unknown lands, and fearful rumours and stories began to spread throughout the Roman rank and file about evil Celtic deities.

But Brutus continued to march north killing and destroying everything he encountered. On crossing the Douro, he penetrated further into an unknown world that was somewhat different from what most of his soldiers were used to. From Velleius Peterculus, we have information that this unknown hostile land was humid, rainy, oceanic and difficult for a people that could barely speak a known language.[10] During the campaign many Iberians who had fought alongside Viriathus spread the word about how the Romans conducted business and fled to the mountains laden with all they could carry. Some decided to resist, resulting in massive loss of life; not only did the men fight, the women also fought and died alongside their men. As for those who quietly surrendered, Brutus pardoned them, but divided up their personal belongs among his army.[11]

Having crossed the Douro River, Brutus continued to march north until he arrived at the Lusitanian city of Citânia de Briteiros.[12] Knowing that the inhabitants were ready to put up an obstinate and ferocious resistance, Brutus decided he would rather take the city peaceably. He sent emissaries to propose peace to the Lusitanians. The Lusitanians responded arrogantly. Brutus answered that if they did not surrender he would burn the city to the ground; still the Lusitanian response was negative.The general ordered the city to be assaulted. The Romans suffered high losses, but Brutus took the city. Many Lusitanians died with their weapons in hand. Upholding his promise, Brutus devastated the city and left not one stone standing.[13] Today the ruins of the old city still exist and on visiting one can still see Brutus' devastation of it.

From this point on the historical record is fragmented, for several classical authors mention Brutus' campaign in a non-chronological order. From what I could put together, Brutus continued to advance north and moved on to the city of Talabriga (Cabeço do Vouga and Marnel near Aveiro).[14] Brutus besieged the city and and promised that no harm would come to its inhabitants if they returned all Roman deserters, released all Roman prisoners and laid down their weapons. In addition, he ordered that all inhabitants leave the city. The city's population peacefully accepted the terms and left the city, whereupon his army suddenly surrounded them, and Brutus made a speech recounting how many times they had revolted and waged war against the Romans, saying because of this he would not be wrong in massacring all of them. Having provoked fear and the belief that he was about to inflict something terrible, he suddenly emancipated them, but took away their horses, grain, money, precious goods and chattels and allowed them to return to their city, quite contrary to what they had expected.[15]

Brutus then for some unknown reason decided to turn slightly east in the direction of the Lusitanian city of Araduca (Guimarães) and Sabroso (São Martinho de Sande), finding the same resistance as in Citânia de Briteiros. Sabroso was completely demolished stone by stone.[16]As for Araduca, though the ancient texts do not mention what happened to this city during Brutus' campaign, according to Tusculano it was also destroyed.[17] While some cities were let off easily because they had surrendered, others were not so lucky.

Those that put up stiff resistance suffered horribly at his hands and were basically burned down and destroyed just as Citânia de Briteiros and Sabroso.[18] According to archaeological evidence, this hill-top fort was completely covered by a thick layer of ash, signifying that during Brutus' campaign, these *castros* were set on fire to make an example of them, so that others would surrender rather than be annihilated.[19]

Valerius Maximus mentions a Lusitanian city by the name of Cinginna (Covilhã) that Brutus came upon. Arriving at its gate, he demanded that if they wanted to remain free they had to surrender all their precious metals. The inhabitants answered that they did not have gold to buy their freedom, but had iron weapons to defend it.[20] The historical record says the *castro* was destroyed; unfortunately Maximus did not leave us details of what happened. But from his words it is clear what Brutus sought was gold.

Since ancient times, the northwest was known to hold large quantities of gold, as confirmed by the studies on *castro* jewellery by Monteagudo and Cuevillas.[21] During the time of Posidonius it was well known that the northwestern region of the Iberian Peninsula was rich in silver, tin and gold.[22] The old Tartestian road that would later become known as the Via de la Plata was in reality the main route for retrieving gold from the northwest. Knowing that this was an untapped region full of wealth was perhaps the reason for Brutus' campaign in northern Lusitania. By the end of the campaign both he and his soldiers had plundered and looted many cities along the Atlantic coast. During this campaign Brutus amassed such a fortune that on his return home he constructed a temple to Mars. Besides booty, Roman legionnaires also took clothing used to protect themselves from the harsh climate and animals that were deemed useful for campaigning, such as horses.

Orosius mentions that during his campaign against the northern Lusitanians, Brutus routed an army of 60,000 Gallaeci and Callaeci near the Douro River; they had come to the aid of the Lusitanians.[23] The classical texts seem to indicate that the defeat was so demoralizing that Lusitanian and Gallaeci resistance against the Romans ended there. Though one classical text makes mention of such a large tribal army, it seems unlikely that the Gallaeci, themselves, could have gathered one so huge. If such an army did exist, it was perhaps made up of other surrounding tribes. As for the Gallaeci coming to the rescue of the Lusitanians, ancient Iberian historian N. Santos writes that it is not surprising. Though they had become allies, they were not part of any Lusitanian tribal confederation or unit, so perhaps the main reason the entire tribe united for this action was not only to support the neighbouring populations in their struggle against Rome but also to prevent the Romans from invading their territory.[24] In the end, this battle shows the great psychological impact the Roman invasion had on the *castro* tribes that lived around the Douro River. It is safe to say, according to Lopez Cuevillas, that the year 139 BC was the entry date of the Gallaeci into the annals of ancient history, the first mention of these people in the Roman historiography.[25]

Unfortunately history has not given us a place were the battle occurred nor produced the time frame that made Brutus a hero. For C. Torres Rodriguez and Alain Tranoy, this major battle took place during the early part of the campaign season.[26] From their research, it may have taken place on 9 June 137 BC, for it was commemorated in Rome a year later, during the inauguration of the construction of Brutus' temple dedicated to Mars.[27] In addition, as proof of Brutus' triumph over these people, he was received as a hero in Rome with the *cognomen* of Gallaicus.[28]

During his rampageous campaign he decided to turn back in a northwesterly direction and advanced across another the River Nimis. From here, Brutus marched against the Bracari, for they had begun plundering Brutus' supply trains.[29] Appian wrote they were the most warlike people of all the Gallaecian tribes. They were so warlike that according to Appian the women (who were now the majority) fought alongside their men in full armour and died bravely.[30] Of the women that were taken prisoner, some killed themselves while others murdered their children before killing themselves, preferring death with honour to slavery.[31] From Tusculano's study on the subject, this heroic resistance occurred at Braga.[32]

Brutus' campaign was in full swing with the subjugation of the northern Lusitanian tribes, until his army came to a complete stop the minute it arrived at the banks of the Lethes (Lima) River, which was known as the River of Forgetfulness.[33] At the banks of the river, Brutus sought to dispose of the myth, for it impeded his military campaign into the area further north. According to several classical texts, his soldiers refused to cross in fear of the River of Forgetfulness; as the story goes, Brutus grabbed the standard from its bearer and crossed with it by himself, persuading them to follow. Having crossed the river, he called out to his soldiers on the other side, one by one, by name. The soldiers, astonished that the general remembered their names, crossed the river without fear.[34] This act proved that the Lima was not as dangerous as the local myths described.

Another incident mentioned by Florus occurred after the 'attempted mutiny' before the Lima River. Brutus continued his advance north, but his progress was finally halted when his army arrived at the banks of the Minho River estuary. Brutus could not go any further because his men's fears intensified with the idea that they were treading at the end of the world and the beginning of the underworld. This idea had been etched into the soldiers' psyche when they had watched in horror as the sun set into the sea, setting its waters ablaze and growing in size, causing panic among many, who had never seen such a sight. It seems that many of Brutus' men had had enough and began to either desert or plan mutiny, leading Brutus to decide to end the campaign at the banks of the Minho River and return homewards.[35]

Perhaps some of the men may have interpreted the sunset as an evil omen. Along with this superstitious fear was the fact that in the rear of Brutus'army,the Lusitanians and the Gallacci were threatening his lines of communication to his bases on the Tagus River. These were the two deciding factors to Brutus ending the campaign. Though he had gone deep into northern Portugal and Spain, putting his supply line under threat, a majority of the northwestern Iberian tribes had been defeated and Brutus was still able to consolidate his conquests during the march back to his base camp. But all good things must come to an end. Even though he was able to consolidate a good portion of what he conquered and had further plans to continue north, his campaign came to an abrupt halt because some cities that had previously surrendered to Brutus began to revolt. He had to subdue them before another large-scale rebellion broke out or got out of hand. Brutus therefore returned south to fight the rebels and reconsolidate this newly gained territory.

Unfortunately we do not have information about Brutus' southward march back toward his base at Olisipo, or about his quelling of the rebellious tribesmen or the consolidation of the newly conquered territory. One thing is certain, though: with the destruction of Lusitanian and Gallaeci towns and cities, their will to continue fighting quickly melted away as soon as Brutus' army was in the vicinity. Perhaps this may be the reason there is a lack of information. With the consolidation of these lands, the northern tribes were forced to accept a peace treaty, whose terms were seen as lenient for the Romans gave them some land to cultivate and a city, just as Caepio had done in the south after Viriathus' death.

The Senate, after this long and difficult war, finally understood that if they wanted to pacify this 'wild country of savages', it was necessary to resolve the social and economic problems that existed there. For this reason it offered new lands to the Lusitanians, this time holding to their word and handing over some land and a city, especially to those who desisted from fighting against Rome or volunteered to fight for Rome.

But instead of giving the Lusitanians land within their borders, Brutus relocated many of the warriors and their families eastward into Spain and established a city named Valentia, which meant 'strength' and 'valour' in Latin.[36] The name came from the Roman practice of recognizing the valour of former Roman soldiers after a war, but this time the Romans were showing respect to an incredible former adversary. The location of the city, as mentioned by Diodorus and Livy, has caused some argument among scholars.

The first site has been identified by some scholars as Valencia de Alcántara in Spain.[37] Some critics cannot accept this and suggest that many of the Lusitanians may have been settled somewhere northeast of the Alentejo in Portugal.[38] Other scholars argue that the other scholars are completely wrong and that Valentia was founded in the second century BC on the east coast of Spain at the site where modern day Valencia is today. The Lusitanians were resettled so far from their homeland because many of the warriors who had fought against Rome were former rebels who had fought in Viriathus' army and against Brutus. To allow them to stay in Lusitania was very risky, so it was a wise decision on Brutus' part to relocate them as far away as possible, to not allow them to regroup and instigate another rebellion.Thus it was important that the Romans invested time in founding Lusitanian towns with *jus Latinum* (Latin rights) and citizenship. The newly signed peace treaty had finally brought the Lusitanian War to an end; no doubt this brought much relief to both sides.

Along with the relocation of the Lusitanians, Brutus also founded a city in his name. At the end of Brutus' campaign, Stephanus Byzantinus mentions that he founded Brutobriga.[39] Besides incorporating 'Bruto', the name implies that the city was established in a Celtic area, because of the use of the suffix 'briga'. The location has not been discovered as of yet, but minted coins bearing the city's name have been found.[40] Since the 1900s there has been argument between Portuguese and Spanish scholars and archaeologists about the location of Brutobriga. On the Spanish side, they claim it was situated somewhere in the district of Viana del Bollo, while the Portuguese say it was built somewhere along the banks of the Lima River. But according to Alarcão, minted coins found in the river's vicinity imply that it may have been a maritime city established somewhere near the river.[41] Unfortunately due to the lack of private and governmental funding, excavations are not possible at the moment. Another point about Brutobriga is that we do not know if the town was intended to be a new settlement for Roman soldiers who had participated in Brutus' campaign or if it was a native town that simply took the Roman commander's name to honour him.

Brutus' victorious expedition against northern Lusitania and Gallaecia was a hard pill to swallow for all the western tribes that had lived on the coast from the Algarve in the south of Portugal to the Minho River in the north, for they had finally become fully aware of Rome's military power and realized that the Romans were going to stay. From this point on, the tribes had now or would become nominal subjects under the authority of the governors of Hispania Ulterior. Though this land had fallen under Roman rule, the emergence of industry such as the amphorae trade in the area of Viana do Castelo (a district located in the northwest of Portugal, bordered by Spain) illustrates the progressive opening of the indigenous world to the outside Roman world.[42] The experience the Roman military had gained fighting the Lusitanians gives us an understanding of the progression of its weaponry and strategy, which would become useful in the next century against other non-tactical barbarian tribes that the Roman army would encounter.[43]

Brutus' advance through this theatre of operation was the largest military conquest of Hispania since that of Scipio Africanus.[44] The final defeat of the Lusitanians was welcomed in Rome and, above all, Baetica, and for the rest of the second century BC and the entire first century BC the Romans consolidated Lusitania through the establishment of military posts and large-scale urbanization projects under Caesar Augustus, some of which would later become *civitates*. But before Rome could consolidate and reorganize the region into administrative centres within the realm of the growing Roman Empire, for Lusitania to be completely subdued, the Celtiberians of Numancia needed to be defeated.[45] Only then would western and central Iberia finally be at peace.

In a nutshell, Lusitania was only conquered at that point because Viriathus was assassinated. If Viriathus had lived or had the Lusitanians elected or found a military leader who was a near equal to Viriathus, it is possible that the Romans would have been stopped at its borders or not have had the chance to disembark on the Lusitanian coast. But although the Lusitanian War may have lasted several more years, eventually Rome would have conquered it.

Campaigns After Brutus

At the end of Brutus' campaign, the Romans believed they had repulsed the barbarians and would now attempt to maintain a control element over the hostile, insubordinate people. Rome would now incorporate into its growing empire the territory between the Douro and Minho Rivers, plus the area extending east along the Douro River further into the peninsula's interior. It also still needed to expand into other unoccupied areas, such as Celtiberia in central Spain, the Basque country in northeastern Spain, Asturias, Galicia and Cantabria in northwestern Spain, which would not occur until the end of the first century BC. Many ambitious Romans considered the new territory a fertile field for political and military promotions and entrepreneurialism. Thus the fall of Lusitania produced a chain reaction that led to a mass migration of Roman citizens, which would lead to the occupation of the rest of the territory, even if it was of little economic interest to Rome. From a military and political point of view it was important for any individual with personal ambition to move up the ranks in the military or gain fame as a politician to be elected to the Senate later on. Thus the Lusitanian territory constituted one of these areas for someone to become somebody in Roman society, if they were willing to serve overseas.

But now that Lusitania was in Roman hands, the Romans began to feed money and provisions into it to keep the peace. This should have been an effective and reasonable way to put an end to the Lusitanian way of life, but it did not always work out because the Romans still treated these 'Romanized Iberians' as second-class citizens. The lack of sensitivity on the part of Rome made the situation worse. Even after Lusitania had been conquered, the Lusitanians did not conform to or agree with the tiny allocation of land given to them, and although without an organized army, they rose up against Rome at various times during the following years.

Though many Lusitanian rebellions are mentioned, only fragmented information about them exists. The reason is that after the fall of Numantia in 133 BC there was little that happened in Spain to pique the interests of our ancient sources for half a century, plus Rome was involved in major conflicts elsewhere that were more interesting than minor rebellions. But when warfare of a sufficiently important nature did arise, it was of a character quite unlike anything that had been seen before on the peninsula. The wars that followed the Roman Republic did not see Romans fighting for glory and wealth against indigenous inhabitants, so much as Romans fighting Romans, for these civil wars had become an extension of the political struggles that racked the capital itself. Hispania was spared such scenes until the arrival of Quintus Sertorius in Citerior in 83 BC, and it was to be involved in a surprisingly immediate way from then on until the murder of Caesar in 44 BC, which, with hindsight, could be seen to mark the end of the so-called 'free republic' of Rome.[46]

But prior to Sertorius, the Romans continued to fight the rebellious Lusitanians off and on. During the praetorships of Caius Marius (114 BC) and L. Calpurnius Piso (112 BC), Ulterior was on fire once again when the Lusitanians rose up in rebellion. These new Lusitanian incursions into Baetica occurred because the Lusitanians seemed to not have been satisfied with the distribution of lands or their treatment by the Romans. The Lusitanians had been treated well straight after the Lusitanian War, but after several years they were an oppressed people once again.[47] The Romans scored several victories against Lusitanian guerrilla attacks under the command of Praetor Gaius Marius and later Decimus Junius Brutus (who replaced Marius in 113 BC) and Piso. The Lusitanians were eventually defeated by M. Iunius Silanus the following year. But once again history has dealt us a blow, for we do not know the places or results of these two campaigns.[48]

Shortly afterwards, in the next decade, we hear of more Lusitanian rebellions, met by the Romans with varying degrees of success. In 109 BC, the praetor to Ulterior, Quintius Servilius Caepio's son Quintius Servilius Caepio the Younger, faced the Lusitanians and achieved such a great victory that on his return to Rome in 107 BC a triumph was celebrated.[49] In 105 BC, another Lusitanian rebellion broke out, resulting in a victory over the Romans, as reported by Julius Obsequens;[50] in 102 BC the Romans defeated the Lusitanians under praetor Marcus Marius, brother of Caius Marius and governor of Hispania Citerior.[51] In 101 or 100 BC, under the governorship of Lucius Cornelius Dolabella and until the preatorship of C. Coelius Caldus in 99 or 98 BC war broke again, proving that the Lusitanians were in a state of agitation and the Romans had a difficult time controlling these warlike people.[52] In 93 BC, Consul P. Licinius Crassus fought the Lusitanians and returned to Rome in triumph.[53] These bits of data prove that relations between the Romans and the Lusitanians remained imbalanced.

Even with the lack of information from the sources, a clear picture of the last fifty year period shows that the Roman praetors in Lusitania had done very little to change the situation since the early and middle second century BC. Warfare was still the main preoccupation of the praetors and consuls who held the two provinces, even though the Romans did what they could to make life better in Lusitania. In spite of all these Roman military victories and their economic and administrative support, the social and political organization of the Lusitanians and their way of life did not disappear completely with the Roman conquest of Lusitania. After a long series of expensive, hostile armed conflicts with the Lusitanians, by the middle of the first century the Romans finally managed to subdue and place the indigenous population of Lusitania within the orbit of Rome's cultural and political policies, forcing most of them to descend from the mountains onto the plains and seeking to improve their situation.[54]

Some modern historians wonder why it took the Romans so long to stop the Lusitanians. The answer is that they were initially ineffective because it was the first time they had encountered a people who did not have a standing army or political agendas (unlike the Carthaginians during the First and Second Punic wars). Also, historians do not take into consideration the natural conditions of the terrain, which had wide areas that were not easily accessible or controllable, meaning the Romans could not quickly commit themselves to a large offensive campaign. But as in most wars, the powers that confronted the unknown enemy eventually adapted and overcame their shortcomings to defeat them.

Once these areas had come under Roman control and the people were being treated somewhat fairly, the warlike Lusitanians, rather than fight the Romans, fought for them as auxiliary soldiers. Many Lusitanians participated in the Sertorian War between the factions of Lucius Cornelius Sulla and Gaius Marius, which had spilled into the Iberian Peninsula in 83 BC.[55] During this civil war, Sertorius, who was a supporter of Marius, led a mixed army of Romans, Libyans, Celtiberians, Cilician pirates from Turkey, Lusitanians and several other Iberian tribesmen against Sulla's incoming army. Like Viriathus, he was murdered by two of his most trusted officers in 72 BC, which ended the war.

Up to this point Decimus Iunius Brutus' campaign did not appear to have led to an effective occupation of Lusitania, nor did the Sertorian War lead to a real Roman domination of the region, especially since his campaign was fought as a civil war instead of a war of liberation or conquest. By the time he arrived in Lusitania his military strength seemed to have declined as it coincided with a moment in which his followers were quarrelling among themselves. So Lusitania only came under full Roman domination under Julius Caesar.

The classical sources are silent about what happened in Lusitania during the years between Sertorius' death and the governorship of Julius Caesar, whose stay there does not have seem to have been as memorable as his stays in Gaul or Egypt. Memorable or not, in 61 BC he broke the peace and attacked the Lusitanins and Callaici by ordering the inhabitants to leave their way of life and their hill-top forts and move onto the plains.[56] Knowing that they would refuse this request,Caesar had found a reason to attack them.

Caesar was still in debt when he was appointed to govern Hispania, and needed to satisfy his creditors before he could leave for his praetorship, so he turned to Marcus Licinius Crassus, one of Rome's richest men, for help. In return for political support in his opposition to the interests of Gnaeus Pompeius Magnus, also known as Pompey, Crassus paid some of Caesar's debts and acted as guarantor for others. To avoid becoming a private citizen and opening himself up to prosecution for his debts, Caesar left for his province before P. Licinius Crassus' praetorship had ended. In Hispania his indebtedness caused him to attack the Callaici and Lusitani, and he was hailed as *imperator* by his troops.[57]

Alarcão suggests that, besides campaigning against the Iberians to take booty from the natives, Caesar's campaign of 61 BC was conducted to subdue the native inhabitants even further. He also suggests that Caesar attempted to guarantee peace for several more years rather than colonize the land with permanent military outposts, with the exception of Scallabis (Santarém) which he established as a base for his campaign.[58] Still, after 61 BC Roman settlements became a reality throughout Lusitania and Rome's legions were frequently moved around between the Tagus and Douro rivers, as the case is when any foreign force occupies another country.

Between the Sertorian War, and to a certain extent during Caesar's praetorship, little was written about the events in Hispania. This changed on the outbreak of Julius Caesar's Civil War (49 BC to 44 BC), during which several large-scale battles were fought, the Lusitanians fighting as auxiliary troops on both sides. The majority of them, according to all the classical accounts that mention the Lusitanians, sided with Pompey as many of the Lusitanians remembered Caesar's campaign of 61 BC. The Lusitanian city of Viseu was the military headquarters of Marcus Petreius (a Pompey supporter during the civil war). After Caesar's victory at Ilerda in 49 BC, his newly appointed governor of Ulterior, Quintus Cassius Longinus, took over the province. Longinus, either through his natural disposition or out of a hatred he had developed during the civil war in Spain due to a wound he had treacherously received as quaestor, decided to start his own campaign against the Iberians.Whether it was based on revenge, greed or both we do not know, but it is certain that he let loose his temper on the natives.[59] It is also said that Longinus was conscious of the discontent around him,[60] and to secure himself against disaffection from his men, he endeavoured to gain their love and respect by promising them a hundred sesterces each.[61] Longinus set off and attacked the Lusitanian town of Medobriga.[62] Soon after, having made himself master of the town, he charged up Mount Herminius, where the Medobrigians had retired. Once the mountain was taken he was saluted by the army as *imperator*, and he gave them another hundred sesterces each.[63] Soon after this campaign (48 BC) Longinus received orders from Caesar to deploy to Africa with his legions from Lusitania and a local auxiliary army.[64] But Longinus would never see Africa, for his quaestor Marcellus mutinied against him.[65] The mutiny came too late, though: his tyrannical government in Hispania greatly injured Caesar's cause when the civil war broke out again.

After Longinus' disgraceful exit from Hispania in 47 BC, Caius Trebonius (a Caesar supporter) was named praetor of Ulterior. Soon after he took office, civil war broke out again in Hispania between Caesar and Pompey's sons, Sextus Pompeius Magnus Pius and Gnaeus Pompeius, along with Caesar's former praetorian legate, Titus Labienus. It seems that the majority of Lusitanians again joined forces with the Pompey faction, for there is an account that at the Battle of Ategua (Espejo, Spain), Munatius Flaccus, one of Pompey's commanders, seeing the inhabitants deserting the city, sent the Lusitanians to punish them: the men were beheaded and the women and children impaled.[66] Iberian cities such as Ategua were caught in the middle of the civil wars; whether they took sides or not is not very clear in the classical accounts, except that on several occasions they seem to have wanted to be left alone or to not get involved. Unfortunately, they were forced into a serious predicament because in every village, town and city a small minority of Romanized Iberians either supported Caesar or Pompey. Thus they suffered the consequences of being besieged or plundered, such as at Ategua and soon Hispalis (Seville).

Caesar marched onto Hispalis and sent deputies to sue for a defensive alliance, which the leaders of Hispalis turned down. Though the citizens assured him that they were able to defend the town for Pompey's forces, Caesar sent one of his lieutenants named Caninius to camp near the city with some troops. In the town, a strong party of Pompeian supporters, who were displeased to see Caesar's troops well received within the city's walls, secretly deputed a zealous partisan of Pompey by the name of Philo to reach Pompey's sons and report Caesar's activities in the area. On his way to report to Pompey, he encountered a well-known Lusitanian leader, Cecilius Niger, who was encamped near the town of Lennio with a strong Lusitanian army. Knowing that the Lusitanians had sided with the Pompeys, Philo begged for his assistance. Niger broke camp and headed out. The Lusitanians arrived at Hispalis by nightfall and surprised the town's sentinels and populace. Well received by the townsfolk, they immediately shut the gates and set up defensive positions.[67]

Several hours later, however, instead of defending the town against Caesar's legion, the Lusitanians suddenly begin to plunder Hispalis. Through military intelligence, Caesar was told what was happening within the city's walls and decided not to press the Lusitanians into a fight just yet. In a war council he laid out a plan to allow the Lusitanians to escape in the night and attack their disorganized withdrawal. For the plan to succeed it had to work in this manner, for Caesar did not want to lose anymore men over some barbarians who had control of a city. Plus he believed that a larger battle was soon to come against the Pompey brothers, so he could not afford to lose Roman soldiers.

Unbeknown to Caesar, the Lusitanians had a plan of their own and it just about ruined his planned ambush. Before they escaped, several Lusitanians snuck past the Roman camp and set fire to their ships docked on the Guadalquivir River. While the Romans were surprised and distracted with extinguishing the flames, the Lusitanians began to escape. But Caesar, being quick on his feet, recovered. While the Roman infantry was busy putting out the fires, the Lusitanians were overtaken by his cavalry. Most of them, according to Hirtius, were cut to pieces.[68]

As mentioned, many Lusitanians fought during the Roman civil war. What is interesting to note is that from this point on the Romans would enlist a massive number of Iberians as auxiliary troops into the Roman legions, especially the Lusitanians, Callaecians and Celtiberians. It has been calculated that of the total of Roman auxiliary troops within its western European army, Iberian soldiers made up thirty per cent.[69]

Following the incident at Hispalis, Ceasar defeated Pompey's sons at the battle of Munda.[70] Near the end of the battle, Pompey's battle line broke and the Pompey brothers fled in disorder with their army. Caesar sent troops after them. Hirtius writes that during the pursuit, a Lusitanian warrior (one who had joined Caesar) discovered the place where one of the Pompey brothers, Gnaeus Pompeius, hid; he was quickly surrounded by Caesar's cavalry and infantry. Seeing himself betrayed, he took refuge in a post fortified by its natural surroundings. Several attempts to storm it were repulsed, so the general in charge decided to besiege the 'fort' instead. Surrounded and his resources cut off, many of Gnaeus' men began to surrender, while those loyal to him fought on to the death. After several days, Gnaeus was captured and beheaded.[71]

After Gnaeus Pompeius' death and Sextus Pompey's escape from Hispania, Caesar was still not able to gain total possession of the Iberian Peninsula. The Lusitanians and other native warriors that had supported the Pompey faction continued to fight Caesar. These remaining natives rallied into an army and advanced against Gaius Didius, Caesar's loyal naval commander, whose ships were docked somewhere near Gades.[72]

Though the preservation of the fleet was his main concern, he became engaged with the troublesome Lusitanians. He was obliged to leave his fort in order to restrain the frequent enemy attacks. These daily skirmishes gave the Lusitanians an opportunity to stage an ambush. They divided their troops into three bodies: one to set fire to the fleet, the other two to come to their relief. Their plan of attack was so well arranged that they could advance into battle formations without anyone seeing them. As the story goes, Didius sallied out according to Roman military custom. When a signal was given by the Lusitanian commander, one of the parties advanced to set fire to the fleet and another, counterfeiting a retreat, drew Didius into an ambush, where he was surrounded and slain along with most of his men, although they fought valiantly. Some of his men managed to escape in boats which they found further down the coast; others reached the galleys that had not caught fire by swimming towards them; once onboard they weighed anchor and sailed out to sea.[73] This was a devastating defeat for the Romans and an incredible victory for the Lusitanians after Viriathus; as booty, they captured a mass quantity of provisions. But this is the last we hear of the Lusitanians as a rebellious lot.

The period of civil war between Julius Caesar and the Pompey family, despite the insecurity of the time and several battles, seems to have led to the eventual Romanization of Lusitania. The need for fresh troops led to the incorporation of Lusitanian men into the ranks of the Roman army, especially the legions of Pompey.[74] Their recruitment into a professional army led them to being granted Roman citizenship and rights. This was also a useful channel for their warlike qualities and traditions. Alarcão said it best when he wrote, 'The war between the Lusitanians and Romans became to a certain extent a war between Lusitanians associated with Romans, against other Romans.'[75] From this unexpected and surprising alliance a strong friendship was forged which led to the extinction of their ancient hatred for one another. This companionship would become so strong that several emperors, starting with Julius Caesar, used Lusitanians, Celtiberians and other Iberian warriors as bodyguards because of their loyalty to their leader.[76]

Chapter 9
The Romanization of Lusitania

At the end of the first century BC — 200 years after the conquest of Hispania had begun — Gaius Octavius Julius Caesar Augustus finally pacified Lusitania, Callaecia, Asturia and Cantabria,bringing them all under Roman control.[1] With Augustus' military campaigns in the northwest successfully concluded, he began to remould Lusitania, which was still mostly pastoral. Augustus instilled many political and administrative structures and policies, some of which are still in use today, such as the welfare system and taxes. The later history of Lusitania from Augustus onwards is practically unknown besides a few literary mentions. Though much has been written about Rome's purpose and development, daily life, religion, art and architecture, inadequate attention has been paid to the Romanization of its satellite states.

The Romanization of the Iberian Peninsula, as well as other future Roman provinces, was a gradual process of cultural assimilation, in which the conquered 'barbarians' (non-Greco-Romans) gradually adopted and largely replaced their own native cultures (which in many cases were quite developed) with the culture of their conquerors. Acculturation proceeded top down, with the upper classes adopting Roman culture first, and though the old ways lingered longest in outlying districts among peasants, they too would become assimilated into Roman culture.

The Creation of Lusitania: Its Boundaries, Districts and Roads

Despite the onset of the Romanization of Lusitania, some tribes continued to rebel until 19 BC. In other cases, small groups broke away from tribes and formed 'guerrilla gangs' as a means of self-defence against the further expansion of the newly acquired Roman state. These 'gangs' were small and mobile, but seemed to lack a fluid social formation, making for weak leadership. Though these two groups were a minor nuisance to Rome, the Romanization of Lusitania was continued by first encouraging (or requiring) its people (i.e. the upper class) within the state's border to form centralized policies to start producing some type of tax, and placing responsibility on local leaders to instil a relationship with other neighbouring states and tribes. But tribal leaders instead of forming their own borders and centralizing Roman administrative policies and political and social institutions within the guidelines given them by Rome, began to misuse the money and power handed to them. Instead of rebuilding their lands they used the money to support a stable army that could fight other states or tribes in an attempt to gain more land and power. This caused a problem to Roman administrators as it incited various tribes, especially the Lusitanians, to fight and defend their land ownership against other tribes.

To prevent these territorial issues between tribes, Augustus instituted a new administrative reorganization. Dio Cassius writes that in 27 BC, Augustus divided Hispania into three provinces: Baetica, which was given to the Senate, and Lusitania and Tarraconensis, which he kept for himself.[2] It seems that the formation of Lusitania as a separate autonomous province may have taken place immediately after the campaigns of 26 to 25 BC that led to the annexation of Callaecia, Asturia and Cantabria; it is also believed that it may have taken plac in 22 BC, under the consulship of L. Sestius Quirinalis Albinianus.[3] In addition, Alarcão, Tranoy and Solana Sainz suggest that the formation of Lusitania may have occurred later, between the years 16 BC and 13 BC.[4] Another possible date, 19 BC, was the year Augustus sent Agrippa to the north of the peninsula to quell the Cantabri tribe.[5] The formation of Lusitania removed all Lusitanian territorial ambitions.[6] It is evident that before the administrative division was carried out by the Romans, the concept of Lusitania was a vague one, since it defined a people, the Lusitanians, and not a territorial constituency that was strictly delimited.

Augustus apportioned the provinces in this way to lead the Roman people away from the idea that he was monarchical in his way of ruling the fledgling empire. Augustus Caesar's took this decision because in his youth he had seen, through his uncle Julius Caesar, what was happening in Hispania. So to control and pacify the area he promised that for the next ten years he would help the Senate by taking over two of the provinces and building and running their governments (along with several other provinces throughout the empire). He promised to reduce his power over them in time, boastfully adding that if they should be pacified sooner, he would sooner restore them back to the Senate's control.[7]

Under Augustus' reign the province of Lusitania was created. He first began to organize the colonial regime by first creating the name Lusitania, after its people, and establishing its borders. Secondly, he founded several

Luso-Roman cities and towns, began an urban development programme of integrating existing Lusitanian cities into *oppida* (a Latin word meaning enclosed space, referring to the main settlement in any administrative area of ancient Rome) and lastly, marked the boundaries of the *civitates* (districts).[8]

The study of the reconstruction of Lusitania's frontier in Roman times poses a problem. Strabo's account says that Lusitania extended from Baetica up to the Douro River.[9] Alarcão believes that Strabo was referring to an earlier administrative union prior to Callaecia's division from Lusitania, which may have been altered by Augustus when he placed the northern boundary of Lusitania at the Douro River after 4 BC.[10] Emperor Augustus made a new administrative division, creating the province of Hispania Ulterior Lusitania, whose capital was to be Emerita Augusta (currently Mérida). Originally Lusitania included the territories of Asturias and Gallaecia, but these were later ceded to the jurisdiction of Provincia Tarraconensis and the former remained as Provincia Lusitania. In the south, the boundaries were the same as that of modern Portugal's.[11] We are not sure exactly how far into Spain the province extended, but it is believed that it may have stretched as far as Toledo and Salamanca.

When Lusitania was organized as a separate province, Augustus divided it into *civitates*. This extended and formalized mapping of the territory defined where the new towns had to be established, but first the territory had to be surveyed and marked out.[12] When new Roman colonies were founded in newly conquered territories, they were centuriated to facilitate the assignation of plots of land to new settlers.[13] This centuriation gave a visible sense of order to the rural landscape.[14] Once these projects were completed it is believed that every provincial community received a copy of a *forma* (map) of its rural territory, which was supposedly kept in the city's archives. A copy was sometimes inscribed on bronze and displayed in public, making the world around the inhabitants visually comprehensible, giving them a greater sense of place.[15]

The Roman genius for administrative organization is well illustrated in Portugal. Like many other Roman provinces, Lusitania was divided into *civitates*, which were usually modelled on the boundaries of pre-Roman tribes or *populi*. Every *civitas* had its own administrative capital that was often an ancient settlement rebuilt on the Roman urban model with the grid-iron street patterns, public monuments and services such as running water and sewers. In the case of Lusitania, the *civitates* seem to have been established by Julius Caesar or Augustus Caesar. Capitals of *civitates* were called *oppida*. They had local assemblies and two to four magistrates, who were regularly elected and in charge of the city administration.[16] The *oppidum* would have had a *territorium* and magistrates to administer its affairs. According to Alarcão it was quite possible that the administration was controlled at a local level by native representatives from different *populi*.[17] To adapt his policies to the local social conditions of his various subjects, Augustus would have established chieftains in some places and magistrates in others, who may have been appointed by the regional administration or elected by councils of elders.[18] After a while the *populi* would have become part of the *civitates* and the tribal princes or elected local officials would have been either replaced by or promoted to municipal administrators with an assembly and elected *duumvirate* (an alliance between two equally powerful political or military leaders).

Once an *oppidum* had become well established it could aspire to become a *municipium* which was basically a self-governing community with several grades of importance and legal rights. Many Luso-Roman towns achieved this status under the reigns of Julius Caesar and Augustus Ceasar. When the *oppidum* was promoted to a *municipium*, the *civitas* was assigned to a Roman voting tribe, the unit into which the citizens were enrolled.[19] The Lusitanians fell into the Galeria and Quiria tribes.[20] Towns that received the status of *municipia* under Caesar and Augustus appear to have had their citizens enrolled in the Galeria tribe; those elevated later on by the Flavians were enrolled into the Quirina tribe and given municipal rights.[21]

The highest ranking a town could achieve was the status of *colonia*, which were settlements of veteran soldiers that were granted citizenship after they had served out their time in the army. Sometimes the *colonia* was established with citizens brought in to help 'civilize' the natives in the newly conquered territories. In Portugal, Pax Julia (Beja) and Scallabis (Santarém) were given this status.[22]

There were also two other city classifications used by the Romans: *vicus* and *castellum*. The word *vicus* was designated to a town or city of less importance than an *oppidum* or a *civitas*, though it could have been bigger, richer, more populous, more industrious or commercial. In addition, a *vicus* usually had a military base attached to it. While the word *castellum*, was used to identify Iberian hill-top forts.[23]

Prior to these classifications and city rankings, between the Lusitanian War and the Sertorian War in the first century BC the Romans created a series of military villages whose names revealed an aspect of military character: *castra* or *castrum* (military camp), *praesidium* (military outpost of fort), and *praetorium* (commanding officer's residence in a fort). Within Lusitanian territory, towns were explicitly mentioned with the term *castra*, supplemented by an adjective derived from the name of the founder of the site (such as

Castra Caepiona, Castra Caeciliana, Castra Liciana and Castra Servilia), which at the time of the Roman occupation of Lusitania were all basically military camps.[24] Thus the military forts in occupied territory later turned into towns and cities promoting the integration of Lusitanian territory into Roman ones due to heavy Roman presence and influences.

Along with these administrative creations, beginning with Augustus Caesar and ending with Vespasian, a new type of administrative district was 'created': the *conventus* (diocese).This was primarily a legal term since the capital of the *conventus* was the place where the governor and his delegates passed judgment on issues that were beyond the capability of the local officials of the *civitates*; moreover, it had an assembly of representatives of component cities to advise, consult and report to the governor.[25] Though the *conventus* was created as an administrative district, its origins can be traced back to the Republican period perhaps beginning Julius Caesar or even earlier.[26] Originally the *conventus* was known as a *conventus civium Romanorum*, which was an unofficial association of Roman citizens in distant lands, who joined together for matters such as trade and defence.[27] These *conventus* were naturally located in major towns and cities where Roman citizens congregated on a regular basis to conduct business, exchange ideas and discuss news about the area. Since these locations acted as central meeting places, it became convenient for the provincial governor or his delegates to visit and dispense their authority during their annual circuit of visits to each town or city.

Under Augustus the *conventus* transformed, becoming a governmental body that primarily dealt with judicial matters.While still centred in a major town or city it referred not to an association but to a geographic region comprised of many lesser towns, whose inhabitants would have to travel to the central towns to engage in lawsuits.[28] In addition to this judicial function, the capital of the *conventus* not only retained its status as a commercial centre but also became an administrative centre with its own *concilium* (parliament). Besides being the administrative centre of the *conventus* it also became an important religious centre to the imperial religious cult within that district, so altars, shrines and temples were built to the protector god or gods of the *conventus* or *flamines* of the imperial cult.[29] Of the twelve *conventus* that were formed in Hispania, three were in Lusitania: Emeritensis, Pacensis and Scalabitanus.[30] There is no written record on the boundaries of the three *conventus*, but it seems reasonable to assume that they included a large number of *civitates*. It is believed that Conventus Scalabitanus incorporated the land between the Douro and the Tagus Rivers, Conventus Pacensis was made up of all of southern Portugal, and Conventus Emeritensis, the smallest of the three, lay west of Scalabitanus and held the region between Serra de Gardunha and Serra de Estrela.

Urbanization

The grounds that I mentioned in the last section may apply in particular to the Lusitanian territory conquered by Rome. From a geographical point of view, Lusitania was an agglomeration of various regions with different levels of wealth. But from an ethnic point of view, Lusitania was comprised of tribes with various degrees of cultural development, boasting an incipient vertex of urbanism at the time of Rome's conquest of Hispania. These people had suffered Celtic and now Roman cultural changes and transformations. They also integrated influences from neighbouring peoples, and although progressive and variable, these influences together with other cultural and environmental elements marked a process that more than ruptured their continuity and development. It is very likely that all these elements and cultural developments shaped the Lusitanians and the various peoples that the classical texts mention as inhabitants of Roman Lusitania.

Cities were the focal point of Roman assimilation thanks to the leadership of the local elite. Most cities in Hispania originated as pre-Roman towns but with the coming of the Romans local leaders seized the initiative to upgrade their communities and status by allowing the Romans to impose their colonial model upon cities' residents. By the end of the age of the Republic these towns were effectively Romanized and the towns within the peninsula's interior and to the west were making an effort to catch up. By the end of Augustus' reign the entire peninsula began to enjoy, under peaceful conditions, the benefits of urban life. Moreover, all Roman citizens and Romanized natives were allowed to participate in local government through popular assembly in electing magistrates. Life in Hispania became so good that even former slaves, though ineligible for magistracies, could become government employees or officials of the imperial religious cult, if they could afford the entrance fee.[31]

By the beginning of the first century AD, Romanization was well underway in southern Portugal. A Senate was established at Ebora (present-day Evora); schools of Greek and Latin were opened; industries such as brick making, tile making, and iron smelting were developed. Gradually, Roman civilization was extended to northern Portugal, as well. The Lusitanians were forced out of their hill-top fortifications and settled in bottom lands in Roman towns (*citânias*). The *citânias* were one of the most important institutions imposed on Lusitania during the Roman occupation. It was in the *citânias* that the Lusitanians acquired Roman civilization, learned Latin and were introduced to Roman culture, administration and religion. All in all, the Roman occupation left a profound cultural, economic, and administrative imprint on the entire Iberian Peninsula that remains to the present day.

Once the invasion and conquest of Hispania was complete, the colonization of the region was comprehensive and permanent. Large numbers of colonists arrived from Italy, an infrastructure of roads and towns was built, and Roman citizenship became universal to all Lusitanians by 73 AD. Iberian and other native languages gradually began to disappear. It seems that the whole of Lusitania, as well as other regions throughout Hispania, were completely Romanized by the beginning of the first century AD. Though we see and understand that Romanization transformed the social and economic structures of pre-Roman populations, we also see that Romanization had produced no profound effect upon Lusitania until the upbringing of the next generation of Lusitanians, known as Luso-Romans.

As for the history of the capital cities of the *conventus* and other major towns of importance, there is little written data on their individual historical evolution or physical development. But it is certain that the Romans did very little to actually build entire towns from scratch and that the Romanization of Lusitanian towns and cities began with Julius and Augustus Caesar, as the archaeological record shows. Romans would usually build on or improve pre-Roman settlements that were already developed, especially in the Algarve and on the Atlantic coastline. But at times they would establish a town to resettle rebellious tribesmen, as we saw with the Lusitanians in the founding of Valencia in the previous chapter, or settling Roman veterans as in Beja (known by the Romans as Pax Julia) where Julius Caesar mixed native Iberians with Roman army veterans and colonists.[32]

It is clear through archaeological and epigraphical evidence that the rebellious Roman praetor Sertorius and the one-time praetor of Hispania Julius Caesar began to develop Lusitania prior to Augustus. But it was not until Augustus Caesar that significant contributions to the urban development of Lusitania were made. Although it was a difficult task, he accomplished it with amazing ambition. Even after the Julio-Claudian dynasty, the Flavian dynasty continued to bring many improvements to Lusitanian urban life. From Augustus' reign to the beginning of the second century AD there was much building and rebuilding within Lusitania's borders. Thereafter, through archaeological and epigraphical evidence, construction stagnated for various reasons. By the end of the third century and the onset of the fourth century AD Lusitania, like much of the western Roman Empire, began to surround its cities with walls and change or destroy many Roman edifices, an architectural occurrence that came with the coming of the barbarian hordes into Roman territory.

These walls not only changed the look of the cities but also changed the type of construction and the quality of city life, making them more crowded. A wall meant that only a small part of the city was enclosed, leaving other homes, amphitheatres, temples, baths and other structures outside the city's defence. As many of these beautiful structures were left out in the open and abandoned, many of the buildings were demolished and used to build the city's wall. Adding to the threat of invasion and the destruction of many Roman architectural wonders was the decline in paganism and the adoption of Christianity as the official state religion. This led to many temples being destroyed or configured into churches that are still in use today. One last example of this large-scale change was that many Roman towns and cities were dependent on a water supply brought in by aqueducts, but the barbarian dangers led newly walled cities to construct large cisterns inside city walls, to guarantee, if only for some time, their survival if the city was besieged.

One must remember that, just like today, the founding of a new city or the rebuilding of a pre-Roman town or city required immense public investment of money and human resources, such as labourers and craftsmen. Such simple tasks as the squaring and fitting of stone blocks, construction of archways, making concrete, plastering walls and other specialized skills were unknown to the local inhabitants, so it was important to bring in colonists to these areas with special incentives. Besides requiring cash and technical expertise to build a Roman style city, it was important to Rome to Romanize the natives in terms of social and cultural norms and mores. Civilizing the local inhabitants required Roman immigrants, whose practice of daily life and customs was the best way to assimilate the natives. Not educating the locals about Roman ways or teaching the required skills would have left all of Augustus' endeavours useless.

Besides spending large amounts of money and time improving Lusitanian cities and towns, the Romans also spent a large amount of effort expanding the road network of its new province by cutting and paving roadways, constructing bridges and placing milestones along the roads. Peripheral regions of the provinces no longer seemed remote and cut off from the rest. Roads now connected many cities and towns, such as those connecting Olisipo (Lisbon) to Bracara Augustus (Braga), and Bracara Augustus to Ebora (Evora), which became major commercial roads.[33] Not only did they interconnect Lusitanian cities — several of these 'highways' connected with roads that led into Spain, and to this day many are still in use. Along these major roads, *miliarium* (milestones) were provided to help guide the traveller, so people were no longer in doubt about where they were going or how far they had to go.[34] In this context it did not matter if people travelled far on these roads. The milestones helped make people aware that they were now linked to a wider and very Roman world.

Though cultural, social and architectural changes were many throughout the Roman occupation, Lusitania escaped the realities of the barbarian invasions of the third and fourth centuries AD, but like the rest of the western Roman Empire during its decline, it did suffer inflation, economic recession and social unrest. It was not until the fifth century AD that the barbarian invasion reached the Iberian Peninsula's borders and change was put into effect by the invading Alans, Vandals, Visigoths and Suebis. One has only to read the chronicle of Hydacius, the Bishop of Chaves, to know a horrid account of these invasions.

Social Classes

THE UPPER CLASS

The Roman Empire was characterized by a social inequality and imbalance of wealth; even the Roman upper class was not homogeneous.[35] In Hispania, the 'Hispano-Roman' upper class was composed of a combination of Roman settlers and Romanized indigenes. The first group, the settlers, became an elite class the minute they set foot in Hispania, for they were basically Roman by birth or veterans who had completed their military service and decided to settle in Hispania's Roman colonies. The second group was made up of local nobility who had become local magistrates, abandoned their ancestral nomenclature and adopted Roman names.[36]As Hispania became more Romanized there is some evidence of the *decurial* class that included wealthy freedmen and their sons, showing that it was possible for local citizens to gain admission into the ranks of the elite providing they had proved their merit through financial success and had built up a network of supporters in the local Senate through business dealings, marital ties, or patron-client relationships.[37] Despite such opportunities for advancement, the *decurions* were not elected to governmental positions like the magistrates but remained an exclusive club for 'socially accepted families'.[38]

FREEMEN

All freeborn Roman citizens that belonged to the lower classes were called *plebs* (commoners). These Roman citizens had *conubium*, the right to contract a legal marriage with another Roman citizen and beget legitimate children who were themselves Roman citizens. But freeborn men and women that lived in Roman territories were called *peregrine*(foreigners). Noncitizens, or *peregrine*, generally remained subject to whatever legal system was in effect when their provincial communities were annexed by Rome. Beginning with the reign of the Emperor Augustus (27 BC to 14 AD), institutionalized practices permitted provincials to become citizens, generally by serving either in the Roman army or on a city council.[39] And because citizen rights were inherited, the number of Roman citizens quickly increased. The group received what was called Latin rights, a form of citizenship with fewer rights than full Roman citizenship granted in Italy, especially Latium (modern region of Lazio, Italy, where Italy's capital Rome is situated). Gradually Roman citizenship extended to communities throughout the empire.[40] These citizens had rights under Roman law, but could not vote, although their leading magistrates could become full citizens because they worked for the Roman government. Free-born foreign subjects, the *peregrini*, followed laws that existed to govern their conduct and disputes. This would change in 212 AD, when Marcus Aurelius Antoninus and Marcus Aurelius Severus Antoninus, also known as Caracalla, extended full Roman citizenship to all freeborn people living within the Roman Empire.[41]

The next class within the *plebs* were the freedmen (*liberti*), freed slaves that had a form of Latin rights. Besides the slave class, freedmen made up the bulk of the Iberian population. Many Iberian freedmen engaged in commerce, amassing vast fortunes that sometimes rivalled those of the wealthiest patricians. The majority of freedmen, however, joined the plebeian classes and often worked as farmers or tradesman. Social mobility beyond the leap from slavery to freedom was limited. Wealthy freedmen could purchase the position of *servi Augustalis*, an official of the imperial religious cult, but could not hold political office.[42] However, local prominent freedmen were sometimes made honorary magistrates, which allowed their sons to enter into the world of Roman politics.[43] They could also improve their status through marriage with someone from a higher rank, such as a freedwoman of a local magistrate, though freedmen could not marry their patronesses.[44] But there were some who enjoyed their freedom and became wealthy men, such as the group belonging to *liberti Augusti*, individuals freed by the emperor. These men played a major role in the imperial civil service. Although freedmen were not allowed to vote during the Republic and the early Empire, children of freedmen were automatically granted the status of Roman citizens. Overall their status varied from generation to generation throughout the Republic.

It is quite ironic that of all the people that made up the bulk of the *liberti* class, the *plebs rustica* (the rural class) are the ones we know least about. Their sole aim in life was to produce enough to pay taxes and rents and provide for their families. In Hispania, as elsewhere throughout the empire, poverty was king, as the classical sources indicate.[45] To further insult this class, they were labelled and scorned by city dwellers as uncultured bumpkins.[46] Though they were seen as a lower class they played an important role in Roman society as their main purpose was food production.[47] Peasant life on a farm was harsh for families living in cramped conditions in rude cottages along with their livestock and had a diet of milk, beer, cheese, vegetables, goat meat and acorn bread.[48]

SLAVES

Little is also known of slaves (*servi*) in Hispania, apart from that they were used as servants, miners, factory workers, construction workers and farmers on large estates. Unlike in modern times, Roman slavery was not based on race, but on conquest of territory. Slaves in Hispania originally were for the most part 'prisoners of war' and conquered people captured during sieges and other military campaigns throughout the Roman Empire. At first they had no rights whatsoever and could be disposed of by their owners at any time. As time went on, however, the Senate and later emperors enacted legislation meant to protect the lives and health of slaves. However, until slavery was abolished Romans habitually used their slaves for manual labour, as gladiators, for servitude and sexual purposes.[49] Though they had no rights they still received a *peculium* (allowance), were permitted to take a slave partner, known as *contubernalius*, and raise a family, thus providing their master with a new generation of slaves, although many *testators* (person who makes a will) freed the slaves that they believed to be their natural children.[50]

Another difference between Roman slavery and its modern variety was manumission — the ability of slaves to be freed. Roman owners freed their slaves in considerable numbers: some freed them outright, while others allowed them to buy their own freedom. The prospect of possible freedom through manumission encouraged most slaves to be obedient and hardworking. Formal manumission was performed by a magistrate and gave freedmen full Roman citizenship. The one exception was that they were not allowed to hold office. However, the law gave any children born to freedmen, after formal manumission, full rights of citizenship, including the right to hold office. Slaves freed informally did not become citizens and any property or wealth they accumulated reverted to their former owners when they died.[51] However, Rome's rigid society attached importance to social status and even successful freedmen usually found the stigma of slavery hard to overcome — the degradation lasted well beyond the slavery itself.

Women and Marriage

Iberian women in the eye of the Romans were seen as tough and unfeminine, weighing against unflattering stereotypes. But tombstone relief sculptures and vase paintings show another side to Iberian women. They were depicted as tough but sensitive and skilful people. Though the Romans saw these women as uncultured with their barbaric customs, under Roman occupation they continued to have many rights and were more likely to be employed than their Roman counterparts.[52]

With regards to intermarriage, barbarians and Romans were perfectly free to marry each other so long as the marriages were 'between persons of equal social status, with no law impeding them.'[53] This notion of marital exclusivity was current in other spheres of contemporary Roman thought. The late-fourth century Spanish poet Prudentius, for example, stated:

> A common law makes us equal ... the native city embraces in its unifying walls fellow citizens (*cives congenitos*) ... Foreign peoples now congregate with the right of marriage (*ius conubii*): for with mixed blood, one family is created from different peoples.[54]

Roman Military Service

Although there was no professional army, the Lusitanians, like the rest of the Iberians, had a long history of serving in foreign armies as mercenaries and auxiliary soldiers. Tacitus observed that their physical strength and excellent fighting abilities made an impact upon the Roman army.[55] Roman military indoctrination helped to Romanize the recruits, qualifying them for Roman citizenship upon discharge from the military.[56] The large number of Iberian men that served in the Roman army illustrates the continuing and integral role the Iberians played in the Roman war machine; some Iberians even served in the emperor's Praetorian Guard and urban cohorts in Rome.[57] The majority of Iberians living in the northern part of the peninsula served in the frontier, particularly in Britain and Germania because they were accustomed to cold and damp climates, while those from the south served in Gaul or the eastern frontier. It has been assumed that, by an unspecified process, some barbarians were granted some type of citizenship after completing their long military service, but many scholars think that perhaps only officers became Roman citizens, not soldiers.[58] Emilienne Demougeot, for example, conjectures that barbarians who became members of the field army held

Roman military or civilian office and were allowed to marry Roman women once they became citizens.[59] Barbarian soldiers were also eligible for veterans' benefits such as land grants and tax breaks.[60]

While military service was a prominent way for many Iberians to leave the peninsula, others left and became merchants selling Iberian goods and leaving a cultural footprint.

There were other Iberian individuals that left their mark on history, such as the famous Lusitanian charioteer, Appuleius Diocles; the rhetorician and poet, Seneca; the writer Columella; the grammarian Quintilius; the poet Martial; and even emperors such as Trajan — showing that Roman influence had a large impact in defining Hispania.

Roman Law

In the world of Roman officialdom during the Roman Republic (509 to 27 BC) and the first few centuries of the Roman Empire, citizenship denoted an elite legal status to which certain rights, privileges and obligations were accrued under the law.[61] For example, in private life, citizens could marry, make wills, and carry on business under the protection of Roman law and bring lawsuits against other Roman citizens. Noncitizens generally remained subject to whatever legal system was in effect when their provincial communities were annexed by Rome. Thus the laws applied to the Iberian population were tribal laws, because the Iberians at the time of the Roman conquest of Hispania were not Roman citizens, and it was only to Roman citizens that Roman law applied. But beginning with the reign of Emperor Augustus (27 BC to 14 AD), institutionalized practices permitted provincials to become citizens by serving in the Roman army or on a city council. And because citizen rights were inherited, the number of Roman citizens quickly increased.[62] Recognition of the legitimacy of such legal foreign systems must have taken place during the formal organization of the province. As the province was being organized, jurisdictional boundaries were established; at the same time a commission oversaw that process and drew the boundaries for assize districts, revenue collection, and a myriad of other purposes.[63]

Though the Iberian tribes still followed their own laws during the early part of the Roman occupation, they began to follow Roman laws as the Romans pacified the western half of the peninsula by forcing certain laws upon the indigenous people, such as a ban on Roman-barbarian marriages. This law was another example of the Roman fondness for prohibiting or regulating marriages between persons from different social, legal, or even religious backgrounds.[64]

Luso-Roman Economy

Lusitania had resources that were very important to the economy of the Roman Empire. The Romans therefore quickly took charge of its economical resources, which were primarily based on agriculture but included two other important industries: mining and fishing. Roman Lusitania developed a large industry of tinned fish and sauces called *garum* that were exported throughout the empire. Mining, meanwhile, gave access to natural resources for the manufacture of items such as weapons.Though the Lusitanians were agriculturalists, the Romans taught them to grow olives for oil and grape for wine.

AGRICULTURE

Agriculture played a significant part in the development of Roman Lusitania, especially in the south and along the coastal strip. With the occupation of Lusitania, the Romans effected deep structural reform by consolidating the deprived land into properties and infusing into the Lusitanians the ideology of profit making. But first they had to introduce the idea of setting up farms, which the Romans initiated by taking up as much rural space one could handle and establishing a large estate. In the north, unlike the south, farmable land was maintained as free pastures and fallowed farmland, only to be used in the spring and summer to grow seasonal vegetables. In the south, especially in the Alentejo region where the Roman occupation was slower, Luso-Roman farming took place in large estates or villas called *latifundia*, of which many still stand today; unfortunately a large number have not yet been excavated. These *latifundias* were characteristic of the Roman Empire and would be most highly developed in Sicily, Spain, and North Africa. Their establishment destroyed many ancient forests and dried up swamp areas, changing these areas into hospitable valleys where settlements were built and conditions cultivated for growing edible food products. In Lusitania, this agricultural system would produce cereals, grains, olives, grapes, legumes, fruits and livestock.

The Alentejo region provided a setting for the construction of *latifundias*, for its rolling hills and flat gentle plains were and still are suited for growing cereals, grains, olive trees and grapes, while in the north the land was (and still is) arable for agriculture. With varying degrees of soil conditions in the Alentejo, a system of crop rotation was used; even though at times the profit margin may have been low this was necessary for it conferred various benefits to the soil.To make up for the losses, pigs were allowed to forage in the surrounding plains of ilex and cork oak, while shepherds herded sheep and goats within the fallow acres of the *latifunda* so that they would be fertilized and be able to produce during the following season. Along with this system of land rotation, olive trees were planted among wheat fields to help in olive oil production. This was the only way a living could be hatched out in this area.

In José María Blázquez Martínez's work on the impact of the Roman conquest on the Peninsula, he writes that after it had been pacified Hispania provided five percent of the grain harvest used by the Roman Empire, which also could now impose taxes on the populace, bringing to Rome a larger profit margin than before.[65] In 124 BC, Gaius Sempronius Gracchus prompted the Senate to sell the wheat sent to Rome by the praetors from Spain, then send the money back to Iberian cities to be used to build public projects.[66] This return was at some point beneficial to the province, but the entire wheat profit was not sent to Hispania but distributed in Rome. Wheat shipments to Rome had become an important resource in this stage of the empire's development for it desperately needed to feed its growing population.

On the Atlantic coast the land was blasted by gale winds and rain, making the soil a bit more hospitable for food production. In addition, the land was particularly excellent for olives, for they thrive well in the limestone-type soils found around Elvas, Moura, Cano and Pavia. Along with the production of olive oil, viticulture was very lucrative for Lusitania. Before the now famous Douro wines became well known, the Romans concentrated their viticulture in the valleys of the Sado and Guadiana Rivers (both in the Alentejo region) and along the main road from Olisipo (Lisbon) to Emerita (Mérida) via Ebora (Evora).[67]

We know very little about life in these *latifundias* or about agriculture in Roman Portugal, but life in the country villa was certainly based on raising cattle, horses, pigs, goats and sheep as well as growing cereals, grains, vines, fruits, olives and vegetables according to the suitability of the soil, and the proximity of towns and cities that provided an income for the landowner. In the end the development of horticulture, viticulture and grain crops was primarily developed to supply the cities' food and export a new food supply to Rome.

One can only imagine that the Roman settlers at the end of the republic and the beginning of the imperial periods brought with them new technology, management techniques and methods for agricultural improvements, along with the introduction of new seeds and animal breeds. Sadly, there has been very little to nothing written about the Roman innovations and technology introduced to Lusitania, such as agricultural implements, field cultivation and fertilization, irrigation, pruning, fruit production, wine making, olive oil production and animal husbandry. But all is not lost; since the late 1980s there have been several in-depth studies about the Roman 'agricultural revolution' in Lusitania, such as Roman hydrology and surviving agriculture tools.

Garum and Salted Fish

Not all villas were limited to agriculture. Along the coast and river outlets that drained into the sea these villas were involved in the production of *garum* and drying and salting fish. They found this industry to be more lucrative than agriculture. Thus many smaller *latifundia*, especially those on the coast and along the estuaries of the Tagus and Sado Rivers, became engaged in the fishing industry as well as preserving fish in fish-salting tanks and producing *garum* sauce.[68]

During the Roman period, Lusitania led the way in establishing the Iberian Peninsula as a major exporter of salted commercial products that supplied salted fish and meats to all of the western empire. According to Leonard Curchin, the fish were gutted and cut into cubes or triangular chunks, with slits in the flesh to aid the penetration of the salt; the pieces were then thrown into large rectangular vats with an equal quantity of salt. The fish was left in these vats for twenty days so that the salt would seep into the flesh for flavour. It was then removed and packed into amphorae and sealed with wood or cork.[69] This process may have also been used to cure meats. The salt used in this processes was undoubtedly obtained by evaporating sea water in huge salt pans called *salinae* and any surplus salt was sold as a food preservative.[70]

Lusitania's productivity was not only evident in its salted meats and fish, but also with the making of *garum* sauce, which was more profitable than salted fish.[71] *Garum* was prepared from the viscera, innards and blood of various fish including mackerel, tuna and eel. Before the process began it may have been a common practice for fishermen to lay out their catch according to the type of fish. This allowed *garum*-makers to pick the exact ingredients they needed.[72] The fish was first macerated in salt, and days later crushed and placed in a bath of brine to allow fermentation. The fish and brine would cure in the sun for one to three months, where the mixture fermented and liquified in the dry warm air, the salt inhibiting the common agents of decay. In some cases, for quicker fermentation, it was stored in a heated room. Concentrated decoctions of aromatic herbs, varying according to the locale, were then added.The end product was a very nutritious thick liquid that retained a high amount of protein and amino acids, along with a good deal of minerals and

B vitamins.[73] After several decantations a black sauce emerged that added great zest to bland dishes. A fine strainer would be inserted into the fermenting vessel, and the liquid was ladled out into amphorae for export.

As it was for both domestic consumption and overseas exportation, this industry was another way for smaller landowners to make an income. Lusitania *garum*, known as *garum hispanicum*, was so popular that *garum* amphorae from Lusitania have been found as far as Palestine. Thus in times before the discovery of the Spices Isles and India, Portugal and coastal Spain were major producers of *garum*; this product was one of the few seasonings available at the time and highly prized. So highly prized that Pliny writes it cost 1,000 sesterces (about US$1,500) for about two *congii* (about 1.5 gallons).[74]

Wine

One of the lasting legacies of the Roman Empire was the establishment of a wine culture in lands that would become world renowned wine regions. Under the Romans, Portugal's wine production started in earnest. Portuguese wines were apparently so popular in Rome that demand outstripped the province's small production, making it a rare commodity. Strabo mentions that vines were grown around the mouth of the Tagus.[75] As for the interior of Lusitania, such as the well-known Douro region, the heartland of today's port wine industry, during the Roman era it was just beginning to grow vines, so there was no wine industry.[76] The Roman influence of new techniques and the development of road networks brought new economic opportunities to Lusitania, elevating winemaking from private agricultural crops for personal consumption to a viable commercial enterprise. Still unlike the rest of Hispania, Lusitania did not develop into a wine-producing region under the Romans until Portugal began to export wine to England at the beginning of the eighteenth century AD when a cut in the duty tax on Portuguese wines happily coincided with a ban on the importation of French wines to Britain.[77]

Manufactured Goods

Some landowners made their income in other ways, making pottery, tiles, bricks, glass and so on, while others turned their land into smelting plants and stone quarry sites. Some entered the textile industry, dying and weaving cloth. As for mining, the state owned the mines but citizens were able to rent the land and buy mining rights.

Amphora Production

The production of *garum* and wine complemented another important export from the Iberian Peninsula, the amphora.[78] Hundreds of amphorae have been found in Portugal, signifying that there existed a major amphora industry in Lusitania. The amphora was a type of ceramic vase with two handles and a long neck narrower than the body, which in this case were used to package and transport *garum* and wine. Because of conserved remains of *garum* found in vases throughout the peninsula and beyond, such as in Italy, Britain and Gaul, archaeologists have been able to better understand the history of this Iberian industry and economy during the Roman occupation. In Lusitania most of the amphora workshops discovered up to this point are on the left bank of the Tagus River and on the right bank of the Sado; both on the lower reaches of these rivers.[79] Though these two areas were the province's major producer of amphorae, there were other sites such as at Salacia (Alcácer do Sal). According to Alarcão, the geographical locations, the types of clay used to make amphorae, and the kilns found in these workshops must have been associated with the preparation of *garum* and salt-fish products which was important in those areas. In the Algarve there are several amphorae 'factories' which were not far from *garum* producers and fish preserving factories.

Pottery

Besides using clay to make roofing tiles and amphorae, pottery was another commodity. This production, especially in northern Lusitania, was of a low-grade quality, labelled *terra sigillata hispanica*, compared to the better quality *terra sigillata* (stamped earth) intended for domestic use.[80] Spanish *sigillata* has been found outside the Iberian Peninsula in Morocco, Algeria, France, Germany, Britain and even Italy, indicating that despite its quality it was largely exported, perhaps due to its low market prices.[81]

Prior to the emergence of a pottery industry in Lusitania, during the onset of the first century AD pottery was imported first from Italy and then southern Gaul. During Brutus' campaign, potters followed the army and the *figlinarius* (potters) attached to the legions were possibly producing their own pottery using 'Spanish' clay. Lusitanian pottery production may have begun before 50 AD but it was not until the second half of that century that the industry reached its high point, involving mass production, before dwindling and in some areas even ceasing at the beginning of the second century AD.[82] In the Alentejo there seems to have been factories that produced imitations of a higher quality ceramic pottery from other areas, such as the Southern Gaulish or Spanish Merida style *sigillata*.[83]

Apart from the domestic decorative pottery produced in certain areas, coarse ware was made all over the country. As pottery for kitchens, as opposed to the tables of the better off, and for all types of people, coarse ware was more likely to be made locally. Oil lamps were mass produced, as well as amphorae for the transportation of liquid goods as mentioned before. Unfortunately the study of Lusitanian coarse ware is lacking, although attempts have been made to push forward the classification of these artifacts and materials.

Glassware

According to Alarcão's study on Roman Lusitania no major glasswork industry has yet been found in Portugal, but glass waste at Braga and the ruins of Conimbriga near Coimbra suggest that there may have been workshops that produced common green glass for everyday glassware such as bottles, jars of all sizes and other popular products.[84]

Jewellery

Jewellery for both the Lusitanians and the Romans was extremely ornamental.[85] Lusitanian jewellers made everything from simple to intricate necklaces, bracelets, armlets, broaches,rings and earrings. The Roman hunger for jewellery prompted the Lusitanians to make it from any raw material they thought precious: gold, silver, copper, bronze, precious stones such as quartz, turquoise and opals, and other materials such amber and even bones. From archeological artifacts found near Monte de São Félix, Portugal, in 1904, it seems that men enjoyed wearing torques or smooth rounded necklaces, armlets and round or flat bracelets.Women wore a much larger variety, but it seems they liked a more intricate type of jewellery.[86] Lusitanian jewellery reveals a developed technique, very similar to that made throughout the Mediterranean, namely using plates and solders, filigree and granulated techniques. Though everyone wore jewellery it did play a part in class distinction.[87]

Textiles

The textile industry in Hispania was praised by the Romans due to Iberian linen, which was popular among men and women — especially men, for it was so sheer that when women wore it they were reproached for wearing 'woven wind'.[88] It is also believed that the Romans used linen for undergarments. The majority of the linen throughout the entire country was homespun, as proven by the discovery of thousands of loom weights and spindle whorls. Although we believe linen was homespun, it is difficult to say whether there were linen factories as a study on the subject has not been conducted.Wool is also mentioned epigraphically. The most famous woolen cloth, according to the Romans, was woven at Salacia (Alcácer do Sal) in Lusitania; its beautiful smooth fleece produced attractive checkered patterns of black and white.[89] Along with the making of linen and wool, dying also played a part in the textile industry, but unfortunately there is little information to indicate whether it was a major factory industry or if there were workshops spread throughout the province that exported their product to Rome.

Mining

Unlike the industries I have mentioned, mining was entirely state run. It was the second most profitable industry in Lusitania, but only after metal ores had been reached. In Roman Lusitania the minerals that were mined were naturally gold and silver, along with copper, lead, tin iron and semi-precious stones.[90] The majority of its mines were state owned, but there were a few, such as Aljustrel, where the state allowed private citizens to have mining rights.[91] But other mines, such as at Vipasca, were leased by the state to individuals who organized themselves into a mining company.[92] With gold mines, the state had a greater interest in having direct control.

'Mining companies' were each legally allowed to control five working mines, either as a maximum or minimum number — we are not sure.[93] On being awarded these concessions, the 'tenants' would have to pay a tax called a *pittaciarium* and start working within twenty-five days of getting their lease.[94] On top of this, there were other stipulations in the contract mining companies signed with the state.[95] Though the mines were state property, the concessionaries were responsible for their upkeep; in one example from the tablet of Aljustrel, concessionaries were forbidden to make holes that would put safety of the miners, the mine or operation of its drainage at risk.[96]

As mining was only profitable once the ore had been reached, the mining company was made to pay a second tax on what they found, for example 4,000 sesterces for silver.[97] Along with these taxes, the concessionary had to pay to the state half the value of the minerals extracted and as there were no state run smelting plants, the ore was weighed at the pithead and then the tax assessed; only when it was paid was the concessionary allowed to transport the ore to the foundry.[98] To avoid in paying this tax it is probable that much smuggling took place, but this was at the risk of the miners for if caught they were severely punished. The policing of the mines fell upon the military. A small garrison was responsible for seeing that no smuggling took place, collecting taxes and making sure the regulations about time limits, transport, pit props, and distance between the pits and drainage were observed. Besides forcing private mining companies to pay several types of taxes, the state also monopolized the service industry: shoemakers, tailors, barbers and anyone else who helped serve the miners had to pay rent for their concessions.[99] With gold mines such as Três Minas, the military had more direct control in running the mine for it administered and disciplined the workers and provided skilled mining engineers. At the same time, unlike the mines at Vipasca, the Romans used slaves in the gold mines instead of private citizens.

Construction and Architecture

During the pre-Roman era building methods in Lusitania were fundamentally simple: rough stone walls put together with or without mortar. Another method used was mud bricks (adobe) and lath and plaster. Roofing was made of straw and wood. But with the Romans all that changed. Technical innovations were introduced such as squared blocks of stone mortar, *opus caementicium* and *opus signinum* (types of concrete), tiles, small clay bricks, stucco and vaulted ceilings. These material novelties lead to the erection of better structures. They also gave rise to the use of new raw materials such as clay, limestone and quicklime.

Architectural forms depended both on materials and construction techniques, as well as the social purposes the buildings were intended for. Temples' shapes varied according to the liturgies celebrated in them; theatres arose out of the requirements of drama and their architecture evolved according to the demands of the type of plays they staged; baths were designed for the needs of Roman bathers; and the amphitheatre's shape determined what type of gladiatorial games would take place within. It is therefore logical to say that because of the Roman conquest of Lusitania and the thorough transformation of its society, a real architectural revolution was brought about.[100] Indeed, advances in architecture on the Iberian Peninsula began with the Romans.

Lath and plaster and bricks continued to be utilized during the occupation of Lusitania. Modelled stucco was employed throughout the Roman Empire. The Romans used mixtures of lime and sand to build up preparatory layers over which finer applications of gypsum, lime, sand and marble dust were made; pozzolanic materials were sometimes added to produce a more rapid set. Lath and plaster was a durable and not a very expensive technique, for the process began with wood laths. These narrow strips of wood were nailed horizontally across the wall studs. Next, temporary lath guides were placed vertically on the wall, usually at the studs. Stucco was then applied, typically using a wooden board. The applier dragged the board upward over the wall, forcing the stucco into the gaps between the lath and leaving a layer on the front of the temporary guides. A helper fed new stucco onto the board, as it was applied in quantity. When the wall was fully covered, the vertical lath 'guides' were removed, and their 'slots' filled in, leaving a fairly uniform undercoat.

The Romans made use of fired bricks, and the Roman legions, which operated mobile kilns, introduced bricks to many parts of the empire. Upon occupying new lands, the Romans would introduce the craft of brickmaking to the local populations.[101] Roman bricks were often stamped with the mark of the legion that supervised their production.They were almost invariably of a lesser height and longer than modern bricks, but made in a variety of different shapes and sizes.[102] Shapes included squares, rectangles, triangles and circles, and the largest bricks found have measured over 3ft in length.[103] Bricks allowed Luso-Romans to build an assortment of houses and buildings. For public buildings, ashlar stone blocks and dressed stone work were the rule; and even when walls were generally made of mud or clay bricks they required stone for their foundations, thresholds and door and window frames.[104]

Stone was also used for many other purposes such as paving roads, making querns for funerary and honorary stelae, and baths, but to construct such magnificent works, stone quarries were needed. Traces of Roman quarrying in Portugal are practically non-existent today and the study of the origins of stone use is very rare. There is however some evidence that stone was quarried in the Alentejo, the Beiras, the modern-day province of Estremadura and in the Algarve. According to Alarcão's in-depth study on Roman Portugal, these quarries produced local stone such as schist, granite, limestone and marble.[105]

Clay was used in a variety of building materials, such as *tegulae* and *imbrices*, both types of tile for coving and roofs. Bricks of various sizes and shapes were used in constructing buildings and roads, and *suspensurae* for hypocausts and columns; terracotta pipes, *tegulae mamatae*, were used for insulating bath houses and so on. Though these clay materials were manufactured in Lusitania, many of the tile and brick factories have not been discovered; the ones that have been found and excavated represents a tiny portion of what must have existed during the Roman occupation.[106]

As for the other building materials used, quicklime and *opus signinum*, there is very little information. Making quicklime may have become an industry in the limestone areas of Portugal, from which it would have been transported to areas of the country where heavy construction took place. During the Roman Empire concrete (*opus caementicium*) was made from quicklime, pozzolanic ash or pozzolana, and an aggregate of pumice. Its widespread use in many Roman structures — a key event in the history of architecture termed the 'concrete revolution' — freed Roman construction from the restrictions of stone and brick material and allowed for revolutionary new designs both in terms of structural complexity and dimensions.[107] In Roman times, gypsum and lime were used as binders, but volcanic dusts such as pozzolana were favoured when they could be obtained. But the type of material used in Rome and Italy was different from that found in the other provinces. In Lusitania, the lack of pozzolanic ash for *opus caementicium* meant other materials were used. According toAlarcão, it seems that the Luso-Romans made their own concrete.[108] To prepare *opus signinum* crushed tiles were mixed with lime, sand, and powdered clay bricks, and at times crushed stones were added. Any builder's yard yielded plenty of broken tiles and bricks, which combined with the sandy terrain of the country meant a major industry developed. But besides using *opus signinum,*which may have been a bit expensive, the Luso-Romans were able to make a low quality cement of sand, water, and artificial pozzolans (broken stones and baked clay).

But for the Romans to build such wonderful buildings, they first had to set up city plans. Much has been written about the purpose, development, daily life and architecture of Roman cities, but inadequate attention has been paid to the role of these factors in Romanizing conquered territories. Cities were the focal point of assimilation that helped form the cultural and social structure of Roman civilization: commerce was centralized, conquered lands were 'civilized'and populations were usually under control. It has also been claimed that urbanization was a deliberate attempt by Rome to rechannel the efforts of the Iberian elite from rebellion to community projects.[109] Somewhat cynical, this statement assumes that the Romans had premeditated intentions to impose cities on the conquered, but apart from a handful of colonies Rome established throughout the empire it could claim little credit in founding cities. Most Romanized cities, in Hispania and elsewhere, began as pre-Roman towns.

Under the peaceful conditions of Augustus' reign and onwards, Iberian cities became satiated with monumental buildings, temples and statues.[110] Not only could the elite enjoy the benefits of urban life, the lower classes could too.

Roman architecture declared a functional and pragmatic spirit that spread out from Rome and conquered the whole known world. It is clear that the Romans adopted Etruscan and Greek influences, but Rome developed its own highly distinctive architectural style by introducing the previously little-used arches, vaults and domes. In Hispania, the urban design of Roman cities followed clear laws of development for public and military services. The Roman city was basically composed of a number of identical components, disposed in a special way — parallel and at equal distance — separated by streets. The whole forms a unit of rectangular designs surrounded by a parametric wall with watchtowers. All the streets were equal except two: the main northsouth one (*cardo maximus*) and the main eastwest one (*decumanus*). Both were wider for at their ends the gates were placed in the city walls.

The centre of the city was where very important social and cultural systems were placed: amphitheatres, theatres, temples, markets, forums and so on. There were also great communal buildings throughout the city, such as *basilicae, termae*, gyms and bathhouses. In addition, housing could be divided into *house, domus, insula* and *villa*. There were also *casae* or housing for lower classes and ex-slaves. Because of modern urbanization many of these building structures have disappeared in our time.

Religion

Luso-Roman Religion

It is said that Rome had more gods than citizens, but Hispania had more gods than Rome.[111] This profusion is attributed to several factors: the plurality of indigenous tribes, each with its own pantheon, the implantation of successive foreign cults, and the polytheistic nature of ancient religions, which allowed all these gods to co-exist without inherent contradiction.[112] Since the Romans were usually tolerant of other people's belief systems they allowed their religion as well as the indigenous gods to flourish throughout the province. Nonetheless there was a tendency to adopt Roman gods, modify indigenous cults to conform with Roman ones, or mix together a native god with a Roman god to form somewhat a new god.

Lusitania, which was among the last region of Hispania to come under Roman control, can be divided into two religious spheres. The first is the south — the Algarve, the Alentejo and the coastal zones between the Tagus and Vouga Rivers; the second comprises the inland area between the Tagus and the Douro Rivers and north of the Douro.[113] This religious division into two contrasting regions, though an over simplification, will be useful for tracing the spread of Roman classical religion.

Roman civilization penetrated the south first, as we can see from the ruins of buildings, numerous villas, their mosaics and the large amount of artifacts that have been found. By the time of Augustus, the north was still predominantly indigenous as demonstrated by the lack of artifacts and mosaics, which are rare. Very few villas have been found and towns are few in the north compared to the south. It may be correct to say that in the north the social structure was different, more rural and with a less developed social system and economy. This division is also discussed by Pliny, who describes Lusitania from the north to south, using the word *populi* (tribes) until he reaches the Vouga River; thereafter *oppida* (towns). It appears that the Vouga was some kind of cultural divide between the Romanized section of Lusitania and the indigenous cultures. Finally, the two regions are marked by an ethnic division. In the north, the native Indo-European pre-Celtic people dominated, in the south, tribes of other origins influenced by more advanced outside civilizations inhabited the area. This was the difference between the two regions by the time the Romans had completed their conquest of Lusitania.

When it comes to religion, it seems that the worship of Roman gods was strongest in the more Romanized south, though it is not clear how this came about. But given Roman tolerance to foreign religions, why was the widespread conversion to Roman deities in Lusitania so strong? We can only imagine that it was in the cities that the Luso-Roman origins began with the coming of Roman colonists, settlers, craftsmen, soldiers and merchants. To some extent there may have been a perception that the gods of the conqueror were more potent or had stronger powers than those of the vanquished.[114] But more importantly the worship of Roman gods was an integral component of Romanization, a *sine qua non* of being accepted as a Roman. Though this is a possible theory, in reality there was not much wholesale abandonment of native gods but reconciliation with the Roman pantheon through the process of conflation that Tacitus termed *interpretatio Romana*.[115] In time these Roman religious beliefs moved into the rural areas as country folk came into contact with Roman gods when they went to the cities. But though the rural regions were becoming Romanized, they likely clung to their traditional gods long after the Roman gods had been transplanted into Lusitanian towns. Religion was and still is among the most conservative institution and usually the last to surrender.

If the less Romanized parts of the peninsula tended to contain the lion's share of indigenous gods, the majority of Roman gods were worshipped along the very much Romanized Mediterranean coast. But one must not forget that this was made possible by the Phoenicians and Greeks who brought their culture to the Iberians, particularly in the south of Spain, thus driving out native gods.[116] So introducing Roman gods into the Iberian pantheon was easy. Of all the Roman gods that came to be in Lusitania, it seems that at least forty played an important part in Lusitanian religion.[117] There were a small number of *nymphae*, *lares* and *genius* that also had a role in Luso-Roman religion, but they were used more frequently in the backwoods of Roman Lusitania.[118] Still, the lack of epigraphic material and sculptures are a serious drawback to our understanding of the exact number of gods that existed in Lusitania and how their cults functioned in the province.

EASTERN CULTS

With the Roman conquest of Hispania, there came other foreigners from the east, such as Egyptians; besides bringing material goods, they brought new ideas, technology and religion to Lusitania's major urban areas. As these towns became cities and capitals of a *conventus* and commercial centres, they began to attract many freemen and foreigners, thus Luso-Roman society was fertile ground for eastern and African religions. Of the eastern religions or cults (*sacra peregrine*) there is evidence of several that made a home in Lusitania, according to inscriptions discovered throughout the years.There seems to have been seven eastern mystery cults that had footholds in Lusitania: Cybele and Attis of Phrygia, Isis and Serapis of Egypt, Mithras of Persia, Caelestis of Carthage, and Astarte of Mesopotamian origin.[119] As Lusitania became more Roman with each passing decade public officials, especially during the Antonine and Severan dynasties, were keen to syncretize religions to make a strong impact on Hispania.

IMPERIAL CULT

The imperial cult was based on the supposed divinity of the emperor, and had essentially the political purpose of strengthening the loyalty of the provinces to the current ruler. In Hispania, the imperial cult was easily reconcilable with Iberian traditions of the *devotio Iberica*, which strengthened the belief in the imperial cult to the point that individuals would die for their leader. Once the indigenous people accepted Roman leadership, it became natural for them to treat an outstanding Roman official — especially a general — as a god. Though Spain was at the forefront of emperor worship in the Roman west, Lusitania was not until Caesar Augustus became *imperatori*. Augustus was staying in Tarraco in 26 to 25 BC when a delegation arrived from Mytilene, Greece to bestow divine honours upon him. Not to be outdone, the people of Tarraco built an altar to him and on one occasion they enthusiastically informed him that a palm tree had miraculously sprung out of it. Sarcastically, Augustus replied that they did not light sacrificial fires on the altar.[120] From this point on, all incoming emperors were paid homage. In Lusitania, the imperial cult may have appeared around 19 BC after Augustus' death via its military governor, L. Sestius Quirinalis Albinianus.[121] Along with this information the oldest inscription that shows Lusitania followed the imperial cult is from 5 or 4 BC, proving its existence.[122]

The imperial cult came to Lusitania in two phases. The first was based on tributes to Emperor Augustus in that altars and statues were consecrated to him and several other emperors that followed. But by the time of Tiberius, the imperial cult in Lusitania had entered its second phase and temples and colleges for priests were beginning to sprout up in several municipalities.[123] But still the Lusitanians used their traditional priests, who were not elected from the local elite, unlike their Roman and Iberian counterparts, but were skilled tradesmen.[124]

These imperial cults not only deified emperors but also the emperor's protective spirit and household gods. This tendency expanded until a large number of gods and goddesses were inducted into the Augustan pantheon, becoming in effect the emperor's own gods.[125] Bearing on the evidence available it seems that the worship of the imperial cult flourished during the first and second centuries AD but declined at the beginning of the third century with the arrival of Christianity.

Language

Assimilation of Latin came later to Gallaecia and Lusitania than the other administrative regions, and further variations in Latin were caused by differing tribal migration patterns and regional dialects.[126] Moreover, Lusitania as a whole was essentially rural in nature and more isolated than the rest of Hispania. This explains in part the differences between modern Portuguese and Spanish.

During the long process of colonization and assimilation, the dialect of the Roman Empire, known as vulgar Latin, diffused throughout the Iberian Peninsula. Vulgar Latin, or *linguaromana* — 'vulgar' in the sense of 'common', or 'of the people' — differed in grammar and syntax from classical Latin, the written and literary language of the Roman Empire, which had been developed in its standard form by Roman writers and grammarians of the first century BC. Vulgar Latin was spread throughout the western provinces of the Roman Empire by soldiers, merchants, travellers and, later on, Christian preachers. Latin in time became a highly varied, mobile and fluid form of spoken discourse. Through the influence of local or pre-Roman languages, Latinized regional variations developed and Rome became dependent on the extent of communications via interpreters or officials that had learned these newly Latinized dialects.[127] With the decline and fall of the Roman Empire, communication in Latin became more erratic as these regional dialects began to form into local languages, later becoming Portuguese and Spanish.

Although some of the pre-Roman Iberian languages became Latinized, many others succumbed and disappeared from human history due to the pressure and prestige of Latin. Of all the dialects that had existed in the Iberian Peninsula, only the Basque language is believed to be still used in its original form. Overall, it has been estimated that from around 600 AD, local dialects of vulgar Latin were no longer mutually intelligible, and, thereafter, many regions began a process of crystallizing these dialects into the early forms of Romance languages, such as Portuguese, Spanish, French, Romanian and several other European languages.

Though Rome had Romanized a major part of the Iberian Peninsula there still existed issues in dealing with Romanization and resistance to it. Strabo boasted that by the early first century AD the inhabitants of Hispania Ulterior were completely pacified, but one must remember that Ulterior by this time had been a Roman province for about 200 years. Though this was applicable to the cities, this was probably not true for the countryside. It is generally believed that the conquest of the entire peninsula was complete by 19 BC, having taken two centuries compared to Julius Caesar's conquest of Gaul in less than a decade. Therefore we can see that Romanization was resisted, and was a slow and gradual process. Though Romanization took hold in political, social and economic spheres, in religion, language and art the old ways died hard. In regions isolated by natural topographical structures such as mountains, by distances and by lower cultural levels, Romanization was an uphill battle.

According to Curchin, Rome was not committed to imposing its culture on the provinces in any thorough or systematic manner.[128] Official policy was chiefly aimed at pacification, justice and tax collection.[129] In religion, he writes that the polytheistic Romans were tolerant of other religions except those that posed a political threat, while in material culture, Roman goods were introduced not by official policy but by free enterprise; Roman exports found new markets.[130] On a social level, Iberians took Roman names and attempted to further their careers via achievements or family prestige. As a community, the Iberians took strides to gain Rome's grants of *ius Latii* for provincial communities, which were handed as a favour rather than an imposition.[131] This said, complete Romanization still failed to take over the entire peninsula.

Curchin writes that it failed in three essential areas: dispersion, depth and durability. Despite the high grade of Romanization in the south and east, the western and northwestern region were only partly assimilated, and other areas such as the Cantabrians and the Basques were never Romanized.[132] Furthermore, although much of the peninsula was Romanized, it was but a superficial veneer, barely masking the indigenous subculture.[133] Lastly, by the Late Empire, the north, central and western regions became de-Romanized and pre-Roman cultures re-emerged.[134] In short, Romanization was not homogeneous, but a process that varied from region to region and from tribe to tribe.

Chapter 10
Viriathus the King and the Legend

Viriathus' Leadership in Hispania Ulterior

What position did Viriathus occupy in the Lusitanian army? His position appears in the ancient sources in different forms. The classical sources habitually use the term '*dux*' (Latin for chief or commander), for example in Frontinus' work he is '*dux Lusitanorum*', or '*dux Celtiberorum*'.[1] This title was given to Viriathus by Frontinus only in 143 BC when Viriathus was already a Lusitanian chieftain and general.

Other Latin authors, including Veleius Paterculus, Eutropius and Diodorus, use the title '*dux latronum*' (chief of thieves). He was also called '*Lusitanus latro*' (Lusitanian thief) by Seneca, who mentions how frustrated he was by Viriathus' attack on Cordova.[2] This title, according to Muñoz, is without a doubt a reference to the type of military strategy (i.e. guerrilla tactics) Viriathus used to fight the Romans and how they despised it, calling the Lusitanian War a *latrocinium* (thief's war) rather then a*bellum iustum* (just war).

Of course the first Latin author to consider him a tribal chief or general was Livy, who wrote that he '*mox iusti quoque exercitus dux factus*' ('was quickly nominated the general of the army'). Justinus shares the same thought, writing: '*in tanta saeculorum series mullus illis hominibus Hispaniae dux magnus praeter Viriathum fuit*' ('in so many centuries there was not one man in Hispania that was a great general, except for Viriathus').

Besides the term *dux*, some Latin author also used the word *imperator* (commander in chief, general, emperor). Florus writes of him, '*ex latrone subito dux atque imperator*' ('from a thief he passed on to be chief and quickly general of the army'). Eutropius expressed the same, while Dio Cassius and Appian use the Greek term *strategós*. Of all the terms used, the word *rex* is very rarely mentioned except by Diodorus and Strabo, but it does not correspond to the terminology that recognizes the denomination of the applied word for king. Though several different words identified Viriathus' leadership position during his eight year war, most historians on the subject conclude that Viriathus was considered a general or chief of the Lusitanian army rather than a king of the Lusitanian people.

The acceptance of his leadership is addressed explicitly by Appian, but with his death his army undid itself and the power of his successor was not the same. Viriathus possessed excellent qualities as tribal chief and military leader. Because of these leadership qualities he has been considered the 'saviour' or 'liberator' of Hispania, but in reality he was never able to become either.

Besides holding a leadership position, after Galba's massacre in 147 BC, Viriathus came to the forefront of history as a military genius and the creator of guerrilla warfare by defeating several Roman praetors and their numerous legions. Following these defeats, Rome attempted to make a pact with the rebels, and although Viriathus was at first opposed to it, in time he became merciful, a wise general and chief who was recognized as not only a tribal leader of Lusitania but of Turdetania also. From this point on, Viriathus was considered by many historians to be 'a chief of the Lusitanians'as well as a leader of various tribes due to his amazing leadership skills and use of military tactics.

But the power that Viriathus had over western Hispania did not last very long. With his brother or father-in-law's death, ordained by Viriathus, the degradation of his authority began. But before his downfall and at the peak of his power, Viriathus celebrated his marriage outside Lusitania — either in Turdetania, or more likely Bastetania — to show the Romans who were invited to the ceremony that he was in control of the reconquered territory.

Though Viriathus showed the Romans his power, could he have been a friend of Rome? This would have been unthinkable for a man like him, who had an internal hatred for Rome. But in 140 BC, at the peak of his political and military career, we do see a change in his attitude in that he sought to make peace with Rome, in an attempt to end to the war.

The signing of the peace treaty of 140 BC was not the result of the Lusitanians tired of war, but of his military advantage that he had over Servilianus, enabling Viriathus to negotiate at that moment conditions for the signature of a peace treaty. It was the first time that he had the Romans totally cornered forcing their hand to sign the peace treaty or else.

Viriathus' treaty with the defeated Servilianus in 140 BC has a tendency to favour him as a peacemaker for he began negotiations with the Romans, bringing a short-lived peace to the Lusitanians, and he imposed on Rome a treaty of equal conditions (*aequis conditionibus*), but unfortunately this treaty was taken to be a disgrace.

But actually Viriathus knew that if he destroyed this Roman army, the war would continue and Rome would send more powerful legions than before to either annihilate his army or wipe out the entire tribe. He also began to detect that his army was weary after their first encounter with Servilianus, having been forced to retreat back across the border into Lusitania in search of provisions and reinforcements. A third reason was perhaps his people's lack of enthusiasm to continue to fight; he realized that if he pushed his people a bit further to continue their fight, it could have ended in mutiny and he may have lost the power he had fought so hard to achieve. In these three scenarios perhaps lie the reasons Viriathus decided to conduct peace negotiations.

The peace treaty reveals that the causes of the problems the Lusitanians faced were poverty and the poor land where they lived. The treaty provided conditions that the Lusitanians would continue to hold onto Baeturia, south of the Tagus River. Had the Romans allowed the Lusitanians to control this area, rather than break the treaty, the chronic lack of good lands for farming and pastures for their herds whould have come to an end, and the war would have ceased.

In the Roman Senate, however, there existed two parties, a hawkish party and one that favoured the peace treaty. The former considered a treaty with such conditions an offence to the Roman state and did not accept it. But the latter seem to have felt they were winners, because their members were more interested in the commercial and economic value of the Iberian coast and in exploration by penetrating the rest of the peninsula's interior. In the eye of these Romans, the land was inhabited by savages who only lived for war, but with the right influences and time they would become 'Roman subjects' who could be exploited. Unfortunately, the following year the Romans broke the peace.

It is indubitable that the peace of 140 BC meant for Viriathus the abandonment of further campaigning against Rome. Thus some historians believe he may have lost some of his power. Although a peace treaty was signed, the Romans had the upper hand and Laenas, an expert on indigenous idiosyncrasy, imposed hard conditions upon the Lusitanians: first, the delivery of hostages and Roman deserters; then, taxes; and finally, the surrender of weapons and Viriathus' betrayal and execution of many of his companions, among them his in-law Astolpas. With these deaths, Viriathus had practically dug his own grave. Perhaps many of his former allies and Lusitanian nobles did not forget this betrayal, and some had a hand in his murder. But this theory is unprovable.

Though Viriathus seems to have constantly tried to maintain his conquered lands, supported by an anti-Roman population, his power over Lusitania and the territories he captured did not remain absolute. In the eyes of his tribesmen, his shameful act no doubt broke oaths that Viriathus and his allies had made to each other. His murder by Audax, Ditalco and Minuro may have had something to do with Viriathus' betrayal of his allies. Viriathus' attempt to make peace by sacrificing some of his allies seems to have backfired, as evidenced by his assassination.

Viriathus did not abandon the idea of trying to achieve a Lusitanian influence on Celtiberian towns such as Tucci and Arsa, but he never got them to come over to his side because they went on to fight their own war of independence. On the other hand he fought for the Lusitanians who sought out agricultural lands to cultivate, which the Romans had promised. But each time these promises were made in an attempt to lure the Lusitanians into peace, it ended in betrayal. Thus Viriathus' tendency to become a 'king' of a state was inevitable, but would only work if he succeeded in defeating the Romans and built an effective and very organized tribal government structure. Unfortunately for the Lusitanians it never reached that point for two reasons: his failure to establish a border for his newly acquired territory and his unexpected death.

Viriathus' tragic death created the total dismemberment of the Lusitanian tribe, which ended their struggle. His successor, Tautalus, elected in a tribal assembly, did not have the personal attributes Viriathus had and soon yielded unconditionally to the Romans.

Besides his leadership skills, Viriathus appears to have been fair in sharing booty, as we saw in Diodorus' work. This was admired by Cícero, who introduced him as an example of justice, austerity and incorruptibility in various paragraphs of his *De Officiis*.

The data on Viriathus' sharing of wealth supports Sanchez Moreno's ideas that the Lusitanians had a complex social and political system that bestowed military prestige, social promotion and wealth upon its leaders. The majority of booty usually went to the tribal chiefs. The spoils were then distributed among their upper class subjects or those who had participated in the campaign. Viriathus, however, distributed wealth equally among his men and the classical writers characterize him as just, fair and equal, which were signs of a good leader. This form of wealth redistribution has been identified as the proper way primitive organizations adopted a socio-economic system of partnerships based on interactions through bartering. In this sense, it is necessary to understand the function of Viriathus' division of spoils.

Viriathus' attitude is explained in the classical texts' mentioning that he shared his booty among his men. Compared to the rest of the tribal leaders, Sanchez Moreno characterizes Viriathus as a moralistic warrior, who was known for his generosity and fairness.

Though he was a warrior's warrior, to gain the fidelity and adhesion of his troops it was important to manipulate the men through gifts or rewards, as deduced by the ancient texts. In this sense, the offerings worked as a commitment of loyalty among individuals and as an element to initiate social relationships between warriors and their people, to consolidate prestige and authority. Besides gaining the confidence of his people, Viriathus also established diplomatic ties with other tribal chiefs, reiterated in the exchange of offerings in political and religious ceremonies. This way, the redistribution of wealth was a reflex of the establishment of personal ties.

Viriathus, the Lusitanian King

Let us think of Viriathus as king of the Lusitanians. Several historical passages in the classical texts about Viriathus express an ideology of royalty, as discussed by Garcia Quintela and Muñoz. To establish that Viriathus was considered a king by his people, it is necessary to establish a comparison and above all to thoroughly analyze testimonies about personality traits Viriathus had that were considered by the classical authors as 'kingly'.

In this analysis, Viriathus is represented first as a bandit chief, followed by his transformation into a military leader and an end result that shifted him into kingship, if not directly at least in terms of an atmosphere of royalty. Most of these ancient testimonies refer to Viriathus not as a *latrine* but as *dynastés*, a term that designated chiefs of smaller political groups (i.e. chief of a group of bandits). As a leader of such a group, Viriathus would have to exercise great responsibilities.

Much of the texts' structures and vocabulary were utilized in relation to the kings of the Hellenistic monarchies. Thus Viriathus is described as if he had acceded into a type of royalty granted by a consensus among his partisans.[3] According to Muñoz, Viriathus has been compared to kings that were sovereigns of their homelands, but whose status was rejected by the Romans who felt that only they could be seen as kings, while all others were uncivilized barbarians.[4]

According to Muñoz and Garcia Quintela, this royal political system was very similar to that of the Celts, where kings came from the warrior class and their position was elective and revocable: though the king was in power, his power was controlled by his subjects. A king did not get to pass on his throne to a relative or son when he died, as in other historical civilizations.[5]

Though Viriathus did not inherit his chiefhood, his election marked an institutional change of bandit chief to tribal chief, granting him a 'kingship' over all Lusitanians. Unlike some other historians, Garcia Quintela concludes that Lusitanian royalty was much more similar to that of the Celts than the Hellenistic monarchies.[6]

He also points out that the classical authors knew how to capture in detail the legend of Viriathus by interpreting indigenous ideology in accordance with traditional Greek ethnography. Stories and anecdotes as well as the structure of Lusitanian sacrificial rites were the vehicles for transmitting the legend of Viriathus.

Overall, these classical stories about Viriathus seem to be an attempt to explain that Lusitanian ideologies went through a mythological process, Viriathus, a leader of men who fought for a cause he believed in, ended up representing a larger glory as a leader of an entire community in a critical situation.The Romans and Greeks that heard of and collected these stories adapted them to their ideologies and the norms of traditional ethnography;

so the excerpts we read today by the classical authors are fragmented traces of those final adaptations.

Was Viriathus the Romulus of Hispania?

Florus declared that Viriathus was a historical personage of Romulus, the creator and father of Rome. These classical authors seem to illustrate through their works that Viriathus played such an important part in the history of Hispania that Florus could compare him to Romulus.[7]

An interesting analytical work comes from Raquel Lopez Melero, who discusses whether Viriathus should be called the Romulus of Hispania, or if this was political rhetoric exaggerated by Florus. This controversial work sent waves among Iberian historians, prompting Lopez Melero to defend her thesis by stating:

> considering Viriathus as someone that almost consolidated a regnum does not seem to be absurd, or an exaggeration. ...for if he had consolidated a strong indigenous power, Rome would have unavoidably been obligated to recognize this new king and establish an independent Iberian state within the Roman realm.[8]

It seems evident that this idea was not unanimously accepted, since it was believed that the Romans would have Lusitania under their submission and quickly Romanize it. This of course did not happen, for Viriathus became the opposition to their conquest. For Rome to control the entire Iberian Peninsula would mean great economic profits and an increase of its power against Carthage, but instead of gaining the expected economic advantage, the Romans began losing their war against Viriathus (including the Celtiberian War), which became a large military expense that surpassed their earnings.

Perhaps had the Roman Senate been a bit more favourable to the ratification of Servilianus' peace treaty of 140 BC, the war would have ended then instead of lasting another year. This of course would have drastically changed Viriathus' fate and the outcome of Luso-Roman relations, but instead the Senate quickly allowed the new governor, Servilianus Scipio, to break the treaty and continue fighting, which resulted in Viriathus'death. This blow to his destiny caused him to become known as 'the Romulus of Hispania'.

Lopez Melero's work on the subject of Viriathus as the Romulus of Hispania puts forward various key points for her hypothesis. Prior to the Lusitanian War, there was no Roman initiative for territorial expansion, and, although it appears that Rome was in total control of the entire territory on the left bank of the Baetis River, the apparent lack of military positions north of the river points to a stabilization of their conquests. But the large-scale 'offensive' raids of the Lusitanians, which started in the middle of the second century BC, revealed the vulnerability of the Baetis defensive line. R. Knapp writes, in his 'Aspects of the Roman Experience in Iberia, 206 – 100 BC', that 'the determining factor of rethinking of the southern border translated into a clear initiative of Roman expansion toward the north.'[9] However, in the early stages of this expansionist process, Rome, occupied by the military needs of other fronts, appeared to have maintained a defensive attitude on the peninsula, believing that the problem was minor and could be resolved by a base of military operations ordered to punish cities and tribes that turned hostile, or the annihilation the indigenous troops or bandit raiders that opposed them.[10] Because of Lusitanian incursion into Roman territory the Romans had to react, hence the start of the Lusitanian War.

Although this is what Roman historiography states, Lopez Melero believes that the Roman conquest of Lusitania went deeper than the Romans claimed. The ability of Rome to overcome any indigenous resistance on the peninsula when given a favourable combination of sufficient troops and a competent command structure meant they were undefeatable. From a military point of view Viriathus and his successors were doomed from the onset of the war, for the behaviour Rome displayed towards the Iberians indicated that their main motive was territorial expansion to economically exploit annexed areas and safeguard Roman citizens.[11]

The decision to extend the territory further north from the Baetis River after the Servilianus peace treaty of 140 BC was made so as to pacify the troublesome Lusitanian tribes once and for all, but more importantly to stop them owning fertile farmland that had been hard fought for when it was taken away from the Carthaginians. Giving it away to a barbarian would have been a disgrace.

An important factor Lopez Melero mentions that helped thwart Viriathus' claim to the title of the Romulus of Hispania was the ethnic identification, social and geographical spread of integrated elements that sided with him. There is a serious documentary deficiency on the subject, not only because of lack of data, but because some of that which exists is not reliable; overall, Roman sources show that Viriathus became a character of legend, and that, moreover, there is a natural tendency of national historiography to rehabilitate the image of the Roman provincial governors, as the enemy who often used foul play in the defence of their interests, to build up their opponent, Viriathus, to a status of hero. All these deviations and adhesions have been adulterated to make up for the gaps in information and the inability to geographically identify many of the cities mentioned in the classical sources as being involved directly or indirectly with Viriathus' campaigns. It is also sad that there is no information to determine who the chieftains under his command were, what areas they were from, their social class or what political relationships they had with Viriathus. And, of course, the question is further complicated when we consider the population centres that were not Lusitanian but joined Viriathus' cause.

Another factor is the connections Viriathus had with indigenous areas that were not Lusitanian.[12] This indigenous involvement in Viriathus' cause suggests that there was a combination of interests between the Lusitanians and cities from the south, on the basis that a unified action was necessary to achieve independence from Rome, which would be beneficial for both parties: the Lusitanians could establish their own state, and the others would be free from the power that oppressed these tribes, thus the presence of those cities that rallied to Viriathus' cause helped to strengthen those ties.[13] This coalition, which began to extend to other Iberian regions, conferred viability to Viriathus' cause, giving him a reasonable chance of victory against Rome; it did not last long, however, for though the cities were united for his cause, it was the cities and not Viriathus' army which truly suffered the punishment from Rome, weakening these strong supporters, who would identify themselves as the losers of the conflict. Had Viriathus effectively doubled his army, his cause may have had the potential to shift the tide of the war in his favour, but as Viriathus did not expand his army, it instead debilitated his war effort, shifting the tide towards the Romans. That is why the balance of Viriathus' rise to power was constantly threatened.[14]

The final assessment of Lopez Melero's statements leads me to list three fundamental factors that stopped Viriathus becoming the Romulus of Hispania: 1) Had Viriathus effectively doubled his army, his cause may have had the potential to shift the tide of war in his favour; but as Viriathus did not expand his army the capacity of his resistance and subversion was limited due to disagreements about who was leader; 2) his capacity to stir up trouble was affected by internal factors of instability that Rome at times capitalized on; 3) Viriathus' death was unquestionably the factor that presented to the Romans the decisive key for completely ending Lusitanian resistance, so it was imperative that the Romans neutralize him as quickly as possible.

Though some historians state that the end of the war was due to an impulse of Lusitanian generosity, others argue that luck put Viriathus in a favourable situation to accomplish his personal ambition: to become absolute ruler of an independent Lusitania. Thus Viriathus took a risk in the hope that the Senate would ratify the treaty. But it did not, making his dream of becoming Romulus of Hispania just a dream.

Unfortunately the terms of the treaty are very ambiguous. But it is probable that it considered Viriathus '*amicu populi Romani*' and allowed his partisans to establish themselves in their own little kingdom as Roman subjects within Roman territory. In some sense, it would have been understandable if the Senate had ratified the peace treaty, because it would have been advantageous to the Romans. As a 'friend of the Romans', Viriathus would not be able to restart his war against Rome, or support any of Rome's enemies, but have to provide Lusitanian support to Roman legionnaires. If the Lusitanians were not uprooted they would draw some advantage from the armistice, for the cities involved in Viriathus' cause would gain some benefits. The treaty would have virtually dashed any possibility of the Iberians returning to lead future hostile actions against the Romans. Though he may have curbed any possible Roman intervention in Lusitania, the bellicose Lusitanians, the destabilizing agents, at least in the south, would have become Roman subjects and thus generators of profits for Rome.

However, this interpretation does not seem to convince some historians, who say it's hard to believe that Viriathus was lucky to find himself in an excellent position to give the Romans a definitive blow by forcing them into a treaty, or that Servilianus, after suffering a major defeat, convinced the Senate to revoke the treaty.

Viriathus'peace terms, as stated by Appian, referred to land concessions for his people.[15] This non-Roman treaty placed demands on Rome that made them think that they were being forced to recognized the independence of former Roman controlled cities and territories that were now in Viriathus' hands; the Romans refused to ratify the treaty which was '*pax in aequibus condicionibus facta*' ('done in conditions of equality') and seen by the Roman Senate as '*deformis*' ('of a shameful peace') as Livy says.[16] The Romans at that time felt that the relinquishing of these lands was not very important compared to the neutralization of Viriathus which was important above all else because to continue their conquest of the Iberian Peninsula they had to defeat Viriathus and the Celtiberians to expand north of the Guadalquivir River. So it is possible the Senate considered him a threat, for they had now to recognize a new independent power in their sphere of influence, so it was necessary that they not ratify the treaty.

Several members of the Senate, as well as Caepio, perhaps understood that Viriathus could increase his domain in Iberian areas that had not submitted themselves to Rome's control, thus increasing his power at Rome's expense. It was imperative, therefore, for Rome to conduct military campaigns to quell Viriathus and reduce the nucleus of Iberian independence that was causing financial difficulties for Rome's other enterprises. Perhaps Caepio and several Senate members saw the dangers of Viriathus becoming known as the Romulus of Hispania. According to Appian, the Senate resisted recommencing hostilities against the Lusitanians in an open fashion, secretly authorizing Scipio to irritate Viriathus into action so he could be blamed for restarting the war.They thought Viriathus would be seen to be breaking his own treaty.

Although I have mentioned why he may have wanted the war to continue, we cannot establish the exact reasons that prompted Servilianus Caepio to seek the necessary authorization of the Senate. Though it is possible that he may have been motivated by simple personal ambition or the aspiration to loot and seek glory and triumph, it is possible that perhaps he saw from a political standpoint that Viriathus was still a threat to Rome if it recognized Lusitania as an independent nation.

This new political situation of breaking the peace treaty may have enhanced Viriathus' power and increased the scope of his domain in areas still not subject to Roman control,which could be annexed by any of the two parties without violation of the *'amicitia'*. Thus Viriathus' growing power could multiply into a major military force to be reckoned with and perhaps later cost Rome dearly, so the decision to break the treaty in 141 BC was of great significance to Rome's expansion of its Iberian empire.

But for us to test this theory, we would have to know the type of political bonds that linked Viriathus to the populations or cities that depended on him. But we know very little in that respect. The only thing that seems clear is that both the Romans and the Iberians had recognized Viriathus as a military leader. It is also probable that Rome foresaw an embryo of a *regnum*, justifying the Senate's desire to destroy the rebellion. The urgency with which the Senate intervened by breaking the peace indicates that he appeared very charismatic and with a strong following.

As for the title *amicus populi Romani*, from the constitutional Roman point of view it was granted on certain occasions to foreign kings and princes who had befriended Rome. It was also at times granted to certain prestigious foreign individuals that had presented themselves in a good light in the eyes of the Senate. Besides this titbit of information, the Latin and Greek sources lack terms that truly expressed Viriathus' royal status, so scholars cannot be sure that he reached something more than just being a tribal chief and rebel general.

The terms that are used in the sources superficially indicate his position as 'king'. Diodorus uses the term *dynastés*. But this word is ambiguous and could classify a *regulus* (a petty king of a small state). The image Diodorus uses is too conventional and does not determine Viriathus' political status. But according to Roman writers he was a 'barbarian king' who had outstanding ethical and individual qualities that functioned socially in an uncomplicated manner. Besides being married to nobility, Viriathus was never pronounced king nor did he descend from a long line of a royal household. Thus the term dynasty is deceptive and does not strictly denote royal origins.

According to most classical authors, Caepio bribed the three future assassins that were sent by Viriathus to negotiate the peace treaty. Diodorus defends the Romans, saying the ambassadors proposed the murder to Caepio in exchange for personal safety and riches. Regardless, the responsibility for Viriathus' death still falls upon the Romans and the three assassins. It is possible that the assassins decided to kill Viriathus not just to guarantee their personal safety or get rich, but to obtain for their city favourable conditions once they returned to their homes.

Diodorus writes that the three traitors were from Urso. According to Appian they appeared before Caepio with a peace proposal, but were bribed. Though Viriathus continued to hold on to his power in Lusitania, he had lost the accession of the southern cities, which were at this point at the mercy of Rome and had began to suffer the costs of repression. It is credible that these three individuals from a southern city decided to assassinate Viriathus not for their personal safety, which was not at the time especially threatened, or to get rich quick, but to obtain for their city favourable conditions from the Romans. This could have been the context alluded to by Diodorus, who blamed the three men for assassinating Viriathus. Viriathus' death, due to an error in his judgment in choosing his companions, left open the question of whether he was truly the Romulus of Hispania.

Viriathus, Warrior King

Viriathus had a series of virtues held by warriors that were admired by populations that lived warrior lifestyles. He was, according to the ancient texts, a warrior who sought a warrior's way of life and the only thing that he wanted was prestige and esteem, measured by the honours his people had rendered to wise and courageous warriors before him. Valour and fighting prowess were fundamentally part of a warrior's life, but to be a king he needed oratory skills and generosity to his people too. These values in the end transformed him into a hero, and at his funeral his followers consecrated him as such. He was exalted to cult status for it was an important and substantial element in Iberian culture to honour the life of a warrior who had given so much to his people.

From an Indo-European ideological point of view, Viriathus' demeanour basically described him as lance-bearing and behaving like a warrior (uncivilized).[17]Various examples exist to support this idea. The first point comes in the form of how he recruited his warriors, who were loyal to their leader until death.[18] The second example is that Viriathus is presented as the warrior chief of a group of warlike people, whose members were personally linked to him through a warrior culture.[19] This shows that his true vocation was not banditry, as most historians claim, but military, putting him in Dumézil's Indo-European trifunctional category of the warrior class. This can be vaguely seen in the classical texts, placing a value on his military virtue in a positive way.

The classical texts make references to the capacities that made him a great leader. The texts give a few examples of him undergoing a life of hard self-discipline, austerity and privacy, making him a true warrior. But on the other hand there is also a negative side that a warrior hero should not follow. Cassius Dio describes 'the three sins of the warrior', things a hero or king should avoid while manifesting the qualities specific to a warrior's character.[20] Viriathus' personality seemed to have avoided them, making him an incorruptible hero. He was admired by Cicero who presented him as an example of justice, austerity and incorruptibility, as seen in various passages, such as in Book 2 of *De Officiis*.

Though Viriathus was from the start a barbaric hero, he came to be considered at the end of his life a king, so to speak. In the classical texts he is characterized by an 'internal beauty', as Muñoz puts it.[21] This is the 'beauty of spirit of the superior man' that correlates with his physical and internal aspects. However, there were negative values present as well.

In the final analysis J. Alvar believes that although the classical texts viewed this ancient Roman enemy as a bandit for many years after his death, his destiny was determined by his virtues, measured largely on the scale of a warrior's value system, and he became a national hero. Viriathus was a popular military leader and effective enough to successfully have faced the Roman army, giving him the attributes of a hero; but his success had not been so pernicious that it provoked a bitterness as well as admiration among his enemies and admirers.

His condition as leader of a 'primitive people' allowed the attribution of all the characteristics of a hero and transformed his story into a model of living in righteous agreement with nature and himself. Diodorus sought in Viriathus the representation of moral good, a mirror that reflected the lost qualities of Rome. Through Viriathus he attempted to recover or make Romans see, if they wanted to read between the lines, that Rome needed to get back on track and become righteous again to assure its political domain and territorial gains throughout the known world.

So the question remains, was Viriathus a warrior hero or a warrior king? One cannot give an exact response, because he lived in a Celtic world that was different from the Roman one. Unlike the Roman leaders, who usually reigned for their entire lives, Celtic kings were usually elected from among the warrior class; the king would have been the best of the warriors and one who did not commit the sins of a man. This can be the case for Viriathus. Viriathus was an excellent warrior, according to the classical texts 'the best of all', and he had the virtues needed to be elected as king. But was he truly king of the Lusitanians? That is for you, the reader, to decide.

Viriathus' Legacy: The Creation of a Legend

Viriathus is not just a historical character, a shepherd who became a warrior and a leader of a nation, but a hero. His life and exploits were transformed by the people into legend. Even during his lifetime, whenever people saw themselves forced to gather strength to defend their homeland from invasion, or suffered misfortunes, stories about Viriathus increased his mythical character. This interesting use of myth turned a simple man into a living legend, which has become an essential part of the Iberian Peninsula's history.

The Iberian Renaissance saw a resurgence in classical archaeology and the study of ancient classical literature. With this, Viriathus and his legend became linked to the Portuguese and Spanish spirit to the point that his name is attributed to the cohesion of nationalistic fervour even when both cultures face internal and external political problems, or during governmental repression brought on by fascist dictatorships, as during the last century. But at what moment did Viriathus become legend? When was his legend created and the myth of Viriathus elaborated? To answer this question, it is necessary to go back to the ancient texts.

Thanks to Diodorus and Appian, we have an idea about the military campaigns and politics of the Lusitanian War as well as about the character and virtues of Viriathus. The classical texts offer two images of the war. One presents the exalted virtues of Rome, which neither an exceptional and virtuous barbarian chief or his people could resist. The other offers the image of a man of exceptional character who had the ability and willpower to defeat Rome, but because of greed and jealously he was betrayed by his own people, showing that corruption still roamed wild. Though many of these ancient authors showed readers the power that Rome was, they still had a special sympathy for the Lusitanians and their leader, to the point that they considered him a model of moral values.

There is no doubt that most of the information about Viriathus' life and character are exemplary representations of a historical figure as a model of virtue. They are also ideas that projected the simple happiness of primitive people who were born in the fields and in contact with nature: frugal, austere, disciplined, capable of resisting the asperities of the time and of controlling their desires.[22] All of the aspects referenced in the classical sources presuppose that the first step in the elaboration of the myth of Viriathus rested on local lore that grew into a full-blown legend in the Iberian Peninsula. In Portuguese and Spanish history, his story was tentatively repeated without end in every regional locality, so in time he became a national symbol.

This idea of a 'national hero' was not the case during Viriathus' lifetime, for Portugal and Spain did not exist yet. But as the centuries passed these local tribes united, thanks to Romanization, and began to form a national identity that brought with it the story of Viriathus and the peninsula's history.

The process of Portuguese appropriation of Viriathus, or the connection of his character to the geographical space known as Portugal, began with André de Resende and Father Bernardo de Brito during the late fifteenth century.[23] It was brought into the twentieth century by A. Guerra and C. Fabião, whoconsidered ancient Lusitania a pre-configuration of modern Portugal.

In the late nineteenth century Augusto Ferreira do Amaral wrote that Viriathus was the voice of the Portuguese Renaissance for he was the embryo of the Portuguese homeland, the first symbol of its identity and of differentiation from the other people on the peninsular.[24] Sergio Franklin de

Sousa Rodrigues claims that the Portuguese oral tradition contributed to Viriathus becoming the mythical hero who founded the Portuguese nation out of the ashes of Lusitania.[25]

However the Spaniards also began to claim Viriathus as their own. The first text to exalt Viriathus and the Lusitanians came from Afonso X in his work on the history of Spain, *Crónica Geral de Espanha* (1344). He represents Viriathus as a herculean hero without a country who fought the Romans to establish a Hispanic nation for his people.

With the onset of the Renaissance, the classics were rediscovered in Portugal and many historians of that age began to identify and recognize ancient Lusitania as Portugal's precursor, such as in a 1532 work entitled Auto da Lusitania by Gil Vicente. Also from these early writings come two epic poems that made Viriathus into a Portuguese hero. The first is the famous *Os Lusíadas* (1572) from Luis Vaz de Camões, in the mid-fifteenth century, and the second is *Viriato Trágico* (1699),written by Brás Garcia of Mascarenhas at the end of the sixteenth century. This last author was an enthusiastic defender of restoring the Portuguese monarchy of João IV from the Spanish — ending the Iberian Union — thus making his poem an authentic nationalistic manifestation that claimed Viriathus, like the king, came from a long line of Portuguese heroes that had defended their homeland from foreign invaders.[26]

Historical study of Viriathus did not start until 1593 with Resende's book, *Antiguidades da Lusitania*. Resende's work marked the beginning of archaeology and anthropology in Portugal, for his studies stated that the Portuguese were descended from the Lusitanians, and Portugal was historical Lusitania. This was followed by Brito's 1597 *Monarquia Lusitania*. He tried to justify the idea of a history of the Portuguese homeland from one of Noah's sons in antiquity to his own time. The second volume of his two-volume book identified the Portuguese and the Lusitanians as one in the same. Though it was 'historical' the main objective of the book was to glorify the Lusitanians and the hero that had opposed the Roman Empire, arguing that the Portuguese should follow their example and free themselves of the Spanish yoke that had occupied Portuguese territory since 1580. It helped stir up patriotic fire for the launch of the Restoration War (1640–1668).[27]

During the eighteenth century, Spanish historian J.F. Masdeus also contributed and reinforced the Portuguese appropriation of Viriathus' legend in a detailed description that proclaimed Viriathus' character to be Portuguese, not Lusitanian. This work enforced the idea that the Portuguese were the true descendants of the Lustianians.[28]

The nineteenth century saw the emergence of major historical studies and archeological science. This was the beginning for many scholars, historians, archaeologists and researchers who began to distance themselves more and more from the imaginative antiquarian. The revision of Portugal's history began to change or debunk many of the myths that had been created. One of the individuals that led this revision was the particularly lucid Alexandre Herculano.

Herculano, the creator of scientific historiography in Portugal, was the biggest advocate of rejecting any continuity between the Lusitanian and the Portuguese — a theory that was then systematically repeated in all the manuals and school curricula in Portugal from the end of the nineteenth century until the early mid-twentieth century. This meant that in the middle of the nineteenth century Viriathus' stature as a national hero underwent a downturn. This refers to the Lusitanian resistance and the episode of Viriathus as a man born from the Lusitanian tribe and not Portuguese.[29] However, Herculano's theory was largely rejected by de Vasconcelos, who continued to proclaim Resende's theory that the Portuguese were related to the Lusitanians.[30] Though he was the first to attempt a systemization of Iberian tribes that inhabited Lusitania, his investigative work was driven by a fundamental objective to prove that there was a direct relationship between the Lusitanians and the Portuguese. De Vasconcelos' claim was re-enforced by Portugal's renowned archaeologist Francisco Martins Samento's archaeological excavations of *castros* in northern Portugal. There are scholars that continue to affirm this identification.

Just as in Portugal, in Spain the Viriathus legend also thrived throughout the ages. At the start of the 1600s, Viriathus was recognized by both the Portuguese and Spanish as the first Iberian hero to become a legend, thanks to two of Miguel de Cervantes' works: *Novelas Exemplares* (1613) and the play *O Cerco de Numância* (1585), in which he uses a character named Viriathus. In *Don Quixote* (1605–1615), the eponymous character advises the *cónego* to stop reading books about cavaliers and instead read accounts of the great heroes from antiquity, among them Viriathus. Another early author to mention Viriathus was Félix Lope de Vega y Carpio who wrote *La Arcadia* (1598), which compared Viriathus to Hannibal and Julius Caesar. This was followed by González Bustos' 1668 comedy entitled *O Espanhol Viriato*. During this same time, Jose Zorrilla dedicated several poems to this ancient hero. A tragedy was written a century and half later by Hernando de Pizarro, titled *Viriato* (1843). All of these have Viriathus as being from Spain. So like the Portuguese, various Spanish authors between have exalted Viriathus; they added a Spanish character and birth to his story. But the first historical work on the subject came from Father Juan de Mariana. In his 1623 history of Spain, known as *História Geral de Espanha*, he called Viriathus 'the liberator of all Spain.'

As a result, by the eighteenth century many Spanish scholars were referring to Viriathus as a Spanish hero, a Celtiberian rather then a Lusitanian. Others were more specific, calling him a Valencian — from the region in south eastern Spain. By the end of the nineteenth century, Spanish authors and artists were representing Viriathus as a Celtiberian. So strong was the belief that he was Celtiberian that the Spanish sculptor Eduardo Barrón González, in 1884 the first person to create a statue of Viriathus, gave his work to the Spanish city of Zamora, which is near the Portuguese border at a site known today as Plaza de Viriato.

The Legacy Continues

At the onset of the twentieth century, Portuguese and Spanish scholars and historians began to debate about what tribe or region Viriathus was from. From this early time period several significant works were written. In 1900, Spanish historian A Arenas Lopez was the first that I know of to write a work that debated Viriathus' regional and national identity and was not lost or destroyed (Mariana had written an entire biography of Viriathus). In Arenas Lopez's book, *Reivindicaciones históicas: Viriato no fué portugués si no celtibero: su biografia*, he indicates that Viriathus was a Celtiberian tribal chief.[31] His 1907 work, entitled *La Lusitania Celtíbera*, claimed that Lusitania was part of the Celtiberian realm.[32] Starting in 1920, Spanish historian M. Peris came to the forefront with four research papers in 1926 stating that Viriathus was from the region of Valencia, but this theory, like the other Spanish and Portuguese regional theories that continued to be produced throughout the twentieth century, was not taken seriously because it mostly dealt with local lore and myth rather than scientific evidence. On the Portuguese side, Teófilo Braga wrote *Viriatho* (1904), a historical novel describing in vivid and colourful detail the war years until the warrior's death. Despite the fact that it was fiction, Braga made strong suggestions throughout the book that Viriathus was Lusitanian.

Surprisingly, one person who contributed most to the incorporation of Viriathus into Portugal's history and psyche — and those of the rest of the western world — was German historian and archeologist Adolf Schulten with his work *Viriato* (1917), translated into Spanish in 1920 and Portuguese in 1927. His work on Viriathus and his three-volume masterpiece on pre-Roman Hispania made a large impact on the Iberian Peninsula's anthropological, archaeological and historical community.

Schulten's work on ancient Hispania has had a profound effect on all those who came after him. In his work he wrote that the Lusitanians were of Celtic origin but had their own identity and culture, unlike the Celtiberians. But opposing Schulten's Celtic hypothesis, some Iberian scholars, historians, archaeologists and researchers have argued that the Lusitanians were of a native Iberian origin. At the very least we can say they were influenced by Celtic migration to the Iberian Peninsula from Central Europe, but the question of origins remains open to this day. As for Schulten, his work remains the basis for historical research on the subject and is the most cited work on the history of pre-Roman Hispania.

Fascism had a major influence on the dictators of Portugal and Spain in their 'struggle for the independence of their people, threatened by foreign domination'. This influence is evident during the Spanish Civil War when a unit of 10,000 Portuguese volunteers chose the name of Viriathus (*Os Viriatos*) under which to fight on the nationalist side during the Spanish Civil War in the 1930s, as well as in the Second World War when Portugal sent Portuguese volunteers to fight alongside Spain's pro-Nazi division, known as the 'Blue Division', against Communist Russia.

The exaltation of Viriathus as a 'Portuguese hero and leader' and commemorations of the foundation of the new Portuguese Republic in 1932 helped give weight to the profile of its charismatic leader, Antonio de Oliveira Salazar. It is in this sense that one should understand the work of A. Athayde, translator of Schulten's work 'Viriathus', who defends the Portuguese origin of the hero. Meanwhile, J. Lopes Dias, in a speech for the inauguration of a Viriathus statue by sculptor Mariano Benlliureat Viseu, hailed Viriathus as Portugal's first national hero, and related this to the coming of the New State, while proclaiming that the region of Beira Alta was Viriathus' homeland.Victor de Tusculano further helped engrave into the Portuguese psyche Virathus as the precursor to Portuguese history.[33] Though all of these individuals follow Schulten's work as historical proof, their theories are more based on nationalistic or regionalistic ideologies than historical accuracy.

But in 1943, Damião Peres published a book titled *Como Nasceu Portugal* (*How Portugal was Born*),which caused some turmoil with the newly established fascist scholarly regime. His work devastated the theory of an umbilical connection between the Portuguese and the Lusitanians. He had the idea that the formation of the nation did not start with Viriathus but with the political will of Portugal's first king, Afonso Henriques. Peres' statement angered Portugal's top scholar, Antonio Augusto Mendes Correia, and the fascist regime, which had revised Portugal's history by contesting Herculano's work and going back to claims that the Portuguese were the true descendants of the Lusitanians and that the Portuguese nation began with Viriathus.

The fascist regime, known as the *Estado Novo* (New State) and lasting from 1932 to 1976, not only took control of the military, administration, press, religion and the people's will, but attempted to revise the the country's entire history. Ignoring past theories about Celtic origins, the fascist revision of history began with the Lusitanians belonging to an early race of hominids that were different from the other known races such as the Neanderthals. There was a 'newly discovered' race of men, the fascist government said, called '*homo taganus*' who had lived on the banks of Riberia de Muge, a tributary of the Tagus River in the district of Santarém.[34]

During the regime of Salazar's *Estado Novo*, the government made the question of race fundamental to national pride within its colonial empire, and so it was important to maintain and propagandize the idea of the umbilical relationship with the Lusitanians. Thus the history taught in primary schools and high schools transmitted the idea that the 'purity' of the Portuguese bloodline began with the *homo taganus* and that the formation of the Portuguese homeland started with Viriathus' Lusitania. It exalted Lusitanian bravery and Viriathus' dedication to his homeland, which all Portuguese citizens should mimic.

The Portuguese state claimed, and still does claim, the honour of being the homeland of Viriathus or at least possessing the grave where he may be buried. Though most Portuguese believe that he was from the region of Beira Alta, where the Serra de Estrela is situated, other regions in Portugal contest this and claim their towns as his birthplace, such as Póvoa Velha, Seia, Gouveia, Loriga, Folgosinho Valenzim, Videmonte, Sena Covilhã Termo de Lumiar and even Viseu. Viseu has been made famous for its ancient military encampment, dubbed Cava de Viriato, which according to local tradition is where Viriathus took refuge during his later campaigns against the Romans.[35]

Though Viriathus has been seen as a Portuguese hero, some historians and scholars refused to follow these nationalistic theories and instead studied the Lusitanian realm through historical evidence. On one side, Portugal is an integral part of occidental civilization, heirs of the Roman legacy and of Romanization; on the other hand, Viriathus represented the opposition to Rome and resistance to Romanization. How can we possibly reconcile both elements into Portuguese history? The solution is to place Viriathus and Romanization in two different chapters. At the beginning of the twentieth century only the story of Viriathus and his resistance to the Roman conquest was taught in the Portuguese school system. It was not until the end of the fascist regime in 1975 that Romanization and its effect on the country began to be taught, impressing on the population not only the Viriathus story but the formation of the Roman colony that would later become Portugal.

Near the end of the dictatorship of the Salazar regime the nationalistic theories of the aforementioned authors became so contradictory it was difficult to understand or make sense of them. When the Portuguese became involved in African colonial wars in the 1960s and 1970s, they faced African rebels who through Portuguese indoctrination had come to identify themselves with Viriathus. His consequential emergence as not just a Portuguese hero but an African one prompted many Portuguese to think about how unjust the colonies were. Little by little, patriotic reverence for Viriathus began to dissipate, and by 1968 it had almost disappeared from school curricula.[36]

With the end of the dictatorship in 1976 a revision of the Viriathus legend emerged with a new generation of historians such as Alarcão, Rui Centeno, M. Cardoza, Gundel and J.L. Inês Vaz. They used historical facts and research about the subject for scholarly purposes instead of for propaganda, and did not use myth and legend as factual data.

In Spain, it was not until the beginning of the twentieth century that the Viriathus legend acquired a new meaning and would be used in the defence of nationalism and regionalism there. Arenas Lopez was the first to state and defend the theory that Viriathus was not Portuguese or Spanish but Celtiberian.[37] Costa also thought that Viriathus was of Celtiberian origin rather than Lusitanian and insisted that these 'facts' were based on ideas already expressed in the works of Mariana and Schulten. Costa's own work, however, was based more on social and economic aspects of Hispania, which were later further developed by J. Caro Baroja and A. Garcia y Bellido in the 1980s.[38] A. Gonzalez del Campo and Vitor Chamorro considered Viriathus a Lusitanian from the Spanish province of Estremadura, and like these two men, many poets and writers from the area proclaimed him to be from there.[39] Though these historians believed that Viriathus was from Central Spain, Peris turned Viriathus into an Iberian from the region of Valencia.[40] Like the Portuguese, Spanish revisionist historians began to theorize that perhaps Viriathus was not from Lusitania but from other regions in Spain. According to J. Osório de Castro there are more than seventy towns across Spain that claim that they are Viriathus' birthplace or place of death.[41]

These nationalist and regionalist ideas were also used by painters and authors inspired by this period in the history of the Iberian Peninsula to contribute to and spread the idolization of Viriathus. The same nationalist ideas about him were placed in Spanish schoolbooks in the 1930s, so the young generation could learn how the poor shepherd became a great commander of the Spaniards and fought against Roman legions for ten years. As with the Portuguese, the revision of the Viriathus story in Franco's Spain was undertaken to instil patriotism and confidence in a generation that had been treated badly for so many years by its former government, and to show that anyone could rise above their status.

The nationalistic Spanish version of Viriathus appears as the precursor of Franco in post-war 1945, when A. Garcia y Bellido published *Bandos y Guerrilhas en las Luchas con Roma*. It showed Viriathus as a warrior who fought for the independence of his people, but the main argument of the work was that guerrilla warfare was something genuinely Hispanic that has been followed by other cultures throughout the centuries.[42]

Schoolbooks of that time transmitted the image of Viriathus as a hero of the independence war of his 'Spanish homeland', pointing out that even the Romans ended up recognizing Viriathus as the leader of the Lusitanian resistance and that only by betrayal did they succeed in putting down this 'rebellion'. Mid-twentieth century Spanish history compared Viriathus and Franco as builders of the Spanish nation.To assure the people's fidelity, the Portuguese and Spanish fascist governments both transformed the myth of Viriathus into one of nationalistic heroism. After Franco's death and the end of his fascist regime, new and revised literature about Viriathus began to appear in the late 1970s, and by the mid-1980s all nationalistic and regionalistic propaganda literature had disappeared. The myth of Viriathus in Spain, just as in Portugal, faded away.

But these nationalistic interpretations should not be confused with historical works in which Portuguese and Spanish scholars have attempted to develop their theories based on fact, despite being seen as anti-Salazar and anti-Franco at the end of the Second World War. It was these educated scholars who began to down play Viriathus' mythical status and place him as a historical figure: a bandit, warrior, general and a ruler of the Lusitanians, not the Spanish or Portuguese.

The myth of Viriathus, which began with the classical authors of ancient Rome and continued through the ages, is built around a man from an ancient society, whose values differentiated substantially from those of the Romans and who fought until the end against the inevitable submission to the might of a much more powerful enemy. Though the Portuguese and Spanish dictatorships ended in the mid-1970s, one can still point out how the fascist interpretation of history had an influence over the Iberian population. For the last thirty-four years both countries have still seen Viriathus as a national hero.

It was not until 2000 that the first realistic biography of Viriathus was published in Spain by Muñoz, a professor and Spanish historian. His work, published in Portuguese and Spanish, was the culmination of previous studies by Iberian historians on more specific aspects of the life and times of Viriathus and the Lusitanians.

As an overall analysis, literary works on Viriathus and the Lusitanians can be seen in three clear phases. From the classical authors to the onset of the Renaissance, Viriathus was represented as the ideal Iberian hero who apparently believed in no borders. But that changed when Portugal and Spain began to compete against one other over land and sea power: Viriathus was portrayed as a national or regional hero who fought an unjust enemy. The idea of him being a national hero lasted until the demise of the fascist governments of both countries at the end of the twentieth century. The nationalistic ideal began to fade away as a new archeological evidence countered nationalistic tradition, ushering in a clearer picture of Viriathus as a product of an ancient people from the Iberian Peninsula: the Lusitanians.

Not only was Viriathus part of the world of history and literature, but also of art. In paintings, sculpture and music, artists were sensitive to Lusitanian culture, but the one problem they did face in the Viriathus myth was his physiognomy: how to create an image of a character known only through texts in which no reference to his physical appearance is made? Still, artists came up with their own renditions of what he may have looked like and what the Lusitanians wore. Viriathus is represented in various ways, from shepherd to warrior.

The oldest artistic representation of Viriathus can be seen in an edition of *Brás Garcia de Mascarenhas*. Viriathus has one hand raised as if taking an oath of revenge, for he is surrounded by the bodies of his compatriots, freshly slaughtered by Galba. In this representation the Lusitanians and Viriathus are in Roman clothing rather than traditional Lusitanian grab. Perhaps the reason the Lusitanians were drawn wearing Roman clothing and not presented visually as barbarians, as the classical texts claim they were, was because Iberian Renaissance painters and scholars did not want to give a bad image of their ancestors.

As time passed it became disgraceful to portray this Lusitanian hero wearing Roman attire after the way he was was treated by the Romans for being their main Iberian enemy. In later drawings the correct, more primitive clothing type, corresponding to Lusitanian rather than Hellenic apparel, was portrayed. The first attempt to depict this type of primitive dress is in Portuguese painter Augusto Roquemont's *Juramento dos Lusitanos*, displayed at the National Museum of Soares of the Reis in Oporto. Viriathus is portrayed in a tunic and leather belt, with a beard and long hair, barefoot and armed with a lance, giving him a character composition of a warrior.

Though over a dozen paintings of Viriathus had been created by the end of the eighteenth century, a sculpture of him was not made until Eduardo Barrón's 1884 work. Viriathus is represented as a Greco-Roman athlete who stands bare-chested, again with his right arm extended as if making an oath, while holding in his left hand a king's sceptre with his tunic suspended over his forearm. The statue is raised on a unfinished, jagged granite pedestal, said to represent the hills where Viriathus walked. At his feet is a symbol of the beginnings of his life, a sheep. At the base of the statue the inscription reads '*Terror Romanorum*'. This is the only Viriathus statue in which he holds a sceptre identifying him as a king. This statue, according to Muñoz, became an important work for other sculptors to follow, for it possesses very concrete iconographic elements that truly characterize the hero — our protagonist.[43]

Another well-known statue of Viriathus stands in Viseu near the famous Cava de Viriato, where the vestige of a former Roman army camp still stands. The Ourivesaria Artisticas Aliança in Oporto commissioned Benliure to create a beautiful piece of work to commemorate the 300th anniversary of Portuguese independence from Spain. The dioramic statue is set around a large piece of granite with small boulders surrounding it, emphasizing that the Portuguese nation is strong and immortal; the high rock also stands for the Serra da Estrela where he had positioned his army against countless Roman legions. As for the statue, a bearded and long-haired Viriathus stands at the top of a rock's ledge in the middle of the 'wild mountains', in an attack position, dressed in a tunic and a fur cloak with his shield and *falcate* at the ready, signifying his invincibility. A man who would have obtained complete victory over Hispania had he not been treacherously assassinated. On the side of the rocky crag that serves as a pedestal, some companions await his signal to attack, while a wolf bares a threatening snarl at the approaching enemy. At the base there is an inscription and a dedication to the *Mocidade Portuguesa* (the Portuguese Youth Movement).[44] The entirety of this beautifully crafted work shows how nature, man and animal share the burning of a warrior's passion to sacrifice himself in the defence of his sacred land, bringing to the Portuguese psyche courage, energy and the untamable feeling of independence.

The statue at Zamora, Spain, presents Viriathus as a king with the artistic classical stance of a warrior.[45] The statue at Viseu, Portugal, is an austere representation of the barbaric highlander in contact with nature, with a face well roasted by time and bad weather.[46]According to Carlos Fabião and Amílcar Guerra, 'It is the most interesting for it corresponds well to the stoic archetype that is found in the Hellenistic historiography.'[46] Both are interesting, for the one in Zamora is of a perfectly classical nude, and the one in Viseu is of a stoic nature.

Since 1940 several other statues have been erected, the most recent in 1998 in the town of Cabanas de Viriato, Portugal. The Spanish post office commissioned a 20 cent euro stamp in 2005 bearing Viriathus, showing its continuous remembrance of the hero. Since the publication of Muñoz's book in 2004 and a second edition in 2006, there has been a popular resurgence of interest in the story, and several other books about Viriathus and the Lusitanian culture have been published. In 2009 a documentary, the first of its kind, was made, followed by a television docudrama series in 2010 on Spanish television channel Antenna 3, which can today be watched online.[47]

All of these representations show the permanence of the values attributed to Viriathus throughout the last few centuries. Historical recognition of Viriathus has placed him among similar heroes from antiquity, along with the necessary romantized sceneries, Greco-Roman decorations and allusions to the 'good savage'. The nationalistic ideas of the nineteenth century vitalized the image of a Lusitanian man who acquired an iconography exclusively from literary knowledge, which made artists capable of painting and sculpting him.

Overall, Roman historians and writers who honoured Viriathus' memory in their writings enhanced his fame by eulogizing his strategy and military tactics, while supplying him with a personality and morals. Thus Viriathus'fame is not lost to us. The Romans recognized his greatness and though their experience in dealing with him improved their military efficacy and their foreign policies when handling other tribes throughout their growing empire.

According to J. Alvar, it is not logical to think that the classical authors transmitted information on their heroic enemies without subjective interpretation.[48] He finds it necessary to discover the motives that led to the creation, adaptation, assimilation, usurpation or rejection of the alienated hero in Roman historiography. After Viriathus' death he was transformed into an *exemplum* (moral) as an example of what a warrior should be. A simple reading of the texts demonstrates that the creation of a historiography of this type is aesthetic. On the other hand, it would be unthinkable to write so much historical information without producing the facts. This creates a larger problem of profiling, for many writers have used a degree of literary manipulation of these facts.

In the history of military warfare Viriathus occupies a place of honour in the category of guerrilla war. He was a master of guerrilla tactics and knew how to choose and plan this type of war. He fought it with amazing aptitude and with a dedicated force of warriors that impeded the Roman army's effectiveness. The free spirit of the Lusitanians and the Iberians in general can be seen in all their successes during those difficult centuries.

In final analysis, Viriathus was neither Portuguese nor Spanish but Lusitanian. He was, is, and will always be known as the 'Iberian' who fought Rome for the independence of not only the Lustianians but of all the tribes that inhabited the Iberian Peninsula.

Notes and References

CHAPTER 1

1   Polybius, 11.20.1; Livy 28.12.4; R. Corzo Sanchez, 'La secunda Guerra punica en la Betica', *Habis* 6, 1975, pp. 234-40

2   Richardson, J.S. *Hispaniae, Spain and the development of Roman imperialism, 218-82 BC*, Cambridge Univ. Press, London, 1986, pp. 54-55

3   Richardson, J.S., op. cit., p. 51; Curchin, Leonard, A., *Roman Spain*, Barnes & Noble Inc, NY, 1995, pp. 28-29

4   For a detailed look at the type of *imperium* that Roman commanders were given in Hispania see Richardson, J.S., op. cit., pp. 55-57, 75-77, 104-112

5   Today Sagunto is the capital of the district of Camp de Morvedre, which is located in the northern part of the province of Valencia. For a better understanding of the siege of Saguntum see http://en.wikipedia.org/wiki/Siege_of_Saguntum; Astin, A.E., 'Saguntum and the Origins of the Second Punic War', *Latomus* #26, 1967, pp. 577-596 and Richardson, J.S., op. cit., pp. 20-30

6   Richardson, J.S., op. cit., pp. 42-43

7   Ibid., p.43

8   For a more detailed look at the patterns of command during the war in Hispania see Richardson, J.S., *The Romans in Spain*, Blackwell Publishers Ltd, Oxford, 1996, pp. 35-43 and *Hispaniae*, p.42-43 and 55-57

9   The *comitia centuriata* was the democratic assembly of the Roman soldiers, while the *comitia tributa* was the democratic assembly of Roman citizens. For a better understanding of these two assemblies see http://en.wikipedia.org/wiki/Comitia_centuriata and http://en.wikipedia.org/wiki/Comitia_Tributa as well as G.W. Botsford, *Roman Assemblies*, New York, 1909. As for the subject of the election process for service in Hispania see, Richardson, J.S, op. cit., pp. 64-70 and 75

10   Livy, 21.61.6-11; 23.48.5

11   Livy, 28.25.9; 29.12; 34.11; for more details see Richardson, J.S., op. cit, pp. 57-58

12   Livy, 21.61.6 – 11; 23.48.5; Richardson, J.S., op. cit., p.57.

13   Livy, 21.60.3; 22.20.10-12; 21.1-8; 22.22.4-21; 23.49.14; 24.49.7-9 Polybius 3.76.2; 3.97.2; Sanctis, G. de., *Storia dei romani*, 4 vols. Turin/Florence 1907-1964, vol. III.2, 236, n.73.

14   Livy, 26.47.1-26.50.7, 28.15.14; Polybius, 10.17.6-8, 18.3-15, 19.3-7

15   Polybius, 10.6.3, 10.7.3 and 10.10.9; Livy, 26.41.20; Diodorus, 25.12

16   Livy, 21.11.13, 23.46.6, 24.47.8, 24.49.5, 24.49.7-8, 26.41.20

17   Ibid.; Polybius 10.6.3; 10.7.3

18   According to Professor J.S. Richardson there seems to be some confusion concerning which city his father and uncle were killed in. Many scholars claim that these two men were killed at Castax (Scipio's father) and Ilyrgia (Scipio's uncle). But in his research on the subject, Richardson writes that the Scipio in fact attacked the town of Castulo (the city was entirely destroyed in 1227 during the Reconquista) and Ilurco (today it is an ancient ruin near Pinos Puente) and not Castax and Ilyrgia, for in Pliny's work Natural History (3.13) he cites that Ilurco was where his uncle funeral pyre took place. As for Castulo, Livy (28.19-20) makes references to this city, while Appian calls it Castax for some unknown reason.

19   Livy 28.19 -20 Castulo and Iliturgi were names used by Appian, while the names of Castulo and Iliturgi where the names for the same city used by Livy, 32.127 and 32.128; as for Scipio's father and uncle's deaths see Appian 16.61 and Livy 25.32-36The details of these campaigns are not completely known, but it seems that the ultimate defeat and death of the two Scipiones was due to the desertion of the Celtiberians, who were bribed by Hasdrubal Barca, Hannibal's brother.

20   Appian, Ib, 32.127; 11 Livy 28.19.1-20.12; Appian Ib 32.127-31; Polybius 11.24.10.

21   Schulten, Adolf, 'Iliturgi', Hermes #28, 1928, pp. 288-301

22   Appian, 32.128; Livy 28.19 and 20 also describes the attack on both towns.

23   Appian, 32.129

24   Ibid., 32.129

25   Appian, 32.130-131; as for who was put in charge of the town, Appian just says a Castacian with a good reputation while Livy, 28.20.11-12, gives his name.

26   Appian, 32.131

27   Appian, 33.132-134

28   Livy, 28.22.18 - 26

29   Ibid.

30   Livy, 28.23.1-6

31   Appian, 33.136

32   Livy, 28.23.9

33   Livy, 28.23.7-8

34   Appian, 43.137; Appian writes that Marcius was elected by Scipio but in Livy's and Polybius' work it is Silanus who was put in charge. Professor Richardson believes the text is defective in that Μάρκος should be read as Μάρκιος, but Appian always writes Silanus as Σιλανός elsewhere. Richardson, J.S., *Appian: Wars of the Romans in Iberia*, Warminster, UK, 2000, p. 132

35   Appian, 34.138; Livy 28.24.5 Livy is the only person who states the location of the mutiny.

36   Gades was the last Carthaginian stronghold in Hispania after the Second Punic War.

37   Appian, 34.137 - 138

38   Livy, 28.24.5. Surco is the Roman name for the Júcar River. According to J.S. Richardson, the location of the camp could not have been the purpose of controlling the tribes that lived on the north side of the Ebro, and they were actually stationed at the mouth of the Júcar River. I agree with Richardson, for if the Romans were based at the Surco River it would have been impossible for 8,000 men to patrol such a vast area - the distance from the Júcar River to the nearest point of the Ebro River is about 140 miles (225 km). If the camp was on the Ebro River it would have made command and control very difficult in an area that was not completely pacified. It also would have made it difficult for military orders to arrive from Carthago Nova, some 248 miles away (400 km). So it is likely that Richardson is correct in his statement that the military base was only 124 miles away (200 km) from Carthago Nova, making it a bit easier to control 8,000 soldiers.

39   Livy, 28.24.9

40   Livy, 28.24.14. This is somewhat different from what Appian writes.

41   Livy, 28.24.16-17 He is the only source that names the mutiny's ringleaders.

42   Livy, 28.24.19-20

43   Appian, 35.141-142

44   Livy is the one who states the number of tribunes that were sent (28.25.5) and what the terms were and what went on during the meeting 28.25.6-15

45   For the entire episode see Appian verse 35 and 36; Livy, 28.26, 28.27, 28.28, 28.29; Polybius, 11.29

46   Appian, 36.146; Livy, 28.26.6For Scipio's speech see W.J., Bryan,' To His Mutinous Troops', in *The World's Famous Orations: Rome (218 B.C.– 84 A.D.)*, Rome, 1906; Livy is the one who mentions that there were five other involved in the mutiny.

47   Livy, 28.24

48   Livy, 28.25.9

49   Livy, 28.31.6-8

50   Livy, 28.34; As many as 2,000 Romans and allies fell in the battle; the wounded amounted to more than 3,000.

51   Appian, 37.148

52   Livy, 28.34.5

53   Livy, 28.34.7

54   Livy, 28,34.10. This is somewhat surprising for it was the traditional practice of the Romans, in the case of a conquered nation with whom no friendly relations had previously existed either through treaty or community of rights and laws, not to accept their submission or allow any terms of peace until all their possessions sacred and profane had been surrendered, hostages given, their arms taken away and garrisons placed in their cities.

55   Livy, 28.34.12

56   See above: this was the restart of the previous military operation against Gades just prior to Scipio's illness.

57   Livy, 28.36.1

58   Livy, 28.36.3-16

59   Livy, 28.37

60   Richardson, J.S., *Hispaniae: Spain and the development of Roman imperialism*, 218-82 BC, Cambridge Univ. Press.

61   Appian, 38.153; Livy 28.24, 28.37 and 32.2; Badian, E., 'The prefect at Gades', *Classical Philology* #49, 1954, p. 250-252; Richardson, J.S., op. cit., p. 61; Pellicer, M., Hurtado, V. and La Bandera, M.L. 'Corte estratigrafico de la Casa de Venus', in Italica: actas de las primeras journadas sobre excavciones en Italica', *Excavaciones arqueologicas in España 121*, 1982, p. 29-73; Richardson, J.S., *The Romans in Spain*, Blackwell Publishers Ltd, Oxford, 1996, p. 39 and 222. As for the founding of Italica, the town would become the forerunner of towns and cities that would eventually 'Romanize' the peninsula, but this would not happen until the reign of Julius Caesar, a century –and-a-half after its founding.

62   Richardson, J.S., *Hispaniae, Spain and the development of Roman imperialism*, 218-82 BC, p.63

63   Livy 28.38.2

64   Gamito, Teresa Júdice, 'The Celts in Portugal', *Journal of Interdisciplinary Celtic Studies*, University of Algarve, volume 6, p. 571-604.

65   Strabo 3.2.1-8; Polybius 34.9.8-11; Schulten, A., *Iberische Landeskunde*, Vol.I, Strasbourg, 1955-1957, p. 195-197. The Sierra Morena is a mountain range which stretches for 400 km east-west across southern Spain, forming the border of the central plateau (Meseta Central) of

Iberia, and providing the watershed between the valleys of the Guadiana River to the north and the Guadalquivir River to the south. It has valuable deposits of lead, silver, mercury, and other metals, some of which have been exploited since prehistoric times.

66   Muñoz, Mauricio P., *Viriato, O Herói Lusitano que lutou pela liberdade do seu povo*, Esfera dos Livros, Lisbon, 2006, p. 39

67   Ibid., p. 39

68   Livy, 29.1.19-20; cf. Appian, 38.156-7 and Diodorus, 26.22

69   Livy, 29.2.1-4

70   Livy, 29.2.6-7

71   Livy, 29.2.8

72   Livy 29.2.9- 11

73   Livy, 29.2.12-14

74   Livy 29.2.15- 20; As for the casualties it is questionable if that is an exact number to be used for propaganda purposes or if it actually happened.

75   Livy, 29.3.1 and 29.3.3

76   Livy, 29.3.2 and 29.3.4

77   Livy, 29.3.5-6; Appian 38.157

78   Livy 29.3.5 – 9

79   Appian, Ib, 38.157

80   Livy, 31.20.1-6

81   Livy, 31.49.7 Livy does not mention about Cethegus' elections but writes that a large Iberian army was routed in the Sedetan district in 200 BC that resulted in 15,000 Iberians being killed in that battle and seventy-eight standards taken.

82   An elected official of ancient Rome who was responsible for public works and games and who supervised markets, the grain supply, and water supply.

83   Livy, 33.27.1-4; Richardson, J.S., *Hispaniae*, p.69

84   Livy, 32.1.6

85   The ovation was a less-honoured form of the Roman triumph. An ovation was granted, when war was not declared on the state level, when an enemy was considered basely inferior, and when the general conflict was resolved with little to no bloodshed or danger to the army. For Lentulus' ovation see Livy 31.20; for Sertinius' ovation see Livy 33.17.1-4; about Blasi's ovation see Sumner, G.V., 'A New Reading in the Fasti Capitolini', *Phoenix* #19, 1965, p. 95-101; on Stertinius' arches see Coarelli, F., 'La Porta Trionfale e la Via dei Trionfi', *Dialoghi de Archeologia* #2, 1968, p. 55-103

86   Livy begins to make references about Hispania as two Spains starting

in Book 33.

87   The Battle of Zama was fought in North Africa around 19 October 202 BC. It marked the final and decisive end of the Second Punic War. A Roman army led by Publius Cornelius Scipio defeated a Carthaginian force led by Hannibal Barca. For more information see http://en.wikipedia.org/wiki/Battle_of_Zama.

88   Livy, 30.41.4-5; Richardson, J.S., *Hispaniae*, p.68

89   Richardson, J.S., *Hispaniae*, p.69

90   Livy, 30.41.4-5; Brunt, P.A., *Italian Manpower, 225 BC – AD 14*, Oxford, 1971, p. 661; Richardson, J.S., *The Romans in Spain*, p. 45-46; Richardson, J.S., *Hispaniae*, p.68

91   Richarson, J.S., *Hispaniae*, p. 57-58

92   Richardson, J.S., *Hispaniae*, p. 20-30, 55-56

93   The word tax in this context does not mean what it did later when the Romans actually began to levy taxes on an annual fixed sum drawn from across the province.

94   For further information see Richardson, J.S., *Hispaniae*, p. 72 and 115-117, Richardson, J.S., 'The Spanish mines and the development of provincial taxation in the second century BC', *Journal of Roman Studies* 66, 1976, pp. 139-152, for on the subject of the stipendium see p. 147-149

95   Livy, 30.3.2 31.4.6-7

96   Richardson, J.S., *Hispaniae*, p. 70

97   Livy, 31.1.6

98   Livy, 33.27

99   For more details about one praetor see Ibid., p. 68-74 and Richardson, J.S., *The Romans in Spain*, p. 46-49

100 Livy, 32.28.11; Pliny the Elder, *Naturalis Historia*, 3.5.56. Beside these two men, four other were elected as praetors; one each was sent to Sicily and Sardinia the other two were positioned as *praetor urbanus* of the city of Roman and *praetor peregrine* to deal with issues about foreigners.

101 For details see Richardson, J.S., *Hispaniae*, p. 54-60.

102 For a more detailed account see: Richardson, J.S., *The Romans in Spain*, p.2-6, 41-50.

103 Stephenson, Andrew, *Public Lands and Agrarian Laws of the Roman Republic*, Baltimore, John Hopkins Press, July-August 1891, Sec. 3. Ager publicus is the Latin for the acquiring of public land for the Roman Republic via expropriation from Rome's enemies.

104 Hill, G.F., *Notes on the ancient coinage of Hispania Citerior*, New York, 1931; Gundan y Lascaris, A.M. de, *La Moneda Iberica*, Madrid, 1980;

Crawford, M.H., 'The Financial Organization of Republican Spain', *Numismatic Chronicle* #9, 1969, p. 79-93; id, 'Money and Exchange in the Roman World', *Journal of Roman Studies* #60, 1970, 40-48; Knapp, R.C., 'The Date and Purpose of the Iberian Denarii', *Numismatic Chronicle* # 17, 1977, p. 1-18

105 Mackie, Nicola, 'Local Administration in Roman Spain', *British Archaeological Report International Series* #172, 1983. This would later be reverted back to the praetors.

106 Livy, 32.28.3

107 Livy, 32.28.14

108 For details see Schulten, A., *Fontes Hispaniae Antiquae* XI Vols., Barcelona, 1935-1987, Vol.III, p.174.

109 Livy, 33.21.6-9

110 Livy, 33.21.8

111 Livy, 33.21.6-9; Tsirkin, J.B., 'Romanization of Spain; socio-political aspect', *Gerion* #10, Universidad Complutense de Madrid, 1992, p. 205-242, p. 214-217 is about Culchas and Luxinius.

112 Tsirkin,J.B., 'The Phoenician Civilization in Roman Spain', *Gerion* #3, Universidad Complutense de Madrid, 1985, p. 245-270

113 Richardson, J.S., *Hispaniae*, p. 79.

114 Livy, 34.10.3

115 33.27.3

116 Livy, 33.25.5. Though the letter stated he was wounded, he ended up dying from his wounds.

117 These soldiers were probably needed in the east to fight in the Second Macedonian War (200–196 BC) which was fought between Macedonia, led by Philip V of Macedon, and Rome.

118 Livy, 33.26.2; Sumner, G.V., Proconsuls and provinciae in Spain, 218 – 195 BC, *Arethusa* 3 (1970) 85-108; Develin, R, 'The Roman command structure in Spain', *Kilo* 62 (1980) 355-367.

119 Livy, 33.26.3

120 Livy, 24.44.4; Appian 10.36. The Turboletae were a warlike people whose tribal name later became a byword for unruly behaviour (trouble), as they were a constant source of trouble to most of their neighbours. Not only did they harass the Belli and Titti, but also raided Iberian tribes in southeastern Hispania, particularly the Edetani city-state of Saguntum. As former allies of the Carthaginians the Turboletae actively participated in the incident that triggered the Second Punic War, the siege of Saguntum in 219 – 218 BC. The Turboletae assisted the Carthaginian troops in the final assault and looting of the city, slaughtering a great deal of its inhabitants.After the Second Punic War the exhausted Turboletae sued for peace and the

Roman Senate forced them to pay a huge compensation to the surviving citizens of Saguntum. Resentment fuelled by the heavy tribute imposed, coupled with the destruction of their capital city in 212 BC (the Romans and their Edetani allies invaded Turboletania, seized the capital Turba and razed it to the ground, selling his residents to slavery - Livy, Ab Urbe Condita, 24.42.11), may account for the Tuboletae revolt of 196 BC.

121   Livy, 33.44.4-5. Some believe that Turda, sometimes pronounced Turta, was the ancient legendary city of Tartessos. This harbour city is believed to have been located at the mouth of the Guadalquivir River. Other scholars claim that Turta was not a city but the name of a ancient region in Andalucía. The remaining Turboletae population appears to have been either obliterated or simply assimilated into the neighbouring tribe for their devastated lands were divided among the Bastetani and Edetani, resulting in their total disappearance from the historical record. Montenegro, Angel, *Historia de España 2 – colonizaciones y formación de los pueblos prerromanos 1200 – 218 a.C.*, Editorial Gredos, Madrid 1989; Motoza Francisco Burillo, *Los Celtíberos – Etnias y Estados*, Crìtica, Grijalbo Mondadori, S.A. Barcelona 1998.

122   Livy, 33.44.5

123   Livy, 33.43.7-8

124   Portus Lunae later became Luni but in 1059 its population abandoned the city due to constant attacks by Muslim pirates and a pitched battle that was fought there against the Muslims and forces from the of Pisa and Genoa.

125   Livy 34.8.4-7; Dennis, George, *The Cities and Cemeteries of Etruria*, John Murray, London, 1848.

126   Appian, 40.161

127   Livy, 34.9.1-10; Almagro, M, *Las Fuentes escritas refrentes a Ampurias*, Barcelona, 1951, 47-60

128   Livy, 34.9.11-13

129   Livy, 34.11.2

130   Livy, 34.11.3

131   Livy, 34.11, 34.12 and 34.13

132   Frontinus, *Strategemata*, 4.7.31. Frontinus says the trick actually worked. See Richardson, J.S., *Hispaniae*, p. 53-54; 67-68 about the Ilergetes' frequent alliances and defections.

133   Livy, 34.13.2

134   Livy, 34.13.3-9

135   Battle details come from Livy 34.14 , 34.15.

136   Livy, 34.16.4-5-9; Appian 41.167-170

137   Livy, 34.16.1

138 Livy, 34.16.2-4

139 Plutarch, *Cato the Elder*, 10.3

140 Livy, 34.16.15; Astin, A.E., *Cato the Censor*, Oxford, 1978, p. 304-05. Turdetania was a region covering the Guadalquivir River Valley which coincided with the former territories of ancient Tartessos. Bergistani was a tribe that lived around foothills of the Pyrenees.

141 Livy, 34.16.16-17

142 Richardson, J.S., *Hispaniae*, p. 84

143 Livy, 34.17.1 This army consisted of not only his but also a part of Praetor Appius Claudius Nero's; Livy, 33.25 and 33,44. The Turdetani rebellion had been going on for at least a year when Minucius Thermus was praetor of Citerior.

144 Livy, 33.43.7; 34.10.1-6; 34.17.1

145 Briscoe, John, *A Commentary on Livy, books XXXIV-XXXVII*, Oxford Univ. Press, Oxford 1981, p.80

146 Livy and Polybius mentions an Appius Claudius Nero who was stationed as a legate in Greece.

147 Livy, 34.17.2; Strabo, 3.2.15

148 Livy, 34.17.3

149 Livy, 34.17.4

150 Livy, 34.17.5-6

151 Livy, 34.17.10-14

152 Livy, 34.19.1-3

153 During the second Punic War Romans and Carthaginians had employed many Celtiberians and Lusitanian mercenaries.

154 Livy, 34.19.12

155 Livy, 34.19.12; Astin, A.E., *Cato the Censor*, p. 43-46

156 Livy, 34.20.1

157 Livy, 34.20.2

158 Livy, 34.20.3-9

159 Livy, 34.21.1-8

160 Appian, 40.161

161 A *foederatus* was a tribe that was nota Roman colony and had not been granted Roman citizenship (*civitas*), but that was bound by a treaty (*foedus*) and expected to provide a contingent of warriors when trouble arose. For more information see: Richardson, J.S., *Hispaniae*, p. 58- 61, 73-74

162 Livy, 34.21.7

163 Nostrand, J.J. van, *Roman Spain, An Economic Survey of Ancient Rome* #3, Baltimore, MD, 1937, p.126-137

164 Livy, 34.21.7

165 Bernhardt, R., 'Die Entwicklung römischer Amici et Socii zu Civitates Liberae in Spainien', *Historia* 24 (1975), p. 411-424; Richardson, J.S, 'The Spanish Mines and the Development of provincial Taxation in the 2nd Century BC', *Journal of Roman Studies* 66 (1976) p. 139-152.

166 Livy, 34.9.12-13

167 Cato, 51-59

168 Livy. 34.21.7; Schulten, A., *Fontes Hispaniae antiquae III*, Barcelona, 1935, p.185, R.Way and M. Simmons, *A Geography of Spain and Portugal*, London, 1962, p. 155-158.

169 Livy, 34.9.12-13; Richardson, J.S., *Hispaniae*, p. 93

170 Livy 34.21.7-8, 42.1; 46.2-3; A thanksgiving to the gods decreed by the Senate. For more information see http://en.wikipedia.org/wiki/Supplicatio

171 Livy 34.43.3, 43.8 and 35.1; Astin, A.E., *Cato the Censor*, p. 47-48; Richardson, J.S., 'The triumph, the praetor and the Senate in the early second century BC', *Journal of Roman Studies* #65, 1975, p. 60-62; Richardson, J.S., *Hispaniae*, p. 95

172 Livy, 34.43.11

173 Livy, 35.1

174 Livy 35.1.1-3

175 Livy, 35.1.3

176 Livy, 35.1.1-12

177 Livy, 35.1.1-16

178 Livy, 35.1.4

179 Richardson, J.S., *Hispaniae*, p. 96

180 Curchin, Leonard, A., *Roman Spain*, p. 31; Richardson, J.S., *Hispaniae*, p. 96

181 Livy, 34.55.6 Flaminius was a veteran who fought in Spain during the 2nd Punic War

182 Livy, 35.2.3

183 Livy, 35.2.5

184 Livy, 35.2.2

185 Livy, 35.7.5-6

186 Livy, 35.7.8. Inlucia, sometimes pronounced Ilucia, is an ancient town in central Spain situated on the bank of the Guadiana River.

187 Livy, 35.7.7

188 Livy, 35.7.6-8

189 Livy, 35.22.9

190 Livy, 35.22.10-11.There is debate over whether the town of Helo, sometimes pronounced Halon, is the modern city of Ayllon. It has an abundance of ancient ruins to see.

191 Livy, 35.22.11

192 Livy 36.39.1

193 Livy, 36.2.3

194 Livy, 36.2.3

195 Livy, 37.2.11 Because of the war in Greece praetors now had to serve two years in Hispania instead of one. At the end of the war, in 188 – 187BC, it reverted back to one year.

196 Next time we read about Flaminius is when he was elected to the Senate and when he is given the task to fight the Ligurians who had been raiding in Northern Italy.

197 Polybius, 32.8

198 Livy, 37.46.8

199 Mommsen, Theodore, 'Bemerkungen zum Decret des Paullus', *Hermes* 3, 1869, p. 261-271; Mishulin, A.V., 'On Interpretation of Aemilius Paullus' Inscription', in Izvestia AN SSSR, 1946, p 166-169, 178-184; *Corpus Inscriptionum Latinarum*, CIL II, 5041; CIL I(2), 614; A. Degrassi, *Inscriptiones Latinae Liberae rei publicae*, Firenze, 1957-1963, no. 514, n. 3. Hasta, also pronounced Asta, was later changed to Asta Regia during Rome's occupation. Today it is the city of Jerez la Frontera. Guerrero, E.M., *Excavaciones de Asta Regia (Mesas de Asta, Jerez): Campaña 1942-43*, Acta Arqueológica Hispánica III, Madrid, 1945; *Excavaciones de Asta Regia (Mesas de Asta, Jerez): Campaña 1945-46: Informes y Memorias de la Comisaría General de Excavaciones Arqueológicas*, no. 22, Madrid, 1950; *Excavaciones de Asta Regia (Mesas de Asta, Jerez): Campañas 1949-50 y 1955-56*, Centro de Estudios Históricos Jerezanos, no. 19, Jerez, 1962.

200 Livy, 37.57.5

201 Livy, 37.57.1 L. Baebius Dives was elected to take over Paulus' praetorship in Hispania, but on his way there he was mortally wounded in an ambush by the Ligurians.

202 Livy, 37.50.11-12

203 Livy, 37.57.6

204 Livy, 37.5.6

205 Livy, 38.35.10

206 Livy, 39.7.5-6

207 Livy, 39.21.1-5

208 Livy, 39.21.6

209 Livy, 39.21.7

210 Livy, 39.21.8-10. Once again these casualty numbers seem to be

exaggerated.

211   Livy, 39.21.10

212   Livy, 39.20.3-4; Brunt, P.A., 'Italian Manpower, 225 BC – 14 AD', p.166.

213   Livy, 39.30.1-2

214   Livy, 39.30.6

215   Livy, 39.30.3-9

216   Livy, 39.30.11-12

217   Livy, 39.30.13-15

218   Livy, 39.30.16 and 39.31.1-4

219   Livy, 39.31.5-6

220   Livy, 39.31.11

221   Livy, 39.31.13-15

222   Livy, 39.31.16-17

223   Livy, 39.31.18

224   Livy, 39.31.19-22

225   Livy, 39.42.1, 39.56.2; 40.2.6

226   Livy, 39.42.2. The ancient Iberian town of Corbio, sometimes pronounced Corbion, is situated near Sangüesa (Navarre).

227   Livy, 39. 56.1

228   Livy, 40.16.18

CHAPTER 2

1   Livy, 40.1.5

2   Livy, 40.1.2

3   Urbicua's ruins lie between Cesaraugusta (Zaragoza) and Libisosa (Lezuza) according to the Antonine Itinerary (see below). But some scholars put it in the heights of Turia, while others in the Oretania country, in the area of Montiel (Ciudad Real). Still others say it is on the banks of the Douro River and south of Ocellodurum (Zamora).

The Antonine Itinerary is a register of the stations and distances along the various roads of the Roman empire, containing directions how to get from one Roman settlement to another. It is seemingly based on official documents, probably of the survey organized by Julius Caesar and carried out under Augustus. Due to the scarcity of other extant sources of this information, it is a very valuable source. Nothing is known with certainty as to the date or author. It is considered probable that the date of the original edition was the beginning of the 3rd century, while that which we possess is to be assigned to the time of Diocletian. Although traditionally ascribed to the patronage of Antoninus Augustus, if the author or promoter of the work is one of the emperors, it is most likely to be Antoninus Caracalla. [wikipedia]

4   Livy, 40.16.12-15

5   Appian, 42.171.Unfortunately Appian does not mention the other tribes except the Lusones, who, being mentioned, perhaps instigated the revolt. But according to Strabo, the Lusones lived along the eastern part of the Tagus River (3.4.13) and not the Ebro River as Appian says. So it is unclear who Flaccus actually fought against.

6   Appian, 42.172. There is a similar story in Diodorus 29.28. As for Complega,there has been debate in identifying it. It has been suggested that it is close to Caravis, while other scholars claim it was the site of Complutum, near Madrid.

7   Appian, 42.173 and 174

8   Livy, 40.30.2

9   Livy, 40.30.3-4

10   Livy, 40.30.5-7

11   Livy, 40.30.7-14

12   Livy, 40.31.1-2

13   Livy, 40. 31.3-11

14   Livy, 40.32.1-4

15   Livy, 40.32.5-10

16   Livy, 40.32.12

17   Livy, 40.32. 13-14

18   Livy, 40.33.1. About the site of Contrebia see: A. Beltran and A. Tovar, *Contrebia Belaisca I: el bronce de Botorrita*, Zaragoza, 1982, 9-33; Fatas, G., *Contrebia Belaisca I: Tabula Contrebiensis*, Zaragoza, 1980, pp. 46-57

19   Livy, 40.33.2-4

20   Livy, 40.33.5-10; Appian 42.171.4; Diodorus Siculus, 29.28

21   Livy, 40.33.11-12

22   Livy, 40.35.5-6

23   Livy, 40.35.7

24   Livy, 40.35.8

25   Livy, 40.35.12-16

26   Livy, 40.36.9-10

27   Livy, 40.36.12

28   Livy 40.36.14

29   Livy, 40.39.1-2

30   Livy 40.39.4-5

31   Livy, 40.39.6

32   Livy 40.39.6-15

33   Livy, 40.40.1-5

34   Livy 40.40.6-11. There are accounts that the Roman cavalry had often performed that manoeuvre and covered themselves with glory.

35   Livy, 40.40.12-14

36   Livy 40.40.14

37   Livy 40.40. 15-17

38   Livy 40.40. 18-21

39   The Celtic city of Caravis is said to have been situated around Mount Moncayo between the Queiles and Huecha River, tributaries of the Ebro River. Mozota, F.B., *Sobre el Territorio de los Lusones, Belos y Titos en el Siglo II a. de C.*, Madrid, n.d., p. 9.

40   Appian, Ib, 43.175-177

41   Appian 43.178. At the present time the spot were the city of Complega was is not known, except that in was in the Ebro River Valley but close to Caravis. Mozota, F.B., Sobre el Territorio de los Lusones, p.9

42   Appian, 40.179

43   Livy, 40.47. Munda is believed by some to be where Montilla is today, but other scholars and archeologists believe that the city of Monda is the site of the ancient Iberian city.

44   Muñoz, M.A., *Viriato: O Herói Lusitano*, p. 41

45   Livy, 40.47.7

46   Livy, 40.47.12-13

47   Livy, 40.47.12-13

48   Livy, 40.47.14-16

49   Livy, 40.48.1-4 to 5-10

50   Livy, 40.49.1-2

51   Livy, 40.49.3 to 7-11

52   For many years now there has been debate on the exact location of Ergavica. One thing is for sure: that it is situated somewhere in the province of Navarre. Some scholars and archaeologists say the location of the Iberian city isArguedas, while other claim it is Berbençana. Others say it is an old Celtiberian/Roman city north of the Ebro River, the ruins of which lie near the city of Fitero. Etayo, J, 'Vestigos de poblaciòn ibero-romana cabr Arguedas', *Boletin de la Comisiòn Provincial de Monumentos de Navarre* #17, 1926, pp. 84-90; Taracena, B. and Vazquez de Parga, L Excavaciones en Navarre: Exploracion del Castejòn de Arguedas, Principe de Viana #10, pp.129-159; Corona Baratech, C.E., *Toponimia Navarre en la Edad Media*, Huesca, 1947; Moret, J de, *Anales del Reino de Navarre 1665–1766*, Pamplona, 1987.

53   Livy, 40.50.2

54   Livy, 40.50.2; The Moncayo or San Miguel is a small mountain system

situated between the province of Zaragoza, Aragón (Spain) and the province of Soria, Castilla León.

55   Livy, 40.50.4

56   Livy, 40.50.5

57   Appian, 43.179

58   A. Garcia y Bellido, 'Las colonias romanas de Hispania', *Anuario de Historia del Derecho Espanol* 29 (1959) 448ff

59   A. Blanco and G. La Chica, *Arch. Español de Arqueologia* 33, 1960, 193-95; Knapp, R.C., *Aspects of the Roman Experience in Iberia 206 – 100 BC*, Vallodolid, 1977, p. 110, n. 18

60   Muñoz, M.A., *Viriato: O Herói Lusitano*, p. 42

61   Polybius, 25.1.1; Strabo 3.4.13; Florus 1.33.9

62   Polybius, 35.2.15; Appian, *Iberika*, 43.179 - 44.183; Plutarch, Ti. Gracchus, 5.2

63   Appian, *Iberika*, 43.179

64   Livy, 40.47.3-10, 40.49.4-7

65   Although previous praetors had brought back tonnes of plunder from Hispania and Cato had introduced a tax on mine production, this is the first reference to a regulatory collection of revenue.

66   Curchin, Leonard, A., *Roman Spain*, p. 32

67   Ibid., p.33

68   For more information on Gracchus' contributions in Hispania see, J.S. Richardson, *Hispaniae*, p. 112-123

69   Livy, 40.50.7

70   J.S. Richardson also states this claim in *Hispaniae*, p. 102

71   Payne, Stanley G., *A History of Spain and Portugal Volume 1, Antiquity to the Seventeenth Century* (Print Edition: University of Wisconsin Press, 1973). The chapter on Ancient Hispania can be read online at The Library of Iberian Resources Online, http://libro.uca.edu/payne1/payne1.htm

72   Livy, 41.9.3, 41.15.11

73   Livy, 41.15.9-10

74   Brunt, P.A., *Italian Manpower, 225 BC – 14 AD*, pp. 661-63

75   Livy, 41.26.1-4

76   Livy, 41.26.5-11

77   Livy, 41.28.5

78   The'Fasti Triumphales' were published in about 12 BC. They contain a list of triumphs from the foundation of Rome down to the reign of Augustus. They are preserved as part of a larger inscription, the Fasti Capitolini, which is now displayed at the Palazzo dei Conservatori,

Capitoline Museum in Rome. This translation is based on the edition by A.Degrassi (*Fasti Capitolini*, 1954).

79   Livy, 41.21.3

81   Livy, 42.1.3, 4.1-3

82   42.9.8

83   Brunt, P.A., *Italian Manpower, 225 BC – AD 14*, p. 662

85   *Lex Baebia de praetoribus* prescribed that praetors would be elected in alternate years; *Lex Baebia de ambitu* involved combating electoral bribery.

86   Mommsen, Theodore, *Römisches Staatsrecht*, vol. 2, Leipzig, 1887-1889, p.194

87   For more information on the subject see J.S. Richardson, *Hispaniae*, pp. 109-112; Scullard, H.H., *Roman Politics 220-150 BC*, (2nd ed.) Oxford, 1973

88   Upon the death of Philip V of Macedon (179 BC), his son Perseus attempted to restore Macedon's international influence and moved aggressively against his neighbours. When Perseus was implicated in an assassination plot against an ally of Rome, the Senate declared the Third Macedonian War. Initially, Rome did not fare well against the Macedonian forces, but in 168 BC, Roman legions smashed the Macedonian phalanx at the Battle of Pydna. Perseus was later captured and the kingdom of Macedon divided into four puppet republics controlled by Rome.

89   Livy, 42.28.5-6; Broughton, T.R.S., *The Magistrates of the Roman Republic*, NY, 1951, p. 421.

90   Livy, 42.2; 42.3

91   Livy,43.2.1-5

92   Livy, 42.2.10-11

93   Livy, 43.2.12-13

94   Richardson, J.S., *Hispaniae*, p.114; Strachan-Davidson, J.L., *Problems with the Roman Criminal Law II*, Oxford, 1912, vol II, pp. 1-4; Gruen, E.S., *Roman Politics and the Criminal Courts*, Harvard, 1968, p. 10.

95   Richardson, J.S., *Hispaniae*, p. 114.

96   Ibid., p. 114

97   Ibid., p. 115; Livy, 43.2.16; Mackie, Nicola, 'Aspects of the Roman Experience in Iberia 206 – 100 BC', *Journal of Roman Studies* # 71, 1981, p. 187

98   Livy, 43.3.1-2

99   Livy, 43.3. 1-4. Below the common people were the freedmen or *libertini*. They had formerly been slaves but had been freed by their masters. Although technically free, the *libertini* had serious restrictions

on their rights and maintained close relationships with their former masters. Nevertheless many of these freedmen were talented and highly educated individuals, and many found their way into high places of power and influence, often to the disgust of traditionalists in Roman society.

100 Florus, *An Epitome of the Histories of Titus Livy*, 1.33.13

101 Livy, 43.12.10-11; 45.4.1 According to Livy each province held a legion of 5,200 infantry and 300 cavalry.

102 Livy, 44.17.5, 10

103 M Cornelius Scipio Maluginensis was expelled from the senate at the next *lustrum* in 174BC (Livy 41.27.2). P Licinius Crassus wished to go to Macedonia as consul in 171 BC to participate in the Third Macedonian War, but it was argued in the Senate that he could not because of the oath he had sworn in 176 BC. (Livy 42.32.1-5)

104 Degrassi, A., *Fasti consulars et triumphales, Insriptiones Italiae*, vol. 13.1, Rome 1947, p. 80-83, 556-557; Richardson, J.S., 'The Triumph, the Praetors and the Senate in the Early Second Century BC', *Journal of Roman Studies* No. 65, 1975, p. 50-63; Develin, R., 'Tradition and development of triumphal regulations of Rome', *Klio* No. 60, 1978, p. 429-438

105 Livy, 45.16.1-3

106 Livy, 45.16.1-3

107 Livy, 45.44.1-2

108 Curchin, Leonard, A., *Roman Spain*, p. 33

109 Schulten, A., *Fontes Hispaniae Antiquae III*, p.230

110 Brunt, P.A., *Italian Manpower, 225 BC – AD 14*, p. 661-63; Richardson, J.S., *Hispaniae*, p. 105.

111 Livy 32.28.2 (197 BC); 33.26.1-3 (196 BC); 33.43.5 (195 BC); 34.43.6-7 (194 BC); 34.55.6 (193 BC)

112 Livy 42.28.5-6

113 Livy, 39.29.4-7;39.38.4-12;40.35.3-36.12

114 For detailed examples of this see Richardson, J.S., *Hispaniae*, pp. 108-09.

115 Livy 43.2.1-11

116 Richardson, J.S., *Hispaniae*, p. 114

117 Griffin, M., 'The Elder Seneca and Spain', *Journal of Roman Studies* 62, 1972, p.17-19; Knapp, R.C., *Aspects of the Roman Experience in Iberia 206 – 100 BC*, p. 120-124; Wilson, A.J.N., *Emigration from Italy in the Republican Age of Rome*, Manchester, 1966, p.16-17

118 See above p. 31; Humbert, M., 'Libertas id est civitas', *Mélanges de l'école française de Rome Antiquité* 88, 1976, pp. 221-242; 'Latin rights'

was a civic status given by the Romans between full citizenship and non-citizen status (*peregrines*). The most important Latin rights were *commercium, conubium,* and *ius migrationis. Commercium* allowed them to own land in any of the Latin cities and to make legally enforceable contracts with their citizens. *Conubium* permitted them to make a marry a resident of any other Latin city. *Ius migrationis* gave them the capacity to acquire citizenship of another Latin state simply by taking up permanent residence there. People with Latin rights were protected under Roman law.

119   Sherwin-White, A.N., *The Roman Citizenship,* 2nd ed. Oxford, 1973, p. 110; Knapp, R.C., Aspects of the Roman Experience in Iberia 206 – 100 BC, p. 116-120

120   Appian, Ib, 44.183

121   Richardson, J.S., *Hispaniae,* Cambridge Univ. Press, London, 1986, p. 125.

122   Appian, 43.179

123   Polybius, 35.2.15; Plutarch, Ti. Gracchus, 5.2; Appian, *Iberika,* 44.182-183.TheNumantine War was a twenty-year conflict between the Celtiberian tribes of Hispania Citerior and the Roman government that began in 154 BC.

CHAPTER 3

1   Arribas, Antonio, *The Iberians,* Frederick A. Praeger Publishing, NY, 1964, p.73.

2   Diodorus, 5.34.7

3   Jones, C.P. 'Stigma: Tattooing and Branding in Graeco-Roman Antiquity.' *Journal of Roman Studies* 77 (1987) 139-155; W. M. Gustafson, 'Inscripta in fronte: Penal Tattooing in Late Antiquity', *Classical Antiquity* 16 (1997) 79-105

4   Ibid.

5   One such example comes from the Picts, for they were famously tattooed (or scarified) with elaborate dark blue woad (or possibly copper for the blue tone) designs, as described by Julius Caesar in Book V of his *Gallic Wars* (54 BC).

6   Octávio da Veiga Ferreira e Seomara Bastos da Veiga Ferreira, *A Vida dos Lusitanos no Tempo de Viriato,* Polis, Lisbon, 1969, p. 175; Leite deVasconcelos, José, 'Medicina dos Lusitanos', *Opúsculos, Volume V – Etnologia (Parte I)* Lisboa, Imprensa Nacional, 1938, p. 291-293; Fontes, Joaqium, 'Contribuição ao estudo da tatuagem', *Arquivo de Antropologia, vol. II & III,* 1914-1915

7   Octávio da Veiga Ferreira e Seomara Bastos da Veiga Ferreira, *A Vida dos Lusitanos no Tempo de Viriato,* p. 180

8   Ibid., pp. 130 – 144 (entire section on Lusitanian funerary rites);

Diodorus, 5.33.21

9   Ibid., pp. 134 – 137

11   Ibid., p. 85

12   Strabo, 3.4.18; Martinez, Rafael T., *Rome's Enemies (4): Spanish Armies*, Men-at-Arms Series #180, Osprey Publishing, Oxford, UK, 1986, p. 40

13   Arribas, Antonio, *The Iberians*, p. 84; Martinez, Rafael T., *Rome's Enemies (4): Spanish Armies*, p. 40

14   Arribas, Antonio, *The Iberians*, p. 84

15   Pidal, Ramon Menendez, História de España vol. I, Espaca-Calpe S.A., Madrid, 1947, p. 36 Martinez, Rafael T., op.cit., p. 40; Octávio da Veiga Ferreira e Seomara Bastos da Veiga Ferreira, op.cit, p. 176

16   Martinez, Rafael T., op. cit., p. 41

17   Weber, S.E. (translated from German), 'Historical Development of the Horseshoe', *Scientific American Supplement* No. 819, Volume XXXII, September 12, 1891 (originally written by district veterinarian named Zippelius of Wurtzburg)

18   Fleming, George, *Horseshoes and horseshoeing: their origin, history, uses and abuses*, London, Chapman & Hall Gasner, 1869; Mgnin, J. P, *De l'origine de Ia ferrure du cheval*, Paris, P Asselin, 1865.

19   Miguel Sanchez de Baêna and Paulo Alexandre Louçao, *Grandes Enigmas da História de Portugal*, Vol. I, Esquilo, Lisbon, 2008, p. 57. Martinez, Rafael T., op. cit., p. 41

20   Strabo, 3.4.18; Martinez, Rafael T., op. cit., p. 40; Miguel Sanchez de Baêna and Paulo Alexandre Louçao, *Grandes Enigmas da História de Portugal*, Vol. I, p. 56.

21   Strabo, 3.4.15

22   Miguel Sanchez de Baêna and Paulo Alexandre Louçao, *Grandes Enigmas da História de Portugal*, Vol. I, p. 57

23   Arribas, Antonio, *The Iberians*, Frederick A. Praeger Publishing, New York, 1964, p. 84-86; Martinez, Rafael T., op. cit., p. 41-42

24   Miguel Sanchez de Baêna and Paulo Alexandre Louçao, op. cit., p. 57

25   Martinez, Rafael T., op. cit., p. 42

26   Miguel Sanchez de Baêna and Paulo Alexandre Louçao, op.cit.,p. 55

27   It is strange that the Romans were the first to create specialized horses for different purposes, such as the hunting horse, the delivery service horse, horses for long and short journeys, the show horse and race horse, but ignored the war horse. All these types of horses, especially racing horses, were carefully bred and selected from the best studs of Rome and the empire. But the war horse was relegated to secondary position when it should have been a priority. Perhaps the Romans did not concentrate on cavalry because their interest in horses was more

based on profitable business ventures than war. The Roman generals
incorporated little cavalry and relied mostly on heavy and light
infantry. As a result, the cavalry was the weakest link in the Roman
Army.

28   Diodorus 15; Livy 21.43.8-9, 24.12 (Italian Campaign); Silius Italius,
     Punica, 3.354-356; Polybius, 3.56, 72; 'Hanno, Los Mercenarios
     Hispanos durante la Segunda Guerra Puncia', Celtiberia.net, Oct. 4,
     2006http://www.celtiberia.net/articulo.asp?id=846; García-Gelabert
     Pérez, M. P. and Blázquez Martínez, José María, 'Mercenarios
     hispanos en las fuentes literarias y en la Arqueología', *Habis* 18-19;
     Sevilla, Publicaciones de la Universidad de Sevilla, 1987-1988, p.257-
     270.

29   Livy, 21.43

30   Livy, 39.56

31   Diodorus, 5.34.6; Martinez, Rafael T., op. cit., p.7; Garcia y Bellido, A.,
     'Bandas y guerrillas en las luchas con Roma', *Hispania*, 21, 1945, p. 19;
     Abengochea, Juan Jose Sayas, 'El bandolerismo lusitano y la falta de
     tierras', *Revista de la Facultad de Geografia e Historia* #4, Universidade de
     Santiago de Compostela, 1989, p.704-714.

32   See Chapter 1

33   Gunn, Robert M., *The Ancient Celtic Warrior of Europe*, Edinburgh, 2004,
     Part 8: Celtic headhunters; Rodrigues, Adriano Vasco, *Os Lusitanos:
     Mito e realidade*, Lisbon, Academia Internacional da Cultura
     Portuguesa, 1998.

34   Diodorus 33.1.1

35   Pérez Vilatela, Luciano, 'Procedencia Geográfia de los Lusitanos de las
     Guerras de siglo II a.C. en los Autores Clásicos (159 – 139)', *Actas del
     VII Congreso Español de Estudios Clásico*, Madrid, 1989, pp. 257-262;
     'Notas Sobre la Jefatura de Viriato en Relación con la Ulterior', *Archivo
     de prehistoria Levantina*, XIX, Valência, 1989, pp. 191-204, *Lusitania:
     Historia y Etnología*, Madrid, 2000, pp. 203-204 (pages 204 – 238 deal
     with Viriathus allies)

36   Diodorus, 2.33.1,7,19,21; Cassius Dio, *Historae*, 73,77, 78; Muñoz,
     Mauricio P., *Viriato: O Herói Lusitano*, Esfera dos Livros, Lisbon, 2006,
     p. 51-52; Schulten, A., 'Viriato', *Boletin de la Biblioteca Menéndez y
     Pelayo*, vol. II, (4part series) #3, pp. 126-149; #4,5,6, pp. 272-281.
     Santander, 1920, In Portuguese it is a book entitled *Viriato* Porto, 1940.

37   Strabo, 3.3.7

38   Appian, 46. 188-193, Valerius Maximus, 2.4.10 and 5.2-4; Garcia y
     Bellido, A., 'Elefantes antes Numancia', *Veinticinco estampas de la
     España Antigua*, Madrid, 1968, p. 58 and in the book *La Peninsula
     Ibérica en los comienzos de su Historia*, Madrid, 1952, p. 335.

39   Quesada Sanz, Fernando, 'Not so different : Individual Fighting

Techniques and Small Unit Tactics of Roman and Iberian Armies', in P.François, P. Moret, S. Péré-Noguès (eds), *L'Hellénisation en Mediterranée Occidentale au temps des guerres puniques, Actes du Colloque International de Toulouse Mars-Avril 2005*; Quesada Sanz, F., 'Innovaciones de raíz helenística en el armamento y táticas de los pueblos ibéricos desde el siglo IIIa.C', in M.Bendala, P.Moret, F. Quesada Sanz (eds.), *Formas e imágenes del poder en los siglos III y II a.C: Modelos helenísticos y respuestas indígenas, in Cuadernos de Prehistoria y Arqueología de la Universidad Autónoma de Madrid no.28-29*, Madrid, 2002-2003,pp.96-94; Quesada Sanz, F., 'Military Developments in the Late Iberian Culture (c.237-45 BC): Helenistic influences via the Carthaginian Military', N. Sekunda (ed.) *First International Conference on Hellenistic Warfare*, Torun, Poland, 2003; Garcia Alonso, F., *La Guerra en la Protohistorica: Héroes, nobles, mercenarios y campesinos*, Barcelona, Ariel, 2003; Hernandez Cardona, F.J., 'La batalla de Ampurias', *Historia* #16, 1991, pp.101-112; Martinez Gazquer, J., *La Campaña de Catón en Hispania*, Barcelona, 1992; P. Moret and F. Quesada (eds), *La Guerra en el mundo ibérico y celtibérico (ss.VI-II a.C. de C)*, Collection de la Casa de Velázquez, Madrid, 2002; Quesada Sanz, Fernando, 'La Guerra en las comunidades ibéricas (c. 237-195 a.C.): Un modelo interpretativo', in A. Morilo, F. Cadiou, D. Hourcade (eds.), *Defensa y territorio en Hispania de los Escipinoes a Augusto*, Casa de Velázquez, Madrid, 2004, pp. 101-156.

40   Martinez, Rafael T., op. cit., p.40.

41   Strabo, 3.4.15; See section on horses in this chapter

42   Martinez, Rafael T.,op. cit., p.42

43   See section on horses in this chapter

44   Appian, 64.262-263

45   Quesada Sanz, Fernando, 'Aristócratas a caballo y la existencia de una verdadera 'caballería' en la cultura ibérica:dos ámbitos conceptuales diferentes', in C.Aranegui (ed.), *Los Iberos, principes de Occidente*, Actas del Congreso Internacional, Barcelona, 1998, pp. 169-183

46   Livy, 37.57.6

47   Octávio da Veiga Ferreira e Seomara Bastos da Veiga Ferreira, op. cit., p 167

48   Schulten, A., 'Las guerras de 154 – 72 AC', Fontes Hispaniae Antiquae IV, Barcelona, 1937; Muñoz, Mauricio P., *Viriato: O Herói Lusitano* p.93

49   Schulten, A. 'Las guerras de 154 – 72 AC', p.110; Gonzalez-Conde Puente, Pilar, *Romanidad e indigenism em Carpetania*, Unversidad de Alicante, 1987, p. 32; Arce, J., 'Las guerras Celtibero-Lusitanas' , *Historia de España: Histoira Romana*, vol II, Madrid, 1988, pp. 79-99; Bonilla Martos, Antonio Luis, 'Poblamiento y Territorio en el suroeste de la provincial de Jaén en época romana', *Arqueologia y Territorio* #1,

Universidad de Granada, 2004, pp.119-133

50   Muñoz, Mauricio P., *Viriato, O Herói Lusitano*, Esfera dos Livros, Lisbon, 2006, p. 68

51   Schulten, A., *Historia da Numantia*, Barcelona, 1945, p. 171

52   Diodorus, 5.34.6, Miguel Sanchez de Baêna and Paulo Alexandre Louçao, op. cit., p. 73; Frye, David, G., 'Rome's Barbarian Mercenaries', *Military History Quarterly*, Spring 2007 Vol. 19, No. 3, pp. 68-81.

53   It is perhaps noteworthy to mention that on many archaeological excavations throughout Spain and Portugal hollowed animal or ceramic horns have been found and are believed to have been used to transmit signals during battle or on a hunt. Martinez, Rafael T., op. cit., p.8; Arribas, Antonio, op. cit. p.74; Miguel Sanchez de Baêna and Paulo Alexandre Louçao, op. cit., p. 73

54   Martinez, Rafael T., op. cit., p.7-8

55   Martinez, Rafael T, op. cit. p.8; Arribas, Antonio, op. cit., p.74.

56   Connolly, P., 'Pilum, Gladius and Pugio in the Late Republic', in M. Feugère (ed.), *L'équipement militaire et l'armement de la République*, *JRMES* #8, 1997, pp.41-57; I. Filloy and E. Gil, *Las armas de las necrópolis celtibéricas de Carasta y La Hoya (Alava, España), Tipologia de sus puñales y prototipos del pugio*, 137-150; Garcia-Gelalbert, M.P., 'Estudios del armamento prerromano em la peninsula Ibérica a través de los textos clásicos', *Espacio, Tiempo y Forma Serie II, Historia Antigua*, 2, 1989, pp.69-80; Quesada Sanz, Fernando, *El armamento ibérico, Estudio tipológico, geográfico, functional, social y simbólico de las armas en la Cultura Ibérica (siglos VI-I a.C.)*, Monique Mergoil, Montagnac, 1997; Quesada Sanz, Fernando, 'Gladius hispaniensis: an archaeological view from Iberia', in M. Feugère (ed.), *L'équipement militaire et l'armement de la République*, *JRMES* #8, 1997, pp. 251-270; Quesada Sanz, F., 'Armamento indigena y romano republicano en Iberia seculos III – I a.C., compatibilidad y abastecimient de las legiones republicanas en campaña', in A. Morillo (ed.), *II Congreso de Arqueologia Militar Romana en Hispania, Producción y abastecimiento en el ámbito military*, Universidad de León, 20-22 Octobro 2004; Quesada Sanz, F., 'Las armas del legionario romano en época de las Guerras Punicas: influencias hispanas y formas de combate', in P. Fernández Uriel (ed.), *Armas, legiones, y limes: el ejército romano. Espacio, Tiempo y Forma (Historia Antigua)*; Sandars, H,' The Weapons of the Iberians', *Archeaologia* #64, Oxford, 1913; Fernando Quesada Sanz '¿Qué hay en un nombre?. La cuestión del gladius hispaniensis.' *Boletín de la Asociación Española de Amigos de la Arqueología* 37, 1997, pp. 41-58; Fernando Quesada Sanz, 'Armamento romano e ibérico en Urso (Osuna): testimonio de una época', *Cuadernos de los Amigos de los Museos de Osuna*, 10, Diciembre 2008, pp. 13-19.

57   Martinez, Rafael T., *Rome's Enemies (4): Spanish Armies*, p. 37.

58   The *xiphos* was a double-edged, single-hand sword used by the
       ancient Greeks. It was a secondary battlefield weapon for the Greek
       armies after the spear or javelin. The blade was around 65 cm long
       and was good for both cutting and stabbing attacks due to its leaf
       shape. It was generally used only when the spear was discarded. The
       straight, double-edged design of the *xiphos* lends it the same overall
       martial versatility found in the swords used by infantry until the
       firearm supplanted the sword on the battlefield. Sandars, Horace, 'The
       weapons of the Iberians', *Archeologia* #25, Oxford, 1913, p.58-62
       Sekunda, Nick, *The Ancient Greeks*, Elite Series #7, Osprey Publishing,
       Oxford, 1986; *The Spartan Army*, Elite Series #66, Osprey Publishing,
       Oxford, 1998; *Greek Hoplite 480-323 BC*, Warrior Series #27, Osprey
       Publishing, Oxford, 2000; *Greek swords and swordsmanship*, Osprey
       Publishing Online, 2004
       http://www.ospreypublishing.com/content2.php/cid=217

59   Sanz, F. Quesada, 'Gladius hispaniensis', JRMES, vol. 8, p. 251-270;
       'Máchaira, kopís, falcata', Homenaje a Francisco Torrent, Madrid,
       1994, pp. 75-94; I. Filloy Nieva & E.Gil Zubillaga, Las armas de las
       necropolis celtibéricas de Carasta y La Hoya, JRMES, vol. 8, pp.137-
       150; A. García y Bellido, Arte Ibérico, Historia de España'. *España
       Prerromana I.3*, Madrid, 1954, pp.422-428. Arribas, Antonio, The
       Iberians, p. 82. (In Arribas' book the useage of the word 'falchion' to
       describe the Iberian straight sword known as an *espada* is incorrect.
       The falchion was not invented until the eleventh century AD.)

60   Martinez, Rafael T.,op. cit., p.38

61   Miguel Sanchez de Baêna and Paulo Alexandre Louçao, op. cit., p. 67

62   As the Romans were pragmatic people they had taken Greek
       technology as their own. The Roman legionnaires at the time were
       equipped with a sword identical to that used by the Greek infantry.
       The Greek sword of that time, mainly used by the cavalry, was longer
       and heavier and its technology was Bronze Age design. Miguel
       Sanchez de Baêna and Paulo Alexandre Louçao, *Grandes Enigmas da
       História de Portugal*, Vol. I, Esquilo, Lisbon, 2008, p. 67

63   For more information on this sword see, Quesada, F., *El Armamento
       Ibérico*, I-II. Madrid, 1996; Viana, Abel, 'Una espada de antennas',
       Portucale vol. II, Porto, 1924; Aguilo, Cabre, 'La espad de antennas tipo
       Alcácer do Sal y su evolución en la necropolis de la Osera, Chamartin
       de la Sierra', *Homenagem a Martins Sarmento*, Guimarães, 1933, p.85

64   This episode dealt with the *falcata*, which the Romans also considered
       as a *gladius hispaniensis*. Seneca, De Beneficiis, V.24; Polybius,
       Histories, 3.144.3-4

65   Miguel Sanchez de Baêna and Paulo Alexandre Louçao, op. cit., p. 64;
       Ethridge, Charles E., *Reinventing the Sword: A Cultural Comparison of*

the Development of the Sword in Response to the Advent of Firearms in Spain and Japan, Louisana State University, 1999, p.10-11

66   There is much debate over the origin of the Roman gladius and there are quite a few theories (about which a book could be written) but in the end they are seen to end up complementing the Spanish sword. The Mainz pattern is thought to have developed from the leaf-bladed short swords used on the Celt-Iberian peninsula (what is now Spain) and adopted for use in the Republican Legions. Rather than fighting as individual warriors (like their opponents, the Continental Celts) the Roman legions eventually developed a new way of fighting — massing together with overlapping shields, using their short stabbing and cutting swords to strike from behind this shield wall. As these battle tactics for the legions changed, a shorter, broader stabbing/cutting sword had to be developed to use in combination with these newer types of shield and new styles of fighting. The Mainz pattern is deeply waisted and has a long point section like the earlier gladius Hispaniensis, but is shorter and broader than its predecessor. Unlike the later Pompeii style, the Mainz pattern was still capable of delivering strong cutting blows, though its primary purpose was for thrusting.

66   Mainz was founded as the Roman permanent camp of Moguntiacum probably in 13 BC. This large camp provided a population base for the growing city around it. Sword manufacture probably began in the camp and was continued in the city; for example, Gaius Gentilius Victor, a veteran of Legio XXII, used his discharge bonus on retirement to set up a business as a *negotiator gladiarius,* a manufacturer and dealer of arms. Swords made at Mainz were sold extensively to the north. They are characterized by a slight waist running the length of the blade and a long point. Blade width 7-8 cm. Blade length 66 cm - 70 cm. Sword mass: 1.2 kg - 1.6 kg.

The Fulham or Mainz-Fulham sword was the type dredged from the Thames near Fulham and must therefore date to a time after the Roman occupation of Britain began. That would have been after the invasion of Aulus Plautius in 43 AD. It was used until the end of the same century. It is considered the conjunction point between Mainz and Pompei. Some consider it an evolution or the same as the Mainz type. Blade length 70 cm blade width: 6 cm at the base, 4 cm in the middle, 7 cm in the end. Pompei (or Pompeianus or Pompeii): Named by moderns after the Roman town of Pompeii, which was destroyed by volcanic eruption in 79 AD. Four instances of the sword type were found there, with others turning up elsewhere. The sword has parallel cutting edges and a triangular tip. Blade length of 60 cm, blade length from circa 75 AD of 68 cm - 71 cm; from circa 100 AD of 83 cm (semi-spatha). From then on the Roman *gladius* will be of middle-length. Verboven, Koenraad S., 'Good for Business: The Roman Army and the

Emergence of a Business Class in the Northwestern Provinces in the first century BC - 3 AD', in Lukas, De Blois & Elio, Lo Cascio, *The Impact of the Roman Army (200 BC - AD 476): Economic, Social, Political, Religious and Cultural Aspects,* Leiden & Boston: Brill, 2007, pp. pages 295-314; Lang, Janet, 'Study of the Metallography of Some Roman Swords', *Britannia* # 19, 1988, 199-216; Burton, Sir Richard F., *Book of the Sword,* Kessinger Publishing, Whitefish, MT, 2006, p. 265-266. these are just a sample of the many book on the subject.

67 Polybius, 2.30.8; 3.144.3-4; 6.23.6; 6.25.8-11; Gellus, 9.13.14; Livy, 22.46.5; 31.34; Aguilera y Gamboa, E., *Las necrópolis ibéricas.* Madrid, 1916, p. 13, 29; Walbank, F.W., *A Historical commentary on Polybius,* Oxford, 1957-79.

68 Miguel Sanchez de Baêna and Paulo Alexandre Louçao, op. cit., p. 67; Fernando Quesada Sanz; E. Kavanagh de Prado 'Roman Republican weapons, camps and battlefields in Spain: an overview of recent and ongoing research' In A. Morillo, J. Aurrecoechea (Eds.) *The Roman Army in Hispania.* University of Leon, 2006, pp. 65-84

69 Miguel Sanchez de Baêna and Paulo Alexandre Louçao, op. cit., p. 67; Fernando Quesada Sanz; E. Kavanagh de Prado 'Roman Republican weapons, camps and battlefields in Spain: an overview of recent and ongoing research', in A. Morillo, J. Aurrecoechea (Eds.) *The Roman Army in Hispania,* University of Leon, 2006, pp. 65-84

70 The Iberian sword had two neuralgic points: point of balance (POB) and center of percussion (COP). The point of balance is simply the sword's center of gravity. This can easily be found by balancing a sword, lengthwise, upon one's hand, for there is an equal mass on each side. The point of balance will vary widely from type to type. An early medieval sword will not balance the same as an eighteenth century sword. Statements to the effect of 'my sword has to have a POB four inches from the guard' will often be heard, but if the aforementioned medieval sword has a POB of two inches below the guard, it probably was not an efficient performer regardless of how 'alive' it felt to the owner. In terms of comparing an early Roman/Greek sword to a Iberian sword, the former's point of balance is located a third below the blade's handle, which in real terms turned the weapon into an unbalanced sword. A sword's point of balance is only one small piece of the complex puzzle that makes up a sword; the next part of the blade's success is the center of percussion. The center of percussion, or sweet spot, of a sword is the point on the blade where cutting is most effective. It is also the division between the 'weak' and 'middle' sections of the blade. Like any solid object, a sword vibrates when impacted (such as during cutting). In a sword, such vibrational waves are typically almost imperceptible. Every wave expressed by a solid object has rotational nodes where the wave reverses at either end of the object. On a properly balanced sword, one

node is in the tang of the sword (inside the hilt), ideally directly under the primary hand. On such a 'harmonically balanced' sword, this means a solid blow can be delivered without causing discomfort in the hands, and therefore ensures greater target penetration. The center of percussion of a sword is related to its center of balance, and both can be moved by employing a heavier pommel or changing the mass distribution of the blade. The more regressive or greater the zone of COP, the better the quality of the blade. Miguel Sanchez de Baêna and Paulo Alexandre Louçao, op. cit., p. 66; Turner, George, *Sword Motions and Impacts: An Investigation and Analysis,* The Association for Renaissance Martial Arts, 2001, http://www.thearma.org/spotlight/GTA/motions_and_impacts.htm

71   Miguel Sanchez de Baêna and Paulo Alexandre Louçao, op. cit., p. 66

72   Diodorous, 5.33.3-4

73   Davies, Oliver, *Roman Mines in Europe,* Oxford, 1935, p. 59

74   Polybius, Histories, 3.144.3-4

75   Pattern welding is the practice in sword and knife making of forming a blade of several metal pieces of differing composition forge-welded together, twisted and manipulated to form a pattern. Blades forged in this manner often display bands of slightly different coloration along their entire length. These bands can be brought out for cosmetic purposes by proper polishing or acid etching. Originally, pattern welding was used to combine steels of different carbon contents, providing the desired mix of hardness and toughness needed for highly demanding tasks such as cutting through armour.

76   Philo, mechaniké syntaxis, IV-V

77   Diodorus reports that the *falcatas* were of such superior quality that no helmet, shield or bone could resist its devastating effect. Seneca, De Beneficiis, V.24, Seneca recounts an episode that demonstrates the terror the *falcata* inspired in Roman legionnaires

78   Martinez, Rafael T., *Rome's Enemies (4): Spanish Armies,* p. 38; Allen, Stephen, *Lords of Battle: The World of the Celtic Warrior,* p.117; Miguel Sanchez de Baêna and Paulo Alexandre Louçao, *Grandes Enigmas da História de Portugal,* Vol. I, p. 69

79   Quesada Sanz, F., 'Gladius hispaniensis: an archaeological view from Iberia' *JRMES,* vol. 8, pp. 251-270; 'Máchaira, kopís, falcata', *Homenaje a Francisco Torrent,* pp. 75-94; 'En torno al origen y procedencia de la falcata ibérica', *Archivo Español de Arqueología #63,* 1990, pp. 63-95; *El armamento ibérico.* Miguel Sanchez de Baêna and Paulo Alexandre Louçao, *Grandes Enigmas da História de Portugal,* Vol. I, p. 69. The oldest examples were found in Villaricos dating from the fifth or fourth centuries BC, they are probably copies of Greek models.

80   Martinez, Rafael T., *Rome's Enemies (4): Spanish Armies,* p. 38; Miguel

Sanchez de Baêna and Paulo Alexandre Louçao, *Grandes Enigmas da História de Portugal*, Vol. I, p. 69

81 Seneca, *De Beneficiis*, V.24

82 Fulgosio, Fernando, 'Armas y utensilios del hombre primitivo en el Museo Arqueológico Nacional', José Dorregaray (ed.), Museo Español de Antigüedades, Madrid, 1872, Vol. I, pp. 75-89.

83 Many falcatas have been found in Portugal and Spain and categorized into two groups based on blade size: A, long-bladed falcatas; and B, short – bladed falcatas. From these two groups they have been placed into three subgroups based on their hilts: I, ending with a bird's head; II, ending with a horse's head; and III, ending with a wolf's head.

84 Miguel Sanchez de Baêna and Paulo Alexandre Louçao, *Grandes Enigmas da História de Portugal*, Vol. I, p. 69

85 Sopeña, G., *Dioes, ética y ritos*, p.94; Quesada, F., *Arma y símbolo: la Falcata Ibérica*, p.38

86 Filon, *Mechaniké syntaxis*, IV-V; Suidas, s.v. machaira; Diodorus, 5.33.3-4; José M. Blázquez Martínez and M. Paz García-Gelabert, 'Estudio del armamento prerromano en la Península Ibérica a través de las fuentes y de las representaciones plásticas', *Hispania Antiqua* 14, 1990, 91-115; Garcia-Gelabert, M.P., 'Estudio del armamento prerromano en la península ibérica a través de los textos clásicos', *Espacio, Tiempo y Forma Serie II. Historia Antigua*, 2, 1989, pp. 69-80; Martinez, Rafael T., op. cit., pp. 38-39

87 The *caetrati* (light infantry) and the *scutati* (heavy infantry) were Iberian soldiers who had been formed into these respective units serving under Hannibal during the Second Punic War.

88 Melinda, Jose, *Arquelogia Española*, Madrid, 1942, p. 244; Arribas, Antonio, *The Iberians*, pp. 78-80; Martinez, Rafael T., *Rome's Enemies (4): Spanish Armies*, p. 36

89 Melinda, Jose, *Arquelogia Española*, p. 244

90 Strabo, 10.1.12

91 Livy, 21.8

92 Martinez, Rafael T., *Rome's Enemies (4): Spanish Armies*, p.37

93 Livy, 21.8

94 Livy, 21.8; Wise, Terence, *Armies of the Carthaginian Wars 265-146 BC*, Osprey Publishing, Oxford, 1982, 21

95 Martinez, Rafael T., *Rome's Enemies (4): Spanish Armies*, p.37

96 Though the bow and arrow was used in the peninsula, arrow-head finds are very rare. Due to archaeological evidence of hundreds of slingshots found throughout the peninsula and ancient literary descriptions, it seems the sling was a common instrument like the sword or spear, but it was not widely used except by the masters of

the sling, the Balearic warriors. The sling has a long history on the Iberian Peninsula, especially in Spain, and during my research I had the opportunity to witness the shepherds of the province of Extremadura, Spain use their skill. For information on ancient slingers of the Iberian Peninsula see Strabo, 3.4.15; 3.5.1; Publius Flavius Vegetius Renatus, *De Re Militari*, 1.16; Coronel Córdoba, José M.G., *Historia del Ejercito Español: Los orígenes*, Vol.1, Servicio Histórico Militar, Madrid, 1981; Cleugh, Eric, *Viva Mallorca: Yesterday and Today in the Balearic Islands*, Cassell, 1963; Wise, Terence, *Armies of the CarthaginianWars 265-146 BC*, p.21; Miguel Sanchez de Baêna and Paulo Alexandre Louçao, *Grandes Enigmas da História de Portugal*, Vol. I, p. 72

97   Miguel Sanchez de Baêna and Paulo Alexandre Louçao, *Grandes Enigmas da História de Portugal*, Vol. I, p. 72

98   Ibid., 73

99   Ibid., 72

100 Ibid., 72

101 Strabo, 3.4.18;Martinez, Rafael T., *Rome's Enemies (4): Spanish Armies*, p.8. Apparently one of the wild members of the parsley family (Apiaceae), i.e. fool's parsley (Aethusa cynapsium), poison hemlock (Conium maculatum), or water hemlock (Cicuta maculata); more likely, poison hemlock. But perhaps the herb should be identified with that deadly Sardinian herb which Pausanias (10.17) says is 'like parsley,' namely, celery-leaved, or marsh, crowfoot, celery-leaved buttercup (Ranunculus sceleratus; see Dioscorides, de Mat. Med. 2.206), and called by the Greeks 'wild parsley.' This Sardinian herb produced a convulsive laughter, with a drawing down of the angles of the mouth (Solinus, *Sertorius* 4.4), and ended fatally, with the proverbial 'Sardonic smile' (Pausanias, l.c.) on the victim's face.

102 Martinez, Rafael T., *Rome's Enemies (4): Spanish Armies*, p.8; Miguel Sanchez de Baêna and Paulo Alexandre Louçao, *Grandes Enigmas da História de Portugal*, Vol. I, p. 74

103 This idea is based on the numerous Iberian statues of warriors that have been found throughout the peninsula.

104 Miguel Sanchez de Baêna and Paulo Alexandre Louçao, *Grandes Enigmas da História de Portugal*, Vol. I, p. 58

105 Ibid., p. 58

106 Miguel Sanchez de Baêna and Paulo Alexandre Louçao, *Grandes Enigmas da História de Portugal*, Vol. I, p. 58

107 Ibid., 59

108 Miguel Sanchez de Baêna and Paulo Alexandre Louçao, *Grandes Enigmas da História de Portugal*, Vol. I, p. 59

109 Diodorus, 5.32.3

110 Strabo, 3.3.6

111 Miguel Sanchez de Baêna and Paulo Alexandre Louçao, *Grandes Enigmas da História de Portugal,* Vol. I, p. 59

112 Strabo, 3.3.7

113 The Montefortino helmet was a type of Roman helmet of the Roman republican era named after Montefortino. It was the first stage in the development of the *galea* (which would become the trademark helmet of the Roman army, as seen in most Roman period movies), and was derived from Celtic helmet design. Similar types are to be found in Spain, Gaul and into northern Italy. Surviving examples are generally found without cheek pieces (either because they had none to begin with, or because they were made a material which did not survive the test of time). Later Montefortino helmets are the first helmets proven to be of Roman origin, particularly through inscriptions found on them (mostly the names of the soldiers who owned them). Earlier helmets of the type are generally more decorated since, as the Roman army moved into the huge period of growth in the Marian reforms at the end of the second century BC, cheap, undecorated but effective helmets needed to be mass-produced for the mainly poor legionaries. Burns, Michael T., 'The Homogenization of Military Equipment Under the Roman Republic', *Digressus, Internet Journal for the Classical World, 'Romanization'? Digressus Supplement* 1, 2003, pp. 60-85; Miguel Sanchez de Baêna and Paulo Alexandre Louçao, op. cit., p. 59.

114 Miguel Sanchez de Baêna and Paulo Alexandre Louçao, op. cit., p. 59

115 Sample of these helmets can be seen at the National Museum of Archaeology in Lisbon and at the Museu de Conimbriga (which is an entire preserved Roman city); Miguel Sanchez de Baêna and Paulo Alexandre Louçao, op. cit., p. 61

116 Dias, Jaime Lopes, *Etnografia da Beira*, vol.III, Centro de Tradições Populares Portuguesas da Universidade de Lisboa, Lisbon, 1929, p. 69; Octávio da Veiga Ferreira and Seomara Bastos da Veiga Ferreira, *A Vida dos Lusitanos no Tempo de Viriato*, pp. 168-9.

117 Sanchez Moreno, Eduardo, 'Algunas Notas Sobre la Guerra Como Estrategia de Interacción Social en la Hispania Preromana: Viriato, Jefe Redistributivo (Parte I)', *Habis* #32, 2001, pp. 149-169; (Parte II) *Habis* #33, 2002, pp. 169-202; Muñoz, Mauricio P., *Viriato, O Herói Lusitano*, p. 74-77; Polanyi, Karl., 'The economy ace instituted process', in Polanyi, K., Arensberg, C.M and Pearson, M.W., (Eds.), *Trade and Market in the Early Empires: Economies in History and Theory*, Chicago, 1957, p.250; Sahlins, M., *Stone Age Economies*, New York, 1972 (edition in Castilian: Madrid, 1977); Renfrew, C., 'Trade ace action in distance', in Sabloff, J.A and Lamberg-Karlovsky, C.C., (Eds.), *Ancient Civilization and Trade*, Alburquerque, 1975, pp.8 and 11-12; Pryar, F.L., The origins of the

economy: to comparative study of distribution in primitive and peasant economies, New York, Sanchez Moreno, Eduardo.

118   'Algunas Notas Sobre la Guerra... Viriato, Jefe Redistributivo (Parte I), *Habis* #32, 2001, pp. 149-169 (Parte II) *Habis* #33, 2002, pp. 169-202.

119   Muñoz, Mauricio P., *Viriato, O Herói Lusitano*, p.76-77

120   Diodorus, 33.7.1

121   Sanchez Moreno, Eduardo, 'Algunas Notas Sobre la Guerra...Viriato, Jefe Redistributivo (Parte I) *Habis* #32, 2001, pp. 149-169 (Parte II) *Habis* #33, 2002, pp. 169-202.

122   Tierney, J.J., 'The Celtic Ethnography of Posidonius', *Proceedings of the Royal Irish Academy*, 60, C, Dublin, 1960, pp.189-275; Garcia Moreno, L.A., 'Organización sociopolítica de los Celtas en la Península Ibérica', Almagro Gorbea, M. (Dir.), *Los Celtas: Hispania y Europa*, Madrid, 1993, pp.331-336; Quesada Sanz, F., 'Vino, aristócratas, tumbas y guerreros en la cultura ibérica (ss.V-II a.C.)', *Verdolay*, 6, 1994, pp.99-124; ID., 'Vino y guerreros: banquete, valores aristocráticos y alcohol en Iberia', Celestino Pérez, S., (Ed.), *Arqueología del vino: Los orígenes del vino en Occidente*, Madrid, 1995 pp.273-296; Dominguez Monedero, A.J., 'Del simposio griego a los bárbaros bebedores: el vino en Iberia y su imagen en los autores antiguos', Celestino Pérez, S., (Ed.), *Arqueología del vino: Los orígenes del vino en Occidente*, Madrid, 1995, pp.23-72.

123   The only person who has actually studied the subject of Viriathus' policy of redistributing wealth is Eduardo Sanchez Moreno in 'Algunas Notas Sobre la Guerra... Viriato, Jefe Redistributivo'

124   Cynicism: The point of life is virtue, not pleasure, and it can only be obtained by independence from all earthly possessions and pleasures. Stoicism: Philosophy is primarily concerned with ethics. The end or purpose of life is *arête* (excellence) or virtue, which is identified with 'happiness' as the central theme is 'indifference to external circumstances.' Lens Tuero, J., 'Viriato, héroe y rey cínico', *Estudios de Filología Griega*, 2, 1968, pp.253-272.

CHAPTER 4

1   Books 36 to 54 are nearly all complete. The book 55 has a considerable gap in it. Books 56 to 60 are complete. Of the next 20, there remain only fragments. The 80th and final book covers the period from AD 222-229 (the reign of Alexander Severus).

2   Muñoz, Mauricio P., *Viriato, O Herói Lusitano*, p. 43, Alberto, Paulo Farmhouse, *Viriato, Vultos da Antiguidade*, Editorial Inquérito, Sintra, 1996, p. 33; Vilatela, Luciano Perez, *Lusitania: Historia y Etnología*, Real Academia de la Historia, Madrid, 2000, p. 263-265; Tusculano, Victor de, *A Luistânia de há dois mil anos: epopeia military de Viriato*, Caxias: Tip. do Reformatório Central, 1950, p.61

3   Muñoz, Mauricio P., *Viriato, O Herói Lusitano*. p.43

4   Ibid., p.43

5   Tusculano, Victor de, *A Luistânia de há dois mil anos: epopeia military de Viriato*, p. 61.

6   Schulten, Adolf, 'Viriatus', Neue jahrbücher für der klassiker' *Altertum*, 39, Heidelberg, 1917, pp. 209-237. It was later translated into Spanish as: 'Viriato', *Boletín de la Biblioteca Menéndez y Pelayo*, II, Santander, 1920 #3, pp. 126-149 and #4,5 and 6, pp. 272-281. In Portuguese it was put together as a book published in Porto, 1940.

7   Diodorus, 33.1.1

8   Garcia Moreno, L., 'Infância, Juventude e Primeiras Aventuras de Viriato, Caudillo Lusitano', *Actas I Congreso Peninsular de Historia Antigua*, Vol. II, Santiago de Compostela, 1988, pp. 373-382

9   Vilatela, Luciano Perez, *Lusitania: Historia y Etnología*, pp. 259-263

10   Today Aeminius is known as Coimbra, Portugal, and the river refers to the Minho River that forms the northern border of Portugal with Spain, so perhaps Viriathus may have been born not in Lusitania but in Galizia, which Pliny considered to be part of Lusitania. All three can be found in Pliny, NH, 4.113, 115, 118.

11   Diodorus, 33.1.1

12   Varro, *res Rusticae*, 2.1.19; Vergilius, *Georgica*, 3.272; Silius Italicus, *Punica*, 3.378 and 16.364; Vilatela, Luciano Perez, *Lusitania: Historia y Etnología*, p. 262

13   Costa, Joaquin, 'Viriato y la Cuestión Social en España en el Siglo II Antes de Jesucristo', *Tutela de Pueblos en la Historia*, Madrid, 1879 and it was again published in *Estidios Ibéricos*, Madrid, 1902; Arenas Lopez, Anselmo, *Reivindicaciones Histórica: Viriato não era Português mas Celtibero*, Guadalajara, 1900 and *La Luistania Celtíbera*, Madrid, 1907.

14   Peris, M., 'La Lusitania Primitiva', 'Campaña Luistana y Viriatense', 'Fin de Viriato' and 'La Patria de Viriato', *Boletín de la Sociedade Castellonense de Cultura*, IV, 1926.

15   Diodorus, 23.1.6; Appian, *Iber.*, 70

16   Orosius, 5.4.1; Florous, 1.33, Diodorus, 33.1.1-4. It seems that this theory came from Bispo-Mor do Reino, *História da Lusitânia*, 1580.

17   Aguiar, João, *A Voz dos Deuses*, 13ª edição, Porto, Edições Asa, 1992

18   Alberto, Paulo Farmhouse, *Viriato, Vultos da Antiguidade*, p. 37.

19   Diodorus, 33.1.1; Cassius Dio, 78

20   Ibid., 33.1.2

21   Ibid., 33.7.3

22   Cassius Dio, 78

23   Cassius Dio, 78

24   Ibid., 78

25   Aguiar, João, *A Voz dos Deuses*, p.130; Muñoz, Mauricio P.,
      op. cit., p. 51.

26   Aguiar, p.130; Muñoz, p.51

27   Aguiar, p.130; Muñoz, p.51

28   Aguiar, p.130; Muñoz, p.51

29   Aguiar, João, *A Voz dos Deuses*, p. 135

30   Diodorus, 33.1.3; Florus, 1.33.15; Dio Cassius, 73; Orosius, 5.4.1;
      Eutropius, 4.6

31   See Garcia y Bellido, Antonio, 'Bandas y Guerrillas en las Luchas con
      Roma', *Hispania*, Vol. V, #trg5, p.540-550; Gundel, H.G.., *Viriato,
      lusitano, caudillo en las luchas contra los romanos: 147-139 a.C.*,
      Caesaraugusta, 1968, pp.175-198

32   Maluquer de Montes, Juan, 'Los Pueblos de la España céltica', *Historia
      de España*, book I, Vol. III, Pt. 1, 1976

33   Unfortunately we do not know the true name of his Astoplas
      daughter / Viriathus' wife, although according to legend her name is
      Tongina and she was a young and very beautiful woman, with dark
      hair and pale radiant skin, who was modest but with great
      'haughtiness and firmness'. We know with certainty that she was
      related to the richest land owner of Betica, who is said to have been a
      powerful and influential man who had many connections with Rome
      and other Iberian tribes. Near the end of this section there is some
      controversy over whether Astoplas was Tongina's father or brother. In
      João Aguilar's book, *A Voz dos Deuses*, there are several references to
      Tongina.

34   Diodorus, 33.7.1-4; As for the word brother / father-in-law being in
      quotation marks, this is because near the end of this section there is
      some controversy over the family status of Astolplas regarding
      whether he was the father or brother of Tongina.

35   Diodorus, 33.7.1-4

36   Diodorus, 33.7.1

37   Diodorus, 33.7.2

38   Diodorus, 33.7.3

39   Diodorus, 33.7.5

40   For more see Lens Tuero, J., 'Viriato, Héroe y Rey Cínico', *Estudios de
      Filología Griega #2*, 1986, pp. 253-272 and *Estudios sobre Diodoro de
      Sicilia*, Granada, 1994, pp. 127-143; Garcia Quintela, M.V., 'Viriato y la
      Ideología Trifuncional Indoeuropea', *Polis #3*, 1993, pp. 111-138

41   Garcia Quintela, M.V., 'Viriato y la Ideología Trifuncional
      Indoeuropea', pp. 111-138

42   Muñoz, Mauricio P., *Viriato, O Herói Lusitano*, pp. 57-58

43   Diodorus, 33.7.4-7

44   It is a story of a man with two wives, one young, one older; the man
      goes bald because the older woman plucks out his dark hairs while
      the younger one plucks out his white hairs, as they both desire him to
      look more like them. *Fabulae Aesopiae* 2.2; According to Liv Yarrow,
      this illustrates how Viriathus had gained wisdom and clarity of
      oration without education, although Diodorus defeats his purpose by
      suggesting that Viriathus could 'intuit' such a common didactic
      illustration. Yarrow, Liv Mariah, *Historiography at the end of the
      Republic: Provincial Perspectives on Roman Rule*, Oxford University
      Press, 2006, p. 335

45   Cassius Dio 75; Muñoz, Mauricio P., *Viriato, O Herói Lusitano*, p. 60.

46   Muñoz, Mauricio P., *Viriato, O Herói Lusitano*, 2006, pp. 60-61

47   Ibid., p. 61

48   Garcia Quintela, M.V, *Mitologia y Mitos de La Hispania Preromana Vol.3
      La Leyenda de Viriato*, Ediciones AKAL, Madrid, 1999; Muñoz,
      Mauricio P., *Viriato, O Herói Lusitano*, p. 60

49   Muñoz, Mauricio P., op.cit., pp. 58-62; Garcia Quintela, M.V., 'Viriato y
      la Ideología Trifuncional Indoeuropea', *Polis* #3, 1993, pp. 111-138;
      Sergent, Bernard, 'Three Notes on the Trifunctional Indo-European
      Marriage', *Journal of Undo-European Studies* #12, 1984, pp. 179-191

50   For more information see Dumézil, Georges, *The Destiny of the Warrior*,
      translated by Alf Hiltebeitel, University of Chicago Press, Chicago and
      London, 1970, and Flamen-Brahman, Paris: Paul Geuthner, 1935,
      Garcia Quintela, M.V., op. cit., pp. 111-138; Sergent, Bernard, op. cit.,
      pp. 179-191

51   Dumézil, G., Flamen-Brahman, Paris, 1929 and Mitra-Varuna, Presses
      Universitaires de France, 1940

52   García Quintela, Marco V., 'http://www.uwm.edu/The Celts in the
      Iberian Peninsula', e-Keltoi, Center for Celtic Studies, University of
      Wisconsin-Milwaukee, Volume 6, August 10, 2005, p. 520 and 'Viriato
      y la Ideología Trifuncional Indoeuropea', *Polis* #3, 1993, pp. 111-138

53   Ibid., p.520

54   García Quintela, Marco V., 'http://www.uwm.edu/The Celts in the
      Iberian Peninsula', p. 520 and 'Viriato y la Ideología Trifuncional
      Indoeuropea', pp. 111-138

55   Ibid., p. 520

56   García Quintela, Marco V., 'http://www.uwm.edu/The Celts in the
      Iberian Peninsula', p. 520 and 'Viriato y la Ideología Trifuncional
      Indoeuropea', pp. 111-138

57   Ibid., p. 520

58   Cassius Dio, 22, fr. 73.4

59   García Quintela, Marco V., 'http://www.uwm.edu/The Celts in the Iberian Peninsula', p. 521 and 'Viriato y la Ideología Trifuncional Indoeuropea', pp. 111-138

60   Diodorus, 33 7.3; This is outlined in Quintela, Marco V., 'http://www.uwm.edu/The Celts in the Iberian Peninsula', p. 521 and at the beginning of this section.

61   García Quintela, Marco V., 'http://www.uwm.edu/The Celts in the Iberian Peninsula', p. 521

62   Refer to the outline in García Quintela, Marco V., 'http://www.uwm.edu/The Celts in the Iberian Peninsula', p. 522 and at the beginning of this section.

63   Ibid.

64   The comparison to the rape of the Sabine Women will be looked into in the next section, 'Other Theories about Viriathus' Marriage'

65   Muñoz, Mauricio P., op. cit., 58-62; Garcia Quintela, M.V., 'Viriato y la Ideología Trifuncional Indoeuropea', pp. 111-138; Quintela, Marco V., 'http://www.uwm.edu/The Celts in the Iberian Peninsula', p. 522; Sergent, Bernard, 'Three Notes on the Tirfunctional Indo-European Marriage', pp. 179-191; Dumézil, Georges, The Destiny of the Warrior.

66   García Quintela, Marco V., 'http://www.uwm.edu/The Celts in the Iberian Peninsula', p. 254. It does not appear possible that there was a relationship between Greek ethnographers and Celtic compilers of Celtic mythology.

67   Ibid., p.254

68   'Bride price' also known as 'bride wealth 'is an amount of money or property or wealth paid by the groom or his family to the parents of a woman upon the marriage of their daughter to the groom. (Compare dowry, which is paid to the groom, or used by the bride to help establish the new household, and dower, which is property settled on the bride herself by the groom at the time of marriage.) In the anthropological literature bride price has often been explained in market terms, as payment made in exchange for the bride's family's loss of her labour and fertility within her kin group.

69   Bermejo Barrera, J.C., *Mitologia y Mitos de La Hispania Preromana I*, 2 vols., Madrid vol. 1, 1986 and vol. 2, 1994; Muñoz, Mauricio P., op. cit., p. 59

70   Muñoz, Mauricio P., op. cit., p. 62

71   The Book of Judges in the Bible; Homer, *The Iliad*; Livy, 'The Rape of the Sabine Women', in Mary R. Lefkowitz & Maureen B. Fant, *Women's Life in Greece and Rome: A Source Book in Translation*, Published by JHU Press, 2005, pp. 176-178. In 326 AD, the Emperor Constantine issued an edict prohibiting marriage by abduction. The law made kidnapping a public offence; even the kidnapped bride could be

punished if she later consented to a marriage with her abductor. Judith Evans-Grubbs, 'Abduction Marriage in Antiquity: A Law of Constantine (CTh IX. 24. I) and Its Social Context', *The Journal of Roman Studies*, Vol. 79, (1989), pp. 59-83, at 59, 65.

72   Legend says that the Romans abducted the Sabine women to populate the newly built town of Rome. This is the first recorded example of bride kidnapping. The conflict that ensued ended only when the women threw themselves and their children between the armies of their fathers and husbands. ('Rape' in this context means 'kidnapping' rather than its modern meaning, see *raptio*.) Muñoz, Mauricio P., *Viriato, O Herói Lusitano*, Esquilo, Lisbon, 2006, pp. 61-62

73   Galba's massacre of the Lusitanians resulted in 9,000 killed and 20,000 sold into slavery in Gaul and Rome. Only 1,000 or so escaped, Viriathus being one of them

74   The reason the Lusitanian War was dubbed the Thieves War was because it was fought by thieves rather than soldiers. In the Roman soldier's view the Lusitanians were more thieves than warriors because of their prior history as bandits. 'The Fiery War' was used because of the ferocity that each side showed to each other.

75   Mommsen, Theodor, *The History Of Rome, Book IV: The Revolution*, Chapter I: 'The Subject Countries Down To The Times Of The Gracchi', translated by William Purdie Dickson, University Of Glasgow, n.d.

CHAPTER 5

1   This is the name given by Polybius and Appian.

2   Polybius XXXIII, 8, 12. For an attempt at a correct understanding of this affair see *American Historical Review*, XVIII.236.The war in question was undertaken by Rome wholly on Massilia's behalf and all the profits of the conquest fell to Massilia.

3   Since Rome later received only half a tithe as tribute in Spain, it is probable that the Punic tribute had also been low. Frank, Tenney, *Roman Imperialism*, New York, Macmillan, 1914, p.73

4   Massiliots were Greeks who founded Marseille.

5   The Roman historians naturally forgot the important role of Massilia in the earlier proceedings, since Rome eventually assumed the whole burden of the quarrel. However, Appian, *Hann.* 2, knew that 'Greeks settled in Spain' first appealed to Rome against Punic encroachment, and these were, of course, the clients of Massilia. Frank, Tenney, *Roman Imperialism*, p.73

6   The Massiliot traders may well have suggested this course to the Saguntines, since a Roman alliance would insure an 'open door policy.' Polybius (III, 30) places the alliance several years before 221, but apparently after the Iber treaty. The city was Spanish, as the

excavations prove, not Greek, as the annalists thought. But it was strong and well governed; Polybius. III, 17.

7   Polybius, III, 11, 12.

8   The Roman province of Illyricum replaced the formerly independent kingdom of Illyria, which stretched from the Drilon River in modern Albania to Istria (Croatia) in the west and to the Sava River (Croatia) in the north. The attack on Saguntum occurred when the Romans were involved in the Second Illyrian War (220 BC to 219 BC). In 219 BC the Roman Republic was at war with the Celts of Cisalpine Gaul, and the Second Punic War with Carthage was beginning. These distractions gave Demetrius the time he needed to build a new Illyrian war fleet. Leading this fleet of 90 ships, Demetrius sailed south of Lissus, violating his earlier treaty and starting the war. Demetrius' fleet first attacked Pylos where he captured 50 ships after several attempts. From Pylos the fleet sailed to the Cyclades, quelling resistance they found on the way. Demetrius foolishly sent a fleet across the Adriatic, and, with the Illyrian forces divided, the Illyrian city of Dimale was captured by the Roman fleet under Lucius Aemilius Paulus. From Dimale the Roman navy went towards Pharos. The Romans routed the Illyrians and Demetrius fled to Macedon where he became a trusted councilor at the court of Philip V of Macedon, and remained until his death at Messene in 214 BC.

9   Livy and Appian, who wish to exculpate Rome, recklessly state that Hannibal broke the treaty of 226 BC by crossing the Iber to attack Saguntum, not knowing that the city lay a hundred miles south of that river. Polybius belittles Hannibal's provocation to attack Saguntum and holds that Carthage should have based her grievance upon the seizure of Sardinia twenty years before. This seems to be a very peculiar argument from a statesman of Polybius' experience, for ancient states did not assume the privilege of annulling old treaties on the ground of severity any more than modern states do. Most modern historians assert that Rome's alliance with Saguntum was an infraction of the spirit at least of the Iber treaty; for they assume that the treaty defined the Iber River as the boundary of the Punic and Roman 'spheres of influence' in Spain. E.g.,Heitland, *The Roman Republic*, I, p. 223; Meltzer, *Gesch. derKarthager*, II, 421; Kromayer in *Hist. Zeitschr.* 1909, p. 237; Ed. Meyer, *Kleine Schriften*, p. 269; Frank, Tenney, *Roman Imperialism*, p.73

According to Frank, this is a grave misconception of third-century international politics. Rome had made the Saguntine alliance several years before the war, and yet not a word of protest had been raised against it. Hannibal attacked Saguntum, not on the grounds that the Saguntine alliance encroached upon the Punic sphere, but on the ground of the wrongs committed by Saguntum against Spanish allies. In no ancient source is there the slightest indication that Carthage considered her rights in Spain to have been infringed by the Saguntine treaty; Frank, Tenney, *Roman Imperialism*, p.73; Polybius (III, 29) goes so far as to claim that the Carthaginian government repudiated the Iber treaty on the grounds that Hasdrubal was not authorized to make it. Frank Tenney says Polybius assumes that Rome had full power to make any alliances she chose with free states in Spain and asserts that all such allies were entitled to security by the terms of former treaties. Nor did Rome know anything of the modern doctrine of 'spheres of influence,' although it may have had some meaning for the ancient monarchies of the eastern Mediterranean. Rome's alliances showed in general an abhorrence of loose ends and always insisted upon clear definitions of boundaries. A penumbra of undefined influence over a hinterland of unexplored territory would have been entirely beyond Rome's understanding at that time. It had hitherto dealt with a patchwork of innumerable city-states and tribes whose petty areas in every case were precisely defined. It had signed at least a hundred alliances with such states, and the jurisdiction of each of these hundred treaties was clearly and definitely known. Not one of them assumed any kind of influence or interest beyond the precise boundaries of the signatories. Accordingly, although an affair like the Saguntine alliance would call for immediate protest during the days of Monroe Doctrines and African protectorates, there is no reason to suppose that in the third century, when it occurred, it involved any infraction of rights or that it could, in any way, have offended Hasdrubal and Hannibal, except in so far as it revealed Rome's success in gaining an ally coveted by them.

10   When the war opened, Rome sent only a small detachment to Spain with the purpose not of conquering the peninsula, but of holding back Spanish reenforcements until the war was settled in Africa. The nations came to blows because the Barcid family — whose war policy had met with defeat in 242 BC and 238 BC — were able to keep alive the bitter feelings aroused by former defeats and to discover a situation at the right moment whereby they could force their government to support a raid of vengeance upon Italy. If a brilliant son of Hamilcar Barcas had not survived to carry on the policy of his father till the favourable moment arrived, there is not the slightest reason for assuming that Rome and Carthage would not have found a *modus vivendi* in the same way that the neighboring powers of the eastern Mediterranean had. Frank, Tenney, *Roman Imperialism*

11   The Barcids, in order to acquire Spain for military purposes, had imposed only a very light tribute and Rome could not expect to win it from Carthage if she increased these impositions. Consequently, the Spanish tribute was always extremely low — only half a tithe upon its poorly tilled fields. Livy, XLIII, 2, 12; Frank, Tenney, *Roman Imperialism*, p. 75

12   Mommsen, Theodor, *Römische Geschichte*, 8 vols., Berlin, 1903,vol. 1 and 3. Translated into Spanish as *Historia de Roma*, Madrid, 1983.

13   It required several decades, however, before Rome became overcrowded again. During the three decades after the war, Rome's citizen body increased only 25 per cent, whereas the acreage of *ager Romanus* increased 100 per cent. See *American History Review*, XVIII, p. 245.

14   The only practical difference was that the *civitates* were allowed to pay Rome specified sums of money as tribute (in this case, based upon an estimate of half a tithe on produce) instead of an annual percentage in kind. This was the usual Seleucid system, probably established in Spain by Carthage. The cities were, therefore, *slipendiariae* rather than *decumanae*. Of course there were favoured cities in Spain as well as in Sicily: several *foederatae, some liberae,* and many which, at an early day, secured the privileges of Latin cities. See Marquardt, *Staatsverwaltung,* I, 251; Frank, Tenney, *Roman Imperialism,* p.76

15   Heitland, E.G., *The Roman Republic,* I, p. 227; Frank, Tenney, *Roman Imperialism,* pp. 79-80

16   Livy, 39.20-21

17   During the first stages of Romanization, the peninsula was divided in two by the Romans for administrative purposes. The closest one to Rome was called Citerior and the more remote one Ulterior. The frontier between both was a sinuous line running from Cartago Nova (now Cartagena) to the Cantabrian Sea. Hispania Ulterior comprised what are now Andalusia, Portugal, Extremadura, León, a great portion of the former Castilla la Vieja, Galicia, Asturias, Cantabria and the Basque Country. Hispania Citerior comprised the eastern part of former Castilla la Vieja, and what are now Aragon, Valencia, Catalonia and a major part of former Castilla la Nueva.

18   Livy, 35.1.4; Muñoz, Mauricio P., *Viriato: O Herói Lusitano,* p. 144

19   Livy, 35.1.1-12. The number of casualties that Livy claims the Romans inflicted on the Lusitani seem a bit much, for upon further reading into his work every time the Romans encountered another army in battle according to Livy they inflicted thousands of casualties upon the enemy. If this were the case I might not be here today. The high numbers were perhaps used for propaganda purposes. It is likely that during this battle 1,200 were killed instead of 12,000

20   Livy, 35.1.1-16

21   Livy, 37.57.1. L. Aemilius Paulus Macedonicus, who with great glory had defeated King Perseus of Macedonia, was assigned to Hispania in 189. It was in Macedonia that he received the nickname Macedonicus.

22   Livy, 37.46.10-12, Lyco, sometimes pronounced Llurco, is located in 'Cerro de los Infantes' in Pinos Puente (Granada).

23   Livy, 37.57.5. As mentioned, the number of Lusitanian deaths is questionable for at times (just as in modern times) the number of enemy killed was exaggerated.

24   García Moreno, Luis A., 'Sobre el decreto de Paulo Emilio y la Turris Lascutana (CIL, 12, 614)', *Epigrafía hispánica de epoca romano-republicana*, 1986, Zaragoga, pp. 195-218

25   Livy, 39.7.6

26   Livy, 39.7.7-9; Muñoz, Mauricio P., *Viriato: O Herói Lusitano*, p. 136

27   Livy, 39.21.3-4

28   Livy, 39.21.1-5

29   Livy, 39.30.2

30   Livy, 39.30.3-7

31   Livy, 39.30.8

32   Livy, 39.42.1

33   Livy, 39.42.3-4

34   See chapter one for details.

35   Livy, 41.47

36   Livy, Per. 46

37   Muñoz, Mauricio P., *Viriato: O Herói Lusitano* p. 146

38   The alleged reason for Rome going to war again was that the Celtiberian town of Segeda had taken to incorporating other smaller towns into its own boundaries. J.S. Richardson, in his stern study on this affair, writes that this seems trivial compared to the Roman response of sending a consul with a consular army of two legions to deal with the situation, and it seems likely that at least part of the explanation lies in the need of the Senate to find somewhere for the consuls to fight in a period of relative peace. Richardson, J.S., *Appian: Wars of the Romans in Iberia*, p.141.

39   Appian 56.234-237

40   Ibid.

41   Ibid.

42   Ibid.

43   Calvert, Albert F., *Toledo: An Historical and Descriptive Account of the 'City of Generations'*, The Spanish Series, J. Lane, London and New York, 1907, p. 4.

44   Tusculano, Victor de, *A Lusitânia de há dois mil anos: epopeia military de Viriato*, p.28

45   Appian, 56.237

46   Ibid.

47   Appian, 57.238

48   Ibid.

49   Tusculano, Victor de, *A Lusitânia de há dois mil anos: epopeia military de Viriato*, p. 28

50   Appian, 57.239

51   Ibid.; The Conii were a sub-group of Celts that lived in the Algarve who were Roman subjects since 174 BC

52   Appian, 57.240

53   Appian, 57.241

54   Ibid. Again, 15,000 casualties seems a bit high.

55   Appian, 57.242

56   Muñoz, Mauricio P., *Viriato: O Herói Lusitano*, p. 149

57   Appian 58.243

58   Ibid.

59   Appian, 58.244

60   Appian, 51.215- 53.225. Lucullus campaigned against the Vaccaei and Caucaei because he was keen for glory and needed money (51.215); this led to the undignified massacre of Cauca, a Caucaei city located between Salamanca and Segovia. When both tribes surrendered they signed a peace agreement that had very harsh conditions and required them to provide hostages, a payment of 100 talons (of what it is not known), and establish a garrison of 2,000 Roman soldiers in the city (Muñoz, Mauricio P., op. cit., p. 148).

61   Appian, 58.244

62   Appian, 58.245

63   Appian, 58.246

64   Ibid.

65   Appian, 59.247

66   Appian, 59.248

67   Appian, 59.248-249

68   Appian, 59.249-250

69   Appian, 59.249-250

70   30,000 is an estimate from other sources, with which many modern historians have come to agree, but in actuality nobody knows the number for sure.

71   Appian, 60.251

72   Appian, 60.252; Orosius, 4.21.10. Many authors agree that the Romans only killed the men, as out of the estimated 30,000 Lusitanians only 8,000 to 9,000 were killed.

73   Appian, 60.253

74 Again the number of casualties and prisoners taken cannot be exactly accurate for several sources (such as Valerius Maximus 9.6.2; Suetonius, *Galba* 3) have different numbers, but all modern historians agree with this count.

75 Appian, 60.255. According to J.S. Richardson's research on the war, this is the only statement about Galba's greed in any classical source. Richardson, J.S., *Appian: Wars of the Romans in Iberia*, p.154.

76 Appian, 60.255

77 Cicero, Brutus, 27.106; *Epistulae ad Atticum* (Letters to Atticus), 12.5(b); Livy, 98-100; Richardson, J.S., *Hispaniae*, p. 137. On the history of *leges repetundarum* see Balsdon, J.P.V.D., 'The history of the extortion court at Rome, 123-70 BC', *Papers of the British School at Rome* #14, 1938, pp. 98-114; Lintott, A.W., 'The leges de repetundis and associated measures under the Republic', *Zeitschrift der Savigny-Stiftung* #98, 1981, pp. 162-212.

78 Livy, 39.40.12 and 49; Appian, 60.255; Gellius, *Attic Nights*, 1.12.17; Cicero, *Divinatio in Caecilium*, 20.66 and *Brutus*, 23.89; *de oratore*, 1.53.227-228; Quintilian, 2.15.8; Valerius Maximus, 8.1.2

79 Livy, *Per.* 49

80 Felicitas was unknown before the mid-second century BC, when a temple was dedicated to her in the Velabrum in the Campus Martius (Field of Mars) in Rome by Lucius Licinius Lucullus, who used booty from his 151–150 BC campaign in Spain. The temple was destroyed by a fire during the reign of Claudius and never rebuilt. Muñoz, Mauricio P., *Viriato: O Herói Lusitano*, p. 152

81 Cicero, *Brutus*, 82 and *de oratore*, 1.58;Appian, 60.255

82 Rodrigues, Adriano Vasco, *Arqueologia da Peninsula Hispanica*, Porto, 1960, p. 409

83 Ibid.

CHAPTER 6

1 Polybius, 35.1

2 Third Punic War (Latin: *Tertium Bellum Punicum*) was the third and last of the Punic Wars fought between the former Phoenician colony of Carthage and the Roman Republic. The war was a much smaller engagement than the two previous Punic wars and primarily consisted of a single main action, the Battle of Carthage, but it resulted in the complete destruction of the city, the annexation of all remaining Carthaginian territory by Rome, and the death or enslavement of the entire Carthaginian population. The Third Punic War ended Carthage's empire.

3 Appian, 60.254

4 Appian, 61.256

5   Córdoba was the capital of the Roman province of Hispania Ulterior
     Baetica. Teófilo Braga, *Viriato: A Lusitânia é a mais poderosa nação da
     Hispânia*, Fronteira do Caos Editores, 2006 p. 32.

6   Appian, 61.257

7   Appian, 61.257 - 258

8   Appian, 61.258 - 259

9   Frontinus, Stratagema, 2.13.4

10   Appian, 62.260

11   Appian, 62.261

12   Appian, 62.262-263

13   Appian, 62.262

14   Appian, 62.263

15   Appian, 62.264

16   Appian, 63.266

17   Sierra de Ronda is situated in the province of Málaga, Spain; this is
     also the source of the Guadiaro River. During the Roman era the
     Ronda pass represented the only line of communication in the
     Guadalquivir Valley to the ancient town Carteia (today it is a ruin
     near the city of Algeciras and San Roque), at a distance of 60 km. The
     location of unknown Tribola: UJH Becker sought it in the area of
     Cadis; J. F. Masdeu in Evora and Beja; Schulten follows Appian's text
     that refers the deep gorges that ran along the Serra de Rhonda
     from Betis to Carteia. In the area, there is no evidence of another road
     than the one that follows along the Guadiaro (Barbesula) Valley.
     Currently the rail line to Antequera – Rhonda runs through this area.
     South of Sierra da Ronda between Sierra da Ronda and Libar, a road
     passes through a long narrow pass in which Vetilius men had once
     passed through in a column formation and according to
     archaeological artifacts this could have been the precise place were the
     Lusitanians ambushed the Romans. There already existed a very
     ancient path that connected Acinipo (Ronda la Vieja) and Arunda
     (Ronda) until Carteia, this route a century later; it would turn into a
     major Roman road that connected Carteia to Corduba. So to find the
     city of Tribola one must seek it not far from Carteia. Muñoz, Mauricio
     P., *Viriato: O Herói Lusitano*, pp. 162-163

18   Appian 63.267

19   Appian, 63.267. It is often assumed that Appian meant Carteia on the
     Bay of Algeciras, close to Gibraltar, because other sources believed
     that it was formerly called by the Greeks, Tartessus, and was ruled by
     King Arganthonius, who is said to have lived 150 years. Richardson,
     J.S., Appian: *Wars of the Romans in Iberia*, p.154.

20   Martinez, Rafael T., *Rome's Enemies (4): Spanish Armies*, p.8; Arribas,

Antonio, *The Iberians*, p.74.

21 Appian, 63.268

22 Carpetania was an ancient region of what is today Spain, located between the Guadarrama, the mountains of Toledo, the River Guadiana and the mountain range of Alcaraz, including approximately the present independent communities of Madrid and Castile. It was inhabited by the Carpetanians, a pre-Roman tribe. To the south dwelt the Oretanians; on the northeast were Celtiberians, to the northwest the Vacceus and Vetones. This area was easily conquered by the Romans and it was quickly integrated culturally and politically. Thus it is practically unmentioned in the literature of the Roman conquest of Hispania. Its main urban nuclei —Toletum (present-day Toledo), Complutum (present-day Alcala de Henares), Consabura (present-day Consuegra), Segóbriga (Saelices and Laminio) — soon after the conquest acquired municipal statutes.

23 Allen, Stephen, *Lords of Battle: The World of the Celtic Warrior*, p.150

24 Tusculano, Victor de, *A Luistânia de há dois mil anos: epopeia military de Viriato*, pp. 73-74

25 Appian, 66.279-280

26 Tusculano, Victor de, *A Luistânia de há dois mil anos: epopeia military de Viriato*, p. 74

27 Braga, Teófilo, *Viriato: A Lusitânia é a mais poderosa nação da Hispânia*, pp. 46, 50.

28 Appian, 64.269

29 Appian, 63.268; Teófilo Braga, op.cit., pp. 67-68; Martinez, Rafael T.,op. cit., p. 16; Muñoz, Mauricio P., op. cit., p. 163

30 Evora has a history dating back more than two millennia. It may have been the kingdom of Astolpas (Saramago, Jose, Évora, Património da Humanidade, 1986 report to UNESCO to make Evora a World Hertiage site). It was known as Ebora by the Lusitanians, who made the town their regional capital. The Romans conquered it in 57 BC and expanded it into a walled town. Vestiges from this period (city walls and ruins of Roman baths) still remain. The Romans had extensive gold mining in Portugal, and the name may be derived from that *oro*, *aurum*, gold. (Newman, Harold, R., *The Mineral Industry of Portugal*, 2002). Julius Caesar called it '*Liberalitas Julia*' (Julian generosity). The city grew in importance because it lay at the junction of several important routes. During his travels through Gaul and Lusitania, Pliny the Elder also visited the town and mentioned it in his book Naturalis Historia as Ebora Cerealis, because of its many surrounding wheat fields. In those days Evora became a flourishing city. Its high rank among municipalities in Roman Hispania is clearly shown by many inscriptions and coins. Braga, Teófilo, op. cit., pp. 83 -85;

Tusculano, Victor de, *A Luistânia de há dois mil anos: epopeia military de Viriato*, pp. 76-77

31   Appian, 64.270

32   Appian, 64.271. According to Professor Schulten, Mons Veneris is what is now known as Sierra de San Vicente, close to Talavera de la Reina, but according to Alarcão it may have been the Sierra de San Pedro between Cáceres and Badajoz (Alarcão, J. de, Roman Portugal, Vol. I, Aris & Phillips Ltd., Warminster, UK, 1988, p. 7 and Melena, Jose L., 'Salama, Jálama y la epigrafia latina del antigo corregimiento', *Symbolae Ludovico Mitxelena Septuagenario oblatae*, Vitoria, 1985, p. 484-485), but Blázquez states that it was located in the well-known area of the Sierra the Serenita, in Gredos, which according to him is geographically more strategic for guerrilla operations, given its location between the valleys of Jerte and the Tormes (Blázquez, J.M., 'La religiosidad de los pueblos hispanos, vista por los autores griegos y latinos', *Emerita XXVI*, 1958, 87); Inês Vaz, Luis João, *Lusitanos no Tempo de Viriato*, Esquilo, Lisboa, 2009, p. 159.

33   Appian, 69.271-272; Diodorus 33.2; The *minuta majestas*, or simply *majestas*, was based on the Roman law of treason. The original text of the law appears to have dealt with what were chiefly military offences, such as sending letters or messages to the enemy, giving up a standard or fortress, and desertion.

34   Appian, 64.272

35   The Sierra de Guadarrama is a mountain range forming the eastern half of the Sistema Central (a mountain range in the centre of the Iberian Peninsula), located between the Sierra de Gredos in the province of Ávila and Sierra de Ayllón in the province of Guadalajara. The range runs southwest-northeast, extending into the province of Madrid to the south, and towards the provinces of Ávila and Segovia to the north.

36   Frontinus, 4.5.22; Orosius, 5.4.5

37   Frontinus, *Stratagems*, 3.10.6; 3.11.4

38   Ibid., 3.11.4

39   Orosius, 5.4.3; Florus, 1.33.15

40   Sextus Aurelius Victor, *De Viris Illustribus Romae*, 71

41   Appian, 65.276; Kornemann, Ernst, 'Die neue Livius-Epitome aus Oxyrhynchus.' *Klio Beiheft*, 2. Leipzig, 1904, p. 98 – 99; Brennan, Corey, 'Notes on the praetors in Spain in the mid-second century BC', *Emerita* 63, 1995, p. 65

42   Richardson, J.S., *Hispaniae*, pp. 188-189

43   Braga, Teófilo, op. cit., p. 83

44   This excerpt was supposedly taken from Cassius Dio's History of

Rome and used in these following historical literary works, Braga, Teófilo, op cit., p. 84; Tusculano, Victor de, op. cit., p. 89-90; Martinez, Rafael T., op. cit., p. 16 and Allen, Stephen, Op. Cit., p.150; Muñoz, Mauricio P., op. cit., p. 165.

45   Braga, Teófilo, op. cit., p. 84; Tusculano, Victor de,op. cit., p. 89-90

46   Tusculano, Victor de, op. cit., p. 88

47   Ibid., pp. 89-92

48   Appian, 65.273-274

49   Appian, 65.274

50   Tusculano, Victor de,op. cit., pp. 78-79

51   Ibid., pp. 84-85

52   Ibid., p. 85

53   Muñoz, Mauricio P., op. cit., p. 166

54   Tusculano, Victor de,op. cit., p. 80

55   Ibid., p. 80

56   Appian, 65.274

57   Appian, 65.275. Melqart, also spelled Melkart or Melkarth, was a Phoenician god, the chief deity of Tyre and of two of its colonies, Carthage and Gadir (Cádiz, Spain). He was also called the Tyrian Baal. Under the name Malku he was equated with the Babylonian Nergal, god of the underworld and death, and thus may have been related to the god Mot of Ras Shamra (ancient Ugarit). During the Roman occupation the temple was dedicated to Hercules.

58   Appian, 65.275

59   Appian, 65.277

60   Tusculano, Victor de, op. cit., p. 81

61   Appian, 65.278; Tusculano, Victor de, op. cit., pp. 81-82

62   Appian 65.278 Cicero, *Brutus*, 84; A. Schulten identified as Baecula (Bailén) situated on the road crossing the Guadalquivir Valley by Serra Morena until the Meseta, before the Despeñaperros Pass. Schulten, A., 'Viriatus', *Neue Jahrbücher* 39, 1917, p. 222.

63   Circero, *Brutus* 84 and *de officiis*, 2.11.40

64   Also see Richardson, J.S., *Hispaniae*, pp.187-189; Goukowsky, Paul, *Appien: Histoire romaine II* (Greek text, French translation, notes), Les Belles Léttres, Paris: 1997, p. LXVI – LXVII

65   Appian, 66.279-280; see Appian 76.322 about the Numantine War; Simon, Helmut, *Roms Kriege in Spanien, 154-133 v. Chr.,* V. Klostermann, Frankfurt am Main, 1962;Pérez,Antonio Alburquerque, *Numancia, The Cradle of Our History,* Madrid, 1984.

66   This is the same hill that had been the downfall of Plautius a few years

before.

67   Appian, 66.281 – 282

68   Appian, 66.282; Bastetania derives its name from one of its cities, Basti. It seems to have been an important Roman foothold, for the territory held the port city of Cartagena. The region is located south-east of the Iberian Peninsula, and was made up of the present provinces of Malaga, Granada, Almeria, and the south-east section of Jaén, the south part of Albacete and south-west of Murcia. In this region there existed ancient cities, as mentioned in the classical texts, such as Arkilaquis, Tutugi, Basti, Acci and Iliberri.

69   Appian, 66.282

70   Muñoz, Mauricio P., op. cit., p. 169

71   Livy, *Oxyrhyncus*, 167; *Obsequens* 22; Astin, A.E., 'The Roman commander in Hispania Ulterior in 142 BC', *Historia* #13, 1964, p. 254

72   Appian, 67.283 -284 and 285

73   Appian, 67.284

74   Baeturia was a region in the valley of the Anas (Guadiana River Valley). Appian, 67.285 and 68.288; Iglesia, L. Garcia, 'La Beturia, un problema geografico de la Hispania Antigua', *AEA* 44, 1971, pp. 86-108

75   Appian, 68.289

76   Appian, 67.285 – 287

77   Appian, 68.288

78   Appian, 68.288-289

79   Appian, 68.290. According to A. Schulten and Muñoz, these are the Celtic names for Astigi (Écija), Gemellae (Guadix), Obulco (Porcuna), but J.S. Richardson follows Pliny (N.H. 3.12) who says Gemella was the name give to Tucci when it became a colony in the age of Augustus. Obulcula identifies it as La Monclova. Eiskadia is unknown except that it should be in the middle of the Guadalquivir Valley.

80   Appian, 68.290

81   Appian, 68.289

82   Appian, 68.289

83   Appian, 68.289

84   Appian, 68.291; Valerius Maximus, 2.7.11;Frontinus, *Stratagems*, 4.1.42; Orosius, 5.4.12

85   Appian 69.292. Some Iberian scholars believe that it is the Celtic name for Arsa, while some claim that its location is unknown.

86   Appian, 69.292-293

87   Appian, 68.294-295

88   Appian, 69.294

89   Livy, *Periochae*, 54

90   Appian,70.297

91   Florus, 1.33

92   Becker, U.J.H., *Die Kriege der Römer in Hispanien, cad. 1, Viriath un die Lusitaner*, Altona, 1826, p. 10

93   Muñoz, Mauricio P., op. cit., p.175

94   Bosch Gimpera, P. and Aguado Bleye, P.,'La Conquista de España por Roma (218 a 19 a.C.)' and Chapter III, 'Las guerras de Lusitanos y Celtiberos contra Roma: Prmer period (154 a 143): Viriato' in R. Menéndez Pidal's book, *História de Espanha*, Madrid, 1962, pp. 89-144

95   Gundel, H.G..'Probleme der Römischen Kampfführung Gegen Viriatus', *Legio VII Gemina*, Diputación Provincial, León, 1970, pp. 111-130

96   Muñoz, Mauricio P., op. cit., pp.177-178

97   This theory is based on J. Costa and A. Garcia y Bellido's detailed study on the agrarian problem in Lusitania; both agree that the main objective of the Lusitanians was the acquisition of land, for there existed a social problem between shepherds and farmers. Because of the lack of good land the Lusitanians resorted to 'bandoleirismo' as mentioned in Chapter 3 under 'Land and Banditry'. Also see Costa, J., 'Viriato y la Cuestión Social en España en el Siglo II Antes de Jesucristo', *Tutela de Pueblos en la Historia*, Madrid 1879 and *Estudios Ibéricos*, Madrid, 1902; Garcia y Bellido, A., 'Conflitos y Estructuras Sociales en la Hispania Antiga', *AAVV*, Madrid, 1977, pp. 13-60.

98   Muñoz, Mauricio P., op. cit., pp.175-176

99   Gundel, H.G..'Probleme der Römischen Kampfführung Gegen Viriatus', pp.111 – 130 and'Viriato, lusitano, caudillo en las luchas contra los romanos. 147-139 a.C.', *Caesaraugusta*, 1968, pp.175-198 (translated by J.M. Blazquez).

100 Ancient Roman military assembly, instituted c. 450 BC. It decided on war and peace, passed laws, elected consuls, praetors, and censors, and considered appeals of capital convictions. Unlike the older patrician *Comitia Curiata*, it included plebeians as well as patricians, assigned to classes and *centuriae* (centuries, or groups of one hundred) by wealth and the equipment they could provide for military duty. Voting started with the wealthier centuries, whose votes outweighed those of the poorer. Muñoz, Mauricio P., op. cit., p.179-180;Alberto, Paulo Farmhouse, *Viriato, Vultos da Antiguidade*, p. 45

101 Livy, Per. Oxy., 54

102 Gundel, H.G.., 'Viriato, lusitano, caudillo en las luchas contra los romanos. 147-139 a.C.', pp. 175-198; . Gundel, H.G..'Probleme der

Römischen Kampfführung Gegen Viriatus', pp.111 – 130; Muñoz, Mauricio P., op. cit., p.181

CHAPTER 7

1   Appian, 70.296; Livy, *Ep. Oxy* 54 and *Per.* 54; Diodorus, 33.1.4. At some point the Romans perhaps believed that Lusitanians were bound to return to their old ways

2   Ibid., 70.297

3   Ibid., 70.297

4   Cassius Dio, *History of Rome*, 22.78

5   Munoz, Mauricio P., op. cit., p.184

6   Alarcão, J. de, *Roman Portugal*, Vol. II, Aris & Phillips Ltd., Warminster, UK, 1988, p.8

7   Munoz, Mauricio P., op. cit., p.184

8   Appian, 70.298

10   Ibid., 70.300

11   Appian, 70.300

12   Tranoy, Alain, *La Galice romaine: Recherches sur le nord-Ouest de la peninsule ibérique dans l'Antiquité*, Paris, 1981, pp. 65-66

13   Munoz, Mauricio P., op. cit., p.184

14   Many historians believe that Viriathus did not fight Laenas, because Appian makes no mention of any type of combat between the two.

15   Cassius Dio 22.78: 'Caepio accomplished nothing worthy of mention against the foe, but visited many injuries upon his own men, so that he even came near being killed by them. For he treated them all, and especially the cavalry, with such harshness and cruelty that a great number of unseemly jokes and stories were told about him during the nights; and the more he grew vexed at it, the more they jested in the endeavour to infuriate him. When it became known what was going on and no one could be found guilty — though he suspected it was the doing of the cavalry — since he could not fix the responsibility upon anybody, he turned his anger against them all, and he commanded them, six hundred in number, to cross the river beside which they were encamped, accompanied only by their grooms, and to bring wood from the mountain on which Viriathus was bivouacking. The danger was manifest to all, and the tribunes and lieutenants begged him not to destroy them. The cavalry waited for a little while, thinking he might listen to the others, and when he would not yield, they scorned to entreat him, as he was most eager for them to do, but choosing rather to perish utterly than to speak a respectful word to him, they set out on the appointed mission. And the horsemen of the allies and other volunteers accompanied them. They crossed the river, cut the wood, and piled it in all around the general's

quarters, intending to burn him to death. And he would have perished in the flames, if he had not fled away in time.'

16   Cassius Dio, 22.75. According to Munoz, Cassius Dio's paragraph does not mention Astolpas but it seems to suggest that many prominent Lusitanians were turned over to Laenas by Viriathus, who seems to have been willing to betray the Lusitanian nobility for a peace treaty for his people. Munoz, Mauricio P.,op. cit., p.185

17   Cassius Dio, 22.75

18   Strabo, 3.3.6

19   Cassius Dio, 22.75

20   Cassius Dio, 22.75

21   Appian, 74; Livy, per., 54; Diodorus, 33.1.4 and 33.21; Velleius, 2.1.3; Valerius Maximus, 9.6.4; Florus, 1.33.17; Eutropius, 4.16 and *de vir*. Ill., 71.3; Orosius 5.4.14

22   Appian, 74.311

23   Diodorus, 33.21

24   Diodorus, 33.21

25   Appian, 74.311

26   Urso was a town in Hispania Baetica, thus a city under Roman domination. Diodorus is the only writer to say where the men were from. When Viriathus gave them all up to Laenas, these Roman deserters and prominent Lusitanians had their right hands cut off immediately or were executed.

27   Diodorus, 33.21

28   Tusculano, Victor de, op. cit., p. 119.

29   Appian, 74.312

30   Appian, 74.312

31   Ibid.

32   Diodorus, 33.21

33   Diodorus, 33.21

34   Diodorus, 33.21

35   Diodorus, 33.21

36   Appian, 74.313

37   Appian, 74.314

38   Appian, 74.314

39   Eutropius, *Breviarium ab urbe condita*, 4.16

40   Valerius Maximus, *Factis Dictisque Memorabilibus*, 9.6.4

41   The Battle of Arausio took place at a site between the town of Arausio (modern day Orange, Vaucluse) and the Rhône Riverin 105 BC.

Caepio and Consul Gnaeus Mallius Maximus led two armies against the Germanic tribes. While marching to Arausio, Caepio plundered the temples of the town of Tolosa, finding over 50,000 15lb. bars of gold and 10,000 15lb. bars of silver. The riches of Tolosa were shipped back to Rome, but only the silver made it; the gold was stolen by a band of marauders, who were believed to have been hired by Caepio himself. The gold of Tolosa was never found, and was said to have been passed all the way down to the last heir of the Servilii Caepiones, Marcus Junius Brutus. At the Battle of Arausio, Caepio refused to co-operate with his superior officer, Gnaeus Mallius Maximus, who was a 'New Man' (the term in ancient Rome for a man who was the first in his family to serve in the Roman Senate or, more specifically, to be elected consul) rather than a member of the Roman Elite. Caepio refused to even camp with Maximus and his troops. When it appeared that Maximus was going to reach a treaty and take the glory for the resolution, Caepio ordered his men to engage the Germans, and the ensuing battle completely destroyed the Roman army.

42   Diodorus, 33.21. He is the only writer to mention where these men were from.

43   Tusculano, Victor de, op. cit., p. 119

44   Ahala was the most famous of the early Servilii family as he saved Rome from tyranny by killing Spurius Maelius in 439 BCE. Smith, Willian, 'Ahala, C. Servilius Structus', in Smith, William, *Dictionary of Greek and Roman Biography and Mythology*, Little, Brown and Co, Boston: 1867, pp. 83;   Livy, iv.13, 14, 21; Joannes Zonaras, vii. 20; Dionysius of Halicarnassus, *Exc. Mai*, i. p. 3; Cicero, *Catiline Orations 1*, *Pro Milone 3*, *Cato Maior de Senectute* 16; Valerius Maximus, v. 3. 2; Cicero, *De re publica* i. 3, *pro Dom.* 32.

45   Tusculano, Victor de, op. cit., p. 118.

46   Viriathus had a habit of not sleeping much, so according to Appian his attendants and the entire camp were surprised he had changed his routine. Perhaps he was the last to sleep and the first to rise and walk among his sleeping men. Appian, 74.315

47   Velleius Paterculus, *Roman History*, II.1.3

48   Appian, 74.315-316

49   Appian, 75.317, Diodorus, 33.22

50   Appian, 75.317; Diodorus 33.2; Gladiatorial games used in funerary rites was first recorded by Livy, who dates the earliest Roman gladiator games to 264 BC, in the early stages of Rome's First Punic War against Carthage. According to Livy, Decimus Iunius Brutus Scaeva had three gladiator pairs fight to the death in Rome's 'cattle market' Forum (Forum Boarium) to honour his dead father, Brutus Pera (Livy, *Per.*, 16;Valerius Maximus, 2.4.6). This is described as *munus* (plural *munera*): a commemorative duty owed a dead ancestor

by his aristocratic descendants. But as for the gladiatorial games, in general, in the late 1st century BC Nicolaus of Damascus believed that these games were of Etruscan origin. But at the same time, Nicolaus cites Posidonius' support for a Celtic origin, while Hermippus' for a Mantinean (therefore Greek) origin (Welch, Katherine E., *The Roman Amphitheatre: From Its Origins to the Colosseum*, Cambridge, U.K.: Cambridge University Press, 2007, pp. 16-17)

51 These are just a few of the many references that I found which have been around for some time.

52 Tusculano, Victor de, op. cit., p. 121

53 Mantas, Vasco Gil, 'Indícios de um Campo Romano na Cava de Viriato?', *Al-Madan*, IIª Série. 12: 2003, pp. 40-42.

54 Diodorus, 33.1.4

55 Ibid.; Appian, 75.320

56 Appian, 75.321

57 Appian, 75.321

58 After the death of Viriathus, many allies of Lusitania split from each other, especially in the north of Portugal and Spain, and continued the war on their own, as we shall see in the next chapter.

59 Appian, 75.321

60 Sayas, J.J., 'Algunas Consideraciones sobre Cuestiones Relacionadas con la Conquista y Romanización de las Tierras Extremeñas', *El Proceso Histórico de la Luistania Oriental en Época Preromana y Romana*, Mérida, 1993, p. 189 and 'El bandolerismo lusitano y la falta de tierras', *Homenaje al Prof. Antonio de Bethencourt y Massieu, Espacio, Tiempo y Forma* #4, 1989, pp. 708-710.

CHAPTER 8

1 Richardson, J.S., *Hispaniae*, p.148 and 184; Munoz, Mauricio P., *Viriato, o Herói Lusitano*, p.191.

2 Strabo, 3.3.1

3 Alarcão, J. de, *Roman Portugal*, Vol. II, p.8; Alberto, Paulo Farmhouse, *Viriato, Vultos da Antiguidade*, p. 53

4 Curchin, Leonard, A., *Roman Spain*, p. 38

5 Strabo, 3.3.1

6 The Gallaeci, Callaeci, or Callaici were pre-Roman Celtic tribe, or various tribes, living in the northwest of the Iberian Peninsula, north of the Douro River in Northern Portugal and Galicia (Spain). The other tribe, the Bracarenses, occupied what is now Galicia and northern Portugal. The Romans began their conquest of the region around 136 BC, and during the times of Emperor Caesar Augustus (around the year 20 BC) the city of Bracara Augusta was founded in

the context of the administrative needs of the new Roman territory. Bracara was dedicated to the emperor, hence its name Augusta. The city of Bracara Augusta developed greatly during the first century AD and reached its maximum extension in the second century. Towards the end of the third century, Emperor Diocletianus promoted the city to capital city of the newly-founded province of Gallaecia.

7   Appian, 71.301

8   Ibid., 71.302

9   Rufus Festus Avienus, 5.1

10   Velleius Peterculus, II5; Vilatela, L.P., *Lusitania: Historia y etnologia,* Royal Academia de la Historia, 2000, p21

11   Appian, 71.303

12   The site is situated on a small promontory called Monte de São Romão near the Ave River, in the Northern region of Portugal, between the *freguesias* (parish or county) of Salvador de Briteiros and Donim, about 15 km north-west of Guimarães. The location provides an extensive view over the navigable Ave River and its valley, and over an early north-south trade and communication path between the Douro and Minho River Valleys. Cividade Hill (153 metres is one of the two hills next to the city of Póvoa de Varzim in Portugal.

13   Tusculano, Victor de, op. cit., p. 131; Alarcão, J. de, *Roman Portugal,* p. 9; Coelho da Silva, Armando, 'A cultura castreja no Noroeste de Portugal: habitat e cronologias', *Portugalia,* 4/5, 1983-84, 128; Flores Gomes, José Manuel & Carneiro, Deolinda, *Subtus Montis Terroso* CMPV (2005), 'Origens do Povoamento' pp.74-76.

14   The site of Talabriga is unknown, but it has been suggested that it stood on the banks of the Vouga River, which spills into the Atlantic Ocean at Aveiro, about 50 km south of Oporto. Alarcão, J. de, op. cit., p.9; Osland, Daniel K., 'Early Roman Cities of Lusitania', Master of Arts thesis, University of Cincinnati, 2005, p. 112 - 114

15   Appian, 73.308-30

16   Florus, 1.33.12; Orosius, 5.5.12; Plutarch, *Quaest. Rom.,* 34; Curchin, Leonard, A., *Roman Spain,* p. 38. Sabroso Castro is the ruins of a former castro that was totally destroyed during Decimus Brutus campaign.

17   Tusculano, Victor de, op. cit., p. 132

18   Hawkes, C.F.C., 'North-western castros: Excavation, archaeology and history', *Actas do II Congreso nacional de arqueologia,* Coimbra, 1971, pp. 283-286; Flores Gomes, José Manuel & Carneiro, Deolinda, *Subtus Montis Terroso* CMPV, 'Origens do Povoamento', 2005, pp.74-76; Coelho da Silva, Armando, 'A cultura castreja no Noroeste de Portugal: habitat e cronologias', *Portugalia,* 4/5, 1983-84, 128; Troncoso, Víctor Alonso, 'Primeras etapas en la conquista romana de Gallaecia', *MILITARIA. Reaismc, de Cultura Militar* n. 8. servicio de

Publicaciunes, 13CM. Madrid, 1996, p. 61

19   Flores Gomes, José Manuel & Carneiro, Deolinda, *Subtus Montis Terroso*, CMPV, 'Origens do Povoamento', pp.74-76; Coelho da Silva, Armando, 'A cultura castreja no Noroeste de Portugal, p. 128.

20   Valerius Maximus 6.4 ext 1; Marco Simón, Francisco, 'Intimidación y terror en la época de las guerras Celtibéricas in Terror et pavor', *Violenza, intimidazione, clandestinità nel mondo antico, Atti del convegno internazionale, Cividale del Friuli, 22-24 settembre 2005*, Pisa, Edizioni ETS, 2006, pp. 197-213; Mera, Josefa Martinez, *Expedicións Militares a Gallaecia na Época Republicana*, Universidade Santiago de Compostela, n.d., p. 311

21   Monteagudo, L., 'Neuves joyas preromanoas del Norte de Portugal', *AEArq.* 18, 1945 ; Lopez Cuevillas, F., *Las joyas castreñas*, Madrid, 1958

22   Strabo 3.2.9

23   Orosius, 5.5.12; Lombardero, Alfonso Carbonell, 'The Gaels in Gallaecia', 2000
http://www.galeon.com/lombardero/Lombardero1.htm

24   Santos Yanguas, N., *El ejército y la romanización de Gallaecia*, Oviedo, 1988, p. 29

25   Troncoso, Víctor Alonso, Op. Cit. p. 56; Lopez Cuevillas, F., Cómo 'Galicia, entró en la historia' *Boletín de la Real Academia Gallega*, 25, 1955, p. 19-30

26   Torres Rodríguez, C. *La Galicia romana*, Coruña, 1982; Tranoy, Alain, *La Galice romaine: Recherches sur le nord-ouest de la péninsule ibérique ´dans L'antiquité*. Paris, 1981, p. 198

27   Ovid, *Fastrum Libre*, VI, 461

28   Ovid, *Fastrum Libre*, VI, 461-462

29   Appian, 72.304. Richardson, Schweighäuser and Goukowsky, three individuals who have studied Appian's work in detail, state that this river is unknown. However Strabo names it as the Baenis, which Appian mentions in paragraph 71.301. Unless it is another of Appian's geographical confusions, this maybe the river Nebis as it is documented by Pomponius Mela, 3.10. But his description of it as 'another river' suggests that this is a river that he had not mentioned before. Richardson, J.S., *Appian: Wars of the Romans in Iberia*, p. 141; Schweihäuser, J., *Appiani Historiae Romanae*, 3 vols., Leipzig 1785, vol.3, pp. 297-298; Goukowsky, Paul, ed., *Appien. Histoire Romaine Livre VI. L'Iberique*, Les Belles Léttres, Paris: 1997, p.66, n. 405. The Bracari were an ancient Celtic tribe of Gallaecia, akin to the Calaicians or Gallaeci, living in the northwest of modern Portugal, in the province of Minho, between the Tâmega and Cávado.

30   Appian, 72.302

31   Ibid., 72.306

32   Tusculano, Victor de, op. cit., p. 121.

33   A number of authors from antiquity say the tiny Lima River near
     Xinzo de Limia in the province of Ourense in Galicia (Spain) had the
     same properties of memory loss as the legendary mythical Lethe
     River.

34   Orosius, Adv px., V, 5, 12; Livy, *Per.* 55 and *Ep.* Oxy 55; Florus, 1.33.12;
     Plutarch, *Quaest. Rom.*, 34; A. M. Romero Masió, X. M. Pose Mesura,
     Galicia nos textos clásicos, Coruña, 1988, *passim*; García Quintela, M., 'El
     rio del Olvido', in J. C. Bermejo Barrera, *Mitología y mitos de la Hispan/a
     prerromana II* Madrid, 1986, pp. 75-86.

35   Florus, 1.33.12

36   Diodorus, 33.1.3; Livy, *Periochae*, 55.4

37   Le Roux, Patrick, *L'armée romaine et l'organisation des provinces ibériques
     d'Auguste á l'invasion de 409*, Paris, 1982, p. 36-37; Ventura Canejero,
     Augustin, 'qui sub Viriatho militaverunt', *Archivo de Prehistoria
     Levantina* #16, 1981, pp. 539-551. Valencia de Alcántara today is a
     Spanish town near the Portuguese border (District of Portalegre)
     located in Cáceres province.

38   Alarcão, Jorge de, 'Sobre a romanização do Alentejo e do Algarve: A
     propósito de uma obra de José d'Encarnação', *Arqueologia* #11, 1985,
     p.100.

39   Fear, A.T., *Rome and Baetica: Urbanization in Southern Spain c.50
     BC-AD 150*, Oxford University Press, 1996, p. 38

40   Stephanus Byzantinus' work can be seen in *Fontes Hispaniae Antiquae*,
     IV, 140 and VII, 427; Alarcão, J. de, *Roman Portugal*, p. 9; Fear, A.T.,
     Rome and Baetica, p. 38

41   José Leite Vasconcellos and L. Figueiredo da Guerra, 'Limia e
     Brutobriga', *O Arqueólogo português, Museu Nacional de Arqueologia
     (Portugal)*, Museu Ethnologico Português (Lisbon, Portugal), vol. V,
     1900, p. 4-6.

42   Naveiro López, L., *El comercio antiguo en el noroeste peninsular*, Coruña,
     1991, pp 175-6.

43   Santos Yanguas, N., *El ejército y la romanización de Gallaecia*, Oviedo,
     1988

44   Vilatela, L.P., *Lusitania: Historia y etnología*, R. Acad. de la Hist., 2000, p.
     218

45   Numancia is the Spanish name of an ancient Celtiberian settlement,
     the remains of which are located 7 km north of the city of Soria, on a
     hill known as Cerro de la Muela in the municipality of Garray. The
     Numantine War was the last conflict of the Celtiberian Wars, fought
     contemporaneously with the Lusitanian War in Hispania Ulterior. It
     was a twenty-year conflict between the Celtiberian tribes of Hispania
     Citerior and the Roman government. When Viriathus' Lusitanian War

had spilled over into Citerior and open warfare was reinvigorated in 143 BC, Rome sent a series of generals to the Iberian peninsula to deal with the Numantines. In that year, Quintus Caecilius Metellus Macedonicus tried and failed to take their main city, Numancia, by siege, but subjugated all the other tribes of the Arevaci instead. His successor, Quintus Pompeius, was inept and suffered severe defeats at their hands, so he secretly negotiated a peace with the city, abiding by the previous treaty. Yet in 138 BC Marcus Pompillius Laenas arrived and when the Numantine envoys came to finish their obligations of the peace treaty, Pompeius disavowed negotiating any such peace. The matter was referred to the Senate for a judgment. Rome decided to ignore Pompeius' peace and sent Gaius Hostilius Mancinus to continue the war in 136 BC. He assaulted Numancia and was repulsed several times before being routed, encircled and forced to accept a treaty. The Senate did not ratify his treaty either. His successors Lucius Furius Philus and Gaius Calpurnius Piso avoided any type of conflict with the Numantines. In 134 BC, the Consul Scipio Aemilianus was sent to Hispania Citerior to end the war. He recruited 20,000 men and 40,000 allies, including Numidian cavalry under Jugurtha, the Berber king of Numidia. Scipio built a ring of seven fortresses around Numantia itself before beginning the siege. After suffering pestilence and famine, most of the surviving Numantines committed suicide rather than surrender to Rome. The great Roman victory over Numantia ushered in an era of lasting peace in Hispania until the Sertorian War over half a century later.

46   Richardson, J.S., *The Romans in Spain*, Blackwell, 1996, pp. 83-126

47   *Fontes Hispaniae Antiquae*, IV, 144 and 145; Guadan, A.M., *Numismática ibérica e ibero-romana*, Madrid, 1969, pp. 128 and 216

48   Ibid.

49   Eutropius, *Historiae Romanae Breviarium*, 4.27; Sources on this triumphs are given by Degrassi, Attilio, in *Inscr. Ital.*, vol. 1, Rome, 1947, pp. 85 and 561-2

50   Julius Obsequens, *Iulii Obsequentis ab anno urbis conditae dv prodigiorum liber*, 42

51   Appian, 100.433

52   Degrassi, Attilio, in *Inscr. Ital.*, vol. 1, pp. 85 and 561-562

53   Ibid., 85 and 562-563

54   Dio Cassius, 37.52-53

55   See Plutarch's lives of Sertorius and Pompey; Appian, *Bell. civ.* and *Hispanica*; the fragments of Sallust; Dio Cassius xxxvi; P. O. Spann, *Quintus Sertorius and the Legacy of Sulla* (1987)

56   Dio Cassius, 37.53-53

57   Plutarch, 11–12; Suetonius, *Julius Caesar*, 18.1

58   Alarcão, J. de, *Roman Portugal*, Vol. II, p. 9

59   Aulus Hirtius, *De Bello Alexandrino* (The Alexandrian War), 48.1-2. Greatly in debt, he resolved to pay it by laying heavy burdens upon the province and made his liberalities a pretense to justify the most exorbitant demands. He taxed the rich at his discretion and compelled them to pay, without the least regard to their remonstrances; frequently making light and trifling offences of all manner of extortions. All methods of gain were pursued, whether great and reputable or mean and sordid. None who had anything to lose could escape accusation; the plunder of their private fortunes was aggravated by the dangers they were exposed to from pretended crimes. It is for this reason that the provincials and even his own dependents formed conspiracies against his life.

60   Ibid., 48.2

61   Ibid., 48.3

62   Ibid., 48.4

63   Ibid., 48.5

64   Ibid., 51.1 and 3

65   Some of his troops revolted under the quaestor Marcellus, who was proclaimed governor of the province. Cassius was surrounded by Marcellus in Ulia. Bogud, king of Mauretania, and Marcellus Lepidus, proconsul of Hispania Citerior, to whom Cassius had applied for assistance, negotiated an arrangement with Marcellus whereby Cassius was to be allowed to go free with the legions that remained loyal to him. Cassius sent his troops into winter quarters and hastened on board ship at Malaca with his ill-gotten gains, but was wrecked in a storm at the mouth of the Iberus (Ebro).

66   Valerius Maxmius, 9.2.4, Today the city is an ancient ruin north of Espejo, Spain.

67   Aulus Hirtius, *Bellum Hispaniense* (The Spanish War), 35

68   Ibid., 36

69   Lombardero, Alfonso Carbonell, 'The Gaels in Gallaecia', 2000 http://www.galeon.com/lombardero/Lombardero1.htm

70   For a decent reading about the battle of Munda see the Wikipedia article at http://en.wikipedia.org/wiki/Battle_of_Munda; Munda is the name of a plain in southern Spain.

71   Aulus Hirtius, *Bellum Hispaniense* (The Spanish War), 38 and 39

72   Aulus Hirtius, *Bellum Hispaniense* (The Spanish War), 40

73   Aulus Hirtius, *Bellum Hispaniense* (The Spanish War), 40 and 41

74   Le Roux, Patrick, *L'armée romaine et l'organisation des provinces ibériques d'Auguste á l'invasion de 409*, pp. 46-47; Alarcão, J. de, *Roman Portugal*, Vol. II, p. 12

75   Alarcão, J. de, *Roman Portugal*, Vol. II, p. 12

76   Appian, *Bellum Civile*, 109, Suetonius, *Augustus*, 49; Saddington
     Dennis Bain, *The development of the Roman auxiliary forces from Caesar to
     Vespasian: 49 B.C.-A.D. 79*, University of Zimbabwe, 1982, p. 26;
     Martinez, Rafael T., op. cit., p.6

CHAPTER 9

1   Le Roux, Patrick, *L'armée romaine et l'organisation des provinces ibériques*
    pp. 52-69; Tranoy, Alain, *La Galice romaine* p. 132-144; Syme, Ronald,
    'The Spanish War of Augustus (26-25 BC)', *American Journal of
    Philology* #55 1934, pp. 293-317; Rodriguez Colmenero, A., *Augusto e
    Hispania: Conquista y organización del Norte peninsular*, Bilboa, 1979, pp.
    24-130

2   Dio Cassius, 53.12.4-5

3   Tranoy, Alain, *La Galice romaine* pp. 149 and 326-327; Alarcão, J. de,
    Roman Portugal, Vol. II, p. 15

4   Dio Cassius, 54.11.2-5; Pliny, 4.118; Tranoy, *La Galice romaine*, pp. 146-
    147; Alarcão, *Roman Portugal*, 15-16; Solana Sainz, Jose Maria, *Los
    Canatabros y la ciudad de Iuliobriga*, Santander, 1981, pp. 116-119

5   Dio Cassius, 54.11.2-5; Solana Sainz, Op. Cit. pp. 116-119. Although we
    know that there was an uprising by the Cantabri and that Agrippa
    waged war against them in 19 BC, this revolt may not have been the
    only reason for the journey of Augustus' son-in-law. Agrippa could
    have also come to reorganize the administration and to found the
    province of Lusitania.

6   Muñoz, Mauricio Pastor, *Viriato: O Herói Lusitano* p. 137

7   Dio Cassius, 53.13.1

8   Romanized urban settlements of native tribes were called *civitates* and
    were usually close to the site of an old, pre-Roman capital. The term
    was applied not only to friendly native tribes and their towns but to
    local government divisions in peaceful provinces that carried out civil
    administration. Land destined to become a *civitas* was officially
    divided up, some granted to the locals and some owned by the civil
    government. A basic street grid would be surveyed in but the rest of
    the development was left to the inhabitants although occasional
    imperial grants for new public buildings would be made. The *civitates*
    were regional market towns complete with a basilica and forum
    complex as an administrative and economic focus. *Civitates* were
    primarily to stimulate the local economy in order to raise taxes and
    produce raw materials. This activity was administered by an *ordo* or
    curia, a *civitas* council consisting of men of sufficient social rank.
    Defensive measures were limited at the *civitates*, rarely more than
    palisaded earthworks in times of trouble, if that.

9   Strabo, 3.4.20

10   Alarcão, J. de, op. cit., p. 16; Alföldy, Geza, *Fasti Hispanienses: Senatorische Reichsbeamte und Offiziere in den Spanischen Provinzen der Römisches von Augustus bis Diokletian*, Wiesbaden, 1969, pp. 9-10

11   Pliny, 3.1.6 and 4.22.115, Pomponiua Mela, 2,87

12   The Romans were the first to use boundary markers (*termini Augustales*) to set up the limits of the new territories to physically mark the landscape of the new Roman world. Besides being boundary markers, in Hispania some were actually used as altars for cultic activity. It seems that the gods were called upon to sanction this new organization of the newly established rural space. Frontinus, *De Agrorum Qualitate*, 4; Aggenus Urbicus, *Commentum de Agrorum Qualitate*, 4; Hyginus, *Constit Limit* 162; J.C. Edmondson, 'Creating a Provincial Landscape: Roman Imperialism and Rural Change in Lusitania', in Jean Gérard Gorges and Manuel Salines de Frias, eds, *Les campagnes de Lusitanie romaine*, Casa de Velázquez, Madrid, pp. 27-28; Stylow, A.U., 'Apuntes sobre epigrafia de época flavia en Hispania', *Gerión* #4, 1986, pp. 285-311

13   The Romans formally divided up the countryside (*territorium*) around newly established *coloniae* into square blocks as allotments for the occupants of the colony. Typically there were 776 yards along each side, the boundaries being formed by roads or substantial fences/hedges. Once established the regular grid pattern usually survived into much later times even though the land tenure system changed. Jean Gérard Gorges, and Manuel Salines de Frías, eds, op. cit., pp. 27-28

14   Centuriation was a system of marking out land in squares or rectangles, by means of *limites* (boundaries), normally prior to distribution in a colonial foundation. (The units of *centuria* are explained by Varro, *De re rustica* 1. 10.)

15   Jean Gérard Gorges, and Manuel Salines de Frías, eds., op. cit., p.27-28; Fernandez, P. Sáez, 'Estudio sobre una inscripción catastral colindante com Lacimurga', *Habis* #21, 1990, 205-227; Nicolet, C., *L'inventaire du monde: Géographie et politique aux origins de l'Empire romain*, Paris, 1988, chap. 7.

16   Alarcão, J. de, *Roman Portugal*, Vol. I, p. 15

17   Alarcão, *Roman Portugal*, pp. 30-31, Tranoy, Alain, *La Galice romaine* pp. 60-74

18   Alarcão, *Roman Portugal*, p. 31

19   Alarcão, *Roman Portugal*, p. 15; Tsirkin, Ju. B., 'Romanisation of Spain: Socio-Political Aspects: Part III Romanisation during the Early Empire', *Gerión* #12, 1994, pp. 217-253; M. L. Genderson, 'Julius Caesar and Latium in Spain', *VDI* 4 (1946), pp. 58, 63, 65, n. 8; F. Vittinghoff, op. dL, 105; E. Ritterling, 'Legio', *RE Hbd*. 23(1924), Sp. 1631.The citizens of Rome were divided into voting groups or tribes.

Originally there were three Romulean tribes but they were likely replaced or reorganized under Servius Tullius with four urban tribes and later increased to 16 rustic tribes, in the *ager Romanus*. Tribes were added a few at a time over the years as new Italian territory was incorporated into the Romans' ever expanding empire, but with the addition of two more tribes in Picenum between 242 BC and 241 BC the number of tribes was set at 35. Each tribe had its own officials, and many important activities were organized on a tribal basis including the *census*, collection of taxes, and voting in the Comitia Populi Tributa and the Comitia Plebis Tributa. They were so important that a Roman's full name included the name of his tribe along with the name of his father and grandfather. Of the thirty-five tribes, four (Collina, Esquilina, Palatina, and Suburana) were urban; the rest are rural tribes. In ancient times citizens who owned land outside the city of Rome were enrolled in rural tribes, while those who lived exclusively in the city belonged to urban tribes. The result was that the urban tribes had much less power in the voting assemblies than the rural tribes had.

20   Ibid.

21   Alarcão, *Roman Portugal*, p.15. The gens Galeria was a very ancient patrician family, which already existed at the time of Romulus, and was probably included in the original hundred gentes remembered by the historian Titus Livius. According to Mommsen the antiquity of this family can be deduced from the fact that it gave its name to one of ancient rural tribes, the homonymous Tribe Galeria. The origin of Gens Galeria was probably Sabin, apparently due to a family group from the area of Rio Galera, a river flowing east of Lake Bracciano, which took its name.
http://www.novaroma.org/nr/Category:Gens_Galeria_(Nova_Roma). The Quirina tribe was preeminent of the Flavian emperors but prior to that it was one of the last tribes to be added to the final count of thirty-five tribes created in 241 BC on territory confiscated from the Sabini. The tribe was original filled with the Sabini that were granted incomplete citizenship at the beginning of the third century, but were later made full citizens. Williamson, Callie, *The Laws of the Roman People: Public Law in the Expansion and Decline of the Roman Republic*, University of Michigan, 2005, p.225

22   Alarcão, *Roman Portugal*, p.15

23   Alarcão, *Roman Portugal*, p.43

24   Munoz, Mauricio P., op. cit., p.199

25   Alarcão, *Roman Portugal*, p.33

26   Suetonius, *Julius*, 7; Caesar, *Bellum Civile*, 2.19.3

27   Curchin, Leonard, A., *Roman Spain*, p.57

28   Curchin, *Roman Spain*, p.58

29 Étienne, Robert, *Le culte impérial dans la péninsule Ibérique, d'Auguste à Dioclétien*, Paris, 1974, pp. 177-185. Curchin, *Roman Spain*, p.58. *Flamen* was a name given to a priest assigned to a state-supported god or goddess in Roman religion.

30 Pliny, NH, 4.117; Alarcão, *Roman Portugal*, p.32

31 Curchin, Leonard, A., *Roman Spain*, p.85 and 105

32 Strabo, 3.2.15

33 Alarcão, J. de, op. cit., p. 49-61; Saa, Mario, *As grandes vias da Lusitania*, 6 vols., Lisbon, 1956; Jean Gérard Gorges, and Manuel Salines de Frías, eds., op. cit., p.27-28.

34 A milestone, or *miliarium*, was a circular column on a solid rectangular base, set more than 60 cm (2 feet) into the ground, standing 1.50 m(5 feet high), 50 cm (20 inches) in diameter, and weighing more than 2 tons. At the base was inscribed the number of the mile relative to the road it was on and the distance to the nearest major city centre. Siliéres, P., les voies de communication de l'Hispanie méridionale, Paris, 1990, pp. 53-57 and 791-794; Jean Gérard Gorges, and Manuel Salines de Frías, eds., op. cit., p.27-28.

35 Roman society's upper class comprised of three classes, senators, equities and *decurions* (local aristocrats), that were based on wealth and free birth.

36 Curchin, Leonard, A., *Roman Spain*, p.78; Etienne, Robert, 'Sénateurs originaires de la province de Lusitanie', *Tituli*, vol. 5, 1982, pp.521-529

37 Curchin, *Roman Spain*, p. 82-83

38 Curchin, Leonard, A., *The Local Magistrates of Roman Spain*, University of Toronto Press, Toronto, 1990, pp. 21-27

39 Mathisen, Ralph W., 'Peregrini, Barbari, and Cives Romani: Concepts of Citizenship and the Legal Identity of Barbarians in the Later Roman Empire', *The American Historical Review* vol.111, no.4, Oct. 2006, pp.1011-1040

40 Latium, the cradle of Rome, consisted originally of the coastal plain from the mouth of the Tiber to the Circeian promontory, and its adjacent foothills. M. Cary and H.H. Scullard, *A History of Rome*, Basingstoke, Hampshire: Palgrave , 3rd ed. 1979, p.31

41 Mathisen, Ralph W., 'Peregrini, Barbari, and Cives Romani', p. 1118; Sasse, Christoph, *Die Constitutio Antoniniana: Eine Untersuchung über den Umfang der Bürgerrechtsverleihung auf Grund von Papyrus Gissensis 40* I, Wiesbaden, 1958; Adam Lukaszewicz, 'Zum Papyrus Gissensis 40 I 9 ('Constitutio Antoniniana'), '*The Journal of Juristic Papyrology* 20, 1990: 93–101; and Garnsey, 'Roman Citizenship and Roman Law,' an expanded version of a section on 'Citizens and Aliens,' in Peter Garnsey and Caroline Humfress, eds., *The Evolution of the Late Antique World*, Cambridge, 2001, pp. 88–91.

42   Curchin, Leonard, A., *Roman Spain*, p. 84

43   Mangas, J.., *Esclavos y libertos en la España romana*, Salamanca, 1971, pp. 388-485; Curchin, L.A., 'Social relations in Central Spain: Patrons, freedmen and slaves in the life of a Roman provincial hinterland', *Ancient Society*, vol. 18, 1987 and *Roman Spain*, p.84

44   Paulus, *Sententiae*, 2.19.9; *Corpus Inscriptionnum Latinarum II*, 4524 and 6014 translated by A. Hübner, Berlin, 1869: Curchin, *Roman Spain*, p. 84

45   Livy, 21.43.8; Appian, 59.249 – 250; Strabo, 3.3.5

46   Curchin, *Roman Spain*, p. 84

47   MacMullen, R., *Roman social relations 50 BC to AD 284*, Yale Univ. Press, New Haven, 1974, pp. 28-32; Curchin, L.A., 'Non-Slave Labour in Roman Spain', *Gerión* vol.4, 1986, pp. 178-181

48   See Chapter 3 about Lusitanian life, also Strabo (3.3.7 and 3.3.5) and Columella (7.2.1) mention how this class lived. As for living with livestock in certain rural areas of the Iberian Peninsula, this is still practiced but the change is that the animals do not cohabit in the same living quarters as people but are placed in the basement of a farmstead.

49   Sheldon, Natasha, 'Roman Slavery in Urban and Rural Pompeii, Archaeological Evidence for the Lives of Roman Slaves', *Archaeology*, Apr. 2009; Mangas, J., *Esclavos y libertos en la España romana*, pp. 130-131

50   Palmer, Bonnie, 'The Cultural Significance of Roman Manumission', *Ex Post Facto: Journal of the History Students of San Francisco State University*, vol. 5, 1996, pp. 23-41

51   Ibid.

52   See Chapter 3 on Lusitanian women; also see Curchin, *Roman Spain*, p. 85-86 and 'Non-Slave Labour in Roman Spain', *Gerión* vol.4, 1986, pp. 178-181 Albertos, M.L., 'La Mujer hispano-romana a través de la epigrafía', *Revista de la Universidad de Madrid* #109, 1977, pp.179-198

53   Mathisen, Ralph W., 'Peregrini, Barbari, and Cives Romani', p.1133

54   Prudentius, *Contra Symmachum* 2.598–614

55   Tacitus, Annals, 3.40; Diodorus, 5.33.2; Vegetius, *Epitoma rei militaris*, 1.1; also see Chapter 5 on Lusitanian influences on the Roman military

56   This comes from a example of a bronze tablet from 89 BC that records the granting of Roman citizenship to an entire Iberian troop of cavalrymen who fought with distinction during the Social War (91-88 BC) under Pompey's father, Gnaeus Pompeius Strabo; Curchin, Leonard, A., *Roman Spain*, p.101

57   Cagnat, René, *L'année Epigraphique*, Collège de France, Paris, 1930, p. 57 and René Cagnat and Maurice Besnier 1933, p. 95

58   Sherwin-White, Adrian N.,*The Roman Citizenship*, 2nd ed., Oxford, 1979, 380ff.; Rosario Soraci, *Richerche sui conubia tra Romani e Germani nei secoli I–VI*, Catania, 1965; rev. ed. 1974; Roger C. Blockley, 'Roman-Barbarian Marriages in the Later Empire,' *Florilegium* 4, 1982, pp. 63–79; Demougeot, Emilienne, 'Restrictions, à l'expansion du droit de cité dans la seconde moitié du IVe siècle,' *Ktema* 6, 1981, pp.381–393, p 387; Peter Heather, *Goths and Romans, 332–489*,Oxford, 1991, pp.164–165; Liebeschuetz, Wolf, 'Citizen Status and Law, in the Roman Empire andthe Visigothic Kingdom,' in Pohl and Reimitz, *Strategies of Distinction*, pp. 131–152, Sirks, A. J. Boudewijn, 'Shifting Frontiers in the Law: Romans, Provincials, and Barbarians,' in Ralph Mathisen and Hagith Sivan, eds., *Shifting Frontiers in Late Antiquity*, Aldershot, 1996, pp. 146–157: p.150 ('Roman and indigenous law still coexisted'); p. 149, states simply, 'they did not become Roman citizens.'

59   Mathisen, Ralph W., op. cit., p.1124; Demougeot, op. cit.,pp.384–387.

60   Mathisen, Ralph W., op. cit.,p.1129; Theodosian Code: for a better understanding of this code see Theodor Mommsen, Paul M. Meyer, and Paul Krüger, eds., *Theodosiani libri* XVI, Berlin, 1902, 5.11.7 (365) 7.20.3 (p.320), 7.20.4 (325), 7.20.8 (364), 7.20.11 (373), 7.20.12 (400).

61   Mathisen, Ralph W., op. cit., p. 1115; For Roman citizenship, see Adrian N. Sherwin-White, *The Roman Citizenship*, 2nd ed., Claude Nicolet, *The World of the Citizen in Republican Rome*, trans. Paul S. Falla, London, 1980; Claude Nicolet, *Le métier de citoyen dans la Rome républicaine*, 2nd ed., Paris, 1989; Paulo Donati Giacomini and Gabrielle Poma, eds., *Cittadini e non cittadini nel Mondo Romano: Guida ai testi e ai documenti*, Bologna, 1996; Jane F. Gardner, *Being a Roman Citizen*, London, 1993; David Noy, *Foreigners at Rome: Citizens and Strangers*, London, 2000; Geoffrey E. M. de Ste-Croix, *Class Struggle in the Ancient Greek World*, Ithaca, N.Y., 1981, pp. 453–461

62   Mathisen, Ralph W., op. cit., p. 1115

63   Ando, Clifford, *Citizens and Aliens in Roman Law*, University of Southern California, 2006, p. 18

64   Gaudemet, Jean,, 'L'étranger au bas-empire', *L'étranger, I, Recueils de la Société Jean Bodin* 9, Brussels, 1958, 99209-235, 223; Demougeot, Emilienne, 'Le 'conubium' et la citoyenneté conféré aux soldats barbares du Bas-Empire', *Sodalitas: Scritti in onore di Antonio Guarino*, 5 vols., Naples, 1984, vol. 4: pp.1633–1643; Bianchini, Maria, 'Ancora in tema di unioni, fra barbari e Romani,'Atti dell' *Accademia romanistica constantiana* 7, 1988: 225–249

65   Livy, 43.2; Cicero, Verr. 3.6; Valerius Maximus 8.7.1; Blázquez Martinez, José María, 'El impacto de la conquista de Hispania por Roma (154-83 a.C.)', *Klio* 41, 1963, p.178 and *Antigua: Historia y Arqueología de las civilizaciones*: (http://descargas.cervantesvirtual.com/servlet/SirveObras/01305020

888359846423802/014615.pdf?incr=1).

At this point the Romans in the provinces of Sardinia, Sicily and Hispania continued with the Carthaginian tax, which was to charge the tenth of cereals. The principle contributions were set by the praetors, but the Roman authorities did not set fixed prices on wheat and did not place tax collectors in the cities (G. Bloch and J. Carcopino, *Des Gracques a Sulla*, Paris 1952, p.126; M. Rostovtzeff, *Historia social y económica del Mundo Romano*, Madrid 1937, p.51; L. Pareti, *Storia di Roma* 3 vols., Turin 1953, vol. 2, p.794).

66 Plutarch, *quaest. Graec.* 6

67 Alarcão, *Roman Portugal*, Vol. I, p. 63

68 Alarcão, *Roman Portugal*, p. 87; Edmondson, J., *Two Industries in Roman Lusitania; Mining and Garum Production*, British Archaeological Reports, Oxford, 1987, pp. 114-115

69 Curchin, Leonard, A., *Roman Spain*, p. 143

70 Eupolis, 186; Curchin, Leonard, A., *Roman Spain*, p. 143; Edmondson, J., *Two Industries in Roman Lusitania*; pp. 114-115

71 Curtis, Robert I., 'In Defense of Garum', *The Classical Journal* #78 (February-March 1983), pp. 232-240

72 Curtis, Robert I., 'The Garum Shop of Pompeii' *Cronache Pompeiane*, XXXI. 94, 1979, pp. 5-23

73 Curtis, Robert I., 'Salted Fish Products in Ancient Medicine', *Journal of the History of Medicine and Allied Sciences*, XXXIX. 4, 1984, pp. 430-45

74 Pliny, 31.43

75 Strabo, 3.3.1

76 Russell Cortez, F., 'As escavações arqueológicas do 'castellum' de Fonte do Milho', *Anais do Instituto do Vinho do Porto*, Vol. 12, 1951, pp. 17-88

77 Robert Joseph, Sophie Blacksell, Sarah Sørensen, *The Wine Travel Guide to the World*, Footprint Handbooks, 2006, p. 108

78 For more information on amphorae in Lusitania see Martín, Julián de Francisco, *Conquista y romanización de Lusitania*, 2nd ed., Salamanca, 1996, p. 348; in Hispania see Beltran, M., *Las ánforas romanas de España*, Zaragoza, 1970

79 Alarcão, J. de, *Roman Portugal*, Vol. I, p. 86-87 and Appendix 3

80 Alarcão, *Roman Portugal*, p. 75; Mezquiriz de Catalán, M.A., *Terra sigillata hispánica*, 2 vols., Valencia, 1961; Mayet, F., *Les céramiques à parois fines dans la Péninsule Ibérique*, Paris, 1975 and *Les céramiques sigillées hispaniques*, Paris, 1984.

81 Ibid.

82 Adília M. Alarcão and Alina M. Martins, 'Uma cerâmica aparentada com as paredes finas de Merida', *Conimbriga* #15, 1976, pp. 91-109

83   Alarcão, J. de, *Roman Portugal*, Vol. I, p. p. 83-84 and 86;Terra sigillata hispanica ranged from a color of rosy beige to bright red to light brown with a variety of shapes and designs.

84   Alarcão, *Roman Portugal*, p. 87; Alarcão,Adília M., *Colecções do Museo Monográfico de Conimbriga*, Conimbriga, 1984, p. 23; J.J. Rigaud de Sousa and Eduardo Alberto Pires de Oliveira, 'Subsídios para o estudo das olarias de Bracara Augusta', *Trabalhos de Antropologia e Etnologia* #24 (2), 1982, pp. 360-370

85   For a detailed history about Lusitanian jewelry see Cardozo, Mario, *Joalharia Lusitana*, Universidade de Coimbra, 1959; Ferreira de Silva, Armando Coelho, 'Ourivesaria proto-histórica em território português', in Jorge de Alarcão (ed), De Ulisses a Viriato: O primeiro milénio a.C., Museu Nacional de Arqueologia, Lisbon, 1996, pp. 139-146

86   In 1904, a bricklayer building a mill at the top of São Félix Mountain, close to the small castro of Laundos, found a *púcaro* with jewels. The jewels were were bought by Rocha Peixoto, who took them to the Museum of As. The torque type necklace worn by men did not signify social class but power and authority within the tribe. Silva, Armando Coelho Ferreira da, *A Cultura Castreja no Noroeste de Portugal*, Museu Arqueológico da Citânia de Sanfins, Paços de Ferreira, 1986; Octávio da Veiga Ferreira e Seomara Bastos da Veiga Ferreira, *A Vida dos Lusitanos no Tempo de Viriato*, p.86.

87   Octávio da Veiga Ferreira e Seomara Bastos da Veiga Ferreira, op. cit., p.86

88   Gaius Petronius Arbiter, *The Satyricon of Petronius Arbiter*, Ch. 55

89   Strabo, 3.2.6; Martín, Julián de Francisco, *Conquista y romanización de Lusitania*, 2nd ed., p. 348

90   Encarnação, José, *Inscrições romanas do conventus pacensis: Subsídios para o estudo da romanização*, Coimbra, 1984, pp. 257-259 and 262-264; Azevedo, Pedro de, 'As pedras preciosas de Lisboa (Belas) na História', *O Archeologo Português* #23, 1918, p. 158-202

91   Alarcão, *Roman Portugal*, p. 73

92   Ibid., 73

93   Ibid., 73

94   Ibid., 73

95   A copy of this contract is on a bronze tablet at the Instituto Nacional de Engenharia, Tecnologia e Inovação, I.P. Centro de Informação Científica e Técnica in Amadora.

96   Ibid.

97   Alarcão, *Roman Portugal*, p. 74

98   Ibid., 74

99   Ibid., 74

100   Alarcão, J. de, *Roman Portugal*, Vol. I, p. 109

101   Walters, Henry Beauchamp and Birch, Samuel, *History of Ancient Pottery: Greek, Etruscan, and Roman*, J. Murray, 1905, pp. 330–40

102   Juracek, Jack, *Surfaces: Visual Research for Artists, Architects, and Designers*, W. W. Norton & Company, 1996, p. 310

103   Peet, Stephen Denison, *The American Antiquarian and Oriental Journal*, Jameson & Morse, 1911, pp. 35–36

104   Alarcão, J. de, op. cit., p. 80

105   Alarcão, J de, op. cit., p. 80-81

106   Alarcão, J de, op. cit., p. 81-82

107   Lancaster, Lynne, *Concrete Vaulted Construction in Imperial Rome: Innovations in Context*, Cambridge University Press, 2005

108   Alarcão, *Roman Portugal*, p. 83

109   Roldán Hervás, J.M., 'Las guerras de Lusitania (155-138 BC) y Celtiberia (153-133 BC)' in R. Menéndez Pidal (ed.) *Historia de España*, 2nd ed., 2 vols., Madrid, 1982, vol. I, p. 115.

110   Curchin, Leonard, A., *Roman Spain*, p.105

111   Curchin, Leonard, A., *Roman Spain*, 1995, p.154

112   Ibid.

113   Alarcão, J. de, *Roman Portugal*, Vol. I, p. 98

114   Vasconcelos, J.L de, *Religiões da Lusitânia*, vol. III, 1913, Imprensa Nacional — Casa da Moeda, Lisbon, 1897-1913, p 193; Curchin, Leonard, A., p. 155

115   Tacitus, *Germania*, 43

116   Curchin, Leonard, A., *Roman Spain*, p.160

117   Vasconcelos, J.L de, *Religiões da Lusitânia*, vol III, p. 220-312. Here are some of the gods that played a role in Luso-Roman religion was Jupiter, Juno, Apollo, Diana, Luna, Soli, Proserpina, Poemana, Ceres, Tellus, Dionysus, Neptune, Mars, Aesculapius, Hygia, Salus, Victoria, Venus, Cupid, Mercury, Minerva, Hercules, Volcanus, Concordia, Pietas, Iuventus, Pax, Fortuna, Eventus, Phoebus, Successa and Fata.

118   Ibid., pp. 254-261 and 291-298

119   Ibid., p. 328 – 358

120   *Inscriptiones Graecae* IV, 39; Quintilian, 6.33.77

121   Pliny the Elder, *Historia Naturalis*, 4.111; Ptolemy, *Geographia*, 2.6.3; Pomponeus Mela, 3.13; Fishwick, Duncan, *The Imperial Cult in the Latin West: Studies in the Ruler Cult of the Western Provinces of the Roman Empire*, volume 3, Brill, 2002. vol 3, p.1-7

122   Encarnação, Jose, *Inscrições romanas do conventus pacensis*: pp. 256-257;

This inscription was consecrated in Salacia to Emperor Augustus by Vicanus, son of Boutius.

123   Fishwick, Duncan, 'An early provincial priest of Lusitania', *Historia* #31, Wiesbaden, 1982, pp. 249-252; Pierre and Monique Lévêque, 'Sculptures', in J. Alarcão and R. Etienne, *Fouilles de Conimbriga II, Épigraphie et Sculpture*, Paris, 1976, pp. 235-247; Etienne, Robert, *Le culte imperial dans la Péninsule Ibérique*, pp. 199-200, 238-239, 252-254; Alarcão, J. de, *Roman Portugal*, Vol. I, pp. 105-107

124   See the Chapter 4 section on religion.

125   Etienne, Robert, *Le culte imperial dans la Péninsule Ibérique*, pp. 346-9; Curchin, Leonard, *Roman Spain*, p. 162

126   Mattoso Camara, Joaquim, *The Portuguese Language*, translated by Anthony J. Naro, University of Chicago Press, 1972, p.8-9

127   Mattoso Camara, Joaquim, *The Portuguese Language*, p. 172

128   Curchin, *Roman Spain*, p. 191

129   Ibid., p. 191

130   Ibid., p. 191

131   Ibid., p. 191

132   Ibid., p. 191-192

134   Ibid., 192

CHAPTER 10

1   Frontinus, *Strategems*, Book 2

2   Meyer, Heinrich, *Anthologia veterum latinorum epigrammatum et poematum, Volume 1, Lipsiae, apud Gerhardum Fleischerum*, 1835, p. 46, paragraph 128.

3   Muñoz, Mauricio Pastor, *Viriato, O Herói Lusitano iberdade do seu povo*, p. 233

4   Ibid. 234

5   Muñoz, Mauricio Pastor, op. cit., p. 235; Garcia Quintela, M.V., 'Viriato y la Ideología Trifuncional Indoeuropea', *Polis* #3, 1993, pp.111-138

6   Ibid.

7   Florus, 1.33.15

8   Lopez Melero, Raquel, 'Viriatus Hispaniae Romulus', *Espacio, Tiempo y Forma, Serie II, Historia Antigua, I*, 1988, pp. 247-262, p. 247

9   Knapp, Robert C., *Aspects of the Roman Experience in Iberia, 206 – 100 BC*, (Vol. 9 of Anejos de Hispania antique), Colegio Universitario de Alava, pp. 29-30

10   Lopez Melero, Raquel, 'Viriatus Hispaniae Romulus', pp. 247-262, p. 251

11   Ibid., p. 248

12 Ibid., pp. 247-262 and p. 252

13 Ibid, p. 253

14 Bermejo Barrera, J.C., *Mitología y mitos de la Hispania prerromana 2*, Madrid, 1986, p. 45

15 Appian, 69.294

16 Livy, *Peri.* 54 and *Epi. Oxy*, 185

17 Garcia Quintela, M.V., 'Viriato y la Ideología Trifuncional Indoeuropea', pp. 111-138

18 Ibid, p. 231

19 Ibid., p. 232

20 Dumézil analyzes the three 'sins' of the warrior in the Indo-European tradition: against the king, against the priest, against the laws originating in the state. The triple sins in this theory are against the three offices of kingship/priesthood, warrior, and state. The hero commits sacrilege of some kind against his sovereign lord, his king, and comes under the ban of heaven and the gods. Then he has to fail as a warrior — fleeing from battle, showing cowardice when faced by a challenger — and loses his strength of arms. Then sinning against the state, meaning against the people, the home, family or even marriage.

21 Muñoz, Mauricio Pastor, *Viriato, O Herói Lusitano*, p. 245

22 Ibid., pp. 213-214

23 Guerra, A. and Fabião, C., 'Viriato: Genealogia de um Mito', *Penélope, Fazer e Desfazer a História* #8, 1992, pp. 9-23

24 Chamorro, Victor, 'Viriato, historia compartida, mito desputado', *Agora Academia*, Cáceres, 2002, p.65

25 Ibid., p. 65

26 Inês Vaz, , J.L., *Lusitanos no Tempo de Viriato*, p. 196

27 The death of young King Sebastian I of Portugal in the Battle of Alcácer Quibir (1578) prompted the 1580 Portuguese succession crisis. Sebastian had no immediate heirs and his body was never found, so a dynastic crisis ensued, with several pretenders to the throne emerging. After a three-year war known as the War of the Portuguese Succession, Phillip II of Spain gained control of the country, uniting Portugal and Spain in the Iberian Union, which would last for sixty years, during which the Portuguese Empire declined. The revolution of 1640 ended the dual monarchy in Portugal and Spain. Between 1640 and 1668 there were periodic skirmishes between the two countries, as well as short episodes of warfare, much of it occasioned by Spanish and Portuguese entanglements with non-Iberian powers. In 1662, Spain committed itself to a major effort to end the Portuguese

rebellion. Portugal, with the intercession of its English ally, sought a truce, but after the Portuguese victory at the Battle of Montes Claros and a Franco-Portuguese treaty in 1667, Spain finally agreed to recognize Portugal's independence on 13 February 1668 with the Treaty of Lisbon.

28   Masdeu, J.F., *Historia Crítica de España y de la Cultura Española*, Madrid, 1783

29   Herculano, Alexandre., *História de Portugal Desde o Começo da Monarquia até ao Fim do Reinado de Afonso III*, 3rd ed. Lisbon, 1868; Inês Vaz, , J.L., *Lusitanos no Tempo de Viriato*, p. 197

30   Inês Vaz, J.L., op. cit., p. 193

31   Arenas Lopez, A., *Reivindicaciones históicas: Viriato no fué portugués si no celtibero: su biografia*, Guadalajara, 1900

32   Arenas Lopez, A., *La Lusitania Celtíbera*, Madrid,1907

33   Muñoz, Mauricio Pastor, op. cit., p. 213-214; Athayde, A., 'Viriato na Realidade Histórica e na Ficção Literária', *Prisma*, Porto, 1937; Tusculano, Victor de, op. cit.

34   The existence of a Neolithic/Mesolithic people in the lower valley of the Tagus River was first discovered in 1863 by Carlos Ribeiro. Under the auspices of the Geological Survey in Lisbon, research and occasional excavations on these people continued on until 1954. During the fascist regime, Antonio Augusto Mendes Correia, the main promoter of the Portuguese/Lusitanian linked ancestry, believed that this prehistoric race had migrated from North Africa to the Iberian Peninsula. But there was some disagreement between what the government wanted to promote and his idea of what the Portuguese family tree was. While the government quickly promoted the people from the Muge, Mendes Correia believed that these people contributed little to the ethnogenesis of the Portuguese nation whose roots should have been sought in the dolmen builder of the later Neolithic period. Inês Vaz, J.L., *Lusitanos no Tempo de Viriato*, 9, p. 200; Correia, Antonio Augusto Mendes, 'Origiins of the Portuguese', *American Journal of Physical Anthropology* 2, #2, 1919, pp. 117-145; Ferembach, Denise, 'Le gisement mésolithique de Miota do Sebastião, Muge, Portugal II', *Anthropologie*, Direcção-Geral dos Assuntos Culturais, Lisbon, 1974; Roche, Jean, *Le gisement mésolithique de Miota do Sebastião, Muge, Portugal*, Instituto para a Alta Cultura, Lisbon, 1960 and *L'industrie préhistorique de Cabeço da Amoreira (Muge)*, Instituto para a Alta Cultura, Porto, 1951; Zilhão, João, 'Muge Shell Middens', P. Bogucki and P.J. Crabtree (eds.), *Ancient Europe 8,000 BC – AD 1000*, (Encyclopedia of the Barbarian World, vol. 1), New York, 2004, pp. 164-6

35   Archaeological excavations conducted in the mid-twentieth century show that this site was a Roman military base founded by Decius

Brutus in his campaign against the Lusitanians and Galaicians in 138 BC, rather than a Lusitanian encampment.

36 Muñoz, Mauricio Pastor, op. cit., p. 218

37 Arenas López, A., *Reivindicaciones Históricas, Viriato no Fue Portugués, si no Celtíbero*, Guadalajara, 1900 and *La Lusitania Celtíbera*, Madrid, 1907

38 Costa, J., 'Viriato y la Cuestión Social en España en el Siglo II Antes de Jesucristo', *Tutela de Pueblos en la Historia*, Madrid, 1879; Caro Baroja, J., 'Regímenes Sociales y Económicos de la España Preromana', *Revista Internacional de Sociología* #1, 1943, pp. 149-152; Garcia Bellido, A., *Conflictos y Estructuras Sociales en la Hispania Antigua*, Madrid, 1977.

39 Muñoz, Mauricio Pastor, op. cit., p. 218

40 Peris, M., 'La Lusitania Primitiva', *Boletín de la Sociedad Castellonense de Cultura*, 1920; *Campaña Lusitania y Viriatense*, 1926; *Fin de Viriato y la Patria de Viriato*, 1926

41 Muñoz, Mauricio Pastor, op. cit., p. 218

42 Garcia y Bellido, A., 'Bandos y Guerrilhas en las Luchas con Roma', *Hispania* vol. V, no. 21, 1945

43 Muñoz, Mauricio Pastor, op. cit., p. 268

44 The *Mocidade Portuguesa* (Portuguese Youth) was a Portuguese youth organization under the right-wing regime of the Estado Novo. Membership was compulsory between the ages of seven and fourteen and voluntary until the age of twenty-five. Founded in 1936, it was originally inspired by the model of the Italian Fascist Opera Nazionale Balilla and the Nazi Hitler Youth. However, in 1940 the Germanophile National Secretary Francisco Nobre Guedes was replaced by the Anglophile Marcelo Caetano, who gave the organization a different orientation, withdrawing from Hitler Youth and abandoning paramilitarism. He approached it via the Catholic Church and other youth organizations as a boy scout movement. It was dissolved in 1974 after the fall of the dictatorship in a democratic military coup called the Carnation Revolution, for it was considered a fascist organization.

45 Vaz, J.L., *Lusitanos no Tempo de Viriato*, p. 208; For information on the Classic Stance see http://www.ludus.org.uk/r/essayclassicstance.html

46 Vaz, J.L., op. cit., p. 208

47 http://www.antena3.com/videos/hispania/temporada-2/capitulo-1.html

48 Alvar, J., *Heróis e Anti-heróis na Antiguidade Clássica*, Madrid, 1997, pp. 137-153

Index

EXPLORE MORE
ANCIENT HISTORY TITLES
ALSO AVAILABLE FROM
PEN & SWORD BOOKS

EDITED BY
CHRISTOPHER MATTHEW & MATTHEW TRUNDLE

BEYOND THE GATES OF FIRE

NEW PERSPECTIVES ON THE BATTLE OF THERMOPYLAE

FOREWORD BY PHILIP DE SOUZA
DEPT. OF CLASSICS, UNIVERSITY COLLEGE, DUBLIN

9781848847910 • HB •
240 pages • £19.99 • $32.95

The Battle of Thermopylae in 480 BC is one of the most famous battles in history. The heroism of the 300 Spartans who opted to remain behind to face the full might of the Persian host while their Greek allies made good their escape has become the stuff of legend. The story still inspires novelists and film-makers today (Frank Miller's 300 was a huge hit in 2007 and the film rights to Steven Pressfield's more historical novel, *Gates of Fire*, were bought by George Clooney). But what is the truth behind the legends and why was this bloody defeat immediately accorded a halo of glory that has endured for nearly two-and-a-half millennia?

Beyond the Gates of Fire brings together experts on the classical period from Australia, New Zealand and the United States to take a fresh look at various aspects of the battle. A substantial introductory section by the editors outlines the background to the conflict as well as the arms, armour and fighting styles of the opposing sides. The following chapters then discuss such questions as whether the defence of the pass really was a suicide mission; the exact topography of the battlefield itself in 480 BC, using the latest geological research and core samples; the impact of the battle on the Greek psyche; commemoration of the war dead; the impact of the original battle on the conduct of later battles in the pass, right up to the German invasion of 1941. For the classical scholar or the general reader whose interest has been piqued by the popular books and films, this book is sure to shed refreshing new light on the most famous last stand in history.

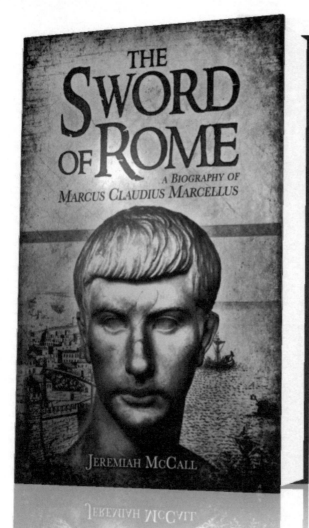

THE
SWORD
OF ROME
A BIOGRAPHY OF
MARCUS CLAUDIUS MARCELLUS

JEREMIAH McCALL

HB 9781848843790 •
Epub 9781783461561 •
Kindle 9781783407927 •
176 pages • £19.99 • $29.95

Marcellus' military exploits were largely unmatched by any other aristocrat of Roman Middle Republic. As a young soldier in the First Punic War, he won a reputation for his skill in single combat. In his first consulship, he earned a triumph for defeating a Gallic tribe, no small feat in and of itself, and also slew the Gallic chieftain Britomartus in single combat. Consequently, he earned the spolia opima, an honor, according to Roman antiquarians, that had only been earned twice before, once by Romulus himself. He went on to defeat the hitherto-invincible Hannibal in a small battle around the central Italian city of Nola, and subsequently led an army to subdue and plunder the powerful city of Syracuse in an epic two year siege (despite the ingenius defensive measures of the inventor Archimedes). Yet, despite his undeniable success as a warrior and commander, Marcellus met with considerable political opposition at Rome.

Marcellus' career not only makes exciting reading, but gives an excellent vantage point from which to view the military and political struggles of the period and the role of military successes in the aristocratic culture of the Roman Republic. His biography will be an important addition to existing works on Roman military history.

HB 9781848844292 •
Epub 9781848849020 •
Kindle 9781848849037 •
208 pages • £19.99

This is a fascinating exploration of how the history of Europe, and indeed the world, might have been different if the Western Roman Empire had survived the crises that pulled it apart in the 4th and 5th centuries.

Dr Timothy Venning starts by showing how that survival and recovery might plausibly have happened if several relatively minor things had been different. He then moves on to discuss a series of scenarios which might have altered the course of subsequent history dramatically. Would the survival of a strong Western Empire have assisted the Eastern (Byzantine) Empire in halting the expansion of Islam in the Middle East and North Africa? How would the Western Roman Empire have handled the Viking threat? Could they even have exploited the Viking discovery of America and established successful colonies there?

While necessarily speculative, all the scenarios are discussed within the framework of a deep understanding of the major driving forces, tensions and trends that shaped European history and help to shed light upon them. In so doing they help the reader to understand why things panned out as they did, as well as what might have been.

9781848843783 • HB
• 224 pages • £19.99

In AD 383, according to Bishop Eucherius of Lyon, flooding caused part of the bank of the River Rhone to collapse, revealing a mass grave. Eucherius identified the bodies as those of legionaries recruited to the Roman army from the Christians of the Theban district in Egypt, whom he claimed had been massacred nearly a century previously (near the modern village of St Maurice-en-Valais in south-western Switzerland) for refusing to obey orders they considered immoral. This incident, asserted by Eucherius as matter of fact, is unrecorded elsewhere. Even the existence of this Theban legion is unclear.

Intrigued by this discrepancy, and suspecting a cover-up by official Roman sources, Dr Donald O'Reilly has spent many years undertaking some historical detective work. Piecing together scattered clues from ancient coins, inscriptions and obscure texts he identifies the Theban legion as fact and sheds light on their fate. In the process he paints a powerful portrait of an empire in turmoil, beset by external enemies and driven by religious and moral uncertainties within.

WHAT THE CRITICS SAID:

'Donald O' Reilly's The Lost Legion Rediscovered is a remarkable book.'
ANCIENT WARFARE MAGAZINE

HB 9781848844278 •
Epub 9781848849082 •
Kindle 9781848849099•
272 pages • £25.00 •
$45.00 • 16 Colour plates

At its height, the Roman Empire was the greatest empire yet seen with borders stretching from the rain-swept highlands of Scotland in the north to the sun-scorched Nubian desert in the south. But how were the vast and varied stretches of frontier defined and defended?

Many of Rome's frontier defences have been the subject of detailed and ongoing study and scholarship. Three frontier zones are now UNESCO World Heritage sites (the Antonine Wall having recently been granted this status - the author led the bid), and there is growing interest in their study. This wide-ranging survey describes the varying frontier systems, describing the extant remains, methods and materials of construction and highlighting the differences between various frontiers. Professor Breeze considers how the frontiers worked, discussing this in relation to the organisation and structure of the Roman army, and also their impact on civilian life along the empire's borders. He then reconsiders the question of whether the frontiers were the product of an overarching Empire-wide grand strategy, questioning Luttwak's seminal hypothesis.

WHAT THE CRITICS SAID:

'This book is without question one of the finest I have read with the Pen and Sword imprint, from the quality of the paper to the quality of the scholarship.'
Ancient Warfare Magazine

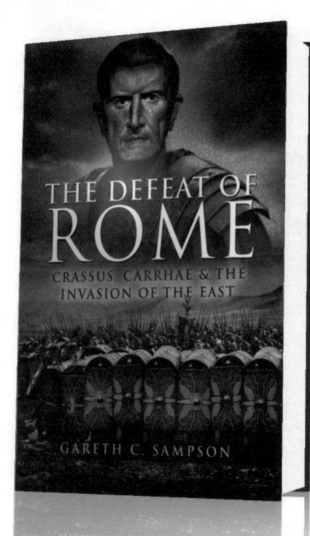

THE DEFEAT OF ROME

CRASSUS, CARRHAE & THE INVASION OF THE EAST

GARETH C. SAMPSON

HB 9781844156764 •
Epub 9781844686346 •
Kindle 9781844686353 •
240 pages • £19.99

In 53 BC the Proconsul Marcus Crassus and 36,000 of his legionaries were crushed by the Parthians at Carrhae in what is now eastern Turkey. Crassus' defeat and death and the 20,000 casualties his army suffered were an extraordinary disaster for Rome. The event intensified the bitter, destructive struggle for power in the Roman republic, curtailed the empire's eastward expansion and had a lasting impact on the history of the Mediterranean and the Middle East. It was also the first clash between two of the greatest civilizations of the ancient world. Yet this critical episode has often been neglected by writers on the period who have concentrated on the civil war between Pompey and Caesar.

Gareth Sampson, in this challenging and original study, reconstructs the Carrhae campaign in fine detail, reconsiders the policy of imperial expansion and gives a fascinating insight into the opponents the Romans confronted in the East - the Parthians.

WHAT THE CRITICS SAID:

'An accessible and cogently written book... Defeat of Rome is an invaluable addition to the literature field.'

WWW.DEREMILITARI.ORG

A STORM OF SPEARS

UNDERSTANDING THE GREEK HOPLITE AT WAR

CHRISTOPHER MATTHEW

HB 9781848842953 •
Epub 9781781594223 •
Kindle 9781781594230 •
336 pages • £25.00 •
24 Colour plates

The backbone of classical Greek armies was the phalanx of heavily armoured spearmen, or hoplites. These were the soldiers that defied the might of Persia at Marathon, Thermopylae and Plataea and, more often, fought each other in the countless battles of the Greek city-states. For around two centuries they were the dominant soldiers of the Classical world, in great demand as mercenaries throughout the Mediterranean and Middle East.

Christopher Matthew's groundbreaking reassessment combines rigourous analysis of the literary and archaeological evidence with the new disciplines of reconstructive archaeology, re-enactment and ballistic science. He focuses meticulously on the details of the equipment, tactics and capabilities of the individual hoplites. In so doing he challenges some long-established assumptions.

This is an innovative and refreshing reassessment of one of the most important kinds of troops in ancient warfare, sure to make a genuine contribution to the state of knowledge.

WHAT THE CRITICS SAID:

'Matthew's work represents an intriguing and original treatment of this subject, supported by a critical evaluation of both models of hoplite warfare... Matthew's conclusions are well-reasoned and interesting.'
ANCIENT WARFARE

AVAILABLE FROM ALL GOOD BOOKSHOPS
OR TO ORDER DIRECT
PLEASE CALL **01226 734222**

OR ORDER ONLINE VIA OUR WEBSITE:
WWW.PEN-AND-SWORD.CO.UK